Property of the Office of Digital Learning
Residential Library

Google® BigQuery Analytics

Jordan Tigani
Siddartha Naidu

WILEY

Google® BigQuery Analytics

Published by
John Wiley & Sons, Inc.
10475 Crosspoint Boulevard
Indianapolis, IN 46256
www.wiley.com

Copyright © 2014 by John Wiley & Sons, Inc., Indianapolis, Indiana

Published simultaneously in Canada

ISBN: 978-1-118-82482-5
ISBN: 978-1-118-82487-0 (ebk)
ISBN: 978-1-118-82479-5 (ebk)

Manufactured in the United States of America

10 9 8 7 6 5 4 3 2 1

No part of this publication may be reproduced, stored in a retrieval system or transmitted in any form or by any means, electronic, mechanical, photocopying, recording, scanning or otherwise, except as permitted under Sections 107 or 108 of the 1976 United States Copyright Act, without either the prior written permission of the Publisher, or authorization through payment of the appropriate per-copy fee to the Copyright Clearance Center, 222 Rosewood Drive, Danvers, MA 01923, (978) 750-8400, fax (978) 646-8600. Requests to the Publisher for permission should be addressed to the Permissions Department, John Wiley & Sons, Inc., 111 River Street, Hoboken, NJ 07030, (201) 748-6011, fax (201) 748-6008, or online at http://www.wiley.com/go/permissions.

Limit of Liability/Disclaimer of Warranty: The publisher and the author make no representations or warranties with respect to the accuracy or completeness of the contents of this work and specifically disclaim all warranties, including without limitation warranties of fitness for a particular purpose. No warranty may be created or extended by sales or promotional materials. The advice and strategies contained herein may not be suitable for every situation. This work is sold with the understanding that the publisher is not engaged in rendering legal, accounting, or other professional services. If professional assistance is required, the services of a competent professional person should be sought. Neither the publisher nor the author shall be liable for damages arising herefrom. The fact that an organization or Web site is referred to in this work as a citation and/or a potential source of further information does not mean that the author or the publisher endorses the information the organization or website may provide or recommendations it may make. Further, readers should be aware that Internet websites listed in this work may have changed or disappeared between when this work was written and when it is read.

For general information on our other products and services please contact our Customer Care Department within the United States at (877) 762-2974, outside the United States at (317) 572-3993 or fax (317) 572-4002.

Wiley publishes in a variety of print and electronic formats and by print-on-demand. Some material included with standard print versions of this book may not be included in e-books or in print-on-demand. If this book refers to media such as a CD or DVD that is not included in the version you purchased, you may download this material at http://booksupport.wiley.com. For more information about Wiley products, visit www.wiley.com.

Library of Congress Control Number: 2014931958

Trademarks: Wiley and the Wiley logo are trademarks or registered trademarks of John Wiley & Sons, Inc. and/or its affiliates, in the United States and other countries, and may not be used without written permission. Google is a registered trademark of Google, Inc. All other trademarks are the property of their respective owners. John Wiley & Sons, Inc. is not associated with any product or vendor mentioned in this book.

Executive Editor Robert Elliott	**Copy Editor** San Dee Phillips	**Business Manager** Amy Knies	**Proofreader** Nancy Carrasco
Project Editors Tom Dinse Kevin Kent	**Manager of Content Development and Assembly** Mary Beth Wakefield	**Vice President and Executive Group Publisher** Richard Swadley	**Technical Proofreader** Bruce Chhay **Indexer** Robert Swanson
Technical Editor Jeremy Condit	**Director of Community Marketing** David Mayhew	**Associate Publisher** Jim Minatel	**Cover Design and Image** Wiley
Production Editor Christine Mugnolo	**Marketing Manager** Lorna Mein	**Project Coordinator, Cover** Todd Klemme	

About the Authors

Jordan Tigani has more than 15 years of professional software development experience, the last 4 of which have been spent building BigQuery. Prior to joining Google, Jordan worked at a number of star-crossed startups. The startup experience made him realize that you don't need to be a big company to have Big Data. Other past jobs have been in Microsoft Research and the Windows kernel team. When not writing code, Jordan is usually either running or playing soccer. He lives in Seattle with his wife, Tegan, where they both can walk to work.

Siddartha Naidu joined Google after finishing his doctorate degree in Physics. At Google he has worked on Ad targeting, newspaper digitization, and for the past 4 years on building BigQuery. Most of his work at Google has revolved around data; analyzing it, modeling it, and manipulating large amounts of it. When he is not working on SQL recipes, he enjoys inventing and trying the kitchen variety. He currently lives in Seattle with his wife, Nitya, and son, Vivaan, who are the subjects of his kitchen experiments, and when they are not traveling, they are planning where to travel to next.

About the Technical Editor

Jeremy Condit is one of the founding engineers of the BigQuery project at Google, where he has contributed to the design and implementation of BigQuery's API, query engine, and client tools. Prior to joining Google in 2010, he was a researcher in computer science, focusing on programming languages and operating systems, and he has published and presented his research in a number of ACM and Usenix conferences. Jeremy has a bachelor's degree in computer science from Harvard and a Ph.D. in computer science from U.C. Berkeley.

About the Technical Proofreader

Bruce Chhay is an engineer on the Google BigQuery team. Previously he was at Microsoft, working on large-scale data analytics such as Windows error reporting and Windows usage telemetry. He also spent time as co-founder of a startup. He has a BE in computer engineering and MBA from the University of Washington.

Acknowledgments

First, we would like to thank the Dremel and BigQuery teams for building and running a service worth writing about. The last four years since the offsite at Barry's house, where we decided we weren't going to build what management suggested but were going to build BigQuery instead, have been an exciting time.

More generally, thanks to the Google tech infrastructure group that is home to many amazing people and projects. These are the type of people who say, "Only a petabyte?" and don't mean it ironically. It is always a pleasure to come to work.

There were a number of people who made this book possible: Robert Elliot, who approached us about writing the book and conveniently didn't mention how much work would be involved; and Kevin Kent, Tom Dinse, and others from Wiley who helped shepherd us through the process.

A very special thank you to our tech editor and colleague Jeremy Condit who showed us he can review a book just as carefully as he reviews code. Readers should thank him as well, because the book has been much improved by his suggestions.

Other well-deserved thanks go to Bruce Chhay, another BigQuery team member, who volunteered on short notice to handle the final edit. Jing Jing Long, one of the inventors of Dremel, read portions of the book to make sure our descriptions at least came close to matching his implementation. Craig Citro provided moral support with the Python programming language.

And we'd like to thank the BigQuery users, whose feedback, suggestions, and even complaints have made BigQuery a better product.

— The Authors

It has been a great experience working on this project with Siddartha; he's one of the best engineers I've worked with, and his technical judgment has formed the backbone of this book. I'd like to thank my parents, who helped inspire the Shakespeare examples, and my wife, Tegan, who inspires me in innumerable other ways. Tegan also lent us her editing skills, improving clarity and making sure I didn't make too many embarrassing mistakes. Finally, I'd like to thank the Google Cafe staff, who provided much of the raw material for this book.

— Jordan Tigani

When I was getting started on this project, I was excited to have Jordan as my collaborator. In retrospect, it would have been impossible without him. His productivity can be a bit daunting, but it comes in handy when you need to slack off. I would like to thank my wife, Nitya, for helping me take on this project in addition to my day job. She had to work hard at keeping Vivaan occupied, who otherwise was my excuse for procrastinating. Lastly, I want to thank my parents for their tireless encouragement.

— Siddartha Naidu

Contents

Introduction

If you want to get the most out of any tool, whether it is a database or a rotary power drill, it is important to know how it works. This lets you develop an intuition about how you can use the tool effectively. The goal of this book is to help you develop an intuition about BigQuery, which can enable you to make your own decisions about when BigQuery is the right tool for the job, how you can improve your query efficiency, and how you can apply BigQuery in unanticipated situations.

It is also important to have good examples that you can incorporate into your code. This book provides source code to help you start using BigQuery in your applications and query examples that can help you solve complex problems in SQL. In addition, we show you how to write code to get your data in, how to query and visualize that data, and how to get it out again.

The target audience for this book is a data scientist who wants to analyze data with BigQuery, a developer who wants to integrate BigQuery into their data pipelines, or someone who is trying to determine whether BigQuery is the right tool to use. Each type of reader might want something different from the book; the "How to Read This Book" section provides guidelines for a custom path through the chapters.

Overview of the Book and Technology

Both of us, Siddartha Naidu and Jordan Tigani, have been part of the BigQuery team since a group of Google engineers sat around a dining room table to brainstorm what kind of product to build. Siddartha, along with another engineer, built the original prototype that he demonstrated in 2010 at Google I/O, Google's annual developer conference. Two years later, also at Google I/O, Jordan was on hand to announce public availability.

In the intervening time, we have both been active contributors to the design and implementation of the BigQuery service. The system has grown considerably, both in the number of users as well as what it can do. We've also helped support the product via mailing lists and the BigQuery area on StackOverflow. We've paid close attention to how the product was used, the kinds of problems that people had, and the interesting applications they found for the technology.

Along the way we built up a collection of cool things you can do using BigQuery: different techniques, ways of querying, and methods of working around limitations. These tricks and best practices are in this book.

This book doesn't attempt to replace the online documentation. Instead, it is a good format to dive deeper into the service and address different audiences, particularly those familiar with traditional data warehousing products. In addition, this book gives you a sense of how BigQuery works and answers some of the "whys" behind the design.

Although BigQuery, as a product, moves quickly, we've written the book with changes (expected and otherwise) in mind. A new version of BigQuery is released every week or so, and each one fixes bugs, adds features, or improves scalability and performance. By the time you read this book, BigQuery may have undergone significant evolution.

The BigQuery team works hard at making sure all changes to BigQuery will be backward compatible. When new functionality is introduced that conflicts with existing behavior, the policy is to ensure the old version continues to work for at least 12 months. The code and examples in this book should continue to work for a considerable amount of time. Both code and SQL queries that were written to interact with BigQuery at the public launch in 2012 still work today.

Even though the BigQuery service maintains backward compatibility, the best way to achieve a particular result sometimes changes as new features become available. We have chosen to document in this book core concepts that are useful independent of details that might change over time. When in doubt, consult the official documentation at `https://developers.google.com/bigquery`.

Moreover, this book describes integration with other technologies, such as R, Microsoft Excel, and Tableau. Although each of these technologies is also evolving, we've tried to include things that will likely continue to work for the foreseeable future. For instance, Chapter 13, "Using BigQuery from Third-Party Tools," describes using BigQuery via an ODBC connection. Although each version of Microsoft Windows may change the user interface slightly around setting up an ODBC connection, ODBC is a stable technology that will still work years down the road.

How This Book Is Organized

This book is divided into four sections:

- **BigQuery Fundamentals (Chapters 1 through 4):** Walks you through how to start with BigQuery and describes the basic abstractions used by the service. If you're familiar with BigQuery, you might want to just skim this section; although, it might be helpful to read it to make sure you have a firm grounding in the primary concepts.

- **Basic BigQuery (Chapters 5 through 8):** Shows how to use the API at a raw HTTP level and via the higher-level clients, as well as how to write SQL queries. This section culminates with an AppEngine app that ties the various pieces of the API together and shows how they are useful in a real-world scenario.

- **Advanced BigQuery (Chapters 9 through 11):** Goes into detail about how BigQuery works, gives advanced query tricks and recipes, and gives advice on data management strategies. This section can help you understand why a query that seems like it should work might return an error, and can help you create queries that can be difficult to express in SQL.

- **BigQuery Applications (Chapters 12 through 14):** Shows how to tie BigQuery in with other systems. For instance, this section shows how to visualize your data with Tableau, how to query BigQuery tables from Microsoft Excel, and how to query your Google Analytics data.

How to Read This Book

You can, of course, read this book straight through from cover to cover. However, depending on your goals, you may want to skip some sections without losing much context. For example, if you are a data analyst trying to learn how to write better BigQuery queries, you may not be as interested in the HTTP API as a developer who wants to mirror a production database to BigQuery. Following are a couple of suggested paths though the book for different user profiles.

Data Scientist

A data scientist is a user who doesn't care about the details of the HTTP API but wants to get the most out of queries. Their primary interaction with BigQuery will be through SQL and the various BigQuery tools provided by Google. The data scientist can follow this chapter progression:

- **Chapters 1–4 (fundamentals):** For anyone not familiar with BigQuery, these chapters describe what BigQuery is and how to start using it. Chapter 4, "Understanding the BigQuery Object Model," is important because the fundamental abstractions in BigQuery differ slightly from other relational database systems.

- **Chapter 7, "Running Queries":** You may want to skim the API portion, but you probably shouldn't skip it completely because it describes what is possible via the API. (And all the API features should be available in the web UI or in the bq command-line client.) Some table management operations that you may expect to be in SQL (such as creating a temporary table) are done via the API in BigQuery. This chapter also discusses how BigQuery SQL is different from standard SQL and walks through a number of BigQuery queries.

- **Chapter 9, "Understanding Query Execution":** This chapter describes the architecture of the systems that underlie BigQuery. If you want to write good queries and understand why query X is faster than query Y, this chapter is important. Most users of relational databases develop an intuition about how to write efficient queries, and because BigQuery uses a different fundamental architecture, some of these previous intuitions could get you in trouble. This chapter can help you develop similar intuition about the types of queries that can run well in BigQuery.

- **Chapter 10, "Advanced Queries":** This chapter shows some queries that you might not think of writing and provides advanced query recipes. You may want to refer back to this chapter when you run into data modeling or query problems.

- **Chapter 11, "Managing Data Stored in BigQuery":** You might want to skip or skim this chapter, but the portions on how to partition your data or how to make use of the query cache may be useful.

- **Chapter 12, "External Data Processing":** The second half of this chapter, which describes running queries from Microsoft Excel and Google Spreadsheets, will likely be interesting if your organization uses a lot of spreadsheets.

- **Chapter 13, "Using BigQuery from Third-Party Tools":** You should read this chapter if you're interested in data visualization, client-side encryption, R, or using BigQuery via ODBC.

- **Chapter 14, "Querying Google Data Sources":** If you have data from a Google project (AdSense, Google Analytics, or DoubleClick) that you want to query, this is the chapter for you.

Software Developer

If you're a developer who wants to integrate BigQuery with your data pipelines or create a dashboard using BigQuery, you might be most interested in the following chapters:

- **Chapters 1–4 (fundamentals):** If you're going to use the API, carefully read Chapter 4, "Understanding the BigQuery Object Model." You need to understand the BigQuery object model, the difference between a Dataset and a Table, and what kinds of things you can do with Jobs.

- **Chapter 5, "Talking to the BigQuery API":** This chapter gives an overview of the HTTP API that you'll use if you write code to talk to BigQuery.

- **Chapter 6, "Loading Data":** If you want to get your data into BigQuery, read this chapter.

- **Chapter 7, "Running Queries":** This chapter discusses the BigQuery query language and the query API. You'll likely want to be familiar with how to run queries via the API as well as the various query options.

- **Chapter 8, "Putting It Together":** This chapter walks you through an end-to-end AppEngine application that uses BigQuery for logging, dashboarding, and ad-hoc querying. If you write code that uses BigQuery, the online resources for this chapter will be particularly interesting because you may cut and paste a lot of the code that is provided.

- **Chapter 11, "Managing Data Stored in BigQuery":** This may be interesting because it gives best practices for how to partition your data effectively, and gives tips and tricks for reducing the cost of using BigQuery.

- **Chapter 12, "External Data Processing":** If you want to process your data outside of BigQuery, this chapter will be useful. Maybe you want to run Hadoop over your BigQuery data, or you want to download your tables locally to process them on-premise.

- **Chapter 13, "Using BigQuery from Third-Party Tools":** There are a number of third-party tools that can make it easier for you to integrate with BigQuery. For example, if you already use ODBC to connect to a database source, the Simba ODBC driver for BigQuery may allow you to run queries without having to write any additional code.

Technology Evaluator

Maybe you're considering using BigQuery and would like to compare it against other options such as Amazon.com's Redshift or Cloudera Impala. Or maybe you're just curious about the architecture. If you're reading this book because you're interested in what the technology can do and how it works, consider the following chapters:

- **Chapter 2, "Big Query Fundamentals"**: This chapter is a good introduction to BigQuery and what it can do. It also describes what BigQuery does not do and gives some comparisons to other technologies.

- **Chapter 4, "Understanding the BigQuery Object Model"**: This chapter will be worth skimming, even if you're interested only in how BigQuery works. Other chapters reference it heavily and assume that you know the difference between a Table and a Dataset.

- **Chapters 5–8 (BigQuery API):** These chapters may be worth skimming, if to see only what BigQuery can do and what the code to use for various features would look like.

- **Chapter 9, "Understanding Query Execution"**: This chapter has architectural comparisons to other Big Data frameworks such as Hadoop. It describes how BigQuery works, including the Dremel architecture, Colossus, and the other building blocks that BigQuery uses to provide a comprehensive service.

- **Chapter 12, "External Data Processing"**: This chapter describes a number of ways to interact with BigQuery; it will be interesting if you want to figure out how to integrate with your existing systems.

- **Chapter 13, "Using BigQuery from Third-Party Tools"**: This chapter gives a survey of visualization, connection, and other types of tools that are built on top of BigQuery.

- **Chapter 14, "Querying Google Data Sources"**: If you use other Google services, such as AdSense or Double Click, this chapter is worth skimming to see how you can access the data you already have within Google via BigQuery.

Tools You Need

If you're an analyst or someone who just wants to use BigQuery directly out-of-the-box (that is, without writing code to interact with it), the only thing you need is a web browser (and perhaps a credit card if your queries exceed the free monthly quota).

If you're a developer who wants to integrate BigQuery into your processes, either by streaming logs into BigQuery, writing dashboards on top of the service, or writing custom Hadoop pipelines that use BigQuery data, you need a bit more. You should have Python installed, at least version 2.7, and should know either Python or another similar language such as Ruby fairly well. The examples in the book are mostly in Python for two reasons: The first is that it is the language that is most commonly used to access BigQuery. The other is that Python is fairly compact (unlike Java) and readable (unlike Perl), so it is easy to see what the important pieces are without a lot of extra boilerplate.

Some chapters have code in other languages where either the code is sufficiently different from the Python code or there is a more natural language to use. For example, Chapter 12, "External Data Processing," uses App Script to demonstrate how to run BigQuery queries from Google Spreadsheets, and Chapter 13, "Using BigQuery from Third-Party Tools," has examples in R and C#. For these sections you will likely need other development environments. For Java code you'll want the JDK, for C# code you'll likely want Microsoft Visual Studio, and for R you'll want R studio.

For the most part, we assume that you've already installed these applications, but for some more specialized environments, such as R, we provide download and installation information. Even if you're not an experienced user of these other languages, you can still follow along with the examples.

If you're not already a BigQuery user, you need to set up a Google Cloud Project. Chapter 3, "Getting Started with BigQuery," walks you through that process. If you intend to use BigQuery heavily, you may need to provide a credit card, but there is a free tier of usage that may suffice for figuring out whether BigQuery meets your needs.

Chapter 8, "Putting It Together," builds both an Android App to stream data into BigQuery from device sensors and an AppEngine App. You can use the Android App as-is, but if you want to tweak it, you need the Android development tools. Chapter 8 goes into more detail about what you need. For the AppEngine portions you need to create your own AppEngine app. Again, the installation information is provided in Chapter 8.

Supplemental Materials and Information

The companion website to this book is hosted at `http://www.wiley.com/go/googlebigquery`. The site contains information about downloading source code and finding sample data used throughout the book. There is also an AppEngine app at `http://bigquery-sensors.appspot.com`, the same one that is built in Chapter 8. It contains links to the BigQuery Sensor dashboard and Android app downloads.

All the code used in the book is hosted at code.google.com at `https://code.google.com/p/bigquery-e2e/source/browse/`. There are two top-level directories:

`samples` and `sensors`. The former contains the code snippets used in the book, arranged by chapter. The latter directory contains code for the Sensors AppEngine and Android apps.

You can navigate to that link and browse through the code, or if you have Git or Subversion installed, you can check out the code to try it on your local machine. Chapter 3 has directions to help you get started. We will update the code periodically to fix bugs or match current best practices. If you find a bug, you can report it at the project issue tracker (`https://code.google.com/p/bigquery-e2e/issues/list`).

If you run into trouble using BigQuery, there are online resources that you can use to get help or report issues with the service. The official BigQuery public documentation is at `https://developers.google.com/bigquery`; the docs there should be the most up to date. If you have questions or concerns, there is an active StackOverflow community populated by BigQuery developers and users at `http://stackoverflow.com/questions/tagged/google-bigquery`. In addition, if you find BigQuery bugs or want to submit a feature request, you can use the public BigQuery issue tracker: `https://code.google.com/p/google-bigquery/issues/list`.

BigQuery Fundamentals

In This Part

The Story of Big Data at Google

Since its founding in 1998, Google has grown by multiple orders of magnitude in several different dimensions—how many queries it handles, the size of the search index, the amount of user data it stores, the number of services it provides, and the number of users who rely on those services. From a hardware perspective, the Google Search engine has gone from a server sitting under a desk in a lab at Stanford to hundreds of thousands of servers located in dozens of datacenters around the world.

The traditional approach to scaling (outside of Google) has been to scale the hardware up as the demands on it grow. Instead of running your database on a small blade server, run it on a Big Iron machine with 64 processors and a terabyte of RAM. Instead of relying on inexpensive disks, the traditional scaling path moves critical data to costly network-attached storage (NAS).

There are some problems with the scale-up approach, however:

- Scaled-up machines are expensive. If you need one that has twice the processing power, it might cost you five times as much.

- Scaled-up machines are single points of failure. You might need to get more than one expensive server in case of a catastrophic problem, and each one usually ends up being built with so many backup and redundant pieces that you're paying for a lot more hardware than you actually need.

- Scale up has limits. At some point, you lose the ability to add more processors or RAM; you've bought the most expensive and fastest machine that is made (or that you can afford), and it still might not be fast enough.

- Scale up doesn't protect you against software failures. If you have a Big Iron server that has a kernel bug, that machine will crash just as easily (and as hard) as your Windows laptop.

Google, from an early point in time, rejected scale-up architectures. It didn't, however, do this because it saw the limitations more clearly or because it was smarter than everyone else. It rejected scale-up because it was trying to save money. If the hardware vendor quotes you $1 million for the server you need, you could buy 200 $5,000 machines instead. Google engineers thought, "Surely there is a way we could put those 200 servers to work so that the next time we need to increase the size, we just need to buy a few more cheap machines, rather than upgrade to the $5 million server." Their solution was to scale out, rather than scale up.

Big Data Stack 1.0

Between 2000 and 2004, armed with a few principles, Google laid the foundation for its Big Data strategy:

- Anything can fail, at any time, so write your software expecting unreliable hardware. At most companies, when a database server crashes, it is a serious event. If a network switch dies, it will probably cause downtime. By running in an environment in which individual components fail often, you paradoxically end up with a much more stable system because your software is designed to handle those failures. You can quantify your risk beyond blindly quoting statistics, such as mean time between failures (MTBFs) or service-level agreements (SLAs).

- Use only commodity, off-the-shelf components. This has a number of advantages: You don't get locked into a particular vendor's feature set; you can always find replacements; and you don't experience big price discontinuities when you upgrade to the "bigger" version.

- The cost for twice the amount of capacity should not be considerably more than the cost for twice the amount of hardware. This means the software must be built to scale out, rather than up. However, this also imposes limits on the types of operations that you can do. For instance, if you scale out your database, it may be difficult to do a JOIN operation, since you'd need to join data together that lives on different machines.

- "A foolish consistency is the hobgoblin of little minds." If you abandon the "C" (consistency) in ACID database operations, it becomes much easier to parallelize operations. This has a cost, however; loss of consistency means that programmers have to handle cases in which reading data they just wrote might return a stale (inconsistent) copy. This means you need smart programmers.

These principles, along with a cost-saving necessity, inspired new computation architectures. Over a short period of time, Google produced three technologies that inspired the Big Data revolution:

- **Google File System (GFS):** A distributed, cluster-based filesystem. GFS assumes that any disk can fail, so data is stored in multiple locations, which means that data is still available even when a disk that it was stored on crashes.

- **MapReduce:** A computing paradigm that divides problems into easily parallelizable pieces and orchestrates running them across a cluster of machines.

- **Bigtable:** A forerunner of the NoSQL database, Bigtable enables structured storage to scale out to multiple servers. Bigtable is also replicated, so failure of any particular tablet server doesn't cause data loss.

What's more, Google published papers on these technologies, which enabled others to emulate them outside of Google. Doug Cutting and other open source contributors integrated the concepts into a tool called Hadoop. Although Hadoop is considered to be primarily a MapReduce implementation, it also incorporates GFS and BigTable clones, which are called HDFS and HBase, respectively.

Armed with these three technologies, Google replaced nearly all the off-the-shelf software usually used to run a business. It didn't need (with a couple of exceptions) a traditional SQL database; it didn't need an e-mail server because its Gmail service was built on top of these technologies.

Big Data Stack 2.0 (and Beyond)

The three technologies—GFS, MapReduce, and Bigtable—made it possible for Google to scale out its infrastructure. However, they didn't make it easy. Over the next few years, a number of problems emerged:

- MapReduce is hard. It can be difficult to set up and difficult to decompose your problem into Map and Reduce phases. If you need multiple MapReduce rounds (which is common for many real-world problems), you face the issue of how to deal with state in between phases and how to deal with partial failures without having to restart the whole thing.

- MapReduce can be slow. If you want to ask questions of your data, you have to wait minutes or hours to get the answers. Moreover, you have to write custom C++ or Java code each time you want to change the question that you're asking.

- GFS, while improving durability of the data (since it is replicated multiple times) can suffer from reduced availability, since the metadata server is a single point of failure.

- Bigtable has problems in a multidatacenter environment. Most services run in multiple locations; Bigtable replication between datacenters is only eventually consistent (meaning that data that gets written out will show up everywhere, but not immediately). Individual services spend a lot of redundant effort babysitting the replication process.

- Programmers (even Google programmers) have a really difficult time dealing with eventual consistency. This same problem occurred when Intel engineers tried improving CPU performance by relaxing the memory model to be eventually consistent; it caused lots of subtle bugs because the hardware stopped working the way people's mental model of it operated.

Over the next several years, Google built a number of additional infrastructure components that refined the ideas from the 1.0 stack:

- **Colossus:** A distributed filesystem that works around many of the limitations in GFS. Unlike many of the other technologies used at Google, Colossus' architecture hasn't been publicly disclosed in research papers.

- **Megastore:** A geographically replicated, consistent NoSQL-type datastore. Megastore uses the Paxos algorithm to ensure consistent reads and writes. This means that if you write data in one datacenter, it is immediately available in all other datacenters.

- **Spanner:** A globally replicated datastore that can handle data locality constraints, like "This data is allowed to reside only in European datacenters." Spanner managed to solve the problem of global time ordering in a geographically distributed system by using atomic clocks to guarantee synchronization to within a known bound.

- **FlumeJava:** A system that allows you to write idiomatic Java code that runs over collections of Big Data. Flume operations get compiled and optimized to run as a series of MapReduce operations. This solves the ease of setup, ease of writing, and ease of handling multiple MapReduce problems previously mentioned.

- **Dremel:** A distributed SQL query engine that can perform complex queries over data stored on Colossus, GFS, or elsewhere.

The version 2.0 stack, built piecemeal on top of the version 1.0 stack (Megastore is built on top of Bigtable, for instance), addresses many of the drawbacks of the previous version. For instance, Megastore allows services to write from any datacenter and know that other readers will read the most up-to-date version. Spanner, in many ways, is a successor to Megastore, which adds automatic planet-scale replication and data provenance protection.

On the data processing side, batch processing and interactive analyses were separated into two tools based on usage models: Flume and Dremel. Flume enables users to easily chain together MapReduces and provides a simpler programming model to perform batch operations over Big Data. Dremel, on the other hand, makes it easy to ask questions about Big Data because you can now run a SQL query over terabytes of data and get results back in a few seconds. Dremel is the query engine that powers BigQuery; Its architecture is discussed in detail in Chapter 9, "Understanding Query Execution."

An interesting consequence of the version 2.0 stack is that it explicitly rejects the notion that in order to use Big Data you need to solve your problems in fundamentally different ways than you're used to. While MapReduce required you to think about your computation in terms of Map and Reduce phases, FlumeJava allows you to write code that looks like you are operating over normal Java collections. Bigtable replication required abandoning consistent writes, but Megastore adds a consistent coordination layer on top. And while Bigtable had improved scalability by disallowing queries, Dremel retrofits a traditional SQL query interface onto Big Data structured storage.

There are still rough edges around many of the Big Data 2.0 technologies: things that you expect to be able to do but can't, things that are slow but seem like they should be fast, and cases where they hold onto awkward abstractions. However, as time goes on, the trend seems to be towards smoothing those rough edges and making operation over Big Data as seamless as over smaller data.

Open Source Stack

Many of the technologies at Google have been publicly described in research papers, which were picked up by the Open Source community and re-implemented as open source versions. When the open source Big Data options were in their infancy, they more or less followed Google's lead. Hadoop was designed to be very similar to the architecture described in the MapReduce paper, and the Hadoop subprojects HDFS and HBase are close to GFS and BigTable.

However, as the value of scale-out systems began to increase (and as problems with traditional scale-up solutions became more apparent), the Open Source Big Data stack diverged significantly. A lot of effort has been put into making Hadoop faster; people use technologies such as Hive and Pig to query their data; and numerous NoSQL datastores have sprung up, such as CouchDB, MongoDB, Cassandra, and others.

On the interactive query front, there are a number of open source options:

- Cloudera's Impala is an open source parallel execution engine similar to Dremel. It allows you to query data inside HDFS and Hive without extracting it.

- Amazon.com's Redshift is a fork of PostgreSQL which has been modified to scale out across multiple machines. Unlike Impala, Redshift is a hosted service, so it is managed in the cloud by Amazon.com.

- Drill is an Apache incubator project that aims to be for Dremel what Hadoop was for MapReduce; Drill fills in the gaps of the Dremel paper to provide a similar open source version.

- Facebook's Presto is a distributed SQL query engine that is similar to Impala.

The days when Google held the clear advantage in innovation in the Big Data space are over. Now, we're in an exciting time of robust competition among different Big Data tools, technologies, and abstractions.

Google Cloud Platform

Google has released many of its internal infrastructure components to the public under the aegis of the Google Cloud Platform. Google's public cloud consists of a number of components, providing a complete Big Data ecosystem. It is likely that in the coming months and years there will be additional entries, so just because a tool or service isn't mentioned here doesn't mean that it doesn't exist. Chapter 2, "BigQuery Fundamentals," goes into more detail about the individual components, but this is a quick survey of the offerings. You can divide the cloud offerings into three portions: processing, storage, and analytics.

Cloud Processing

The cloud processing components enable you to run arbitrary computations over your data:

- **Google Compute Engine (GCE):** The base of Google's Cloud Platform, GCE is infrastructure-as-a-service, plain and simple. If you have software you just want to run in the cloud on a Linux virtual machine, GCE enables you to do so. GCE also can do live migration of your service so that when the datacenter it is running is turned down for maintenance, your service won't notice a hiccup.

- **AppEngine:** AppEngine is a higher-level service than GCE. You don't need to worry about OS images or networking configurations. You just write the code you actually want running in your service and deploy it; AppEngine handles the rest.

Cloud Storage

These cloud storage components enable you to store your own data in Google's cloud:

- **Google Cloud Storage (GCS):** GCS enables you to store arbitrary data in the cloud. It has two APIs: one that is compatible with Amazon.com's S3 and another REST API that is similar to other Google APIs.

- **DataStore:** A NoSQL key-value store. DataStore is usually used from AppEngine, but its REST API enables you to store and look up data from anywhere.

- **BigQuery (Storage API):** BigQuery enables you to store structured rows and columns of data. You can ingest data directly through the REST API, or you can import data from GCS.

Cloud Analytics

Google's cloud analytics services enable you to extract meaning from your data:

- **Cloud SQL:** A hosted MySQL instance in the cloud

- **Prediction API:** Enables you to train machine learning models and apply them to your data

- **Cloud Hadoop:** Packages Hadoop and makes it easy to run on Google Compute Engine
- **BigQuery:** Enables you to run SQL statements over your structured data

If you find that something is missing from Google's Cloud Platform, you always have the option of running your favorite open source software stack on Google Compute Engine. For example, the Google Cloud Hadoop package is one way of running Hadoop, but if you want to run a different version of Hadoop than is supported, you can always run Hadoop directly; Google's Hadoop package uses only publicly available interfaces.

Problem Statement

Before we go on to talk about BigQuery, here's a bit of background information about the problems that BigQuery was developed to solve.

What Is Big Data?

There are a lot of different definitions from experts about what it means to have Big Data; many of these definitions conceal a boast like, "Only a petabyte? I've forgotten how to count that low!" This book uses the term Big Data to mean more data than you can process sequentially in the amount of time you're willing to spend waiting for it. Put another way, Big Data just means more data than you can easily handle using traditional tools such as relational databases without spending a lot of money on specialized hardware.

This definition is deliberately fuzzy; to put some numbers behind it, we'll say a hundred million rows of structured data or a hundred gigabytes of unstructured data. You can fit data of that size on a commodity disk and even use MySQL on it. However, dealing with data that size isn't going to be pleasant. If you need to write a tool to clean the data, you're going to spend hours running it, and you need be careful about memory usage, and so on. And as the data size gets bigger, the amount of pain you'll experience doing simple things such as backing it up or changing the schema will get exponentially worse.

Why Big Data?

Many people are surprised at how easy it is to acquire Big Data; they assume that you need to be a giant company like Wal-Mart or IBM for Big Data to be relevant. However, Big Data is easy to accumulate. Following are some of the ways to get Big Data without being a Fortune 500 company:

- **Over time:** If you produce a million records a day, that might not be "Big Data." But in 3 years, you'll have a billion records; at some point you may find that you either need to throw out old data or figure out a new way to process the data that you have.

- **Viral scaling:** On the Internet, no one knows you're a small company. If your website becomes popular, you can get a million users overnight. If you track 10 actions from a million users a day, you're talking about a billion actions a quarter. Can you mine that data well enough to be able to improve your service and get to the 10 million user mark?

- **Projected growth:** Okay, maybe you have only small data now, but after you sign customer X, you'll instantly end up increasing by another 2 orders of magnitude. You need to plan for that growth now to make sure you can handle it.

- **Architectural limitations:** If you need to do intense computation over your data, the threshold for "Big Data" can get smaller. For example, if you need to run an unsupervised clustering algorithm over your data, you may find that even a few million data points become difficult to handle without sampling.

Why Do You Need New Ways to Process Big Data?

A typical hard disk can read on the order of 100 MB per second. If you want to ask questions of your data and your data is in the terabyte range, you either need thousands of disks or you are going to spend a lot of time waiting.

As anyone who has spent time tuning a relational database can attest, there is a lot of black magic involved in getting queries to run quickly on your-favorite-database. You may need to add indexes, stripe data across disks, put the transaction log on its own spindle, and so on. However, as your data grows, at some point it gets harder and harder to make your queries perform well. In addition, the more work you do, the more you end up specializing the schema for the type of questions you typically ask of your data.

What if you want to ask a question you've never asked before? If you are relying on a heavily tuned schema, or if you're running different queries than the database was tuned for, you may not get answers in a reasonable amount of time or without bogging down your production database. In these cases, your options are limited; you either need to run an extremely slow query (that may degrade performance for your entire database), or you could export the data and process it in an external system like Hadoop.

Often, to get queries to run quickly, people sample their data—they keep only 10 percent of user impressions, for example. But what happens if you want to explore the data in a way that requires access to all the impressions? Maybe you want to compute the number of distinct users that visited your site—if you drop 90 percent of your data, you can't just multiply the remaining users by 10 to get the number of distinct users in the original dataset. This point is somewhat subtle, but if you drop 90 percent of your data, you might still have records representing 99 percent of your users, or you might have records representing only 5 percent of your users; you can't tell unless you use a more sophisticated way to filter your data.

How Can You Read a Terabyte in a Second?

If you want to ask interactive questions of your Big Data, you must process all your data within a few seconds. That means you need to read hundreds of gigabytes per second—and ideally more.

Following are three ways that you can achieve this type of data rate:

1. Skip a lot of the data. This is a good option if you know in advance the types of questions you're going to ask. You can pre-aggregate the data or create indexes on the columns that you need to access. However, if you want to ask different questions, or ask them in a different way, you may not be able to avoid reading everything.

2. Buy some *really* expensive hardware. For a few million dollars or so, you can get a machine onsite that will come with its own dedicated support person that can let you query over your terabytes of data.

3. Run in parallel. Instead of reading from one disk, read from thousands of disks. Instead of one database server, read from hundreds.

If you use custom hardware (solution #2) and you want it to go faster, you need to buy an even bigger data warehouse server (and hope you can sell the old one). And if you rely on skipping data (solution #1) to give you performance, the only way to go faster is to be smarter about what data you skip (which doesn't scale).

BigQuery, and most Big Data tools, take approach #3. Although it may sound expensive to have thousands of disks and servers, the advantage is that you get exactly what you pay for; that is, if you need to run twice as fast, you can buy twice as many disks. If you use BigQuery, you don't need to buy your own disks; you get a chance to buy small slices of time on a massive amount of hardware.

What about MapReduce?

A large proportion of the Big Data hype has been directed toward MapReduce and Hadoop, its Open Source incarnation. Hadoop is a fantastic tool that enables you to break up your analysis problem into pieces that run in parallel. The Hadoop File System (HDFS) can enable you to read in parallel from a lot of disks, which allows you to perform operations over Big Data orders of magnitude more quickly than if you had to read that data sequentially.

However, Hadoop specifically and MapReduce in general have some architectural drawbacks that make them unsuited for interactive-style analyses. That is, if you want to ask questions of your data using MapReduce, you're probably going to want to get a cup of coffee (or go out to lunch) while you wait. Interactive analyses should give you answers before you get bored or forget why you were asking in the first place. Newer systems, such as Cloudera's Impala, allow interactive queries over your Hadoop data, but they do so by abandoning the MapReduce paradigm. Chapter 9 discusses the architecture in more detail and shows why MapReduce is better suited to batch workloads than interactive ones.

How Can You Ask Questions of Your Big Data and Quickly Get Answers?

Google BigQuery is a tool that enables you to run SQL queries over your Big Data. It fans out query requests to thousands of servers, reads from tens or hundreds of thousands of disks at once, and can return answers to complex questions within seconds. This book describes how BigQuery can achieve such good performance and how you can use it to run queries on your own data.

Summary

This chapter briefly documented the history of Google's Big Data systems and provided a survey of scale-out technologies, both at Google and elsewhere. It set the stage for BigQuery by describing an unfulfilled Big Data analytics niche. This chapter deliberately didn't mention BigQuery very much, however; Chapter 2 should answer all your questions about what BigQuery is and what it can do.

BigQuery Fundamentals

This chapter introduces you to BigQuery, describing what it can do, when to use it, when *not* to use it, and even a bit about why it is so fast. Because you may be evaluating whether BigQuery is the right tool for you, this chapter spends a bit of time comparing it to other systems and other architectures. It discusses the performance and types of workloads best-suited to BigQuery, and also how BigQuery fits with other offerings in the Google Cloud Platform.

This chapter concludes with an introduction to an AppEngine and Android App that is used as the basis of many of the examples throughout the book. This sample app demonstrates several ways that BigQuery can be integrated into an application—from log collection and analyses to dashboard development and correlation of multiple data streams.

What Is BigQuery?

BigQuery, like many tools, started with a problem. Google engineers were having a hard time keeping up with the growth of their data. The number of Gmail users is in the hundreds of millions; by 2012, there were more than 100 billion Google searches done every month. Trying to make sense of all this data was a time-consuming and frustrating experience.

Google is hugely a data-driven company. Decisions ranging from café menus to interview strategies to marketing campaigns are made by analyzing data.

If you have a great idea but you don't have data to back it up, you're going to have a hard time convincing anyone to implement your suggestion. However, if you have data on your side that says people click more ads with a particular shade of blue background, your shade of blue will likely become the new official standard.

As Google grew exponentially, the amount of data available also grew exponentially. Despite spending a lot of money on hardware and software for relational databases, it was often difficult to ask simple questions of the data. Despite having invented MapReduce to help analyze large datasets, it was still difficult to get answers interactively, without waiting minutes or hours for a long batch job to complete.

The data problem led to the development of an internal tool called Dremel, which enabled Google employees to run extremely fast SQL queries on large datasets. According to Armando Fox, a professor of computer science at the University of California at Berkley, "If you told me beforehand what Dremel claims to do, I wouldn't have believed you could build it." Dremel has become extremely popular at Google; Google engineers use it millions of times a day for tasks ranging from building sales dashboards to datacenter temperature analyses to computing employees' percentile rank of how long they've worked at the company.

In 2012, at Google I/O, Google publicly launched BigQuery, which allowed users outside of Google to take advantage of the power and performance of Dremel. Since then, BigQuery has expanded to become not just a query engine but a hosted, managed cloud-based structured storage provider. The following sections describe the main aspects of BigQuery.

SQL Queries over Big Data

The primary function of BigQuery is to enable interactive analytic queries over Big Data. Although Big Data is a fuzzy term, in practice it just means "data that is big enough that you have to worry about how big it is." Sometimes the data might be small now, but you anticipate it growing by orders of magnitude later. Sometimes the data might be only a few megabytes, but your algorithms to process it don't scale well. Or sometimes you have a million hard drives full of customer data in a basement.

BigQuery tries to tackle Big Data problems by attempting to be scale-invariant. That is, whether you have a hundred rows in your table or a hundred billion, the mechanism to work with them should be the same. Although some variance in execution time is expected between running a query over a megabyte and running the same query over a terabyte, the latter shouldn't be a million times slower than the former. If you start using BigQuery when you are receiving 1,000 customer records a day, you won't hit a brick wall when you scale up to 1 billion customer records a day.

BigQuery SQL

The lingua franca for data analyses is the SQL query language. Other systems, such as Hadoop, enable you to write code in your favorite language to perform analytics, but these languages make it difficult to interactively ask questions of your data. If you have to write a Java program to query your data, you'll end up spending a lot of time compiling, debugging, and uploading your program, rather than figuring out what data you need.

Despite being somewhat intimidating at first, SQL is also easy to use for nonprogrammers. Many software engineers are surprised when someone from marketing comes up with a sophisticated query to figure out why sales are slumping. However, it is actually quite common for non- or semi- technical people to be SQL wizards.

Oddly enough, the ones who often have the most difficulty with SQL are the programmers themselves. SQL is a declarative language; that is, you declare what results you want, and it is up to the software to figure out how to get those results. For programmers, this reverses the natural order; we're used to telling the computer exactly what we want it to do so that it gives us the results that we want. SQL leaves the method of execution up to the underlying query engine. This turns out to be advantageous for BigQuery because it allows the Dremel query engine to perform the analysis in a different way from traditional relational databases.

It can be surprising that a model we often have trouble understanding would be accessible to people in other disciplines. But after seeing sales, marketing, and even pointy-haired managers wielding RIGHT OUTER JOINS, we grudgingly have to admit that people who aren't programmers are still quite intelligent.

BigQuery uses an admittedly nonstandard dialect of SQL. Speaking for all the engineers who currently work on or ever have worked on BigQuery or Dremel, if we could go back and change one thing, it probably would be to stick to something closer to standard SQL. If there was one prediction we could make about a breaking change in the future, it would be that BigQuery would deprecate some of the nonstandard quirks, such as a comma for table union, in favor of more standard SQL. That said, if such a change was made, there would be lots of advance warning, and the old dialect would continue to work for a long time after the new dialect was released.

How Fast Is BigQuery?

One of the main limitations of database query performance is the sequential nature of most query execution. Although most databases can make use of multiple processors, they often use their available parallelism to run multiple queries at once, rather than taking advantage of multiple processors for a single query. That said, even if they did parallelize single query execution, the database would still be limited by disk I/O speeds—if your data is stored on a single disk, reading the disk from multiple places in parallel may actually be slower than reading it sequentially.

The SQL query language is highly parallelizable, however, as long as you have a way to take advantage of it. The Dremel query engine created a way to parallelize SQL execution across thousands of machines. Chapter 9, "Understanding Query Execution," describes in detail how it works, but the central principle is that it is a scale-out solution. If you want your queries to run faster, you can throw more machines at the problem. This is a contrast to a traditional scale-up architecture, where when you want more performance, you buy fancier hardware.

When run in the Google infrastructure, the Dremel architecture scales nearly linearly to tens of thousands of processor cores and hundreds of thousands of disks. The performance goal of the system was to process a terabyte of data in a second; although peak performance numbers have not been published, those goals have been met and exceeded.

Of course, this doesn't mean that you'll automatically see performance in that range; the Dremel clusters used by BigQuery are tuned for serving multiple queries at once rather than single queries at peak speed. A rough estimate for performance you can expect is on the order of 50 GB per second for a simple query. More complex queries—JOINs, complex regular expressions, and so on—will be somewhat slower. That said, 95 percent of all queries in the public BigQuery clusters finish in less than 5 seconds. However, unless you reserve capacity, you may find that performance fluctuates significantly due to load on the system.

BIGQUERY RESERVED CAPACITY

BigQuery offers the ability to reserve processing capacity in a dedicated virtual cluster in units of 5 GB processed per second. This might sound strange, since we just said that the rough goal is to process 50 GB per second for on-demand. Does that mean reserved capacity charges you more for less performance?

There are a couple of things to note with respect to reservations:

■ Reserved capacity gives you the ability to run queries that preempt other users, up to your capacity limit.

■ Reserved capacity gives you the optional ability to 'burst' over your capacity rate. This means your queries can use the pool of on-demand resources in addition to reserved resources.

■ On-demand (non-reserved) capacity is best-effort only. Performance may vary significantly from day to day, even from query to query, based on load of the overall system. Reservations give you the ability to be first in line for resources and to expect more stable performance.

Query performance should continue to scale sublinearly (that is, if you double the size, it will take less than double the time) up to at least 500 GB of data processed in the query. So if you have a 100 MB table that takes 3 seconds to query and you increase the size a thousand times to 100 GB, it might take only 5 seconds to query. Increasing the size of the table will allow BigQuery to use more hardware to run the query.

There is a limit to the number of execution nodes that will be assigned to any one query, however. Based on current cluster sizing, that limit comes at approximately one-half a terabyte of data processed. If you start with a 1 TB table that you can query in 20 seconds and double it to 2 TB, your queries will now likely take 40 seconds. Note that the relevant size here just includes the fields that are touched. If you have 100 fields but just read one of them, the effective size is just the size of that single field.

There isn't actually a hard maximum table size you can process in BigQuery, other than saying that after a certain point, querying the tables may take longer than you're willing to wait. Multiterabyte queries are fairly common; multi-petabyte queries are not.

Performance Benchmarks

Google doesn't publish benchmarks against BigQuery because when a company publishes its own benchmarks, people have a tendency to not believe them. In addition, if Google published performance numbers, it could be construed as a promise that users will see similar numbers. Because there seemed to be a lack of available performance information, we decided to run a simple benchmark of our own. Figure 2.1 shows a graph of how query execution time varies with the number of rows processed in a table for two different queries.

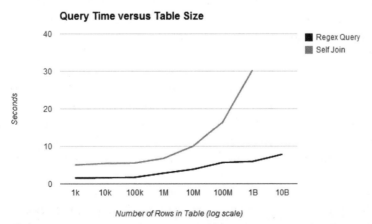

Figure 2.1: Query execution time versus table size

The benchmark used a real dataset: daily page views for Wikipedia in 2011. Each run of the benchmark used a sampled set of rows from the underlying dataset and increased by roughly an order of magnitude in size. The smallest table was 1,192 rows; the largest was more than 10 billion rows. The tables are in a publicly available dataset: `bigquery-samples:wikipedia_benchmark`. You should be able to reproduce similar results on your own (although you should note that several of the tables are large, and it can be easy to run up a serious bill by querying them).

The lower line on the chart corresponds to timings for a simple query that does a regular expression over the title field, groups by the language field, and sorts by the number of views. Here is the query that was used (where `<size>` ranged from 1k to 10B):

```
SELECT language, SUM(views) AS views
FROM [bigquery-samples:wikipedia-benchmark<size>]
WHERE REGEXP_MATCH(title, "G.*o.*o.*g")
GROUP BY language
ORDER BY views DESC
```

We used a reasonably complex query because we didn't want it to be something that could be done with a simple filter or index, and we wanted to make sure the query engine wouldn't be able to use any tricks to skip data.

From the chart, you can see that each order of magnitude increase in the table size roughly corresponds to an additional 1 second of query time (the x-axis is plotted in log scale). The final point on the right corresponds to a 10 billion-row table (10,677,046,566 rows, to be exact). Querying this table scans almost one-half a terabyte of data (446 GB).

This query would be extremely slow on a relational database; there isn't a way to precompute the regular expression results, so a relational database would have to do a table scan. In BigQuery, the query over the largest table took less than 8 seconds, on average, to read half a terabyte and perform 10 billion regular expressions.

We mentioned that there is a size after which you'll start seeing linear performance. To show this, we added another table, this one with more than 100 billion rows, and re-ran the same query. This query processed 4.4 TB and took 69 seconds on average, which is about ten times as long as the query with one tenth the data took. While we didn't go further than the 100 billion row table in our tests, there are a number of customers who routinely query over tens or hundreds of terabytes at a time.

You should not assume that all queries will run this quickly, however. JOIN queries or queries that produce a lot of results may run much more slowly. Some queries will run out of memory; others may hit other limits in the system. For example, in order to test JOIN performance, we ran the following self-join against the same tables from the previous query:

```
SELECT wiki1.year, wiki1.month, wiki1.day, sum(wiki2.max_views)
FROM [bigquery-samples:wikipedia-benchmark<size>] as wiki1
```

```
JOIN EACH (
    SELECT title, MAX(views) as max_views
    FROM [bigquery-samples:wikipedia-benchmark<size>]
    GROUP EACH BY title
    ) AS wiki2
ON wiki1.title = wiki2.title
GROUP EACH BY wiki1.year, wiki1.month, wiki1.day
```

The timing of these queries can be seen as the `Self Join` line in Figure 2.1. They take longer than the simple queries, but still increase slowly until about 100 million rows. Increasing from 100 million to a billion rows takes about double the time—still faster than linear but a significant slowdown. You can see, however, that the line ends at the 1 billion row point; this is because the query against the larger 10 billion row table failed with an Insufficient Resources error. Chapter 9 gives much more information about which queries will work well, which won't, and why. That chapter also provides some pointers for what to do when you hit errors like this one.

Cloud Storage System

In addition to being a way to run queries over your data, BigQuery is also a place to store your structured data in the cloud. Although this aspect of BigQuery grew out of necessity—if your data didn't live in Google's cloud then, you couldn't query it—it has grown into a significant and useful subsystem.

Your data is replicated to multiple geographically distinct locations for improved availability and durability. If a Google datacenter in Atlanta gets shut down because of a hurricane, that shouldn't cause a hiccup in your ability to access your data. Data is also replicated within a cluster, so your data should be virtually immune to data loss due to hardware failure. Of course, the BigQuery service may not have perfect uptime, and if your data is important, you should make sure it is backed up. You can back up your tables by exporting them to Google Cloud Storage for safekeeping, or you can run a table copy job in BigQuery to save a snapshot.

Data Ingestion

Data used in BigQuery must be loaded into the system before it can be queried. The load process transforms your data into a format that is optimized for querying and stores it in locations in physical proximity to the Dremel compute clusters.

There are three ways to get your data into BigQuery: streaming, direct upload, and through Google Cloud Storage. The most reliable and predictable is likely the latter. If your data is already in Google Cloud Storage, the load step is merely a transfer between two systems already within Google's cloud, so ingestion is very fast.

Direct upload can be an easier route if you don't want to go through Google Cloud Storage, because you can follow a standard resumable-upload HTTP protocol. Streaming is the easiest method; you can post individual rows, which will be available for query immediately. That said, for large load operations, or cases in which you want all your data to be available atomically, streaming may not be the best mechanism. For more information about how to get data into BigQuery, Chapter 6, "Loading Data," describes the various options in detail.

Structured Data Storage

BigQuery is a system that stores and operates on structured data; that is, data that follows a rigid *schema*. A spreadsheet is an example of structured data, as is a database table. An HTML document, even though it may have predictable fields, is unstructured. If your data doesn't have a schema, or can't be coerced to a schema, there may be other tools that are better-suited for your use case.

BigQuery schemas describe the columns, or *fields*, of the structured data. Each field has a name and a data type that indicates the kind of data that can be stored in the field. Those data types can be either primitive or record types. Primitive types are basic types that store a single value—a string, a floating-point number, an integer, or a boolean flag.

A record type, however, is a collection of other fields. For the most part, a record is just a way of grouping your fields together. For example, if you store location as latitude and longitude, you could have a location record with two fields: lat and long. Fields can also be repeated, which means that they can store more than one value.

These last two features—record types and repeated fields—distinguish BigQuery from most relational databases, which can store only flat rows. Records and repeated fields enable you to store the data in a more natural way than you might in a relational database. For example, if your table contains customer orders, you might want to store an entire order as a single record, even though there were multiple items in the order. This makes it easier to perform analysis of the orders without having to flatten the data or normalize it into multiple tables.

Collections of rows of data following a single schema are organized into *tables*. These tables are similar to tables in a typical relational database but have some restrictions. The only way to modify BigQuery tables is to append to them or rewrite them—there is no way to update individual rows. BigQuery also doesn't support table modification queries, like ALTER TABLE, DROP TABLE, or UPDATE TABLE.

Collections of tables with similar access restrictions are organized into *datasets*. Many relational database systems allow you to have multiple database catalogs.

For instance, if you have a MySQL database with your financial data you might want that to be a separate catalog from your user data.

These catalogs map quite well to a BigQuery dataset. Datasets can be shared with other users and groups. Collections of datasets owned by a single user or organization are organized into *projects*. Projects are a Google Cloud Platform concept that indicates a single billing entity with a team of users in various roles. Chapter 4, "Understanding the BigQuery Object Model," discusses these abstractions in much more detail.

Distributed Cloud Computing

Google has a lot of hardware in their datacenters. A number of people have tried to figure out just how many machines Google has by taking into account things like global PC sales and maximum power capacity of various known Google datacenters. It is a large number. Very few, if any, organizations can match the scale and, as importantly, the organization of Google's datacenters. Google's Cloud Platform allows people outside of Google to take advantage of this scale and manageability.

Harnessing the Power of Google's Cloud

When you run your queries via BigQuery, you put a giant cluster of machines to work for you. Although the BigQuery clusters represent only a small fraction of Google's global fleet, each query cluster is measured in the thousands of cores. When BigQuery needs to grow, there are plenty of resources that can be harnessed to meet the demand.

If you want to, you could probably figure out the size of one of BigQuery's compute clusters by carefully controlling the size of data being scanned in your queries. The number of processor cores involved is in the thousands, the number of disks in the hundreds of thousands. Most organizations don't have the budget to build at that kind of scale just to run some queries over their data.

The benefits of the Google cloud go beyond the amount of hardware that is used, however. A massive datacenter is useless unless you can keep it running. If you have a cluster of 100,000 disks, some reasonable number of those disks is going to fail every day. If you have thousands of servers, some of the power supplies are going to die every day. Even if you have highly reliable software running on those servers, some of them are going to crash every day.

To keep a datacenter up and running requires a lot of expertise and know-how. How do you maximize the life of a disk? How do you know exactly which parts are failing? How do you know which crashes are due to hardware failures and which to software? Moreover, you need software that is written to handle failures at any time and in any combination. Running in Google's cloud means that Google worries about these things so that you don't have to.

There is another key factor to the performance of Google's cloud that some of the early adopters of Google Compute Engine have started to notice: It has an extremely fast network. Parallel computation requires a lot of coordination and aggregation, and if you spend all your time moving the data around, it doesn't matter how fast your algorithms are or how much hardware you have. The details of how Google achieves these network speeds are shrouded in secrecy, but the super-fast machine-to-machine transfer rates are key to making BigQuery fast.

Cloud Data Warehousing

Most companies are accustomed to storing their data on-premise or in leased datacenters on hardware that they own or rent. Fault tolerance is usually handled by adding redundancy within a machine, such as extra power supplies, RAID disk controllers, and ECC memory. All these things add to the cost of the machine but don't actually distance you from the consequences of a hardware failure. If a disk goes bad, someone has to go to the datacenter, find the rack with the bad disk, and swap it out for a new one.

Cloud data warehousing offers the promise of relieving you of the responsibility of caring about whether RAID-5 is good enough, whether your tape backups are running frequently enough, or whether a natural disaster might take you offline completely. Cloud data warehouses, whether Google's or a competitor's, offer fault-tolerance, geographic distribution, and automated backups.

Ever since Google made the decision to go with exclusively scale-out architectures, it has focused on making its software accustomed to handling frequent hardware failures. There are stories about Google teams that run mission-critical components, who don't even bother to free memory—the amount of bugs and performance problems associated with memory management is too high. Instead, they just let the process run out of memory and crash, at which time it will get automatically restarted. Because the software has been designed to not only handle but also expect that type of failure, a large class of errors is virtually eliminated.

For the user of Google's cloud, this means that the underlying infrastructure pieces are extraordinarily failure-resistant and fault-tolerant. Your data is replicated to several disks within a datacenter and then replicated again to multiple datacenters. Failure of a disk, a switch, a load balancer, or a rack won't be noticeable to anyone except a datacenter technician. The only kind of hardware failure that would escalate to the BigQuery operations engineers would be if someone hit the big red off button in a datacenter or if somebody took out a fiber backbone with a backhoe. This type of failure still wouldn't take BigQuery down, however, since BigQuery runs in multiple geographically distributed datacenters and will fail over automatically.

Of course, this is where we have to remind you that all software is fallible. Just because your data is replicated nine ways doesn't mean that it is completely immune to loss. A buggy software release could cause data to be inadvertently deleted from all nine of those disks. If you have critical data, make sure to back it up.

Many organizations are understandably reluctant to move their data into the cloud. It can be difficult to have your data in a place where you don't control it. If there is data loss, or an outage, all you can do is take your business elsewhere—there is no one except support staff to yell at and little you can do to prevent the problem from happening in the future.

That said, the specialized knowledge and operational overhead required to run your own hardware is large and gets only larger. The advantages of scale that Google or Amazon has only get bigger as they get better at managing their datacenters and improving their data warehousing techniques. It seems likely that the days when most companies run their own IT hardware are numbered.

Multitenancy and Parallel Execution

When you run a query on MySQL that takes one second, you get to occupy a single processor core for one second. If you have eight processors, you can run eight queries at once. Amazon Redshift lets you run a single query in parallel, but on a fixed number of cores that are all yours for the entire time you are renting the Redshift instance.

BigQuery operates on a fundamentally different model; your query will run on thousands of cores in parallel. If you have eight queries, those may all run on a thousand cores in parallel. The query engine will time-slice the operations and make progress on some queries while others are waiting for disk or network I/O. All queries perform a mix of I/O and processing; waiting for I/O would mean that the processor would sit idle. The Dremel engine underlying BigQuery can maximize the throughput of the system by pipelining queries so that as some queries are waiting for I/O operations, other queries will use the processor.

By allowing your queries to run on *all* the hardware in a compute cluster, you can see performance far beyond what you otherwise could see unless you were willing to pay for a dedicated similarly sized cluster. There just isn't another way you can process hundreds of gigabytes per second without a massive amount of hardware. If you want to build it yourself, it would cost millions of dollars to build and maintain. (Licenses for on-premise solutions like Netezza generally run in the seven figures.)

If you did buy and build your own compute cluster so that you could get BigQuery-like performance, you probably wouldn't be able to run it at capacity—it would probably get much less usage overnight and on the weekends for example. If you could run it at capacity, you'd likely have times of day when demand outstripped supply, and then you'd be sacrificing performance.

Keeping a giant compute cluster around in order to run a few queries once in a while seems wasteful. One of the key concepts of the BigQuery query engine is multitenancy. That is, multiple queries from multiple different users are all running at once. By multiplexing usage across multiple customers, who are all on different schedules and with different data usage patterns, BigQuery can keep its hardware running at a high-level of utilization. Also, BigQuery can easily grow and shrink its capacity by taking advantage of extra resources within a datacenter (that is, from other Google services), or by spinning up new clusters in other datacenters.

Analytics as a Service (AaaS?)

There are a lot of acronyms in Cloud Computing, from IaaS (Infrastructure as a Service) to PaaS (Platform as a Service). BigQuery, if you were going to give it a similar acronym, could be called Analytics as a Service (AaaS). We're not particularly excited about this moniker catching on, but as a description, it is quite apt.

BigQuery is a service that you use to perform your analytics tasks. It operates at a higher level than most other Big Data analytics offerings. For example, tools such as Impala and Presto require you to manage your own virtual hardware and your own data. Even Amazon Redshift, although it is hosted, requires you to manage a database instance.

Global Data Namespace

One advantage to performing your analytics in the cloud is that it becomes easy to share data without moving it around. All BigQuery tables sit in the same namespace. This may seem like a minor detail, but it is actually extremely useful. Every table in BigQuery can be joined against every other table in BigQuery, as long as the user running the query has access to both tables. This means that if someone publishes a table with weather data, you can join that weather table against your sales data to determine how the weather affects your sales. There are a number of public datasets that have things like financial information and GitHub commit history. Researchers can mine these sources or combine the data with their own for new insight.

Any dataset can be shared with any user just by making an API call or using the UI to edit the access control settings. If you want someone in a different continent to run queries against your data, you don't have to ship it to them or let them log into your servers. You just share the dataset with them, and they can run queries against the data directly. You have the option of requiring them to pay the BigQuery bill for any queries they run (just add them to the Access Control List) or allowing them to run queries that are billed to you (add them to your project). These concepts will be clearer in later chapters, but we bring them up now to whet your appetite.

Web UI

BigQuery provides a web UI at `https://bigquery.cloud.google.com`. This interface allows you to perform most of the operations in the API: Browse available tables, read their schema and data, share datasets with other users, load data, and export it to Google Cloud Storage. It also allows you to create and edit queries.

Although it may seem like an afterthought to have a web UI for a database, it means that anyone can use it from any web browser—there is no need to download any client side software or install anything. Many users will perform all the tasks they need directly from the web interface. Figure 2.2 shows the BigQuery web UI.

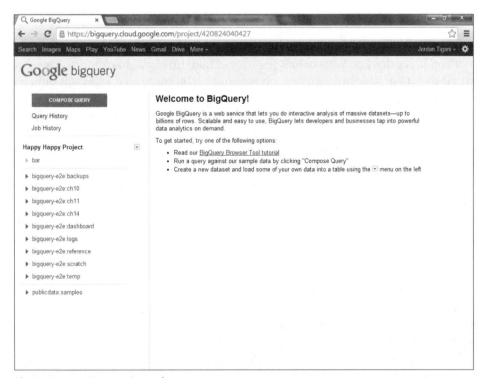

Figure 2.2: BigQuery web interface

HTTP API

Whether they realize it or not, users interact with BigQuery by sending HTTP requests—the same type of HTTP requests they use when browsing the web or filling out a web form. The BigQuery developer documentation describes the particular format of these requests and where they need to be sent. There are client-side tools that make it easier to interact with the service, but if you're happier using the raw HTTP operations, that is an available option. BigQuery's API follows a REST model, meaning that the interface is designed for humans to understand, not just computers. REST means a lot more, too, but we'll get into that in Chapter 5, "Talking to the BigQuery API."

The nice thing about using standard HTTP is that it is, well, a standard. If your company has firewalls that limit the kinds of network traffic that can be sent, HTTP will pass right through. The response codes that are sent are standard, the headers are standard, and various operations have a standard interpretation. This should make it easier to learn the API and develop an intuition about how it should work. It also makes it easier to debug when something is going wrong. An HTTP 404 is always Not Found, so you can handle a 404 from BigQuery the same way you do from another HTTP API, like Google Cloud Storage.

Asynchronous Job Execution

The last important piece of BigQuery is the asynchronous job manager. Everything that BigQuery does on your behalf that might take time, might run into errors, or might cost a variable amount of money, runs in the context of a job. All queries that you run are jobs, for example.

Most other query frameworks force you into a synchronous model, where you start the query and wait for the response, which contains the query results. When running queries synchronously, if you hit a network error or the request times out, you have to retry the query from scratch.

BigQuery jobs are asynchronous; that is, you start a job and then check on the progress of the job until it is done. All jobs have a unique name, either provided by the user or generated by BigQuery. This name can be used both to determine the status of the job and to read the results. Moreover, because you have a name for the job, you don't have to read all the results in one request; you can request one page at a time. Paging through results is important because BigQuery queries can return terabytes of data.

Although asynchronous interfaces can be slightly more difficult to use, they can be much more flexible and resistant to errors. For instance, if you use AppEngine, all requests must complete within 60 seconds or AppEngine kills them. If you used a synchronous model, you would have no way of running a query that took longer than AppEngine allowed. When running asynchronously, however, you can start the query and then poll until it is done, which can all be done in shorter requests that don't bump up against AppEngine time limits.

What BigQuery Isn't

We think that BigQuery is an extremely versatile and useful tool. Like any tool, however, there are some jobs where it is a better fit than others. And then there are some jobs where it is no help at all. BigQuery is not a replacement for health insurance, nor should you consult it for legal advice. If that comes as a surprise, we should probably also tell you that BigQuery is not likely to provide psychiatric services either.

We often hear from customers evaluating BigQuery for projects that BigQuery isn't well suited for. Although we don't like telling people not to use BigQuery, we'd rather have customers who are happy because it meets their needs rather than disappointed because it doesn't support their workloads.

That said, sometimes with a bit of elbow grease and duct tape, BigQuery can work well in cases for which at first glance it didn't appear to be the best solution. We also have had a number of these types of customers who have slightly idiosyncratic usage. By working closely with them, we have helped evolve BigQuery to meet their needs more naturally.

Neither OLTP nor OLAP

While BigQuery performs updates transactionally, it is still a far cry from what you'd consider an Online Transaction Processing (OLTP) system. OLTP systems usually handle simple queries and have high rates of updates. BigQuery supports only append and truncate operations, so the types of row-level updates required in an OLTP system are not directly supported. In some cases, however, you can simulate row-level updates by making your queries more complex.

BigQuery is closer to Online Analytics Processing (OLAP), supporting many of the same types of use cases as an OLAP system. BigQuery's nested and repeated fields can approximate the data cubes in OLAP but allow querying via a more familiar SQL dialect rather than MDX. In a bit of trivia, Mosha Pasumansky, the inventor of the MDX query language, works on the Dremel query engine underlying BigQuery.

Neither Relational nor NoSQL

BigQuery is not a good replacement for a relational database. You shouldn't use BigQuery to store your list of customers or use it for your order-processing pipeline. Relational databases need to update individual rows and often need to perform subsecond queries. The Dremel query engine used by BigQuery actually can run queries in much less than 1 second, but to make sure the system has enough capacity for all users, the number of concurrent queries that can be done by a single user is generally throttled.

So if BigQuery isn't a relational database, it must be NoSQL, right? BigQuery uses a dialect of the SQL language to query data, so it can't actually be called NoSQL, either. NoSQL refers to a group of semi-structured storage technologies designed to scale better than relational databases but which in exchange are awkward or impossible to query. BigQuery makes different trade-offs than NoSQL and goes in the opposite direction. To improve scaling, rather than making it more difficult to query, BigQuery makes it more difficult to update. In exchange, however, BigQuery can query over much larger datasets than traditional SQL databases.

Not Even MapReduce

One of the questions that we heard most often when we released BigQuery was, "So, does BigQuery use MapReduce under the hood?" The open source implementation of MapReduce—Hadoop—has become increasingly popular in helping people perform computation over their Big Data. People are understandably interested in the similarities between the two technologies.

BigQuery doesn't use MapReduce, however. MapReduce is fundamentally a batch-oriented technology. In other words, it is designed for long-running batch jobs and not interactive ones. The particular differences and reasons behind the different performance profiles are somewhat technical—they are discussed in much more detail in Chapter 9.

Although MapReduce is usually going to be at least an order of magnitude slower than BigQuery, it does have a more flexible architecture. That is, there are a number of things that are difficult to compute in SQL, but MapReduce gives you the option of writing whatever code you want in whatever language you choose to perform your computation. Although we don't usually comment about unreleased features, we can make a prediction that the expressiveness of computations that you can perform in BigQuery will increase substantially in the near future.

Not Open Source

One of the criticisms of BigQuery that we've seen in the press and in blogs is that it isn't open source. If Google was serious about open systems, the thinking goes, surely it would want to contribute the source code back to the community. However, open sourcing would both be harder and less useful than you would imagine. There are a lot of internal closed-source systems that would be difficult to separate from the query engine.

For example, if there was no discovery service that told BigQuery when machines were offline, it wouldn't rapidly adjust the serving tree topology. If there was no massive distributed filesystem, running a query over a large dataset would likely be slower than on a traditional relational database system.

Although there certainly would be ways of partitioning the system so that it could work with HDFS or other open source tools, this would be a large undertaking. The Google technology stack, for better or worse, is specialized, and it would be a huge undertaking to separate out the technology-independent portions of it.

Even if BigQuery (or the Dremel query engine) was open source, you'd still need a place to run it. Dremel is most useful when run on hundreds or thousands of machines. A large portion of the value of BigQuery is in providing a slice of a huge managed compute cluster. While you could run this on your own hardware or in another vendor's cloud, it would be expensive and have considerable service-management overhead.

We hope that in the future we will be able to open source portions of the system as Google's Cloud Platform releases more of the building blocks used by Google's internal systems to the outside world. In the meantime, users who want an open source alternative should consider the Apache Drill open source Dremel project, which aims to be compatible with BigQuery's SQL dialect and API.

BigQuery Technology Stack

Google has an extremely comprehensive and impressive set of internal infrastructure tools, many of which, such as Spanner, Megastore, and GFS, have been disclosed in research papers. Some of these tools, such as Bigtable and GFS, have open source versions. Users often wonder how BigQuery relates to these technologies: Are BigQuery tables Bigtables, for example? Is user data stored in GFS?

This section attempts to answer, at a high level, how BigQuery relates to the Google infrastructure stack. Chapter 9 goes into more detail about the architecture; if you're interested in how these systems work, you may want to skip ahead. If Chapter 9 isn't enough detail for you, it provides references to the research papers that Google has published on the underlying technologies.

Metadata Storage

BigQuery stores data about your tables (although not the data itself) in Megastore: a consistent, transactional, globally replicated datastore. Megastore is Google's version of a NoSQL database that supports transactional reading, writing, and updating of entities, but complex queries are impossible. Most other NoSQL offerings lack either strong consistency or transactions. Megastore uses Paxos to ensure strong consistency and has transactional update semantics (although the transactions have more limits than a traditional relational database).

Google infrastructure projects are layered, sometimes to an absurd degree. Each layer adds something that the lower layer doesn't have. Megastore is built on top of Bigtable and adds transactions and consistent replication. Bigtable has the disadvantage of just being available in one datacenter. If that datacenter goes down due to a natural disaster or becomes unreachable because someone cuts a fiber optic cable with a backhoe, the data is essentially unavailable until the problem is repaired. Megastore replicates data synchronously to multiple datacenters so that the data is always available.

Megastore usage is widespread throughout Google products. Cloud Datastore is a thin layer on top of Megastore that allows schema-less and semi-structured tables. It is likely that BigQuery metadata operations will move to Spanner at some point, which is the next-generation globally replicated transactional data store. When and if that move happens, it will be transparent to users of BigQuery. The only visible change will likely be additional data locality options that would be enabled by Spanner.

Table Storage

BigQuery table data is stored in Colossus. So far, Google has been secretive about the details of Colossus, other than to say that it is a successor to the Google File System (GFS). At a high level, Colossus is a distributed filesystem that stores data on an enormous number of disks and makes the data available over a network. Data within a Colossus cell is replicated, providing durability in the event of disk failures. BigQuery also replicates your data to multiple Colossus cells, which preserves the ability to access your data in the event that a datacenter goes down.

The most important feature of Colossus as it relates to BigQuery is the ability to read data in parallel. Because Colossus stores data on many different disks, you can read the data much faster than you could read from a single disk by reading from multiple different locations at once.

Not all your data is stored in Colossus, however. Data that is streamed into BigQuery is temporarily stored in Bigtable. Small tables may be stored inline in Megastore along with the metadata. And, of course, a number of other storage systems at Google may be in use now or in the future to store your table data. Although this may sound cryptic or vague, the bottom line is you shouldn't make any assumptions about where or how your data will be stored. You can, however, assume that Google will continue to invest in storage systems that improve reliability, durability, and performance.

As important as the "where" of data storage is the "how." BigQuery uses a proprietary columnar storage format called ColumnIO. ColumnIO is tuned to the usage patterns for BigQuery, and allows you to read just the columns that are needed to execute a query. This not only improves performance, but it also is what allows BigQuery to charge just for access to columns that get referenced in a query.

Networking

As more people move to scale-out architectures for Big Data, they realize that network connections between machines become a big bottleneck. This mostly follows from common sense—when moving from a single machine to multiple machines, the effective bandwidth you have available to get to your data ends up going down by a couple of orders of magnitude. Even in a Non-Uniform Memory Access (NUMA) machine, memory in another node is much cheaper to access than data that resides on another machine in the network. If you invest more heavily in the network components that carry data from one machine to another, you can more closely replicate the single-machine performance in a clustered network environment.

In a large network cluster, however, it is harder to ensure that you have a fast network path between all combinations of machines. Many Big Data suites, such as Hadoop, allow you to tune the way they run to take into account network topology and physical distance between machines. If two machines share the same physical rack, for instance, the bandwidth between them is likely to be much higher than if they are in opposite sides of the datacenter.

Google guards the details of its datacenter hardware extremely closely. That said, from public benchmarks that people have run on Google Compute Engine, it is clear that one of the main distinguishing factors in the Google cloud is the extraordinarily fast network. It also is clear that the network is much less sensitive to physical locality than you might expect. These super-fast internal connections enable BigQuery to execute multiterabyte queries in seconds.

The connections between datacenters are as impressive as the connections within the datacenter. Google bought up a lot of unused fiber-optic cable around the world and uses it to move data between datacenters. For users of BigQuery, this allows your data to be replicated to different geographical regions extremely quickly so that your data will be available even in the event of a natural disaster or large-scale power outage.

Query Computation

We mentioned that BigQuery's query computation engine does not use MapReduce. And it clearly isn't a relational database…. So how does it work? The computation engine is Dremel, a parallel, distributed, column-oriented query engine that Google has used internally since 2006. The principal innovation is the tree-structured architecture that allows queries to be processed in parallel in the leaves but aggregates results at the higher levels of the tree. The tree architecture also enables multiple queries to run at once within the tree, which lets different users share the same hardware. Chapter 9 discusses Dremel and how it works in considerable detail.

Google Cloud Platform

BigQuery is one component of Google's Cloud Platform. The other principal products are Compute Engine, AppEngine, Cloud Storage, Cloud SQL, and Cloud Datastore. It can be confusing, at first, to figure out what all of these products are, how they fit together, and when to use one versus another. This section walks through the Google Cloud Platform offerings and describes how they work with BigQuery or when you might want to use them instead of BigQuery. Figure 2.3 shows the relationship between BigQuery and various Google Cloud Platform offerings. The ones that are not listed are services that do not have any direct connection to BigQuery (such as Google Prediction API).

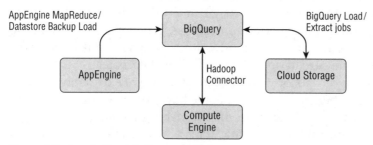

Figure 2.3: Google Cloud Platform and BigQuery

Google Compute Engine (GCE)

Google Compute Engine is the solution for people who want to control all aspects of the software stack. You get a standard Linux virtual machine running in Google's cloud. You can install anything you'd like on that machine and run it however you choose. You pay for the amount of virtual hardware you need and the amount of data transferred out of the system.

Because you can run any software you like on virtually any number of machines, you can run other Big Data analysis and transformation suites. This can be complementary to BigQuery. For example, you can use the BigQuery Hadoop connector to read your BigQuery tables, process them with Hadoop, and write them back to BigQuery. This is a popular option for customers who want to perform transformations on their data that are difficult or impossible to do in BigQuery SQL. This is also a good way to do Extract Transform and

Load (ETL) operations to translate source data into a format that can be easily ingested by BigQuery.

If you prefer, of course, you could run Impala, Presto, or Apache Drill on your Google Compute Engine instances. We believe that there are performance and manageability advantages to BigQuery. However, alternatives do exist, even within the Google cloud. If you choose to use a non-Google cloud, the most comparable alternative is Amazon EC2.

Chapter 12, "External Data Processing," briefly describes using Google Compute Engine to run Hadoop over BigQuery data. The same example would likely work well in Amazon's cloud; although, the performance might suffer because the data has to cross the public Internet.

Google Cloud Storage (GCS)

As mentioned, BigQuery is a structured storage system, which is great if your data is organized into rows and columns. Google Cloud Storage, however, is unstructured storage. That is, it can be used to store any data—from backups of your photos to websites to gene sequences. Google Cloud Storage is directly API-compatible with the Amazon S3 storage service, but it also has a number of additional features that are only available in GCS.

GCS can also be used to get data in and out of BigQuery. If you have data in GCS in any format that BigQuery understands (currently CSV and newline-delimited JSON), you can import it directly into BigQuery. Likewise, you can also export BigQuery tables to GCS. Exporting can be useful if you want to back up your data, or you want to use it elsewhere. (For example, you want to download it into a local database.) Several examples in this book use Google Cloud Storage to get data in and out of BigQuery.

AppEngine

Google AppEngine was the first piece of the Google Cloud Platform to be released. AppEngine is a fully managed web app hosting environment; with very little code you can build a standalone website or back end for a mobile application. AppEngine has its own structured data storage mechanisms such as Cloud Datastore and Cloud SQL. Many AppEngine users log data to BigQuery for analytics and reporting. The BigQuery End-to-End application that is a companion to this book is an AppEngine app that stores data in Cloud Datastore but analyzes data with BigQuery. Chapter 8, "Putting It Together" walks through the code for this app in detail.

AppEngine is often called Platform-as-a-Service because it abstracts away so many of the details about where the software is running. Users write their own code, but they don't have to worry about actual hardware or operating system infrastructure. AppEngine takes care of scaling its service, spinning up new instances as demand increases.

Cloud Datastore

Cloud Datastore is a NoSQL data store; you can think of it as key value storage. Although it does have some support for queries and indexes, it is not well suited to ad-hoc queries over your data. It is, however, fast for point lookups and indexed queries, and it scales virtually infinitely. Cloud Datastore is backed by Google's Megastore distributed consistent storage system.

If you want to run analytics queries over your Cloud Datastore storage, you can export it to BigQuery. Chapter 11, "Managing Data Stored in BigQuery," shows one way of exporting AppEngine data automatically, whereas Chapter 12 shows another mechanism you can use if you want to transform the data in the process. A number of BigQuery customers store their data both in BigQuery and Datastore by writing simultaneously to both locations. Although this seems like unnecessary duplication, it allows for both fast point-lookups (via Datastore) and fast ad hoc queries (via BigQuery).

Cloud SQL

Google Cloud SQL is a cloud-hosted MySQL database. The query language is MySQL, and the performance characteristics are similar to MySQL. However, running it in Google's storage infrastructure helps it scale better than a stock MySQL instance.

Cloud SQL is extremely helpful if you're migrating an existing application to Google's cloud. If your application is currently using a relational database (like MySQL or PostgreSQL), it might be difficult to switch to using a NoSQL store like Cloud Datastore. Cloud SQL allows you to run the same SQL queries you're used to but within Google's managed cloud.

Although it has a familiar interface, Cloud SQL has many of the scaling limitations of MySQL, and if you have a large amount of data you might consider using Cloud Datastore and/or BigQuery instead. Table 2.1 has a comparison of the features between BigQuery and Cloud SQL to help you decide which one is better for your application.

Table 2.1: A Comparison between BigQuery, Cloud SQL, and Cloud Datastore

FEATURE	BIGQUERY	CLOUD DATASTORE	CLOUD SQL
Data scale	Unlimited	Unlimited	< 10 GB
Supports ad-hoc queries	Yes	No	Yes
Supports fast data lookups	No	Yes	Yes
Can be used as a Hadoop source or sink	Yes	No	No

FEATURE	BIGQUERY	CLOUD DATASTORE	CLOUD SQL
Replicated across geo-graphical areas	Yes	Yes	Yes
Choice of datacenter locations (EU and US)	No	No	Yes
Supports row-level updates	No (Append- only)	Yes	Yes
Built-in historical snapshots	7 days of history	No	No
Query UI	Yes	Yes (but not full SQL)	No
Visualization via Tableau	Yes	No	Yes

BigQuery Service History

BigQuery releases a new update every week. Usually, the changes are small: bug fixes, minor features, and other incremental changes. The rationale behind this frequent release cycle is that it allows problems to be caught early, allows major features to be phased in, and gives trusted testers the ability to try out new functionality before it is released to the public.

This constant stream of updates is one advantage of a managed service like BigQuery versus running the analytics software yourself; bug fixes get applied automatically, and the system gets faster and more fully featured over time. In addition, Google constantly upgrades its hardware and improves its infrastructure components; this will translate into faster queries and larger scale.

Version History

About once a quarter BigQuery launches a new version with new functionality. The history of BigQuery major releases follows:

- **May 2010:** BigQuery prototype launched to Trusted testers at Google I/O. At this point, BigQuery provided only a synchronous interface for querying data stored in Google Cloud Storage.
- **May 2012:** Version 1.0. BigQuery launched to the public at Google I/O 2012. This release included the current HTTP API. This release had asynchronous query and job execution and included the principal abstractions of Project, Dataset, and Tables.
- **June 2012:** Billing added. After this, users actually had to pay to use BigQuery.
- **August 2012:** Version 1.1. Batch queries added along with a Microsoft Excel connector.

- **October 2012:** Version 1.2 Imports via JSON added as well as from AppEngine Datastore backups. Querying and manipulation of nested and repeated fields also added.

- **March 2013:** Version 1.3. Added the ability to join two large tables and removed limits on distinct elements for GROUP BY operations. Timestamp data type also added.

- **June 2013:** Version 1.4. Support for large query results. Also analytic and windowing functions added.

- **September 2013:** Version 1.5. Streaming ingestion added to the API. Table decorators also released.

- **March 2014:** Version 1.6. Table views, table wildcards, and partitioned export were all added. Streaming ingestion limits were raised by two orders of magnitude. A number of query improvements such as support for multi-JOIN were also made.

We mention this history to show the rapid evolution of the BigQuery service. Although queries and API calls that were written for BigQuery version 1.0 would still work today, many of the limitations of the service have been removed. For example, BigQuery used to support only JOIN operations where one of the tables was smaller than 8 MB. Now, BigQuery can join tables of virtually any size. Table 2.2 summarizes the expanded functionality.

In addition, quota sizes have been raised considerably over time. When launched, BigQuery supported only 2 concurrent queries, and 100 load jobs per day that could import only 50 GB at a time. Now, BigQuery supports up to 20 concurrent queries per project, and 1,000 load jobs per table per day. Each load job can import up to 1 TB. If you're using the streaming interface to add data, you can insert up to 100,000 rows per second per table.

Table 2.2: Removing Limits

LIMITATION	DATE CHANGED	DESCRIPTION
JOIN operations required one table to be smaller than 8 MB.	March 2013	Now, JOINs of virtually any size can be used via the EACH keyword.
GROUP BY operations that resulted in more than a few million distinct results could cause out-of-resources errors.	March 2013	GROUP BY operations of virtually any size supported via the EACH keyword.
Query results required to be smaller than 128 MB.	June 2013	The allowLargeResults flag was added to allow results of virtually any size to be returned.
Streaming inserts limited to 1000 rows per second.	March 2014	Limits were raised to 100,000 rows per second, per table.

Future Predictions

By the time you read this, some of the exciting new features that the BigQuery team is working on now will be released. Google has a policy of not speculating about new features before they happen. That said, we want to give you a couple of hints about what you might expect from BigQuery in the future. Rather than reveal particular features, we'll just describe what kinds of things are important to us and that we'll be working on improving.

- **Reliability and predictability:** BigQuery should be just as reliable as your local database instance. It also should be predictable—if a query runs in 2 seconds today, it shouldn't take 5 seconds tomorrow.

- **Reducing limitations:** There are cases now in which BigQuery gives out-of-resources errors or runs into size limitations. We'd like to get rid of these; when you run a query, it should just work, no matter how big the data is or what you've requested.

- **Getting closer to standard SQL:** There are a couple of nonstandard SQLisms that can be frustrating for new users. We'd like to make BigQuerySQL look more like SQL-92 or standard SQL that you're familiar with. This also means we'd like to stop requiring the usage of size hints like `EACH`.

- **Interaction with code that isn't SQL:** Right now, if you want to run an algorithm that is difficult to express in SQL, you've got to export your data out of BigQuery, transform it, and import it back. We'd like to remove steps from this process.

- **Features requested by users:** The BigQuery team monitors the `google-bigquery` tag on `StackOverflow.com`. Feel free to chime in there if you have feature requests. There is also an external bug tracker that can be used to report bugs and feature requests at `https://code.google .com/p/google-bigquery/issues/list`. Alternately, if you have a support arrangement with Google Cloud Support; you can let your support representative know your pain points. Customer feedback helps decide priorities for new features and the direction of the product.

BigQuery Sensors Application

To illustrate the different ways that BigQuery can be used in a web application, we have built a BigQuery Sensors sample app that accompanies this book. The application is described in detail in Chapter 8, but examples are used throughout the book, so we'll describe it briefly here. This application shows BigQuery in use to solve real problems; hopefully this can inspire you to come up with ways that it can be used in your own applications.

The code for the application is also open source, hosted on `code.google.com`. If you are interested, you can download the code or browse it online to see how it works. Even better, because the code has been released into the public domain you can take it and extend it however you choose. Although the sample application doesn't exercise the full range of BigQuery features, it does include some advanced usage features and shortcuts that might not be obvious from just reading the documentation.

There are two parts to the sample application: the data collection mechanism and the reporting site. In a real application, you'd also have a site that does something more interesting, but for our purposes, the collection and reporting are the only parts we care about. BigQuery is a service for analyzing data; clearly we need to collect some data. Although we could use a publicly available data source, it is more representative of BigQuery customers to have the data generated within the application.

The data collection piece is an Android app that monitors sensors on Android devices and logs them to BigQuery tables. The app runs in the background and reports status like running applications, acceleration, and coarse-grained location. The reporting piece is a dashboard where you can visualize this data and monitor how the site is used. The dashboard is updated in real time; as connected Android devices log new data, that data will be available for immediate querying. In addition, because the tables that are written are normal BigQuery tables, they can be accessed via the BigQuery web UI to perform ad-hoc queries over the data.

Chapter 8 shows how to build the app, how to use it, and how it works. This section merely introduces the app and what it does. Many of the examples in the book reference concepts from the app or use the schema from the data collection tables, so it helps to have a good understanding of what the app does and what data is collected. The code for the website and the Android app (along with all the other code used in the book) can be browsed or downloaded from `https://code.google.com/p/bigquery-e2e/`.

Sensor Client Android App

Android phones and tablets have an array of sensors available to apps—from location and wireless signal strength to temperature and humidity. The sensor collection app runs in the background on an Android device and reports the values of a number of these sensors directly to BigQuery.

This app is not intended to track users; it is merely an interesting data source that enables distributed data collection and can showcase the streaming ingestion features of BigQuery. For the sake of privacy, location is reported only at a coarse ZIP code level, and the app gives users the ability to turn off the collection of individual sensors. The application also enables you to change the rate at which the sensors are reported; by default, they are sampled once every 5 minutes.

Chapter 8 shows how to install the app on your own Android devices. The default settings log to the main BigQuery Sensors app at `http://bigquery-sensors.appspot.com`, but you can change it to point to your own AppEngine instance after you have that up and running. The app will log, periodically, the coarse-grained location of the user, the applications the user has running, and the values of various sensors. More information about the application and the schema of the data collected is in Chapter 4, in the section entitled "Data Model for End-to-End Application."

If you're not comfortable running the sensor collection app on your phone, no worries; you can always copy the sample data from the `bigquery-e2e` public project. It still may be useful, however, to browse the source code that posts the sensor data directly to BigQuery. The code is written in Java because that is the standard development language for Android apps.

BigQuery Sensors AppEngine App

The main part of the BigQuery Sensors application is the AppEngine data reporting web app, which demonstrates how BigQuery can be used in a real-world application. It uses most of the major features of the BigQuery API, from managing tables to running queries to importing AppEngine Datastore backups.

The application generates custom charts and reports for a set of BigQuery tables. You can see a histogram of the number of different ZIP codes users visited during a day, or track which applications are most popular. Of course, because this application is not widely deployed, there may not be great geographic coverage, but there should be enough to whet your appetite to see how it can apply to your own purposes.

We use GViz and Dygraph to generate the graphs. If you are more comfortable using another graphing utility, it is relatively easy to adapt the graphing display to another framework. Our goal is to show off BigQuery, not graphing APIs, so the charts are fairly rudimentary. They should demonstrate, however, that it is possible to make some nice graphs without a lot of effort. Figure 2.4 shows some of the default graphs for the sensor data application.

The web application is hosted at `http://bigquery-sensors.appspot.com` if you'd like to check it out. If the usage isn't self-explanatory, Chapter 8 goes into more detail about how to interact with it, and by the time you get there you should know more about how to use BigQuery. The code for the website is written in Python. Because Python is a fairly concise and readable language, it should be easier to find and follow the BigQuery-specific sections than if the website was written in another language such as Java.

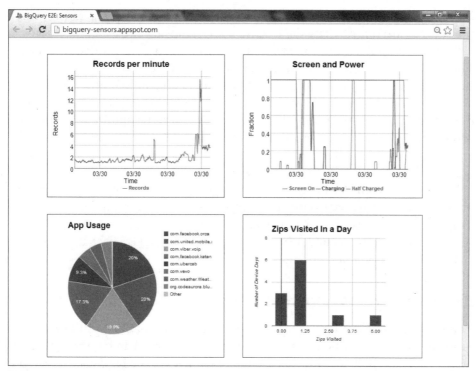

Figure 2.4: BigQuery End-to-End reporting page

Running Ad-Hoc Queries

The AppEngine and Android apps aren't doing anything magical with respect to BigQuery; they just populate and query standard BigQuery tables. The tables used by the BigQuery Sensors application are publicly accessible by anyone with a BigQuery account. You likely will want to lock down your data more tightly, but for the purposes of the book, we wanted to make the underlying data as available as possible.

To access these tables, you can open the BigQuery web UI at `https://bigquery.cloud.google.com` and select Switch to project ⇨ Display project from the project menu on the left tab. Then enter `bigquery-e2e` as the project ID. The datasets used by the End-to-End application display on the left panel. Chapter 3, "Getting Started with BigQuery," has more information about setting up your account for using BigQuery, so if it isn't clear how to start, detailed instructions are on the way. Figure 2.2, earlier in the chapter, shows what the web UI looks like.

As you work through the examples in the book, it may be useful to browse these tables; look at their schemas, look at the contents, and run a couple of sample queries on them. Note that running queries costs money if you go above the "free" 1 TB per month quota. All the examples in this book should use relatively small data sizes to keep you under the 1 TB cap, but you should know that after you exceed that limit, you're on your own for any query charges that are incurred.

Summary

This chapter introduced BigQuery and walked through the various components of the service: the query engine, the cloud-based data warehouse, and the HTTP API.

The chapter also evaluated BigQuery for prospective customers by describing the types of problems it is good for and the types of problems it isn't good for. We compared it to other Big Data systems such as Hadoop and NoSQL databases.

This chapter also discussed the technology that BigQuery is built on top of, such as Dremel, Colossus, and Megastore, which may be interesting to those who follow Google's technology disclosures. It mapped out the various components of the Google Cloud Platform and described how they interoperate with BigQuery.

Finally, this chapter introduced the Android app and Sensors AppEngine application that are the basis for the examples in this book, and whose source code can be helpful in bootstrapping your own applications leveraging BigQuery.

At this point, you've probably had enough about what BigQuery is and are eager to find out how to use it. Chapter 3 will get you up and running.

Getting Started with BigQuery

Throughout this book, features of BigQuery are explained using sample commands and code that you can use to develop a solid understanding of how the service works. This chapter covers the setup necessary to use the examples. This chapter focuses on quickly getting to a working environment, so you shouldn't worry if terms or concepts seem unfamiliar. Detailed explanations follow in later chapters. If you have worked with the Google Cloud Platform, you can skip sections that seem familiar. If you use BigQuery and want to understand advanced features, you can safely skip this entire chapter.

Creating a Project

BigQuery is a part of the Google Cloud Platform suite of services. To start you need a Google account. If you have an existing Google account, for example an `@gmail.com` e-mail address, you can use it; otherwise, you can create one at `https://accounts.google.com/`. This account will be your primary identity when using the service. Next, you need to set up a *project* to enable and manage Google APIs and cloud services.

SAFEGUARDING YOUR PASSWORD

You should never enter your Google account password anywhere other than the Google login page in a browser. It is not uncommon to see passwords for databases or web APIs embedded in source code. However, this should never be the case when working with Google APIs.

Google APIs Console

The project management console is located at `https://console.developers.google.com/`. If you haven't created a project before, you will be prompted to create one. Even if you have an existing project, it is probably a good idea to create a separate one for trying the examples in this book. When you create a project you have the option of choosing a unique ID or accepting a randomly generated unique ID. You will use this ID in the examples shown in this book so you may want to pick a memorable ID. Keep in mind that like an e-mail address, this ID must be unique across all Google Cloud Platform projects, so you might find that common words are already reserved. After the project is created, you are presented with a couple of samples to help you quickly get started. You can skip the samples and just directly enable BigQuery. Select the APIs & auth entry in the navigation panel on the left. This displays the list of available APIs (Figure 3.1) and indicates which have been enabled for the project.

Enable the BigQuery API entry. The first time you enable the API, you are presented with the BigQuery terms of service agreement. After you accept the terms, you return to the services console, and BigQuery will be enabled. Be aware that this is a per-project setting and that you will need to enable the service for each new project. None of the other cloud services are strictly required, but we recommend you also enable Google Cloud Storage (GCS), which enables additional ways to get data in and out of BigQuery.

Before proceeding to the next step, it is useful to understand how to navigate the console. The navigation menu is on the left of the main panel and lists the various sections of the console:

- **Project title:** Displays the name of the currently selected project. This is also the link back to the project list view.
- **Overview:** Summary of the project settings and sample wizard
- **APIs & auth:** Manage the set of services enabled and access credentials.
- **Permissions:** Manage project members and permissions.
- **Settings:** Set up billing details. Also delete the project when you no longer need it.
- **BigQuery:** BigQuery web application.

Project Title

Enable Services

Navigation Panel

Figure 3.1: Google cloud services control panel

There are a couple of additional sections but they are not relevant to using BigQuery. By default, the project is assigned the name My Project, which appears at the top of the navigation panel. It will be helpful to rename the project to BigQuery Examples so you can refer to it easily in later sections. To do this, navigate to Settings and select Rename. Enter the name **BigQuery Examples** in the dialog that opens and save it.

Before you can try any samples that involve API access, you need to set up authentication keys. Navigate to the APIs & auth section. A Credentials entry will appear in the navigation panel. Selecting this entry will bring up a panel that allows you to manage access keys and identities. Clicking on Create New Client ID launches a dialog that allows you to select the type of client you require.

The details of each type are beyond the scope of this chapter; for now, just select Service Account (Figure 3.2) and create the identity. After the account is created, your browser will receive the secret key and prompt you to save the file. You will also see a message containing the password for the secret key, which is always "notasecret." The password is not intended to be a strong password. The downloaded file, on the other hand, contains the secret key that will be used to assert the identity of this service account and should be stored securely. Save the file to a secure location and remember where you put it—you will need it later in the setup process. After you download the key, you return to the API Access section, and there is an entry for the newly created service account.

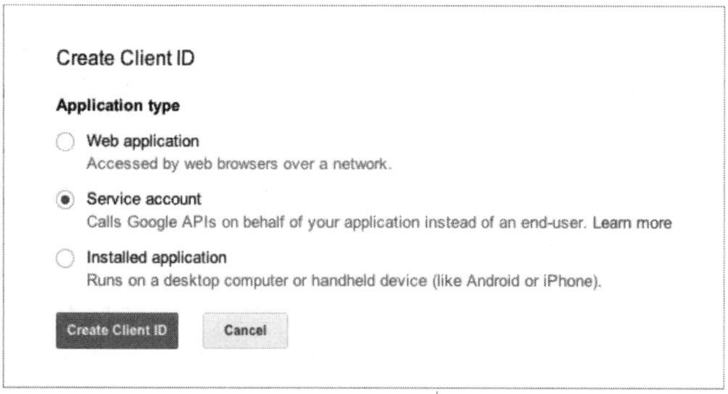

Create Client ID

Application type

○ **Web application**
Accessed by web browsers over a network.

● **Service account**
Calls Google APIs on behalf of your application instead of an end-user. Learn more

○ **Installed application**
Runs on a desktop computer or handheld device (like Android or iPhone).

[Create Client ID]   [Cancel]

Figure 3.2: OAuth client type selection

CLIENT TYPES

The web and installed application client types enable developers to request access to user data in Google accounts. The service account is more like a user account and can appear in team and access control lists. The installed client credentials are the simplest to use with hand-built HTTP requests. In Chapter 5, "Talking to the BigQuery API," you construct such requests to explore the details of the API. However, you do not need to create a credential of this type because you can use one set up for the examples in this book.

This information, shown in Figure 3.3, needs to be saved so that it can be used in the code samples for authentication. The simplest way is to download a JSON file describing the account using the link in the account information panel. Alternatively, you can just record the e-mail address for the service account.

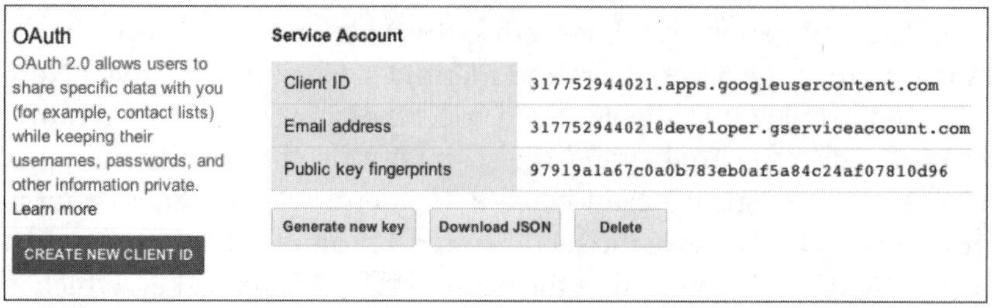

OAuth
OAuth 2.0 allows users to share specific data with you (for example, contact lists) while keeping their usernames, passwords, and other information private.
Learn more

[CREATE NEW CLIENT ID]

Service Account

Client ID	317752944021.apps.googleusercontent.com
Email address	317752944021@developer.gserviceaccount.com
Public key fingerprints	97919a1a67c0a0b783eb0af5a84c24af07810d96

[Generate new key]   [Download JSON]   [Delete]

Figure 3.3: Service account information

By default, the service account is added as an *editor* to the project team. If you navigate to the Permissions section of the project, as you can see in Figure 3.4, the service account appears in the list of project members. The additional entries with unusual addresses are also service accounts, but they are associated with App Engine and Compute Engine and cannot be used directly.

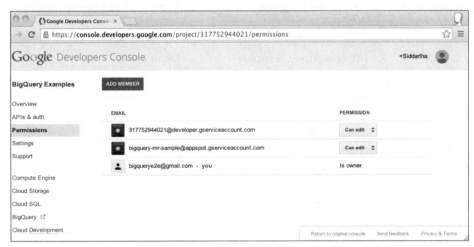

Figure 3.4: Service account permissions

Although the default service account permission works fine for the samples in this book, it is useful to understand that the service account has specific project permissions that can be managed just like any other project member.

There is one final piece of project information that you must record for use in the examples. Navigate to the project overview section and look for the field labeled Project ID. This ID uniquely identifies the project and will be used when you need to refer to the project. Save this ID in a text file so that you can access it in the following steps. Also note that there is a field labeled Project Number, which is an alternate ID for your project and can be used in place of the Project ID. This is mostly a legacy of the old project management process, and you can simply stick with using the Project ID.

Free Tier Limitations and Billing

At this point you have a fully configured project but have not yet set up billing. This means the project you created will be limited to the BigQuery free usage level, which we refer to as the *free tier*. A significant number of examples in this book require access to a project with billing set up. However, you do not have to enable billing right away because you can always return to this section if you would like to explore the features not available in the free tier. Table 3.1

summarizes the quotas for various operations available in the free and billed tiers. Note that these are just quotas and that in the billed tier there are charges associated with usage.

Table 3.1: Comparison Quotas for Free and Billed Tiers

FEATURE	FREE TIER	BILLED TIER
Query	100 GB/month	10 TB/day
Storage	Only anonymous results	Unlimited
Load	None	10 K/Day
Export	1 K/Day	10 K/Day

All users have to access a few public datasets made available by the service to allow users to experiment with queries. In addition, you can access any table shared with your account. However, none of the data storage and management features are available in the free tier. To enable those features you need to set up billing. Even with billing enabled the 100 GB/month free allowance still applies. In addition, there is no fixed cost; if you do not actually store any data in the service, no charges will accrue. The details of the BigQuery pricing model are available at `https://developers.google.com/bigquery/pricing`. Concretely, the cost of running through most of the examples in this book in a month should be well under $10, and anything that can generate nontrivial charges is mentioned.

To turn on billing, select the Settings ➪ Billing section in the project navigation panel. Until you actually set up billing, the link to the section will be highlighted with a warning icon. The section contains a single button to Enable Billing, and clicking the button walks you through the setup flow. You need to register a credit card, which will be charged monthly for the resources used in the prior month. After you submit all the required information, you return to the main project page. Setting up billing on the project enables billing for all the services that have been switched on in the project, and you will receive a combined invoice broken down by service usage. You can monitor your recent BigQuery usage by clicking on the gear icon next to the BigQuery entry in the APIs panel (under APIs & auth).

This completes the project setup. Sections in this book that require a project with billing enabled highlight the requirement. If you choose not to turn on billing, you can simply skip the examples in these sections. For additional information on the Google APIs consoles and project management visit `https://developers.google.com/console/help/`.

Running Your First Query

BigQuery is an "API-first" service. All its functionality is available via its public API, and its features are designed for programmatic access. However, for convenience and ease of use, there is a web application provided by the service that makes it simple to try various features of the service. It is similar in function to MySQL Workbench and similar products that give you the ability to quickly view the layout of your database and run queries. You can use this application to verify that your project is set up correctly and to try your first simple query. Navigate your browser to `https://bigquery.cloud.google.com/`.

When you arrive at the BigQuery web application homepage, you should see a screen similar to the one in Figure 3.5. If you instead see a message directing you to set up a project, then it is likely you did not enable the BigQuery API on the project you created. If so, you will need to head back to the APIs console and enable it.

Figure 3.5: BigQuery Welcome screen

You can navigate the data in your projects using the left side panel. If you have only one BigQuery-enabled project you can access, it should already be selected by default. If this is the case, the project you just created, BigQuery Examples, should appear in the navigation panel to indicate that it is the current project. If you have more than one project, you can switch between them by clicking the arrow next to the project title and selecting Switch to Project.

Because your project was just created, there is no data under the project, so there is not much to see. However, all BigQuery users have access to a public dataset containing tables that can be used to try BigQuery. Click the link `publicdata:samples` to open the dataset. You see a list of names appear under the link corresponding to tables available in this public dataset. The datasets referenced in the sample code in this book are available publicly so that you can query them without having to load your own versions. To view them in this interface, click the arrow next to the project title, and select Switch to Project ⇨ Display Project. In the dialog that appears, enter **bigquery-e2e** in the Project ID field and click OK. You see additional datasets appear in the navigation panel.

Now that you have access to a couple tables, you can explore the data in those tables. Click the `natality` table under `publicdata:samples` to see that the main panel changes to display the schema of the table. This table contains birth records collected by the U.S. government. Click the Details button that appears on the top-right corner of the main panel to see a summary of the table and a sample of the records contained in this table. This view can be useful if you ever want to peek at a table referenced in an example.

It is time to run your first query. Click the Query Table button in the top-right corner. A query editor displays filled in with a skeleton query. On the right, just below the text box containing the query, you can see a red exclamation icon. This indicates that the query currently entered is invalid. Pay attention to this icon as you perform the next step. Modify the contents of the box so that it contains the following query:

```
SELECT
   state, COUNT(state) Num
FROM [publicdata:samples.natality]
GROUP BY 1
ORDER BY 2 DESC
```

Notice that after you update the contents of the text box, a green check mark icon replaces the red exclamation icon, indicating that the query is valid. Click the green icon to reveal additional validation information. The message indicates how much data will be processed to compute the result of the query. It is important to pay attention to this value because it is the amount of processing you will be charged for when you run the query. If you have not enabled billing on your project, you should be especially careful because this amount will be deducted from your limited query quota. Chapter 4, "Understanding the BigQuery Object Model," explains this in more detail; however, the main thing to note here is how to locate this information. Now run the query by clicking Run Query.

Congratulations; you have run your first query using BigQuery. Close the query editor by clicking the X icon (Figure 3.6) located at the top left corner of the editor. This fills the main panel with the results of the query. You can page through the results using the navigation elements below the results table. Now that you have run a query, your query history will no longer be empty. Select the Query History item in the navigation panel. You should see a single entry, unless you experimented with other queries. Selecting an entry from the query history expands it and presents various options to reuse the query. You can edit it if it needs to be modified or simply run it again. However, if you just want to return to the results of the query, you can use the button labeled "Show Previous Results", as long as the results are still available (they expire after 24 hours). If you select a query that is more than 24 hours old, you have to rerun the query to see the results. Each project has an independent per-user query history, so you are seeing only the queries run from your account under the currently active project.

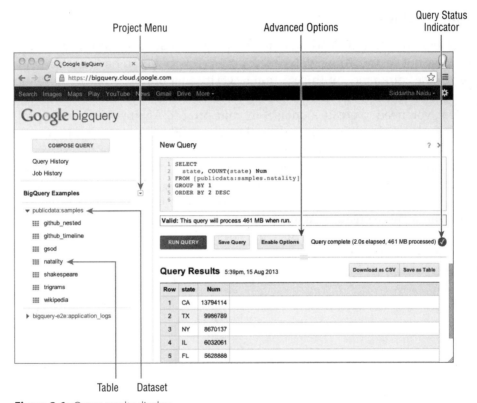

Figure 3.6: Query results display

If you want to experiment with the query editor, consider using the shakespeare table under publicdata:samples. The table contains word frequencies across a couple of works by Shakespeare. The advantage is that it is a small table, so the cost of querying the table is negligible. The query editor supports a couple of common convenience features:

■ Syntax highlighting

■ Indenting support for formatting

- Tab completion of fields and functions
- Parenthesis matching

These simple features make it a convenient tool for data exploration and prototyping queries. If you are interested in trying variations of queries presented in the examples, it is convenient to copy them into the editor and modify them. Some of the examples refer to additional options available when running queries. Many of these options can be controlled in the advanced options panel opened by clicking Enable Options. These options will be covered in Chapter 7.

Loading Data

BigQuery only permits loading data into projects that have billing enabled. If you have not set up billing, you can skip this section. If you have enabled billing try the commands in this section to verify that billing is correctly set up for your project.

First, you need to create a dataset in your project. Again, open up the project menu by clicking the icon next to the project title. Select the option Create new dataset. You see a dialog asking only for the name of the dataset; enter **reference** and click OK. Under the project title you can see an entry for reference appear. Hovering over this entry displays two icons, a plus and a drop-down arrow. Clicking the drop-down icon displays a menu for managing the dataset. Now you want to create a table, so select Create new table. The plus icon is a shortcut for creating a table. This launches the Table Creation Wizard. Follow these steps to complete the wizard:

1. Specify the table to be created (Figure 3.7). Set the table name to `zip_codes`.

Figure 3.7: Table to create

2. Set the source location for the data (Figure 3.8). As part of the support-ing material on this book's website, you can use a file containing ZIP code information made available in Google Cloud Storage. To use this data select the Google Storage option, and set the location to `gs://bigquery-e2e/data/zip_code_data.csv`.

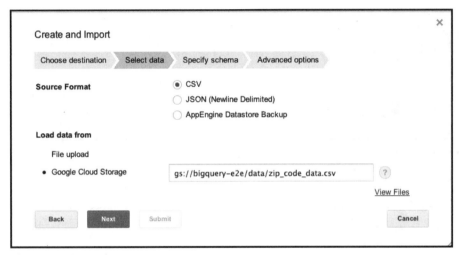

Figure 3.8: Source locations

3. Describe the data contained in the file (Figure 3.9). This is a string describ-ing the fields present in the data. The string is somewhat long, so it is best copied from the download materials for this chapter. Just look for Zip codes schema in `queries.txt`. Be sure not to submit at this point because there is one advanced option that still needs to be specified. Click Next to see these options.

4. Indicate that the data has a header row (Figure 3.10). Set Header Rows to Skip to 1. Now click Submit on the wizard.

You see the `zip_codes` table appear under the reference dataset with an annotation that it is being loaded. In addition, the Job History panel changes to indicate that a job is running. Navigate to Job History (Figure 3.11) to see the list of jobs you have created. There should be an entry for the one you just started. The icon on the left of the entry indicates if the job is in progress or complete. If it succeeds, a green check icon appears next to the job. You can click the job to expand it to inspect additional details. If the job failed, the details contain the error message explaining the failure. This job should succeed assuming there are no issues with the project billing setup or the schema that you entered. When the job completes click the `zip_codes` table to see what it contains.

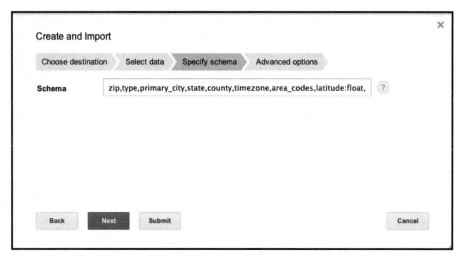

Figure 3.9: Schema

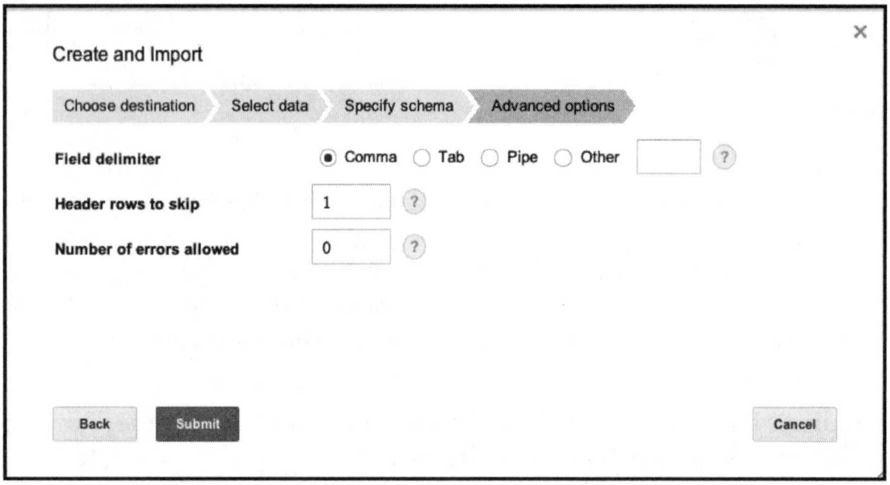

Figure 3.10: Advanced Options

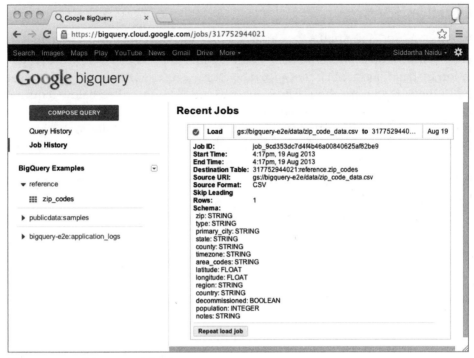

Figure 3.11: Job history and details

Using the Command-Line Client

Having accessed the BigQuery web interface to run a query, you have confirmed that your account and project are correctly set up. It is also useful to have the BigQuery command-line client installed because it will be used extensively in the samples. The client is a Python application built using the Python Google APIs client library. The code for the client is open source, so in addition to being a useful tool, it is also a good reference for BigQuery API usage. The next section walks you through the setup process.

Install and Setup

Because the client is a Python application, you need to have Python installed. If your platform does not come with Python installed, you can follow the installation instructions at `http://www.python.org/getit/releases/2.7.5/` to set up Python on your machine. The Google Cloud SDK described below requires Python version 2.7.x and the samples in the book have been tested with this version, so the link is for that specific version. If you have multiple versions of Python installed, ensure that your `python` command is referring to the appropriate version. On Mac OS X, for example, the version distributed with the OS is located at `/usr/bin/python` and the one set up by the Python installer is located at `/usr/local/bin/python`. Adding an alias to your shell initialization script allows you to directly use the commands that follow without specifying the full path.

```
alias python=/usr/local/bin/python
```

The code for the BigQuery client is open source and is hosted at `https://code.google.com/p/google-bigquery-tools/`. The client is distributed as part of the Google Cloud SDK, which is available at `https://developers.google.com/cloud/sdk/`. The SDK site has platform specific installations. Since the details of the installation are likely to change over time, we have not reproduced those instructions here. You will be given the option of installing a language-specific Google AppEngine SDK. If you want to try the AppEngine examples in this book, you should select the Python option. The installation script will ask if it should modify your PATH environment variable to include the SDK bin directory. If you skip this step you will need to manually add:

```
<install directory>/google-cloud-sdk/bin
```

to your path because the examples use the tools in this directory. Once you are done with the installation, launch a new terminal so that your environment is updated.

With the tools set up, you need to configure them with the Google account to use when talking to the service. It uses the installed client OAuth flow, which requires that you use a browser to complete authentication. You initiate the setup by running:

```
$ gcloud auth login
Your browser has been opened to visit:

    https://accounts.google.com/o/oauth2
    /auth?scope=https%3A%2F%2Fwww.googleapis>

You can view your existing projects and create new ones in the Google
Developers Console at: https://console.developers.google.com. If you
```

```
have a project ready, you can enter it now.

Enter your Google Cloud project ID (or leave blank to not set): project

You are logged in as xyz@gmail.com.
```

When you run the tool it will launch your web browser and open a web page (Figure 3.12) informing you that a client application is requesting permission to manage Google Cloud Platform services under your account. This is similar to how websites delegate access to user data. After you grant permission, authentication is complete and a credential is stored on your computer that enables you to access the service using the command-line client. Additionally, the login process prompts you to enter the ID of the project you will be using. This is the ID of the project you created in the "Creating a Project" section.

Figure 3.12: Online authorization page

You can revoke this access at anytime from any computer that has access to the Internet. Visit `https://www.google.com/settings/security` and navigate to the section Account permissions. Click View all, and you see the list of applications that you have authenticated with a button to revoke access. Clicking the Revoke

Access button next to the Google Cloud SDK entry disables the client on every machine you have set it up on. To revoke access on a specific computer you run:

```
$ gcloud auth revoke
```

This has to be run on the computer for which you wish to disable access. Also if you have multiple Google Cloud Platform projects you can always change the default project you selected at setup.

```
$ gcloud config set project <project id>
```

Returning to the setup of the client, notice that it printed a list of projects with BigQuery enabled. If you have only a single project available, it automatically selects that project as your default project for your operations and finishes the setup process. If you have access to more than one BigQuery project, it asks you to select a project from the list. You should choose the project you created earlier in the chapter, which should be called BigQuery Examples.

Using the Client

You can always find out what operations are supported by bq by running:

```
$ bq
```

The output is a list of commands with a brief description of their purpose and usage. Every bq command has the following general structure:

```
bq [global flags] <command> [command flags] [command arguments]
```

The global flags control options that apply across commands and affect the overall behavior of the tool. They must appear before the command; otherwise they are treated as invalid command flags. You can see a list of these flags by running:

```
$ bq --help
```

You can get help on any specific command by running:
```
bq help <command>
```

Now start by using the client to inspect the contents of the project that you were viewing in the web application. The command you need to use is ls, which applies across various collections in the service. The -p option is used to list the projects you can access.

```
$ bq ls -p
   projectId        friendlyName
-------------- --------------------
 317752944021   BigQuery Examples
```

The bare command, without any arguments, lists datasets in the default project. If specify a dataset name, it lists the tables in that dataset.

```
$ bq ls
  datasetId
  -----------
  reference
$ bq ls reference
    tableId
  -----------
  zip_codes
```

You can use the same command with the -j option to see the list of recent jobs that have been run in a project.

```
$ bq --format=csv ls -j
jobId,Job Type,State,Start Time,Duration
job_9cd353dc7d4f4b46a00840625af82be9,load,SUCCESS,19 Aug 16:17:04,0:00:>
job_2f4aa76f1bef48268080677a556a1dbd,query,SUCCESS,15 Aug 17:39:15,0:00>
```

Observe that both the load job you ran and the query you issue from the BigQuery web UI are listed. As discussed later, queries are a type of job. For now, just keep in mind that the command-line client, unlike the web application, does not actually distinguish between different kinds of jobs for operations. Also the command demonstrates how you can control the output of the client via the --format option. By default it uses tabular formatting that is easy for humans to read, but it also supports options that are more convenient for scripting.

Another difference between the client and web application is that the client does not have a way to list additional datasets you might have access to outside the currently configured project. In the web application you saw that the publicdata:samples dataset appeared in the navigation panel. This dataset, although not easily discoverable, is still accessible via the command-line client.

```
$ bq ls publicdata:samples
      tableId
  -----------------
  github_nested
  github_timeline
  gsod
  natality
  shakespeare
  trigrams
  wikipedia
```

You will have the opportunity to try all the commands available in the client over the course of the book. This section covered sufficient ground to verify that your client is correctly configured to access the project you can use to try the examples in this book.

Service Account Access

In the project setup step, you created a service account that is used as the identity talking to BigQuery in most of the sample code. The advantage of using service account authentication is that it doesn't require any user input, just a private key. It may be useful to run the command-line client under the service account identity to debug the samples or any other code you write that uses these accounts. This section covers the credential setup for the service account you created.

When you ran the client initialization command and stepped through the authentication flow, you installed credentials for your Google account in a configuration file saved on your machine. On Mac and Linux machines, this file is $HOME/.bigqueryrc, and on Windows machines it is %USERPROFILE%\ .bigqueryrc. Try viewing this file in any text viewer, for example:

```
$ cat $HOME/.bigqueryrc
project_id = 317752944021
credential_file = /Users/siddartha/.bigquery.v2.token
```

Remember that every invocation of the client can include global flags that are specified before the command. This file is simply a list of global flags that are applied by default at every invocation. Any flags that are repeated on the command line override the default value specified in this configuration file.

To authenticate as a service account, you need to create a separate configuration file. First, you need the client e-mail address, which you can find in the JSON file that you downloaded with the account information. It looks like *<service-account-id>*@developer.gserviceaccount.com. Create a configuration file for the service account called $HOME/.bigqueryrc.*<service-account-id>* with the following contents.

```
service_account = <service-account-id>@developer.gserviceaccount.com
service_account_credential_file = <location for token file>
service_account_private_key_file = <location of downloaded private key>
project_id = <project-id>
```

The download for this chapter contains a script to help you generate this file from the client secrets you downloaded from the APIs console. You have to copy or move the private key you downloaded to the location specified by the second argument to the script ($HOME/.bigquery.privatekey.p12), which ends up as the value for the service_account_private_key_file flag. It is a good idea to make this file readable by your account only, especially if it is a shared machine.

```
$ export SERVICE_ACCOUNT_ID="<account-id>"
$ python make_service_account_rc.py \
```

```
<path to client_secrets.json> \
<path to private key file> \
>$HOME/.bigqueryrc.$SERVICE_ACCOUNT_ID
```

SETUPTOOLS

Under the hood these commands rely on the Python setuptools (https://pypi
.python.org/pypi/setuptools) package. This package simplifies Python package management and is used again later in this chapter to install the client libraries.
You should install this package in your system Python library so that it is easily accessible. You may also want to consider pip (https://pypi.python.org/pypi/pip),
which is an alternative that has some advantages but is not available for all operating
systems.

Now you can run a command as your service account by specifying the new
.bigqueryrc file:

```
$ bq --bigqueryrc=$HOME/.bigqueryrc.$SERVICE_ACCOUNT_ID ls
```

If you get an error complaining that service accounts require the Python
OpenSSL library (https://pypi.python.org/pypi/pyOpenSSL), then you need
to install that module before proceeding. The easiest way to do that is to use
the setuptools Python package distribution framework. With this package
manager installed you just need to execute:

```
$ easy_install pyOpenSSl
```

This fetches and sets up the necessary packages. If you are unable to install
packages in a system-wide Python library location, you will need to modify
this command to install the library in a private location that is included in the
PYTHONPATH environment variable. After this is complete you can try rerunning
the client command.

The ls command you just ran generates the same output you would get when
running the command under your own Google account. If you try to list jobs,
however, you can see that there are no jobs run by the service account yet.

```
$ export BIGQUERYRC=$HOME/.bigqueryrc.$SERVICE_ACCOUNT_ID
$ bq ls -j
$ bq query '
    SELECT zip FROM [bigquery-e2e:reference.zip_codes]
    WHERE area_codes CONTAINS "425" LIMIT 3'
+-------+
|  zip  |
+-------+
| 98004 |
| 98005 |
| 98006 |
+-------+
```

```
$ bq --format=csv ls -j
jobId,Job Type,State,Start Time,Duration
bqjob_r11253d471625_0140a50036d1_1,query,SUCCESS,22 Aug 00:49:48,0:00:00
```

In the command above, you set the BIGQUERYRC environment variable, which is equivalent to passing the -bigqueryrc global flag to the client. You can clear this environment variable by running:

```
$ unset BIGQUERYRC
```

After running a query the job list is no longer empty. When you switch back to your account, by clearing the environment variable, the job list does not contain the jobs run by the service account. Keep in mind that setting the environment variable from the command line only affects the current terminal session.

If you ran all the commands in this section without errors, then you have your client configured for service account access.

Setting Up Google Cloud Storage

You can do quite a bit with BigQuery without enabling any other services in the Google Cloud Platform. However, to get the most out of the service, it is best used with other components of the platform. Google Cloud Storage is particularly useful because it effectively serves as the *hard disk* for the Google Cloud Platform. This service provides a useful staging area for data that you plan to import into and export from BigQuery. Unfortunately, it has no free tier, so if you have not set up billing, this section is not relevant. If you have set up billing, enabling Google Cloud Storage is simply a matter of enabling it in the services panel of the Google APIs console, the same place you enabled the BigQuery API. There is also a Google Cloud Storage JSON API that you can ignore. Like BigQuery, no charges accrue unless you actually store data in the service.

After the service is enabled, an entry for Google Cloud Storage appears in the left navigation panel of the Google APIs console. Clicking this item expands this entry and displays two links. One link is for the web-based storage browser and one takes you to the GCS Project dashboard. Clicking the Storage Browser link displays a page (Figure 3.13) where you can create a *bucket* to hold files in GCS.

Click New Bucket, which opens a dialog asking you for a name. This name has to be globally unique across the service. A reliable option is to use the project number that appears below the project title BigQuery Examples in the top-left corner. If you assigned an ID to the project you created, you can use that ID. After you click Create, the new bucket appears on the page. Clicking the bucket takes you to the contents of the bucket. This will be empty because you just created it. To test that this bucket works with BigQuery, export some data from BigQuery into this bucket. Using the command-line client execute:

```
$ bq extract bigquery-e2e:reference.zip_codes gs://<bucket>/zip_codes.csv
Waiting on bqjob_r14fa7ecfc2d8c12d_00000140a539e06f_1 ... (25s)
Current status: DONE
```

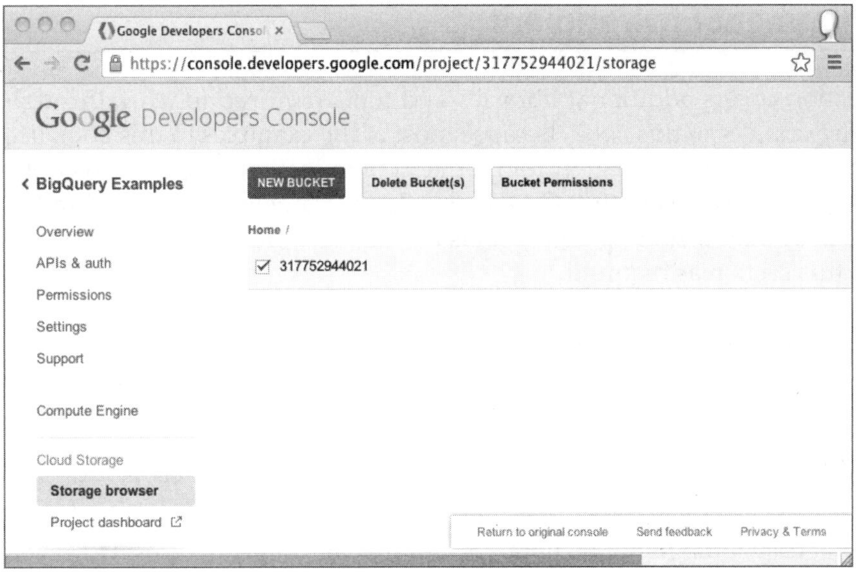

Figure 3.13: Google Cloud Storage Manager

Refresh the content lists by reloading the page. You can see that a file named `zip_codes.csv` appears in the bucket. Clicking this file downloads it to your machine. This is how you can use Google Cloud Storage to get data in and out of BigQuery.

Like BigQuery, Google Cloud Storage has a Python-based command-line tool that is convenient to use for some tasks. The tool is installed as part of the Google Cloud SDK and uses the credentials you configured when you set up the SDK. You can use the tool to inspect the file you created by extracting data from BigQuery.

```
$ gsutil ls
gs://317752944021/
$ gsutil ls gs://317752944021/
gs://317752944021/zip_codes.csv
$ gsutil cat -r 0-300 gs://317752944021/zip_codes.csv
zip,type,primary_city,state,county,timezone,area_codes,latitude,longitu>
```

```
00501,UNIQUE,Holtsville,NY,Suffolk County,America/New_York,631,40.81,-7>
00544,UNIQUE,Holtsville,NY,Suffolk County,America/New_York,631,40.81,-7>
```

Now you have both BigQuery and Google Cloud Storage set up with the ability to move data between them. For additional information on Google Cloud Storage, see the service documentation at `https://developers.google.com/storage/`.

Development Environment

This section covers additional libraries and tools required to work through the code examples in this book. Because most of the examples in this book use Python, it is a good idea to go through the Python section. The other sections cover setup for Java and other Google developer frameworks covered in the book. Rather than installing all the tools at once, it is probably better to come back to this section as required.

Python Libraries

In addition to the client tools, you need to install the Google API client libraries for Python. To install the latest version, follow the instructions at `https://developers.google.com/api-client-library/python/start/installation`. For general development you should install the libraries using this method since it makes it easy to upgrade the libraries and manage dependencies. However, for working on the examples in this book, it is simpler to install the zip file containing the code that accompanies this book that also includes the version of the libraries used in the examples.

```
$ DOWNLOADS="http://storage.googleapis.com/bigquery-e2e/downloads"
$ curl ${DOWNLOADS}/bigquery_e2e_samples.zip -O
$ unzip bigquery_e2e_samples.zip cd bigquery_e2e_samples
# To use the API libraries that are packaged with the samples.
# Command assumes that you are currently in the samples directory.
$ export PYTHONPATH=${PYTHONPATH}:$(pwd)/lib
```

The `bigquery_e2e_samples` directory contains all the samples organized by chapter and directory with required libraries. The last command in the snippet above can be used to set up your PYTHONPATH environment variable to point to these libraries.

Java Libraries

If you are specifically interested in the sample Java code, chances are you already have a working Java development environment (`http://docs.oracle.com/javase/7/docs/webnotes/install/`). In addition, you need the Java BigQuery client libraries. Unlike the Python Google APIs client library, which is a single library for all the APIs, the Java libraries are distributed as a set of common (OAuth and HTTP) libraries and separate per-API packages. The latest version of the BigQuery library is located at `https://developers.google.com/api-client-library/java/apis/bigquery/v2`. This page also has instructions on setting up the libraries under a variety of development frameworks. The samples download described in the previous section also contains the Java libraries required by the chapters that have Java examples.

Additional Tools

Over the course of the book, you develop a substantial application built on the Google AppEngine platform and Android platform in addition to BigQuery. The details of setting up the development tools for these platforms are beyond the scope of this book. However, many online resources are available to help with the process.

Google AppEngine (`https://developers.google.com/appengine/`) is an application platform that simplifies building scalable web services. It supports a number of runtime environments, but this book uses only the Python run time. To work through the AppEngine examples in this book, you need the Python SDK available at `https://developers.google.com/appengine/downloads#Google_App_Engine_SDK_for_Python`. To actually deploy the sample code to your application, you can follow the instructions at `https://developers.google.com/appengine/docs/python/gettingstartedpython27/uploading`. Note that AppEngine has a free usage level, so you can try this at no cost.

Android (`http://www.android.com`) is Google's mobile platform, and as part of the sample application in this book, you develop a mobile client for Android. Developing for Android requires a substantial tool chain, and setup is covered in detail on the Android site. This book supplies an Eclipse project that you can import after you have the Android plug-in set up to experiment with the client. In addition, the client is available in the Android App Store so that you can use it without actually having to build it. The details are covered in Chapter 8, "Putting It Together," which explains the example mobile client and web application.

Summary

This chapter covered the account setup and tools required to work with BigQuery and try the examples in this book. The basic account and project configuration within Google Cloud Platform was explained. Then the tools you use to interact with the service were described. They include:

- BigQuery web client
- bq, the command line client
- gsutil, the Google Cloud Storage command line client

Finally, the development environment and SDKs you need to install to work with the code discussed in later chapters was covered.

Many of the details described in this chapter will change over time, and in some cases will likely change quite often. Wherever possible, we have included pointers to online resources where you will find the latest instructions. So if you find that something is not working as described, consult these resources to see if there are updated instructions.

Understanding the BigQuery Object Model

To understand how to use BigQuery, it is helpful to know a bit about the principal abstractions that it uses and a little bit of terminology. This chapter explains the key objects used by BigQuery and establishes a language for talking about them, which will be useful in subsequent chapters.

BigQuery is a structured data store; that is, it divides data into rows and columns. A collection of rows of data is called a *table*, just like in any relational database. Tables have a *schema* describing the columns of data they contain. Tables are grouped into *datasets*, which are logical collections of tables that can be shared. Datasets are owned by *projects*, which control billing and serve as a global namespace root, meaning all of the object names in BigQuery are relative to the project. Finally, all asynchronous operations BigQuery performs on behalf of users are done via *jobs*. Figure 4.1 shows the relationship between the primary BigQuery abstractions. This chapter describes these in more detail, starting with projects, then delving into data, and finishing up with jobs and what BigQuery can do with your data.

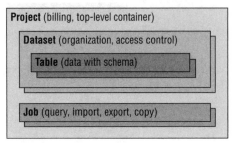

Figure 4.1: BigQuery API abstractions

Projects

You've already seen and created a project in Chapter 3, "Getting Started with BigQuery," but what is a project exactly? Projects combine a number of some-what disparate functions—naming, billing, and access control—into a single entity. Projects are managed via the Google Developers Console (`http://console.developers.google.com`), which is a central location to control access to Google APIs. For the most part, after a project has been set up and configured, most users don't need to bother with it. However, when starting, it is helpful to understand how projects are used and configured.

Project Names

A project serves as the root of the namespace for all other BigQuery objects; that is, in order to talk about other objects, you need to specify which project it belongs to. The names are visible when using the raw BigQuery HTTP API; the URLs for all BigQuery accesses include `projects/<project id>` to indicate which project is being addressed. Because objects such as tables or datasets from different users will be in different projects, they don't have to worry about naming collisions. Project names are guaranteed to be unique by the Google Developers Console.

Projects have two or even three names, which can be a cause for confusion. The first name is the project's *friendly name*, which is the name you specify when you create the project. This name is not unique; it is just an easy-to-remember string. However, because it can be ambiguous, the friendly name is not useful to BigQuery in naming objects.

The second name is the *project number*. All projects have a 64-bit number that uniquely identifies them. These numbers are assigned when the project is created; they are visible at the end of the Google Developers Console URL (for example, `https://console.developers.google.com/project/`**857243983440**) and also can be seen on the project overview status page. Everywhere in BigQuery where you can specify a project, you can use this 64-bit number. Most of the time, unless you construct API requests by hand, you do not need to use this number directly. The BigQuery web UI enables you to select the project to use from a drop-down of your available projects, and the command-line client saves your default project number in a local file. If you access BigQuery programmatically, you'll likely have the project number stashed in a constant somewhere.

Because it can be a pain to type and even more difficult to remember a 64-bit number, the Developers Console provides another way to name a project: the *project ID*. These IDs can be more convenient to type than project numbers and also make it easier to know at a glance what the project contains. For example, the project for the sample application used in this book is called `bigquery-sensors`, which is easier to remember than 1036853159133.

Project IDs are carved from a single global namespace. If I name my project `bigquery-samples`, no one else can ever use this name for their project. There are some restrictions around project IDs; for example, you should not name your project after another company's trademark. In addition, after a project ID is assigned, it cannot be changed, so choose wisely. Both the project ID and the project number can be used interchangeably with BigQuery. Figure 4.2 shows a screenshot of the Google Developer Console showing the three project names.

Figure 4.2: Project names, numbers, and IDs in the Developer Console

Project Billing

One of the primary purposes of projects is to know who to bill for accesses to Google APIs. Although BigQuery and a number of other Google APIs have a limited amount of free usage, some operations require a credit card to be entered and billing to be set up before they can be used. For example, although BigQuery enables up to 1 TB of free queries per month, users cannot use the streaming insert API unless they sign up for billing. Enabling billing on a project can be done via the Developers Console's billing tab and is generally as simple as entering valid credit card information. Large customers may prefer to be billed via invoice. This is possible to set up but requires contacting a Google sales representative.

Project Access Control

Projects can also be used to authorize specific users to access data and perform operations on behalf of the project. The Permissions tab in the Google Developers Console provides a way to add users as either viewers, editors, or owners. Everyone in the team list can run jobs (including queries) on behalf of the project. Users who intend to access BigQuery from an AppEngine app should add their AppEngine service account to the list. (The service account will look like account@appspot.gserviceaccount.com.) The project permissions page will look something like Figure 4.3.

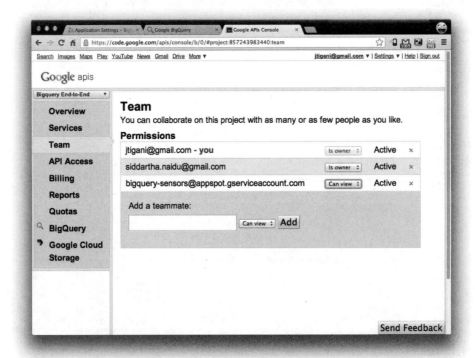

Figure 4.3: Developer Console Team page

The permissions listed in the project become a default access control list (ACL) for datasets in the project. Viewers get read access, editors get write access, and owners get owner access. Note that this is just the default ACL; the dataset ACL can be updated to change or remove any of the default project entries. To prevent a situation in which the people responsible for paying the bills for a project can be required to pay for something they don't have access to, project owners have some special rights. Project owners can always modify object ACLs, so they can add themselves back to the dataset ACL if necessary.

Projects and AppEngine

Google AppEngine automatically creates a project for developers when they sign up. Older AppEngine apps may not have a one-to-one mapping to projects, but newer ones should always have an associated project. AppEngine creates a special nonuser account created for every project, called a *service account*. This can be particularly useful in accessing BigQuery because it can automatically communicate with BigQuery without the need to manage credentials. However, the service account must be explicitly authorized to access BigQuery by adding it to the project permissions. Chapter 8, "Putting It Together," walks through the authorization options from AppEngine in more detail.

BigQuery Data

Data in BigQuery follows a strict hierarchy: Rows of raw data that follow a schema are stored in a table; tables are grouped into datasets; and datasets belong to projects. Projects belong to whoever is paying the bills for the data storage. This hierarchy is visible in the URL paths used in the BigQuery REST API, as well as in the names of objects. The REST paths are described in much more detail in the next chapter; this section gives a rundown on how BigQuery objects are named.

Naming in BigQuery

There are two ways to refer to objects in BigQuery: as *identifiers* and as *references*. In a query, the identifier of the object is used. Take, for example, this query:

```
SELECT message FROM [bigquery-e2e:logs.latest]
```

The field `message` is selected from table `latest` in dataset `logs` in project `bigquery-e2e`. This syntax is used in queries because the table identifiers need to be compact and easy to type by humans. Identifiers are usually referred to as "IDs" and can be relative or fully-qualified. A relative ID is relative to the parent, while the fully-qualified ID is the full name of the object, which can be used to find it in any context. The table in the previous example has a relative ID of `latest` and a fully-qualified ID of `bigquery-e2e:logs.latest`.

In the API, however, the name components are split to make it easier to create and parse names. For example, if you have the fully-qualified ID `bigquery-e2e:logs.latest` and you want to find out the dataset ID, you'd have to figure out a way to extract only the portion you need from the full name. This extraction is an error-prone process, and relies on knowing exactly what characters are expected to be in the different portions of the ID. To prevent you from having to try to parse identifiers, the API returns a JSON object with the individual name components. These JSON objects are called *references*. The reference corresponding to the table `bigquery-e2e:logs.latest` is:

```
{"projectId": "bigquery-e2e", "datasetId": "logs", "tableId": "latest"}
```

The `datasetId` field can be easily extracted from this result. In Python, to extract the dataset ID from the table reference, you can treat the reference as a dict:

```
dataset_id = table_ref["datasetId"]
```

In Java, if you use the BigQuery client library, the `TableReference` object would have a `getDatasetId()` method:

```
String datasetId = tableRef.getDatasetId();
```

Table 4.1 shows the identifier and reference format for BigQuery objects.

Table 4.1: BigQuery Object Names

OBJECT TYPE	REFERENCE COMPONENTS	FULLY QUALIFIED IDENTIFIERS
Project	`projectId: bigquery-e2e`	`bigquery-e2e`
Project (Google Apps for Your Domain)	`projectId: google .com:bigquery-e2e`	`google .com:bigquery-e2e`
Dataset	`projectId: bigquery-e2e` `datasetId: logs`	`bigquery-e2e:logs`
Dataset (Google Apps for Your Domain)	`projectId: google .com:bigquery-e2e` `projectId: logs`	`google .com:bigquery-e2e:logs`

OBJECT TYPE	REFERENCE COMPONENTS	FULLY QUALIFIED IDENTIFIERS
Table	projectId: bigquery-e2e datasetId: logs tableId: latest	bigquery-e2e:logs.latest
Job	projectId: bigquery-e2e job_id: job-abcdefg0001	bigquery-e2e:job-abcdefg0001

Schemas

BigQuery schemas control what type of data the tables are allowed to contain. Schemas contain zero or more *fields,* which are strongly typed columns of values. The primitive field types are INTEGER, FLOAT, BOOLEAN, STRING, and TIMESTAMP. INTEGER values are all signed, 64-bit values. FLOATs are IEEE 754 double-precision values. BOOLEANs are simple flags; they can be either true or false. STRINGs are UTF8-encoded string values. If you want to query over binary data, you should base64-encode it first (or hex-encode it for easier querying). TIMESTAMPs are microsecond-resolution UTC timestamps. Figure 4.4 shows a table with a simple, flat schema.

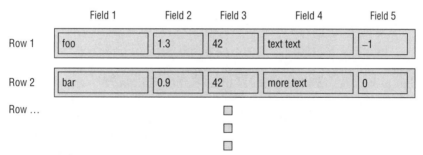

Figure 4.4: Simple table with flat schema

Fields have a mode indicating whether they are REQUIRED, NULLABLE, or REPEATED. Trying to load a null field into a REQUIRED field will result in an error. NULLABLE fields, on the other hand, are allowed to have null values. REPEATED fields can be thought of as arrays of values. An empty REPEATED field is semantically equivalent to a null value.

Fields can also be nested; these are given a type of RECORD, indicating they have a subschema. RECORDs can be repeated as well. Although repeated fields can be useful when the data is hierarchical, it is often a good idea to avoid unnecessary repeated fields. Repeated RECORD fields often become difficult to work with and query after they get beyond the first or second nesting level. Nested fields are referred to by dots; for instance if RECORD outer_field has a field called inner_field, which is also a RECORD containing the field inner_inner_field, you could access the innermost field via the name outer_field.inner_field .inner_inner_field. Figure 4.5 shows a typical nested schema.

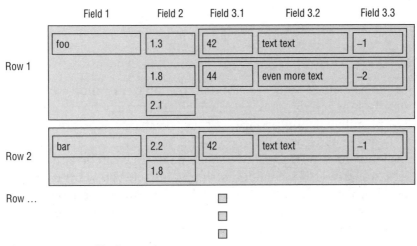

Figure 4.5: Nested BigQuery schema

Tables

Tables in BigQuery are similar to tables in a relational database–they are collections of rows and columns of structured data. Being structured means they have a schema, which applies to all the data in the table. BigQuery supports nested schemas, meaning you can have a row of data that has arrays of values or nested records. Table schemas are generally specified when the table is created and can be updated only in limited ways. The Tables.update() API method enables you to add new columns to the table and to relax REQUIRED fields to make them NULLABLE.

BigQuery tables do not support row-level updates. Tables can be appended to, so they can continue growing after they are created. Appending may be useful if you have data being generated periodically; you can add to the table as new results come in. Tables can also be truncated, which means that a single atomic operation can delete them and replace them with new data. The truncate operation is useful, for example, if you mirror data from an external data store and want to always replace the table with the latest version.

Query results in BigQuery are themselves tables. Any operation you can perform on a BigQuery table can be performed on a query result. By default, query results are "anonymous," meaning they are given a random name belonging to a hidden dataset and will expire after 24 hours. However, queries can also specify named destination tables, in which case the results will stick around until the destination tables are deleted.

In addition to data, tables have some additional interesting metadata. A table can specify an expiration time, which enables it to be automatically garbage collected after it expires. Tables also have a row count and a last modified time, which can be used to tell whether they have been updated recently.

Datasets

BigQuery datasets are collections of tables. They are logical groupings of tables, which can be thought of as similar to a database. Unlike databases, however, a dataset doesn't provide any indication of where or how the underlying tables are stored, and there are no restrictions about combining data (via copy, the SQL JOIN operation, and so on) in different datasets.

Dataset Access Control

Datasets are the primary unit of sharing in BigQuery because they control access to all underlying tables. Datasets have ACLs that specify readers, writers, and owners for the dataset. Readers are allowed to read data from tables in a dataset and run queries against those tables; writers have the same permissions as readers but are also allowed to create and modify tables; and owners have the same permissions as writers but are also allowed to change the ACL on the dataset.

By default, the ACL on a dataset specifies only the project permissions set up in the Google Developers Console. The project owners map to dataset owners; project editors map to dataset writers; and project viewers map to dataset readers. These ACLs can be changed, however, and the project permissions entries can be removed from the dataset. As previously mentioned, project owners have some special rights. Because the project owners pay for the dataset, they always have the option to delete it. This prevents people from having a dataset they are obliged to pay for but cannot remove.

If a user is not a member of the project team, in order to run queries against tables in a dataset, they need to be a member of some other project team that will get billed for their queries. If you allow a user to read your tables, this will not give them permission to do anything that may cost you money; for them to do that, they must be a member of your project's team.

For example, suppose you give Alice access to read your Logs dataset, but Alice is not a member of the project team. She can read values out of the dataset, but if she wants to run a query, she needs to run in some project where she is a member of the team. Then, if Bob is an editor on the project team but you remove him from the ACL of the Sekret dataset, Bob cannot run queries against, read data from, or even see that the Sekret dataset exists.

Jobs

In BigQuery, when you want to get something done—adding data, running a query, copying a table, and so on—you use a *job*. Jobs are asynchronous operations that BigQuery performs on a user's behalf. Some jobs, like Query jobs, may have convenient API wrappers that make them appear to be synchronous, but under the covers they're still asynchronous operations. You can check their status while they're running, and you can come back and get the results later via a separate API call.

Job Components

Jobs have four main parts: a reference, which is a unique name for the job; a configuration that tells BigQuery what to run; status of the job, which includes errors and warnings; and job statistics to provide information about what the job accomplished. Let's consider each of these job parts in turn.

Job References

Job references are immutable names for a job. They can be used to look up the status of a job when it is running or statistics when the job has completed. They can be used by project owners to figure out what was run in their project and by whom. Job references are also useful when contacting BigQuery support about a problem; the support engineer or BigQuery developer can use the job ID to look up what happened and figure out what went wrong.

There are two parts of a job reference: a *project ID* and a *job ID*. Project IDs can be either the project number or project ID discussed earlier in this chapter (not the project friendly name, however). All jobs run in the context of a project that indicates who is responsible for paying the bills for any work done by the job. Job IDs are strings of letters, numbers, and underscores that must be unique per project. This uniqueness constraint for job IDs within a project is important. By carefully controlling the job IDs, you can know whether something has already run and can prevent duplication.

THE CASE FOR SPECIFYING YOUR OWN JOB ID

After you submit a job insert request, BigQuery starts processing the job on your behalf. A number of things can go wrong that would prevent BigQuery from communicating back to you the status of the job unless you have a pre-arranged name to refer to. For instance, your wireless network could disconnect. Your wired network could have a hiccup. A BigQuery server could crash. Your machine could crash. A traffic management algorithm could decide to drop packets that are crossing intercontinental fiber-optic cables in order to make way for something more important.

All these things may look, to you, like errors starting the job. However, because BigQuery runs the job asynchronously, when you get an error, it might actually still complete successfully. If the job is a query, maybe this isn't important; you can just run the job again. But if the job were appending data to a table, you want to know whether you need to run it again or whether the import actually succeeded.

The way to avoid these types of problems is to create your own job ID for each task. When you run the `Jobs.insert()` API, you can specify a unique ID for the job that will be created. This can give you a way to refer to the job if a connection error occurs. Usually, coming up with a unique name is easier than it sounds—just use the current time or the pathname of the file you're importing.

If you have a known job ID, you have two ways of figuring out whether the job ran successfully. The first is the simplest: Just try running it again with the same ID. Because job IDs are enforced to be unique, you cannot run a job with the same name twice. If the job actually started, the second call to `Jobs.insert()` will fail with an Already Exists error. The following transcript shows an example of what happens when you try to create the same job twice. (We first generate a job ID based on the date so that it will start out as unique.)

```
$ JOB_ID=job_$(date +"%s")
$ bq --job_id=${JOB_ID} query --max_rows=0 "SELECT 17"
Waiting on job_1394690025 ... (0s) Current status: DONE
$ bq --job_id=${JOB_ID} query --max_rows=0 "SELECT 17"
BigQuery error in query operation: Already Exists:
    Job bigquery-e2e:job_1394690025
```

The second way to tell whether a job creation operation actually succeeded is to use the `Jobs.get()` API to look up the status. If the job does not exist, you'll get a Not Found error. If the job did run and has an error, that error will be present in the job status. Next is an example of running a job that doesn't actually manage to contact BigQuery because the network is down (we yanked out our network cable). After the network has been repaired, the command `bq show` tells us whether it actually ran. In this case, it did not, so we can retry the query.

```
$ JOB_ID=job_$(date +"%s")
$ bq --job_id=${JOB_ID} query --max_rows=0 "SELECT 42"
Network connection problem encountered, please try again.
```

Continues

(continued)

Once we plug the network cable back in, we can try again:

```
$ bq show -j ${JOB_ID}
BigQuery error in show operation: Not Found:
    Job bigquery-e2e:job_1394690102
```

Both the bq **command-line client tool and the BigQuery Web UI create job IDs automatically before starting jobs. The** bq **tool also has a mechanism for using a fingerprint of the job to prevent re-execution of the same job unintentionally. This is discussed in more detail in Chapter 6, "Loading Data."**

Job Configuration

The *job configuration* section specifies what should get run. BigQuery may tweak the configuration—it might canonicalize path names, for example—but after the job has been created (that is, Jobs.insert() has returned successfully) the configuration will never be changed.

There are four types of jobs: Query, Load, Copy, and Extract. Every query that you run is a *Query job*. *Load jobs* import data from outside of BigQuery. *Copy jobs* make fast copies of tables. *Extract jobs* can be used to make entire tables available outside of BigQuery.

The job configuration has a subsection for each type of job that can be run. The presence of the particular subsection is the signal for BigQuery to run that particular type of job. Only one per-job-type configuration section should be present at a time. For example, a Query job configuration may look like this:

```
{"query": {"query": "SELECT 17"}}
```

Alternately, a Load job configuration may look like this:

```
{"load": {
    "sourceUri": "gs://foo/bar.csv",
    "destinationTable": {
        "projectId": "bigquery-e2e",
        "datasetId": "logs",
        "tableId": "latest"}}}
```

Don't worry about the exact fields that are present here. Individual job types are discussed in more detail in subsequent chapters: Query jobs in Chapter 7 ("Running Queries"), Load jobs in Chapter 6, Copy jobs in Chapter 10 ("Advanced Queries"), and Export jobs in Chapter 11 ("Managing Data Stored in BigQuery").

For now, we will limit discussion to a few settings that are common across job types: `dryRun`, `createDisposition`, and `writeDisposition`.

Dry Run

The `dryRun` flag is one of the only settings present on the top level of the job configuration, and its purpose is to instruct BigQuery to not actually run the job. Instead, dry run requests will perform validation and authorization checks to determine whether the job is likely to succeed, and then return to the user without creating a persistent job or starting the work of the job. Dry run requests may also return some statistics so that callers can estimate the amount of resources that would be used by a job. This can be useful to estimate the cost of running a job or to validate a query without actually running it. The BigQuery web UI uses the `dryRun` flag to validate queries as you type them, and you can use `bq` to do the same, as shown here:

```
$ bq query --dry_run --format=json "bad query"
Error in query string: Encountered " <ID> "bad "" at line 1,
column 1.
Was expecting:
<EOF>
```

Create Disposition

Create disposition controls when tables get created as the result of a job. There are two values for `createDisposition`: `CREATE_NEVER` and `CREATE_IF_NEEDED`. These values determine what BigQuery should do if a table doesn't exist. `CREATE_NEVER` requires a pre-existing table for the job to run. `CREATE_IF_NEEDED` is usually the default; it means that if a table doesn't already exist, go ahead and create it, atomically, when the job is ready to complete.

Write Disposition

The `writeDisposition` flag controls how and when to write to a table and has three possible values: `WRITE_APPEND`, `WRITE_TRUNCATE`, and `WRITE_EMPTY`.
If the write disposition is `WRITE_APPEND`, the job will append any new data to the end of the table. You can run multiple jobs appending to a table in parallel without worrying that they will interfere with each other or corrupt the table.

If the write disposition is `WRITE_EMPTY`, if the table currently has data in it, the write will fail. This can be useful to make sure that multiple jobs all creating the same table don't end up appending their results together, if you want only one of them to succeed.

Finally, `WRITE_TRUNCATE` will atomically replace the data that is currently in the table with the results of this job. This can be useful, for example, to reload data in a table. An analogy to WRITE_TRUNCATE is the scene in the first Indiana Jones movie where he takes the golden idol from the temple—as he takes it, he replaces it with a bag of sand that seems to be about the same size as the idol. Hopefully, your usage of WRITE_TRUNCATE will have a better outcome than in the movie.

The bq tool does not give control over write dispositions directly. By default, for example, load jobs run as WRITE_APPEND. It does however allow you to change the disposition to WRITE_TRUNCATE by passing the --replace flag:

```
$ echo a,b,c > temp.csv
$ bq load --replace scratch.table1 temp.csv "f1,f2,f3"
Waiting on bqjob_r1ef2a0ae815fa433_000001401128cb0b_1 ... (36s) Current
status: DONE
```

All table write operations in a job happen atomically at the end of the job. That is, when the job completes, either all write operations are performed at once or none of them are. For example, if you use WRITE_TRUNCATE, there will be no period of time when the table is empty—other callers will either see all the original data or all the replaced data. Moreover, if there is a WRITE_APPEND job happening at the same time as a WRITE_TRUNCATE job is running, the expected behavior depends on which one finishes first. If the append completes first, the truncate also truncates the appended data. If the truncate job completes first, the appended data will be present in the table along with the results of the truncate job.

Job Status

Job status entries have three fields: state, errorResult, and errors. The state is the state the current job is in; jobs start as PENDING, progress to RUNNING when they are actually being acted upon, and then are marked DONE when the job completes. There is no error state. If the job failed, the state will still be DONE, but the errorResult field will be populated. Figure 4.6 shows the usual job state transitions, both when the job runs successfully and when there is an error.

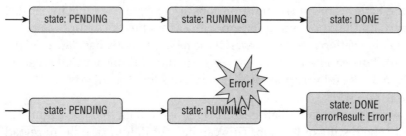

Figure 4.6: Job states and errors

You can use the `bq` tool to inspect job state by using the `show -j` command. The following code snippet creates a load job that will fail because the data doesn't match the schema, and get the status of the job during each of the three job phases.

```
$ JOB_ID=job_$(date +"%s")
$ bq --nosync -job_id=${JOB_ID} \
    load scratch.table1 temp.csv "f1,f2"
Successfully started load bigquery-e2e:job_1394420275
$ bq show -j ${JOB_ID}
Job bigquery-e2e:job_1394420275
```

Job Type	State	Start Time	Duration	Bytes Processed
load	PENDING			

```
$ bq show -j ${JOB_ID}
Job bigquery-e2e:job_1394420275
```

Job Type	State	Start Time	Duration	Bytes Processed
load	RUNNING	21 Jul 15:32:14		

```
$ bq show -j ${JOB_ID}
Job bigquery-e2e:job_1394420275
```

Job Type	State	Start Time	Duration	Bytes Processed
load	DONE	21 Jul 15:32:14	0:00:05	

```
Errors encountered during job execution. Too many errors encountered.
Limit is: 0.
Failure details:
 - Too many columns: expected 2 column(s) but got 3 column(s). For
   additional help: http://goo.gl/RWuPQ
```

The `errors` field is a list of problems that occurred while running the job. These problems may or may not be fatal; like compiler warnings, they may be ways to tell you something went wrong in case you want to deal with it, but it didn't affect the outcome. The job may actually have completed successfully (if so, the `errorResult` field will be empty) but the `errors` list might still report errors.

An example of a successful job with the `errors` list populated is a job that loads data from a CSV file but had a couple of bad rows (but still below the `maxBadRecords` threshold). The following snippet shows an example running the same load command as before, but with one bad record allowed, which lets the job succeed. The `errorResult` field is not present; there are warnings in the `errors` stream:

```
$ JOB_ID=job_$(date +"%s")
$ bq --job_id=${JOB_ID} \
    load --max_bad_records=1 scratch.table1 temp.csv "f1,f2"
Waiting on job_1394723344 ... (25s) Current status: DONE
 $ bq show -j --format=prettyjson ${JOB_ID}
{
...
"status": {
    "errors": [
      {
        "location": "File: 0 / Line:1",
        "message": "Too many columns: ...",
        "reason": "invalid"
      },
      {
        "message": "Input contained no data",
        "reason": "invalid"
      }
    ],
    "state": "DONE"
  }
}
```

Job Statistics

The jobStatistics sub-message is the simplest part of the job object. As you probably have guessed, jobStatistics reports various statistics about how the job has run. For instance, it includes startTime, which is the time in milliseconds since 1/1/1970 that the job started. (That is, the state went from PENDING to RUNNING.) It also includes endTime, which is the time that the job completed.

Other fields are specific to the type of job that was run, but we'll call out one here: totalBytesProcessed. For Query jobs, this is the number of bytes that were read from the source tables, which is a number that is directly related to the cost you get charged to run the query. See the "BigQuery Billing and Quotas" section later in this chapter for how the total bytes processed number can be interpreted.

Job Access Control

To run a job, a user must be a member of the project team, in any role (reader, editor, or owner). But what do we mean by user? A user can be anyone with a Google account, which includes GMail accounts and Google Apps For Your Domain accounts. A user might be a service account that runs on behalf of an application but is considered to be a user by BigQuery for authentication purposes.

A user may or may not be an end user who is using a web app. For example, in our sensor data application, visitors to the website may trigger BigQuery queries to be run, but they are not members of the project team. Instead, the application itself authenticates to BigQuery (via the service account), which then runs the queries and displays the results to the user.

There is one additional user requirement to run a job: The user must have the rights to operate on the data used by the job. If you want to run a job that creates a table, you must have write access on the table's enclosing dataset. It doesn't matter which project that table is in—you could be running the job in one project but writing tables in another one—but you must have write access to anything you are modifying. Likewise, you must have read access to anything you are reading. If you are a member of the project's ACL, you may have rights conferred via the default ACL inherited from the project, but if the dataset ACL has been customized, you may not. For more information about ACLs and access rights, see the "Datasets" section earlier in this chapter.

BigQuery Billing and Quotas

BigQuery users are currently charged for two things: storage and queries. Both are proportional to data size. Storage costs can be incurred even if you're not actively using BigQuery; processing costs get incurred only when you actually run queries. The cost models are described in more detail next; although this book does not mention prices because these are subject to change. Up-to-date information about BigQuery pricing is available at https://developers.google .com/bigquery/pricing.

Storage Costs

Storage is measured in the number of bytes stored in all your tables multiplied by the amount of time the tables are live. The price for storage is quoted in terabytes (for the pedantic, this is actually tebibytes, or 2^{40} bytes) per month. If you create a table that is 3 TB, and that table is around for 2 days before you delete it, you'll be charged for 1/5 of a TB-month [3 TB * 2 days / (30 days/month)]. If you load a big file but it fails, you will not be charged for the failed load. You are only charged for data stored in BigQuery, not for jobs that store data.

If you have a 10 MB CSV file and you load it into BigQuery, how much do you actually get charged for? The answer depends on the type of data you're loading. Numeric data types (FLOAT, INTEGER, and TIMESTAMP) are charged at 8 bytes per value. String (STRING) values are charged at the length of the UTF8-encoded string plus 2. (The 2 bytes at the end are for null-termination.) BOOLEAN values are charged at one byte per value. Null values, regardless of type, are not charged at all. You can see how many bytes were loaded by looking at the load statistics of a successful load job.

```
$ JOB_ID=job_$(date +"%s")
$ echo 1,1.0,foo > temp.csv
$ bq --job_id=${JOB_ID} \
     load scratch.table2 temp.csv "f1:integer,f2:float,f3:string"
Waiting on bqjob_r11463cdf65f08230_00000140037462c6_1 ... (36s) Current
 status: DONE
$ bq --format=prettyjson show -j ${JOB_ID} | grep outputBytes
      "outputBytes": "21",
```

Here you can see that 21 bytes were loaded—that includes 8 bytes for each of the two numeric fields, plus 3 bytes for "foo" plus 2 bytes for the null-terminator.

Processing Costs

BigQuery charges you for the number of bytes scanned by a query. This is roughly proportional to the amount of work that BigQuery does for each query because all queries are essentially table scans—that is, they must read all the rows in the table.

Each column in a table is stored separately, however, so BigQuery needs to read only the columns that are directly referenced by the query. This selectivity can make it somewhat difficult to know how much a given query will cost, especially because the number of bytes per column is not exposed to users, only the total number of bytes in the table.

Luckily, there is a mechanism to determine query cost (in bytes processed): running the query in dry run mode. Dry run reports the amount of resources that would be used by a job but does not actually run the job. This comes in handy to figure out how much a query would cost. The command shown here uses bq in dry run mode to find out how much it would cost (in bytes) to query over the title field of the public Wikipedia table:

```
$ bq query --dry_run --format=prettyjson \
    "select title from publicdata:samples.wikipedia" \
    | grep totalBytesProcessed
      "totalBytesProcessed": "7294285723"
```

The lazy (and perhaps spendthrift) way to determine the cost of the query is just to run the query. As mentioned in a previous section, the totalBytesProcessed field in the job statistics will tell you how many bytes were processed in queries that have been run. The BigQuery web UI reports this number for all queries in the status bar above the query results.

There is no charge for queries that do not complete successfully. Similarly, dry run queries are also free.

Query RPCs

Using the jobs API to run a query can involve a lot of steps: First start a job, then poll for completion, and then read the results when the job is done. Because running queries is such a fundamental part of BigQuery, there are special APIs that provide an easier way to query and read query results: the `Jobs.query()` and `Jobs.getQueryResults()` RPC methods. These APIs don't do anything that you couldn't do via other methods. In fact, they provide less functionality because some features, such as batch mode and named destination tables, are not supported using the `Jobs.query()` RPC.

That said, for many simple query situations, it can be significantly easier to just call the `Jobs.query()` RPC to run a query and get results in one step. If you have long-running queries, or you are using a framework that doesn't allow you to wait for a long period of time on a single HTTP request (AppEngine is an example—it limits all HTTP requests to 60 seconds or less), `Jobs.query()` may not be sufficient. If the `Jobs.query()` timeout expires, you can call the `Jobs.getQueryResults()` RPC to wait for the query to complete and return the results in a single step. This can prevent the need for a polling loop or using the `TableData.list()` method to extract query results. Both `Jobs.query()` and `Jobs.getQueryResults()` APIs are discussed in more detail in Chapter 7.

TableData.insertAll() RPCs

The only BigQuery API to be charged on a per-invocation basis is `TableData.insertAll()`. Unless you are adding a massive amount of data, the costs will be minimal, however. The announced cost is $.01 per 100,000 rows inserted, so for $1 a day you can insert 10 million rows into a table. If you are adding much more data than that, you may be better off batching up your inserts and adding the data via a Load job.

Data Model for End-to-End Application

The BigQuery end-to-end sensor app uses the objects described in this chapter to organize its data for querying and display. This section describes the project setup, the datasets, the tables, and the schemas that are used for the sensor application.

Project

The project used by the sensor data app has the project ID `bigquery-e2e`. The project number and project name are visible in Figure 4.2. The BigQuery and

Cloud Storage APIs have both been enabled via the services tab (hence you can see them in the left panel), and billing has been enabled via the billing tab (which is necessary to load data).

The project permissions configuration (refer to Figure 4.3) is relatively straightforward: The two authors of this book are both owners; the service account from the BigQuery Sensors AppEngine app is a reader. The service account is a reader instead of an editor as a security precaution that prevents it from updating data unintentionally or maliciously. Having reader-level access does allow a user to run queries and other jobs that may cost the project owner money—so be careful when adding people to your team!

Datasets

There are four datasets used in the sensor app: `logs`, `reference`, `dashboard`, and `backup`. The `logs` dataset contains the streamed data from mobile sensors, with one table per day. The `dashboard` contains a cache of values used for rendering charts in the app. The reference dataset contains reference tables that have been downloaded from external sources. Finally, the `backup` dataset contains backups from the app's AppEngine datastore. All these datasets have been locked down via custom ACLs.

The `logs` dataset contains sensitive data, so the default project reader and project writer ACL entries have been removed. Project owners are still on the ACL so that we (the owners) can query the data to diagnose problems with the app. The logs are read by the sensor data AppEngine app, so the app's service account (`bigquery-sensors@appspot.gserviceaccount.com`) has been added as a reader on the dataset ACL.

It was tempting to give write access to All Authenticated Users so that anyone could stream data directly to the logs tables, but that would mean that anyone could write anything they want to our tables and we'd end up paying for it. It also means that anyone could falsify the data; for our purposes that isn't important, but in many others, it would be a serious risk. Instead, we have a service account write updates on behalf of our streaming users; the logs are written to by a different service account than is used for reading (`857243983440-...@developer.gserviceaccount.com`). We give that account write access. Figure 4.7 has the sharing setup for the `logs` dataset.

The `backups` dataset is locked down even more; it is only writable by project owners. The `reference` and `dashboard` datasets are considered less sensitive, so they have default access left in place. They will be read and written by service accounts (via the AppEngine app), but those service accounts are members of the project, so we don't need to set any special ACL entries.

We've also added read access for All Authenticated Users to all of these datasets. Normally, this entry would not be present in any of the datasets. However, we opened up access to grant our readers the ability to look at the data. (It wouldn't be much use for teaching people about BigQuery otherwise.)

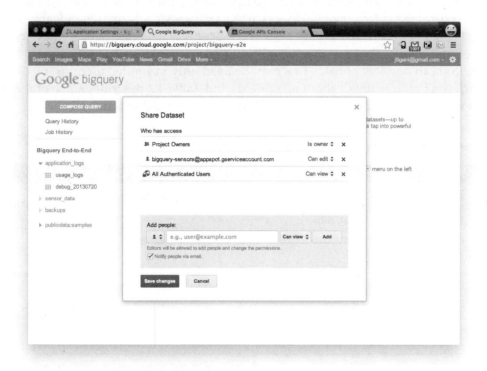

Figure 4.7: Sharing setup for logs dataset

Tables

There are a number of tables used in our application, but we'll discuss only one type of table here: the `logs.device_*` tables. These tables contain the daily sensor data streams. We use the `*` wildcard on the table names when describing them because the new tables are created every day, and the table names include the date. For example, the February 24, 2014 debug log table would be `logs.device_20140224`. The other tables used in the application will be introduced in later chapters when they are needed.

As previously mentioned, a new `logs` table is created every day. This means that you can have a lot of tables accumulating in the logs datas, and often the old ones aren't interesting any more. To avoid having too many tables that you're unlikely to care about (and unlikely to want to pay for), we set the table expiration time to 30 days in the future when the table is created. This means that after a month, the tables will expire and you won't have to worry about seeing them or paying for them any longer.

The sensor data table has all of the sensor and application information that has been streamed in from mobile devices. It has a very wide schema. One advantage of BigQuery's columnar storage system is that empty fields are "free"—they are free to store, and they cost money only in queries when they are explicitly used. So you can add lots of fields that may be used only in limited circumstances. We won't go into detail about all of fields, but Table 4.2 describes some of the more interesting data points collected from the mobile devices.

Table 4.2: Sensor Data Schema (Abridged)

FIELD	TYPE	DESCRIPTION
id	STRING (REQUIRED)	ID of the device recording its data
time	TIMESTAMP (REQUIRED)	Time the sensor data was recorded
screen_on	BOOLEAN	Whether the device screen was on
memory	RECORD	Memory usage and capacity information
memory .avaiable	INTEGER	Amount of memory on the device, in bytes
memory .used	INTEGER	Amount of memory currently in use, in bytes
running	REPEATED RECORD	Record containing running application information on the device
running .name	STRING	Name of the running app
running .memory	RECORD	Information about memory used by the app
running .memory .total	INTEGER	Total amount of memory used by the app, in bytes

This table will be referenced throughout the book; you'll see how it gets created in Chapter 8.

Summary

This chapter discussed the principal abstractions used by BigQuery: projects, datasets, tables, schemas, and jobs. This chapter talked about the relationships among these objects, how they are used, and how access to them can be controlled. Understanding these abstractions is important when using BigQuery, and it may be helpful to refer back to this chapter if something about these objects doesn't make sense. We also introduced the data model of our sensor data application and described how the BigQuery tables, datasets, and projects are set up.

Basic BigQuery

In This Part

Talking to the BigQuery API

The last chapter described the principal abstractions used by BigQuery: projects, datasets, tables, and jobs. This chapter shows you how those concepts map into interaction with the BigQuery service. We introduce the BigQuery REST API by describing the raw underlying HTTP format. We show that there is no magic involved: The BigQuery service is just a server that accepts HTTP requests and returns JSON responses. After reading this chapter, you should understand the API model and be able to interact with the service.

If you do not plan to write code to access BigQuery—that is, you plan to use only tools such as bq or the BigQuery web interface to use BigQuery—you may want to skip this chapter. That said, understanding how the BigQuery API works may make your interaction with BigQuery tools make more sense because those tools use the BigQuery API underneath the covers.

Introduction to Google APIs

Google has a number of externally facing APIs for accessing Google products: the Maps API, a Google+ API, several AdSense APIs, and more. You can see a list of them all in the Google Cloud Console. (Go to `https://console.developers .google.com.` click the name of a project, then click the APIs & auth tab.) BigQuery is just one of these APIs and shares a lot in common with other Google web services.

This section gives information about the basics of accessing any of the REST-based Google web APIs, with a focus on how these operations work in BigQuery. We demonstrate raw access using the UNIX `curl` command so that you can see what actually happens at the API level. When an example requires stringing together multiple commands, we use Python code instead, which will likely be closer to the code you'd write to solve tasks yourself. If you're familiar with other web APIs, you should feel comfortable quickly.

We run all of the commands in this chapter in the `bigquery-e2e` project, but if you try them out yourself, you should substitute your own project ID. We define a shell environment variable for the project ID in order to save typing and make it easy to substitute a different project:

```
$ PROJECT_ID=bigquery-e2e
```

After you've set this environment variable, all the commands in this chapter should work as-is using your project instead of ours.

Additionally, some of the examples require setting up state using concepts we haven't introduced yet. For these commands, we'll use the `bq` command-line client for the sake of expediency. For example, let's start out by creating a scratch dataset that we'll use for storing tables in this chapter.

```
$ bq --project_id=${PROJECT_ID} mk -d scratch
```

Authenticating API Access

The first thing that a Google API front-end server does, after it validates that you sent it a well-formed request, is authenticate the user to figure out who is making the request. On a good day, this is a simple process. On a bad day, authentication can be the most frustrating part of trying to get two systems to talk to each other. Sometimes you have all the data you need to call an API, but trying to convince the other API you're who you say you are can be far more complex than you expect.

AUTHENTICATION VERSUS AUTHORIZATION

It is easy to confuse *authentication* (how do I know you're who you say you are?) and *authorization* (how do I know what you're allowed to do?). The term "auth" is often used so that you don't have to try to remember which one is correct. Part of the problem is that the words look similar, but they also are easy to mix up because most physical examples you have do both types of "auth" at the same time. For example, your driver's license is a token that both authenticates you (establishes your identity) and authorizes you to drive a car (certifies you passed your driving requirements in your state).

To see how authentication and authorization can be separated, imagine what happens when your driver's license expires. You obviously shouldn't drive without getting it renewed. But it is only the authorization portion that has expired. It should be (although I wouldn't try arguing this with a bouncer at a bar) completely acceptable as a form of authentication; it still uniquely identifies you as the person on the card.

In BigQuery, authorization and authentication are distinct mechanisms. Authorization is done via project teams and dataset ACLs, which are described in Chapter 4, "Understanding the BigQuery Object Model." Authentication is done via the mysterious mechanisms described next.

Why Is Authentication So Hard?

To understand why authentication can be so tricky, it helps to consider some history. Back in the wild and freewheeling days of the World Wide Web, you didn't need fancy authentication schemes. You just sent your username and password as part of the URL request and everyone loved it. This was called HTTP Basic Authentication, which was easy to use. Of course, from a security perspective, it is terrible—your password is sent in the clear on every request. It is easy for someone listening on the network to get your password, and from then on, they can impersonate you.

Most interactive web access moved to a different model; you send your password to the server once in an encrypted session and get a token or cookie back that you then use to talk to the server. This doesn't provide a whole lot more security than before—if someone can steal that cookie, he can impersonate you. That is essentially what a cross-site-scripting (XSS) attack does. A mitigation that is often used is that the cookie times out after a period of time, which is why you have to log back in to Gmail every couple of weeks.

For API access, however, you don't want to re-login. You want to just log in once and have the API continue to work. Some Google APIs allow a mechanism similar to cookie-based login, called ClientLogin. BigQuery does not support ClientLogin because it is not considered secure enough; the long-lived ClientLogin tokens are too vulnerable.

The other problem with ClientLogin is that you have to send a password to each site you log in to. This is similar to using the web when you have to create a new username and password to do everything from bank transfers to buying movie tickets. Hopefully, you use a different username and password for the movie site than you do for your bank account, but soon password management gets difficult. One of the goals of more "advanced" authorization protocols is that they limit the proliferation of passwords by limiting the number of places you have to trust to send your password to.

While discussing your authentication wish lists, you also might want to be able to delegate narrow access to a third party. Maybe you would like to authorize a third party to print out your photos from Picasa. You trust them with your photos, but you don't trust them with your Gmail. You also don't want to send them your Google password. You hear about sites with bad password management policies all the time, and you'd rather not have your Gmail account become a vector for a spammer in Nigeria.

Now the requirements are starting to get tricky. You want to reduce the number of sites you need to trust with your password; you want to give third parties the ability to perform certain actions on your behalf without having to trust them completely; you don't want to send a long-lived token over the wire; and you don't want to send your password unless you have to. In software engineering, when things start getting complex, people want to build the "one" solution so that no one else has to implement it again. Often, this just leads to more complexity. OpenID, for example, attempts to be a distributed authentication mechanism. It is, however, used more for end-user web browser authentication rather than APIs, which are often called by programs other than browsers. OAuth and its successor OAuth2 attempt to solve the same problems as OpenID but for API access.

If you want to talk to BigQuery, you need to use OAuth2. OAuth2 satisfies the requirements listed previously, with, of course, a cost in terms of implementation complexity.

OAuth2

Describing the OAuth2 protocol in detail is beyond the scope of this book; instead, we provide the basics. If you hunger for more information, you can check out the official OAuth website at `http://oauth.net/2/`.

FRIENDS DON'T LET FRIENDS RE-IMPLEMENT OAUTH2

If you find yourself implementing the OAuth2 protocol yourself, you should strongly consider using one of the published OAuth2 libraries instead. They're listed on this page: `https://developers.google.com/accounts/docs/OAuth2`, which also has helpful information about OAuth2 as it applies, specifically, to Google APIs.

As mentioned in the last section, authentication protocols try to reduce the number of systems you need to trust. In OAuth2, you need to trust only the Google Authorization Server. (Yes, that's Authorization not Authentication, sorry.) OAuth documentation tends to use the word "Authorization" instead of "Authentication," even though that isn't how it is used in BigQuery. One way to think of it is that OAuth is authorizing you to access the API, and then BigQuery authorizes you to access the resources (tables, datasets, and so on).

Client Secrets

In Chapter 3, "Getting Started with BigQuery," you saw how to set up a Client ID for Installed Applications via the Google Cloud Console. If you skipped that step, you should go read it now, because you are going to need it here. The Client ID contains information that can identify your application to Google APIs. On the Cloud Console page for your project, if you click Credentials under APIs & auth, you can see the Client ID for your project. Click the Download JSON link in the Client ID section to download a client_secrets.json file. The client secrets JSON file for the BigQuery end-to-end project looks like this:

```
$ cat client_secrets.json
{
    "installed": {
        "client_id": "857243983440.apps.googleusercontent.com",
        "client_secret": "9z0P5eC1WjYtRug90aKiejns",
        "redirect_uris": ["urn:ietf:wg:oauth:2.0:oob"],
        "auth_uri": "https://accounts.google.com/o/oauth2/auth",
        "token_uri": "https://accounts.google.com/o/oauth2/token"
    }
}
```

Despite being called "secret," we've included the client_secret for our project. That is because, as used by BigQuery, the client_secrets.json file doesn't contain any important secrets. If you use other Google APIs such as Google Maps, this information may be more sensitive. In BigQuery, the client ID and client secret fields serve only to identify the application making the request. For instance, if you look through the sources for bq.py, the client secret is provided right there in the source:

```
$ grep client_secret bq.py
    'client_secret': 'wbER7576mc_1YOII0dGk7jEE',
```

The reason this "secret" is not so secret is that all access control and authentication is done with respect to users making the request, not the application. So if someone steals your client_secret, she can impersonate your application (which has no special rights) but not any users.

The auth_uri and token_uri fields in the client_secrets.json file tell the OAuth flow which Authorization Server to talk to. The redirect_uris field can be considered opaque. In a normal OAuth flow, a redirect URI is provided to tell the Authorization Server what page to go to after authorization is complete. When you authorize for an installed client, however, this isn't needed. The urn:ietf:wg:oauth:2.0:oob value is just a special identifier that says there isn't a page to go to, and instead, it should show the result of the authorization flow.

OAuth Flow

There are a few different types of OAuth flow; however, as mentioned before, you should likely not try to implement them yourself. Here we walk you through the installed application flow, but the other types of flows (service account and web server) are similar. The way to perform OAuth2 authorization in Python is to use your `client_secrets.json` file to create a `flow` object:

```
$ python
>>> from oauth2client.client import flow_from_clientsecrets
>>> BIGQUERY_SCOPE = 'https://www.googleapis.com/auth/bigquery'
>>> flow = flow_from_clientsecrets('client_secrets.json',
...    scope=[BIGQUERY_SCOPE])
```

The `scope` parameter is what tells the authorization process that you want to access BigQuery. If you want to access a different service as well as use the same credentials, you could pass additional scopes here.

You likely don't want to rerun the full authorization flow each time you run the application. The `oauth2client` storage object provides mechanisms to save your credentials:

```
>>> from oauth2client.file import Storage
>>> storage = Storage('bigquery_credentials.dat')
>>> creds = storage.get()
```

In this case, we save the credentials to a file called `biguery_credentials.dat`. If that file doesn't exist or doesn't have valid credentials (which it will not the first time you run `storage.get()`), you can run the flow to fetch new credentials:

```
>>> from oauth2client.tools import run
>>> creds = run(flow, storage)
Your browser has been opened to visit:
    https://accounts.google.com/o/oauth2/auth?scope=https%3A%2F%2Fwww.go
+ ogleapis.com%2Fauth%2Fbigquery&redirect_uri=http%3A%2F%2Flocalhost
+ %3A8080%2F&response_type=code&client_id=857243983440.apps
+ .googleusercontent.com&access
+ _type=offline

If your browser is on a different machine then exit and re-run this
application with the command-line parameter

  --noauth_local_webserver

Authentication successful.
```

This opens your browser window, prompts you to log in (if you're not already logged in), and prompts you to allow the application access to your BigQuery data. When you accept, the flow automatically completes.

This step may seem like black magic; you went to a web page and somehow your Python client knew about it. What is actually happening here? A request gets sent to the Authorization Server (the `auth_uri` from your `client_secrets .json`). This request doesn't actually know anything about you and doesn't include your username or password. It does send some identifying information about your project (the `client_secret` and the `client_id` from `client_secrets.json`).

As a response, the Authorization Server returns an access URL. The access URL must be visited in a web browser. This is a security precaution; because you may need to enter your password, you want to make sure that no one captures your password and sends it to their servers in North Korea. When you visit the access URL in the browser, it asks you whether you want to grant access to the scopes that were requested by the flow (in this case, just BigQuery).

If you accept, the Authorization Server then issues a redirect to a localhost address. This is where the black magic comes in. When you called `run()` on the `flow` object, it started up a web server on your computer. When the Authorization Server redirects your browser to your local web server, it provides the credential information as part of the request. The `run()` operation listens for this request, and after it receives the credentials, shuts down the web server and returns.

Everything you need to talk to BigQuery is now in the `creds` object, and also saved in a file called `bigquery_credentials.dat`.

OAuth2 Credentials

Now that you've seen how to run an OAuth2 flow to get credentials, look at what the credentials actually contain.

```
>>> import json
>>> print json.dumps(json.loads(creds.to_json()), indent=2)
{
  "_module": "oauth2client.client",
  "token_expiry": "2013-08-11T18:07:59Z",
  "access_token": "...",
  "token_uri": "https://accounts.google.com/o/oauth2/token",
  "invalid": false,
  "user_agent": null,
  "client_id": "857243983440.apps.googleusercontent.com",
  "id_token": null,
  "client_secret": "9z0P5eC1WjYtRug90aKiejns",
  "_class": "OAuth2Credentials",
  "refresh_token": "1/_V43XWglqRtCQCJ2X_AWyajZK1i1NcpRt2DyhIBYLC4"
}
```

OAuth2 uses a split-token technique to keep your credentials secure. That is, your credentials are split into two pieces: a long-lived *refresh token* and a short-lived *access token*.

The only thing that the refresh token does is enable you to create more access tokens. Because the refresh token is a long-lived credential, you want to keep it secret. That means sending it only to the Google Authorization Server, not an API such as BigQuery directly. Instead, you send another request to the Authorization Server, providing your refresh token in order to get a new token: an *access token*.

The access token, finally, is what you use to access BigQuery. At a raw, HTTP level, the access token should be passed in the Authorization header as a Bearer token. The file auth.py, included in the downloads for this chapter, performs the OAuth2 authentication dance and prints out an HTTP Authorization header containing the access token. For example:

```
$ python auth.py
Authorization: Bearer ya29.1.AADtN_V2kFUrjX8wghCSPJng7XR2k7t...
```

You can run the auth.py command from within a curl command to fetch the access token and set it as the Authorization header in an HTTP request. The following command lists projects available for use with BigQuery; it is a good test to see whether authentication worked.

```
$ curl -H \
  "$(python auth.py)"\
  https://www.googleapis.com/bigquery/v2/projects?alt=json
```

The access token, however, has two limitations: It has a limited scope, meaning that it is valid only to access BigQuery, and it has a limited lifetime, usually approximately 5 minutes. (This is what the token_expiry field in the credentials object refers to). After your access token expires, you need to call the Authorization Server with your refresh token to get a new access token.

Split tokens may seem strange; however, you do often encounter them in physical access situations. For example, when you go to the Department of Motor Vehicles to get a driver's license in the United States, you need to bring your birth certificate. This is your long-lived, secure credential. You use this credential to acquire a driver's license, which has a limited expiration time, and it is what you need to use to actually drive a car. The driver's license is a lower value credential; it is relatively easy to replace if lost, as long as you still have your birth certificate. Likewise the birth certificate is a higher value credential, even though you cannot use it if you get pulled over for speeding.

Just as renewing your driver's license can be a pain, renewing your access token whenever it expires can also be a lot of work. This is another reason to use a standard OAuth2 library, which takes care of renewing your access tokens automatically. In Python, you can wrap the httplib2.Http() object you use to make your HTTP requests with one that does the access token bookkeeping and adds authorization to all your requests:

```
>>> import httplib2
>>> http = creds.authorize(httplib2.Http())
```

The resulting `http` object can be used to talk to BigQuery or any other Google API without worrying any further about authentication.

If this protocol sounds complicated, it is even more complicated than it sounds, since some details are omitted. As mentioned elsewhere, you probably shouldn't implement this yourself. The Google APIs client libraries are available for most programming languages and can dramatically simplify the process of getting a fresh access token. Listing 5.1 shows the full process of getting OAuth2 credentials in Python.

Listing 5.1: OAuth2 credential authorization (auth.py)

```
'''Handles credentials and authorization.

This module is used by the sample scripts to handle credentials and
generating authorized clients. The module can also be run directly
to print out the HTTP authorization header for use in curl commands.
Running:
  python auth.py
will print the header to stdout. Note that the first time this module
is run (either directly or via a sample script) it will trigger the
OAuth authorization process.
'''
# for the saved credentials. If the user has never completed
# OAuth authorization this module will initiate the process.
import httplib2
import json
import os
from apiclient import discovery
from oauth2client.client import flow_from_clientsecrets
from oauth2client.client import SignedJwtAssertionCredentials
from oauth2client.file import Storage
from oauth2client.tools import run

BIGQUERY_SCOPE = 'https://www.googleapis.com/auth/bigquery'

# Service account and keyfile only used for service account auth.
SERVICE_ACCT = ('<service account id>@developer.gserviceaccount.com')
# Set this to the full path to your service account private key file.
KEY_FILE = 'key.p12'

def get_creds():
  '''Get credentials for use in API requests.

  Generates service account credentials if the key file is present,
  and regular user credentials if the file is not found.
  '''
  if os.path.exists(KEY_FILE):
    return get_service_acct_creds(SERVICE_ACCT, KEY_FILE)
  else:
```

Continues

Listing 5.1: *(continued)*

```
return get_oauth2_creds()

def get_oauth2_creds():
  '''Generates user credentials.

  Will prompt the user to authorize the client when run the first time.
  Saves the credentials in ~/bigquery_credentials.dat.
  '''
  flow  = flow_from_clientsecrets('client_secrets.json',
                                  scope=BIGQUERY_SCOPE)
  storage = Storage(os.path.expanduser('~/bigquery_credentials.dat'))
  credentials = storage.get()
  if credentials is None or credentials.invalid:
    credentials = run(flow, storage)
  else:
    # Make sure we have an up-to-date copy of the creds.
    credentials.refresh(httplib2.Http())
  return credentials

def get_service_acct_creds(service_acct, key_file):
  '''Generate service account credentials using the given key file.

  service_acct: service account ID.
  key_file: path to file containing private key.
  '''
  with open (key_file, 'rb') as f:
    key = f.read()
  creds = SignedJwtAssertionCredentials(
    service_acct,
    key,
    BIGQUERY_SCOPE)
  return creds.refresh(httlib2.Http())

def print_creds(credentials):
  '''Prints the authorization header to use in HTTP requests.'''
  cred_dict = json.loads(credentials.to_json())
  if 'access_token' in cred_dict:
    print 'Authorization: Bearer %s' % (cred_dict['access_token'],)
  else:
    print 'creds: %s' % (cred_dict,)

def build_bq_client():
  '''Constructs a bigquery client object.'''
  return discovery.build('bigquery', 'v2',
                         http=get_creds().authorize(httplib2.Http()))

def main():
  print_creds(get_creds())

if __name__ == "__main__":
    main()
```

The method `get_oauth2_creds()` will create user credentials, while the method `build_bq_client()` can be used to build an authenticated BigQuery client. This BigQuery client can be used directly to make requests to BigQuery with no further authentication or credential manipulation necessary. If you run this file as a standalone Python script, it will perform authentication and print out an OAuth2 access token. This mechanism is used in many of the examples in this chapter in order to be able to make raw HTTP requests using `curl`. This code is available in the file `auth.py` in the supplemental materials for this chapter.

Service Account Authorization

An alternative way to perform authorization is to use a service account. This method requires a little more work to set up, but less code. A service account has a cryptographic key pair that authenticates requests. If you know the private key, you can authorize without generating any refresh or access tokens. There is a caveat, though: You don't connect as yourself; you connect as a special type of account called a service account. You need to add the service account to your project team in the Google Developer console in order to allow the service account to access your project.

In Chapter 3 you set up a service account, generated a key pair, and downloaded it somewhere safe. The e-mail address of the service account (for example, `long-random-address@developer.gserviceaccount.com`) and the private key file (in PKCS#12 format) are all you need to perform authentication. The method `get_service_acct_creds()` in Listing 5.1 can turn a service account e-mail address PKCS#12 file and a service account e-mail address into valid OAuth2 credentials that can be used the same way as the OAuth2 credentials generated in the previous section.

RESTful Web Services for the SOAP-Less Masses

Most Google APIs, including BigQuery, adhere to a REST model. REST is one of those acronyms where knowing what it stands for doesn't actually help you understand what it is. If you casually read the Wikipedia page for Representational State Transfer (`http://en.wikipedia.org/wiki/Representational_state_transfer`), you might not come away from it knowing much more about REST or what people mean when they say they have a REST API. Part of the problem is that REST can mean a variety of different things, from the very broad to the very narrow. Here's an explanation of REST in Google API context.

If you've been coding web services for a while, you likely have encountered SOAP, which is a standard for describing and transmitting web API requests. There are probably some good things about SOAP. It has a number of downsides, however; it is complex to implement, highly verbose, and most unfortunately, it uses XML. SOAP's popularity has been declining, largely because people want an easier way to interact with their APIs while still providing some structure.

Although REST has been around since HTTP 1.1 was defined in 1999, its widespread use in web services is a much more recent phenomenon. People realized that instead of creating fancy XML API descriptions to implement SOAP, they could just make their web API look like something that was already well understood—collections of files in the World Wide Web. As many Java servlet developers realize, when you respond to a GET request on a URL that ends with `foo.txt`, there doesn't have to be a file named `foo.txt`—you can serve up whatever data you want to in response. Moreover, the path portion of the URL, (for example, `google/apis/v2/foo.txt`) can carry important information, as well as can the trailing query string (as in `foo.text.?start_row`).

This is the central principle of REST—that you can make APIs that look like requests for files, with URLs that provide key information about what resources are requested. Sometimes, however, it requires a little bit of wrangling to make an API fit a REST model.

REST Collections

To make an API RESTful, you can take the main objects—`users`, for example—and expose operations on them as operations on collections of those objects. The endpoint that responds to those operations is a simple URL, usually with the name of the collection as part of the URL. For instance, the method to create a user wouldn't be called "create." It would be an insert operation into the `users` collection (called *Users.insert()*) that you'd send to the `users` URL.

REST collections respond to a standardized set of operations, or HTTP verbs. The verb is the first portion of the HTTP protocol. When you open a web page in your browser, it sends a GET request to the server you're accessing. If you are updating data—submitting a form, for instance—it uses the POST verb instead. The HTTP 1.1 specification describes a few more verbs that can come in handy when accessing REST collections, as shown in Table 5.1.

Table 5.1: REST Verbs

METHOD NAME	VERB	DESCRIPTION
insert()	POST	Adds a resource to the collection
get()	GET	Gets a single resource in the collection
list()	GET	Lists resources
update()	PUT	Updates an entire resource
patch()	PATCH	Updates a portion of a resource
delete()	DELETE	Deletes a resource

To list objects in a collection, you send a GET request to the base URL of the collection. For instance, in BigQuery, there is a Projects collection, representing the projects that are visible to the logged-in user. To list your projects, you can send an HTTP GET request to `https://www.googleapis.com/bigquery/v2/projects`.

To read a particular object in a REST collection, send a GET request to the URL of the object. In BigQuery, the Datasets collection is nested under the projects collection; you can read the metadata for the dataset *bigquery-e2e:application_logs* object by sending a GET request to `https://www.googleapis.com/bigquery/v2/projects/bigquery-e2e/datasets/application_logs`.

Similarly, POST can add an object to a collection, PUT and PATCH will update an object, and DELETE will delete an object. Not all operations will be valid on all collections, but the important part is that the model is consistent.

Although the REST collection-based model sounds great in practice, what do you do if your API doesn't look like collections of objects? This point is where REST stops becoming a technology and starts becoming a philosophy. Advocates of REST would say that the act of turning your API into a set of collections actually makes it a cleaner, more understandable API. They say that the benefits of an easy-to-describe API outweigh the ugly bits when you try too hard to make something fit the model. Furthermore, even if you follow REST, you can have non-REST operations by adding custom RPC methods.

BigQuery tends to follow the REST model closely; it has collections for Projects, Datasets, Tables, Table Data, and Jobs. A couple of API methods that don't fit the model nicely are added as RPCs: `Jobs.query()` and `Jobs.getQueryResults()`. These collections are described in more detail in Chapter 7, "Running Queries."

REST URLs

Another of the main design tenets of REST is that URLs used to interact with the API should be human readable. This is different from other RPC mechanisms such as SOAP and JsonRPC, in which you send data to a fixed URL. Google APIs REST URLs consist of six or seven parts: protocol, host, API selector, version, path, method (optionally), and query string, as shown in Figure 5.1.

Figure 5.1: Google APIs REST URLs

Protocol

The protocol used by BigQuery is HTTPS, which is a security layer that uses SSL on top of raw HTTP. This means that all requests and responses are sent encrypted. Some Google APIs may be available via HTTP, but in BigQuery, all of the data is considered sensitive, so it must be sent encrypted. In the past, people cited performance reasons for avoiding HTTPS. Now, most people believe that the security gained (prevention against man-in-the-middle attacks, authentication of both client and server, and so on) is worth the 1 or 2 percent performance hit.

Host

The hostname for all BigQuery requests is `www.googleapis.com`. Most, if not all, Google APIs use the same domain. They are not hosted at `google.com` for security reasons. If BigQuery was hosted at `google.com` and there was a cross-site-scripting (XSS) vulnerability in some Google web product (Picasa, for example), then an attacker could gain access to your data in BigQuery, or any other Google API. Although XSS vulnerabilities in Google sites are rare, it is safer to remove them as a possible risk. By hosting APIs on a domain that does not have any web properties, `www.googleapis.com` should be immune from XSS attacks.

API Selector

The API selector is how the Google API front-end servers can route your calls to the right API. There are two parts of the API selector: name and version. For BigQuery, the API name is, somewhat obviously, `bigquery`. The BigQuery beta version introduced at Google IO in 2010 was version `v1`, but ever since it was launched publicly, the version has been `v2`. In the future, the active version number may change if breaking changes are introduced.

The BigQuery team's philosophy on changes tends to be that API additions can be made without a version number revision. For example, the ability to run queries in dry run mode was added via an additional flag passed into the query. Because there was no breaking change—it would only affect users who explicitly used the flag—there was no need to change the version. Other Google APIs have different criteria for increasing the version number.

One thing to note about the API version is that when it does change, the old version is usually left running for a significant period of time—usually six months to a year. Users of the old version may not use new features, but they should continue to use the old feature sets without problems. This is why the version number is included in the path, rather than just using something like "latest," because it enables running multiple versions side by side and means that new versions can be added without breaking old ones.

Path

The path to get to a REST object should mirror the object hierarchy. For example, in BigQuery, tables belong to datasets, which belong to projects. So the path portion of the URL to read table `latest` in dataset `logs` in project `bigquery-e2e` looks like `projects/bigquery-e2e/datsets/logs/tables/latest`. The pattern, as you may notice from the table URL, is usually *collection name/object name/sub collection name/object name*. Although it may seem redundant to pass the collection name each time, it makes it easy to add new collections at various levels of the hierarchy and can resolve ambiguity. In addition, the collection names in the URL path serve as a way of self-documenting the URL, at the expense of only a few bytes in the request.

Method

The method portion of the URL is an optional component that tells BigQuery what operation to perform. The method is not present in pure REST requests because REST API calls specify the operation to perform via the HTTP verb: GET, PUT, POST, DELETE, and so on. Some BigQuery operations don't fit well in a REST model, so they use custom methods. An example of this is the `Jobs.query()` operation, which is a shortcut for inserting a job in the Jobs collection, waiting for the job to complete, and reading the results. The path and method portion of the `Jobs.query()` operation URL looks like `projects/{project ID}/query`.

Operations that have a method name are often referred to as RPC methods to distinguish them from pure REST calls. Some of them use HTTP GET, but most of them use the HTTP POST verb because GET requests are supposed to be *nullipotent*, meaning they do not change any state. Perhaps surprisingly, the `Jobs.query()` RPC method is a POST for reasons that are described in Chapter 7.

Query

The final portion of the URL is the query string. This should not be confused with a BigQuery query. The query string is used only for HTTP GET requests (either RPC-style requests or REST `get()` and `list()` operations) as a method of passing parameters to the API method. When you make a POST request, you send the posted data to the server in the body of the request. In a GET request, on the other hand, the only way you can send information to the server is by including it in the request URL.

Query strings, when present, are always the last part of the URL, after the portion that describes the resource being accessed. Query strings begin with the ? character and contain any number of key-value pairs of the format *key=value*, separated by the & character. For example, the following URL . . . `/projects/bigquery-e2e/`

`datasets/logs/tables/latest/data?prettyPrint=true&maxRows=10` lists 10 rows from the table `bigquery-e2e:logs.latest` and pretty-prints the results.

REST Transport

Most RPC frameworks, such as SOAP, are designed to be transport-agnostic. That is, they are designed to work regardless of how the messages are being delivered—raw TCP, HTTP, or Post-it notes sent via carrier pigeon. This follows good network systems design where you want to keep different layers of the protocol stack independent of each other.

REST, on the other hand, is intricately tied to HTTP as the transport layer. In the real world, there are real advantages to creating tight coupling between the layers of network protocols. The advantage of HTTP is that it plays so nicely with other systems. For example, most corporation firewalls are configured to allow HTTP traffic through. Caching and proxying of HTTP data is well defined and well understood. There are also a number of open standards for authentication, such as OAuth and OpenID. REST is designed to reuse as much of the HTTP infrastructure as possible and can take advantage of advanced HTTP features, such as ETags, which are discussed in the section entitled "Common Operations" later in this chapter.

REST Encoding

Although REST doesn't define an encoding standard for data sent and returned, in practice it is almost always JSON. Google APIs in general, and BigQuery in particular, use JSON encoding unless you specify otherwise via the `alt` query parameter. JSON has a number of advantages; it is reasonably compact, it is easy to parse, it is human-readable-and-writable, and it has a simple and open standard. Dynamic programming languages such as Python can automatically turn JSON values into typed objects that make parsing trivial. For example, in Python, the following code snippet turns a JSON string into a `dict` object letting you access the fields as keys:

```
>>> import json
>>> json_str = '{"a": 3, "b": "foo"}'
>>> json_dict = json.loads(json_str)
>>> print json_dict['a']
3
```

The choice of encoding is another advantage REST has over SOAP—SOAP generally uses XML, which is much more difficult to parse. The code in almost any programming language would be much more complex to parse than the same values encoded in XML.

REST Resources

As previously mentioned, REST collections are collections of resources. But what is a resource? A *resource* is any object that you want to perform operations on. In BigQuery, the resources are the same as the principal abstractions discussed in Chapter 4: project, dataset, table, table data, and job.

All Google API resources have a number of common fields. Because these fields are considered boilerplate, many of the examples in this chapter omit them to just highlight the more interesting aspects of the API. Here is a `curl` request that gets the dataset object for the scratch dataset we created earlier, showing only the common fields discussed in this section (we also set up a couple of handy environment variables in order to save some typing):

```
$ BASE_URL=https://www.googleapis.com/bigquery/v2
$ PROJECTS_URL=${BASE_URL}/projects
$ PROJECT_URL=${PROJECTS_URL}/${PROJECT_ID}
$ DATASETS_URL=${PROJECT_URL}/datasets
$ DATASET_URL=${DATASETS_URL}/scratch
$ curl -H "$(python auth.py)" \
    "${DATASET_URL}"
{
 "kind": "bigquery#dataset",
 "etag": "\"4PTsVxg68bQkQs1RJ1Ndewqkgg4/KOb9IHTeiiCy_ICxng0jrzYn6Zk\"",
 "id": "bigquery-e2e:scratch",
 "selfLink": "https://www.googleapis.com/bigquery/...",
 "datasetReference": {
  "datasetId": "scratch",
  "projectId": "bigquery-e2e"
 },
 ...
}
```

The first field you'll notice is `kind`, which, in this case, is `bigquery#dataset`. The general pattern is that the `kind` is the API name followed by the # sign followed by the resource type. This field is not particularly interesting by itself because you usually know what object type you're expecting. That said, it could make it easy to write code that handles several different types of responses by inspecting the `kind` field.

The `etag` field is the next common field in the resource. This is a hash of the resource object and can be useful for detecting when a resource changes. The section titled "ETags and the If-None-Match Header" has more information on how the `etag` field can be useful.

Next is the `id` field, which uniquely identifies the resource within that collection. In BigQuery, there is always a reference field that is a better way to refer to the resource. For this dataset, the `id` is `bigquery-e2e:application_logs`.

Although this name seems straightforward, if you want to extract only the project ID portion, it can be tricky to parse. The datasetReference field would help you here, since it has the datasetId and projectId fields listed individually.

Finally, there is a selfLink field. This is a URI that you can use to read the resource later. This tends to not be very useful; if you just read the object, you probably already know which URL to use to get the object. However, it can sometimes be useful as the result of a list operation, because it tells you how to get the individual resource from the listing.

Discovering Google APIs

There is an advantage, however, that SOAP has over REST APIs. Although REST APIs are often easier to develop intuition about, there is no common description language for them. SOAP APIs, on the other hand, have a well-defined XML description that can tell you everything you need to know to call the API.

Google attempts to bridge this gap in API description via the discovery page. If you navigate your web browser to https://www.googleapis.com/discovery/v1/apis/bigquery/v2/rest, you can find the discovery document for the BigQuery API. In fact, if you read and understand this page, much of the rest of this chapter will be redundant. (Although hopefully you'll find the rest of the chapter more interesting than 2000 lines of JSON.)

Unlike this book, however, the discovery document is designed to be read by programs, not necessarily by humans. That said, it is easy for humans to understand it, since one of the principles of REST is human-readability. Official documentation can sometimes be missing or out of date, but the discovery document is the actual definition of the API, and as such, it is always up to date. It can be useful if you want to read about the different arguments to various API calls or to find out what various fields mean. For example, near the top of the discovery document is a section that looks like:

```
"prettyPrint": {
 "type": "boolean",
 "description": "Returns response with indentations and line breaks.",
 "default": "true",
 "location": "query"
},
```

This snippet tells you about an undocumented feature: that you can add prettyPrint=true to the query portion (that is, the part after the ?) of any BigQuery URL, and it will cause the response to be returned in a format that is easier for humans to read (as opposed to more compact, which is easier for computers to read and more efficient to transmit).

The description of the API in the discovery document is rich enough to enable automatic generation of client libraries in a variety of programming languages.

The page at `https://developers.google.com/bigquery/client-libraries` has a number of links to these auto-generated client libraries for languages from Java to PHP to Ruby. The Python library, in particular, is used in many of the samples in this book. For the most part, you should use the client libraries instead of coding directly against the API. It will be easier, it will be type-safe (in languages that are statically typed), and it will let you know in the event that some behavior in the API changes.

There is, however, a downside to an automatically generated client: The code that gets generated might not be the code that you'd write if you were writing a client from scratch. Some operations may be awkward; others may not use language features as cleanly as you'd like. For example, in the Java client, the `JobStatus.getState()` method returns a `String`, when it would be cleaner to return an `enum` containing the possible values. That said, the generated client is often convenient, especially when using a modern code editor that can auto-complete or display documentation.

From Python, to use the automatically generated BigQuery client, just import `apiclient.discovery` and call `build()`:

```
>>> from apiclient.discovery import build
>>> service = build('bigquery', 'v2')
```

You can then use the generated client to call BigQuery:

```
>>> service.projects().list().execute()
{u'totalItems': 3, u'kind': u'bigquery#projectList', ...}
```

Common Operations

Several operations are common across the BigQuery collections and are generally common across other Google APIs as well. This section describes a number of them as they apply to BigQuery and demonstrates their usage with `bq.py` and `curl`.

Paging through Collections

Often there are more results in a collection than are convenient to return at a single time. When this is true, the results will be truncated—you'll get only the **first** page of results. If you have run 10,000 jobs, you may only care about the **most** recent ones, so you might be okay with just these limited results. Other times, however, you really do want to see all the resources in the collection. The mechanism to access other pages of results is called *paging*. BigQuery, like other Google APIs, supports paging primarily via the `maxResults` and `pageToken` arguments. It also has limited support for index-based pagination. These flags are described next.

maxResults

The first tool that you can use for paging is the maxResults parameter, which controls the maximum number of results that can be returned. This flag is accepted on all BigQuery collections. Let's create a new scratch dataset so we have more than one to list:

```
$ bq --project_id=${PROJECT_ID} \
    mk -d "scratch_2"
```

Now, to list datasets in the your project but limit the results to the first one, you can run the following curl command:

```
$ curl -H "$(python auth.py)" \
    "${DATASETS_URL}?maxResults=1" \
{
...
"datasets": [
  {
    "kind": "bigquery#dataset",
    "id": "bigquery-e2e:scratch",
    "datasetReference": {
     "datasetId": "scratch",
     "projectId": "bigquery-e2e"
    }
   }
  ]
 }
```

If the number you give is larger than the largest accepted by BigQuery, you get BigQuery's maximum rather than an error. This makes it easier to say "give me as many results as possible."

startIndex

The simplest form of pagination is index-based pagination, using the startIndex parameter. If you got 10 results last time, you can specify that the next request start on the 11th value. Note that startIndex can give unexpected results when the underlying collection is changing. For example, if you use indexed pagination to get results 1-10, then request results 11–20, if the underlying results have changed, you might not see the values you expect. You might skip some results or see some of the same results you saw last time.

Because it is difficult to do a stable listing, indexed pagination is discouraged. It is supported only on the TableData.list() operation because often you do care about the 100th row in the table, especially when looking at the results from a query. To demonstrate this, let's first run a query that will generate some results to page through. This query computes percentile distribution of word counts in Shakespeare's plays.

```
$ bq query \
    --destination_table=scratch.table1 \
    --max_rows=0 \
    "select quantiles(word_count) from publicdata:samples.shakespeare"
Waiting on bqjob_r8717055dd1ebad8_0000014070d5e4b8_1 ... (0s) Current
status: DONE
```

Once we have created the table, we can read the 100th row which is the 99th percentile.

```
$ TABLES_URL=${DATASET_URL}/tables
$ TABLE_URL=${TABLES_URL}/table1
$ TABLEDATA_URL=${TABLE_URL}/data
$ curl -H "$(python auth.py)" \
    "${TABLEDATA_URL}?maxResults=1&startIndex=99"
{
 "kind": "bigquery#tableDataList",
 "etag": "\"yBc8hy8wJ370nDaoIj0ElxNcWUg/vk5JRNdt-25J-ICZ34R0Dqpt1Fc\"",
 "totalRows": "100",
 "rows": [
  {
   "f": [
    {
     "v": "995"
    }
   ]
  }
 ]
}
```

pageToken

Specifying a large number of results isn't actually a paging mechanism however; it is just a way of controlling the size of a page. (Although it might mean you don't have to do paging because you could get all the results at once.) The preferred way to page through results is to use a *page token*. This is an opaque value that is returned by each list operation and tells BigQuery where to start in the list the next time the API is called. For instance, if you get `pageToken=@53579480` from a `TableData.list()` operation when reading the first 10 rows from a table, you can read the next 10 rows by passing the same `pageToken` value in your next request. Although sometimes the value of the page token may seem predictable, you should treat it as opaque because the format can change at any time.

Because you have a value threaded through the chain of `list()` calls, token-based pagination can give you a stable snapshot of the results. The BigQuery `TableData` collection gives you a stable listing; that is, the data you see when paging will be exactly the data that was present when you started paging, even if the underlying table changes. Because providing a stable list operation requires keeping around extra state, the token may be only valid for a certain period of time—generally 24 hours.

Here you can use `curl` to get the first row in a table:

```
$ curl -H "$(python auth.py)"\
    "${TABLEDATA_URL}?maxResults=1"
{
  "kind": "bigquery#tableDataList",
  "etag": "\"yBc8hy8wJ370nDaoIj0ElxNcWUg/hDRfxHX8yY1GRPpTthhjzhvMMj8\"",
  "totalRows": "100",
  "pageToken": "1@1376284335714",
  "rows": [
   {
    "f": [
     {
      "v": "1"
     }
    ]
   }
  ]
}
```

You can get the next row via the following command (substituting your page token for the one here):

```
$ curl -H "$(python auth.py)" \
    "${TABLEDATA_URL}?maxResults=1&pageToken=1@1376284335714"
{
  "kind": "bigquery#tableDataList",
  "etag": "\"yBc8hy8wJ370nDaoIj0ElxNcWUg/wkrQkIirE3G6Vvv0_ZnfZOk_V64\"",
  "totalRows": "100",
  "pageToken": "2@1376284335714",
  "rows": [
   {
    "f": [
     {
      "v": "1"
     }
    ]
   }
  ]
}
```

The TableData collection allows you to page through a consistent snapshot of a table. The BigQuery Projects, Tables, Datasets, and Jobs collections give a softer guarantee of consistency while paging. They never skip values if new values arrive, but they might include values that arrive after paging starts. The way this is done is that the pagination token describes the last value returned; future list operations begin pagination at that value. You can tell when you get to the end of the listing because you won't get a `pageToken` in the response.

Updating Resources

The standard way to update a REST resource is the HTTP PUT verb. This allows you to replace the entire object with a new one. Of course, there may be rules governing which fields you are allowed to change—you can't generally update a creation time of an object, for example.

The problem with updating an entire object is that it becomes easy to have a race condition with another update operation. For example, if Alice updates the table `bigquery-e2e:logs.latest` to add a description, and meanwhile Bob is updating the same table to change the schema, either Alice's or Bob's updates might be lost. Bob and Alice may have both read the original copy, made their changes on that copy, and replaced the old version with their new one. Whoever's update runs first will be overwritten by the next update.

The way to prevent this type of race condition is to use the HTTP PATCH verb. When using PATCH, you need to specify only the values you want to change, not the entire resource. So Alice could specify just the table description, and Bob could specify just the schema modification, and both operations would complete successfully without the possibility of clobbering each other.

In BigQuery, the only collections that support updates (via update or patch) are Tables and Datasets. Update operations just modify metadata; they don't modify data in the tables.

Response-Control Options

Some resources in Google APIs can be quite large; for instance, query Job resources include the query text, which can be up to 100 kB. If you want to list 10,000 jobs that all have 100 kB of queries, you might end up reading a lot of data. What's more, there is a good chance you don't care about the actual query text, so most of what you're reading isn't useful. BigQuery supports three mechanisms to help reduce the amount of data returned and to focus on the interesting data: projections, field restrictions, and ETags.

Projections

Projections are predefined views of a resource that include only a subset of the resource's fields. The Jobs collection is the only collection in BigQuery that supports projection. It defines two projections: `full` and `minimal`. The `full` projection returns the entire job, which may include a lot of data—the full text of queries, full table schemas, and so on. The `minimal` projection, on the other hand, omits a lot of potentially expensive fields and just returns the fields that are likely to be more interesting—the job status, the statistics, and so on. When listing jobs, the default projection that is returned is the minimal one. If you want to see the full projection, you can specify `projection=full` in the URL query string.

Here is an example that returns the minimal projection of a single job:

```
$ JOBS_URL=${PROJECT_URL}/jobs
$ curl -H "$(python auth.py)" \
    "${JOBS_URL}?maxResults=1&projection=minimal"
{
 "kind": "bigquery#jobList",
 "etag": "\"yBc8hy8wJ370nDaoIj0ElxNcWUg/UakzbU_RhC8kGP0ve9SOqAWE6Ls\"",
 "nextPageToken": "1374677424654-...",
 "jobs": [
  {
   "id": "bigquery-e2e:bqjob_r1ef2a0ae815fa433_000001401128cb0b_1",
   "kind": "bigquery#job",
   "jobReference": {
    "projectId": "bigquery-e2e",
    "jobId": "bqjob_r1ef2a0ae815fa433_000001401128cb0b_1"
   },
   "state": "DONE",
   "statistics": {
    "startTime": "1374677431634",
    "endTime": "1374677458425",
    "load": {
     "inputFiles": "1",
     "inputFileBytes": "3",
     "outputRows": "1",
     "outputBytes": "0"
    }
   },
   "status": {
    "state": "DONE"
   }
  }
 ]
}
```

Likewise here is the same job with the full projection:

```
$ curl -H "$(python auth.py)" \
    "${JOBS_URL}?maxResults=1&projection=full"
{
 "kind": "bigquery#jobList",
 "etag": "\"yBc8hy8wJ370nDaoIj0ElxNcWUg/ytdMysUYGZY_OZKW01VMUuMdT0k\"",
 "nextPageToken": "1374677424654-...",
 "jobs": [
  {
   "id": "bigquery-e2e:bqjob_r1ef2a0ae815fa433_000001401128cb0b_1",
```

```
"kind": "bigquery#job",
"jobReference": {
 "projectId": "bigquery-e2e",
 "jobId": "bqjob_r1ef2a0ae815fa433_000001401128cb0b_1"
},
"state": "DONE",
"statistics": {
 "startTime": "1374677431634",
 "endTime": "1374677458425",
 "load": {
  "inputFiles": "1",
  "inputFileBytes": "3",
  "outputRows": "1",
  "outputBytes": "0"
 }
},
"configuration": {
 "load": {
  "schema": {
   "fields": [
    {
     "name": "f1",
     "type": "STRING"
    },
    {
     "name": "f2",
     "type": "INTEGER"
    },
    {
     "name": "f3",
     "type": "FLOAT"
    }
   ]
  },
  "destinationTable": {
   "projectId": "bigquery-e2e",
   "datasetId": "scratch",
   "tableId": "table1"
  },
  "writeDisposition": "WRITE_TRUNCATE",
  "maxBadRecords": 0
 }
},
"status": {
 "state": "DONE"
}
}
]
}
```

The full projection includes the configuration, which may contain a lot of data. This particular job is a Load job, so it has the table schema, which can be hundreds or thousands of fields. Query jobs have the SQL query that was run, which also can take up a lot of space in the response.

Field Restrictions

Projections are a somewhat coarse way of specifying the fields you care about. Field restrictions, on the other hand, allow you to specify exactly the fields you want. The advantage of projections is that they are easy to use—you don't have to know exactly what you want. The advantage of specifying exact field lists is that you have control over exactly what you get in response. All BigQuery collections support field restrictions for all operations. To specify the set of fields you want to see in the result, list them as a comma-delimited URL query parameter, as in `fields=field1,field2,...`. Nested fields can be specified via parentheses. For example, to list just the `id` and `totalItems` fields from the Projects collection, you can specify:

```
$ curl -H "$(python auth.py)" \
    "${PROJECTS_URL}?alt=json&fields=projects(id),totalItems"
{
 "projects": [
  {
   "id": "bigquery-e2e"
  },
  {
   "id": "420824040427"
  }
 ],
 "totalItems": 3
}
```

ETags and the If-None-Match Header

One of these advanced HTTP features that can come in handy with BigQuery is the combination of ETags and the If-None-Match HTTP header. Sometimes, you want to know if a resource or list of resources has changed since the last time you read it. ETags are a convenient mechanism to do this; they are fingerprint values that are returned in the API call. If you read the same object twice and it has the same ETag, it has not changed. Here is an example of the ETag returned from a BigQuery `Tables.get()` call:

```
$ curl -H "$(python auth.py)" \
    "${TABLE_URL}?fields=etag,lastModifiedTime"
{
 "etag": "\"yBc8hy8wJ370nDaoIj0ElxNcWUg/gS3ul2baST3PwOoDSGXgugy2uws\"",
 "lastModifiedTime": "1374677458335"
}
```

You may ask, what is the use of an ETag when you could just match the results yourself? Although sometimes it can be more convenient to use the ETag than computing your own hash, the principal value can be in saving network traffic when you combine it with a request that specifies the `If-None-Match` HTTP header. For the ETag previously returned, this would look like:

```
$ ETAG=\"yBc8hy8wJ370nDaoIj0ElxNcWUg/gS3ul2baST3PwOoDSGXgugy2uws\"
$ curl -H "$(python auth.py)" \
    -H "If-None-Match: ${ETAG}" \
    -w "%{http_code}\\n" \
  "${TABLE_URL}?fields=etag,lastModifiedTime"
```

This uses the `-w` option to `curl` to return the HTTP status code. It returns the HTTP status code `304 Not Modified` with an empty response. If you run a job to update the table, the ETag changes, and the same command returns a value again:

```
$ echo foo,1,1.0 >foo.csv
$ bq load --replace scratch.table1 foo.csv \
    "f1:string,f2:integer,f3:float"
Waiting on bqjob_r1acbcee37ed9abeb_000001407034129d_1 ... (26s)
Current status: DONE
$ curl -H "$(python auth.py)" \
    -H "If-None-Match: ${ETAG}" \
  "${TABLE_URL}?fields=etag,lastModifiedTime"
{
 "etag": "\"yBc8hy8wJ370nDaoIj0ElxNcWUg/rlB4v5eu0LBEfFBRBW7-oRFArSQ\"",
 "lastModifiedTime": "1376270939965"
}
```

Batch Requests

It is common to want to request a number of results from an API in parallel. Maybe you have a list of jobs or tables that you'd like to look up. Although you could do this by setting up and sending multiple API requests, there is also a built-in Google API mechanism called a *batch request*. Batch requests enable you to send multiple separate requests and get the responses back for all of them at once.

The raw HTTP mechanism to deal with batch requests is a little bit tricky. You can read more about it at https://developers.google.com/ api-client-library/python/guide/batch. Here you just see the Python version, which wraps a lot of the complexity in an easy-to-use API. Creating a batch request is simple; just create a new `BatchHttpRequest()`, add the individual API requests you want to make to the batch request, and then call `execute()`. If you provide a callback method, you get one callback for each response, providing the ID of the request and the response. This can be convenient so that you don't have to try to separate the responses on your own.

The following Python code can read the metadata for two tables in a single HTTP request:

```
>>> from apiclient.http import BatchHttpRequest
>>> batch = BatchHttpRequest()
>>> def batch_callback(request_id, response, exception):
...     if exception is not None:
...       print "Exception: %s" % (exception,)
...     else:
...       print "Request %s Response %s" % (request_id, response)
...     pass
...
>>> batch.add(service.tables().get(projectId='bigquery-e2e',
...     datasetId='application_logs',
...     tableId='debug_20130720'), callback=batch_callback)
>>> batch.add(service.tables().get(projectId='bigquery-e2e',
...     datasetId='application_logs',
...     tableId='usage_logs'), callback=batch_callback)
>>> batch.execute(http=http)
Request 1 Response {
  ...
  u'tableReference': {
    u'projectId': u'bigquery-e2e',
    u'tableId': u'debug_20130720',
    u'datasetId': u'application_logs'},
  u'numRows': u'3',
  ...}
Request 2 Response {
  ...
  u'tableReference': {
    u'projectId': u'bigquery-e2e',
    u'tableId': u'usage_logs',
    u'datasetId': u'application_logs'},
  u'numRows': u'3'
  ...}
```

Before we move on, let's clean up our scratch dataset so we can start the next section with an empty project:

```
$ bq rm -r -f -d scratch
$ bq rm -r -f -d scratch_2
```

BigQuery REST Collections

As mentioned earlier in this chapter, there are five BigQuery REST collections: Projects, Datasets, Tables, Table Data, and Jobs. The objects contained by these collections are called *resources*; the REST operations in the collection can investigate and manipulate resource objects. This section describes each of these collections in turn, describes the valid operations, demonstrates how they are used, and shows additional ways to control their behavior.

In the REST model, a collection maps to a URL. Figure 5.2 shows a high-level view of the relationships between BigQuery collections and their URLs. These collections are discussed from the outside in, starting with Projects, which is a container for all the other collections.

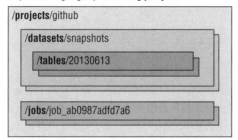

https://www.googleapis.com/**bigquery**/v2

/projects/github

/datasets/snapshots

/tables/20130613

/jobs/job_ab0987adfd7a6

Figure 5.2: BigQuery collections and their URLs

Projects

The Projects collection is the simplest of the BigQuery REST collections; it has only a single method: `Projects.list()`. Projects are containers for all the other objects in BigQuery, but because projects are configured via the Google Developers Console (not in BigQuery), the BigQuery API doesn't have any operations on projects other than to list them. In fact, if there was a better way to get a list of projects that had BigQuery enabled, the Projects collection would likely be unnecessary. At a later date BigQuery may store information on a per-project basis; if so, the Projects collection would become more interesting. The Projects collection is summarized in Table 5.2.

Table 5.2: Projects REST Collection

METHOD	URL	HTTP VERB
Projects.list()	. . . /projects	GET

Project Resource

The Project resource contains only the project name fields: `projectId`, `projectNumber`, and `friendlyName`. If it seems confusing that a project would have three different names, read the section on project references in Chapter 4. At some point in the future, the resource may reflect the project ACL as well, but currently it contains only the name fields, which are all immutable. Table 5.3 contains field descriptions for the Project resource.

Table 5.3: Project Resource Fields

FIELD	TYPE	DESCRIPTION
projectId	string	Unique name of the project. This may be a numeric ID or the project ID that was set in the Google Developers Console.
projectNumber	number	Unique number identifying the project.
friendlyName	string	Friendly name for the project. Not unique.

Projects.list()

The `Projects.list()` method returns a list of all the projects you are a member of (that is, in the project team as either an owner, editor, or reader) that also have BigQuery enabled. There is no way to list projects for a different user other than by logging in as them. As mentioned in Chapter 4, all members of a project team can run jobs billed to the project, so you can run jobs in any project returned by the `Projects.list()` operation.

Although you probably won't be a member of enough projects for it to matter, you can page through `Projects.list()` results using the `maxResults` and `pageToken` parameters, which are described earlier in this chapter in the section "Paging through Collections."

```
$ curl -H "$(python auth.py)" \
  https://www.googleapis.com/bigquery/v2/projects?alt=json
{
"projects": [
  {
   "kind": "bigquery#project",
   "id": "540617388650",
   "numericId": "540617388650",
   "projectReference": {
    "projectId": "540617388650"
   },
   "friendlyName": "API Project"
  },
  {
   "kind": "bigquery#project",
   "id": "bigquery-e2e",
   "numericId": "857243983440",
   "projectReference": {
    "projectId": "bigquery-e2e"
```

```
    },
    "friendlyName": "Bigquery End-to-End"
  },
"totalItems": 2
}
```

USING BQ --APILOG TO UNDERSTAND THE BIGQUERY API

Sometimes you try running something against the BigQuery API that you're pretty sure should work, but for some reason you get back a cryptic error. One way of figuring out what is wrong is to compare it against a tool that you know works.

The `bq` command-line client has an `--apilog` flag that can be used to see exactly what requests and responses are sent. It does skip a couple of details, such as the authorization header (as a security precaution), but, in general it is useful to understand what is happening at the raw HTTP level.

For example, the way to list projects in `bq` is to run `bq ls -p`. If you just add the `--apilog=-` parameter (the "-" tells it to output to `stdout`), and you can see the HTTP request that was sent:

```
$ bq --apilog=- ls -p
...
INFO:apiclient.discovery:URL being requested:
https://www.googleapis.com/bigquery/v2/projects?alt=json
INFO:root:--response-start--
INFO:root:status: 200
...
INFO:root:{
...
"projects": [
  {
    "kind": "bigquery#project",
    "id": "540617388650",
    "numericId": "540617388650",
    "projectReference": {
     "projectId": "540617388650"
    },
    "friendlyName": "API Project"
  },
  {
    "kind": "bigquery#project",
    "id": "bigquery-e2e",
    "numericId": "857243983440",
    "projectReference": {
     "projectId": "bigquery-e2e"
    },
```

Continues

(continued)

```
    "friendlyName": "Bigquery End-to-End"
  }
 ],
 "totalItems": 2
}
```

This response is virtually identical to the `curl` response shown for `Projects` `.list()`. When something is not working, it is often helpful to compare the request you send with the request sent by `bq`.

Datasets

Datasets are containers for tables with some minor metadata and an access control list (ACL). The Datasets collection offers the full range of RESTful operations: `insert()`, `get()`, `list()`, `update()`, `patch()`, and `delete()`. A dataset belongs to a project; any storage used by the dataset is billed to the project. Table 5.4 summarizes the REST methods available in the Datasets collection.

Table 5.4: Datasets REST Collection

METHOD	URL	HTTP VERB
`Datasets.insert()`	`. . . /projects/<project_id>/ datasets/`	POST
`Datasets.get()`	`. . . /projects/<project_id>/ datasets/<dataset_id>`	GET
`Datasets.list()`	`. . . /projects/<project_id>/ datasets`	GET
`Datasets.update()`	`. . . /projects/<project_id>/ datasets/<dataset_id>`	PUT
`Datasets.patch()`	`. . . /projects/<project_id>/ datasets/<dataset_id>`	PATCH
`Datasets.delete()`	`. . . /projects/<project_id>/ datasets/<dataset_id>`	DELETE

Dataset Resource

The Dataset resource contains fields that can be divided up into four parts: the dataset reference, which specifies the dataset name; the dataset ACL, which controls who has access to the dataset; dataset statistics, such as creation and modified times; and user metadata, such as description and friendly name. The interesting fields of the Dataset resource are described in Table 5.5.

Table 5.5: Dataset Resource Fields

FIELD	TYPE	DESCRIPTION
`datasetReference`	`object`	Components of the dataset name. Immutable after the dataset has been created.
`datasetReference` `.datasetId`	`string`	Name of the dataset, unique within the project.
`datasetReference` `.projectId`	`string`	Unique name or number identifying the project the dataset belongs to.
`access`	`object` `array`	Dataset ACL. Exactly one of `specialGroup`, `domain`, and `userByEmail` must be set.
`access.role`	`string`	Access role: One of `READER`, `WRITER`, or `OWNER`.
`access` `.specialGroup`	`string`	Group being given access. Either `projectReaders`, `projectWriters`, `projectOwners`, or `allAuthenticatedUsers`.
`access.userByEmail`	`string`	E-mail address of user being given access. Must be a `gmail.com` or Google Apps For Your Domain address.
`access.domain`	`string`	Name of domain (for example, `google.com`) where all users are given access.
`creationTime`	`number`	Creation time of the dataset, in milliseconds since 1/1/1970. Set automatically.
`lastModifiedTime`	`number`	Last time the dataset metadata was modified, in milliseconds since 1/1/1970. Does not get updated when tables get created or updated. Set automatically.
`friendlyName`	`string`	Friendly name for the dataset. Not unique.
`description`	`string`	Free-text description of the dataset.

Datasets.insert()

The `Datasets.insert()` operation is the only way to create a new dataset. The only fields you need to specify are the dataset and project IDs, but if you choose to specify an ACL or a friendly name, those will also work. The dataset inherits the project ACL by default; project readers become dataset readers, project editors become dataset writers, and project owners become dataset owners. If you specify an ACL with no owners, you will be added as an owner. Here is the output of using `curl` to create a dataset:

```
$ DATASET_REF="{'datasetId': 'scratch', 'projectId': '${PROJECT_ID}'}"
$ DATASETS_URL=${PROJECT_URL}/datasets
```

```
$ curl -H "$(python auth.py)" \
    -H "Content-Type: application/json" \
    -X POST \
    --data-binary "{'datasetReference': ${DATASET_REF}}" \
    "${DATASETS_URL}"
{
...
"datasetReference": {
  "datasetId": "scratch",
  "projectId": "bigquery-e2e"
},
"access": [
  {
   "role": "READER",
   "specialGroup": "projectReaders"
  },
  {
   "role": "WRITER",
   "specialGroup": "projectWriters"
  },
  {
   "role": "OWNER",
   "specialGroup": "projectOwners"
  }
],
"creationTime": "1376367421192",
"lastModifiedTime": "1376367421192"
}
```

Datasets.get()

The `Datasets.get()` API returns the current state of the dataset. You can use
field projections to return only certain fields, or use the `If-None-Match` header
to return only the result if the dataset has changed. Both of these options
are described earlier in this chapter. Following is an example that reads the
`scratch` dataset object but limits the returned fields to the dataset ID and the
creation time:

```
$ DATASET_URL=${DATASETS_URL}/scratch
$ curl -H "$(python auth.py)" \
    "${DATASET_URL}?fields=creationTime,datasetReference(datasetId)"
{
 "datasetReference": {
  "datasetId": "scratch"
 },
 "creationTime": "1374439672882"
}
```

Datasets.list()

The `Datasets.list()` operation returns the datasets in the project. This is an eventually consistent operation—that is, if you create a dataset and do a list operation immediately afterward, you may not see your new dataset in that list right away. With the exception of `Datasets.list()` and `Tables.list()`, all operations in the BigQuery API are guaranteed to be consistent.

The list operation doesn't return the full Dataset resource; it returns only the dataset reference fields. If you need to see the full resource—for example, if you want to see the dataset ACLs—you need to call `Datasets.get()` on the dataset you want to read.

Note that `Datasets.list()` returns only datasets that you have access to. BigQuery must do an access check for each dataset, which is a somewhat expensive operation. For this reason, the total number of datasets in the collection is not returned. This lets BigQuery return a page of results without having to do the access checks on all the datasets in the project. It can just return when it has found enough datasets to satisfy the `maxResults` parameter. The way to tell whether more datasets are available is that the response contains a `pageToken` field, which you can then use to page through the results.

Following is a `curl` transcript showing a `Datasets.list()` request that is limited to the first result:

```
$ curl -H "$(python auth.py)" \
    "${DATASETS_URL}?maxResults=1"
{
 "nextPageToken": "scratch",
 "datasets": [
  {
   "kind": "bigquery#dataset",
   "id": "bigquery-e2e:scratch",
   "datasetReference": {
    "datasetId": "scratch",
    "projectId": "bigquery-e2e"
   }
  }
 ]
}
```

Datasets.update()

The `Datasets.update()` operation enables you to modify the mutable fields of a dataset. The only directly modifiable fields are the ACL (the `access` field) and the friendly name and description of the dataset (the `friendlyName` and `description` fields, respectively). Any attempt to modify an immutable field is ignored. Updating the dataset (via `Datasets.update()` or `Datasets.patch()`) causes the last modified time to be set to the time the operation occurred.

UPDATING ACL OWNERSHIP

A dataset must always have at least one owner. If you try to remove all owners from the ACL, you will be magically added back as the owner. (This is less strange than it sounds because you must have been an owner in the first place to change the ACL.) Furthermore, project owners can always update the ACL, even if they're not actually on the ACL. This is to prevent a situation in which the people paying for the storage of the dataset cannot delete it or exercise control over it.

The `Datasets.update()` method has one more quirk: It will not update the ACL unless an ACL is specified in the update request. This makes it behave more like the `patch()` operation. This behavior was necessary for backward compatibility and to make it easier to update other dataset fields. A dataset with no access control list is not valid, so there should be no ambiguity about what the user actually wanted (because they cannot clear the `access` field).

The following command updates a dataset to set the friendly name to "my dataset":

```
$ curl -H "$(python auth.py)" \
    -H "Content-Type: application/json" \
    -X PUT \
    --data-binary "{'datasetReference': ${DATASET_REF}, \
        'friendlyName': 'my dataset'}" \
    "${DATASETS_URL}/scratch"
{
 "datasetReference": {
  "datasetId": "scratch",
  "projectId": "bigquery-e2e"
 },
 "friendlyName": "my dataset",
 "access": [
  {
   "role": "READER",
   "specialGroup": "projectReaders"
  },
  {
   "role": "WRITER",
   "specialGroup": "projectWriters"
  },
  {
   "role": "OWNER",
   "specialGroup": "projectOwners"
  }
 ],
```

```
    "creationTime": "1376367421192",
    "lastModifiedTime": "1376369547951"
  }
```

Datasets.patch()

Patch operates just like update, except you don't need to provide all the fields; instead you just need the ones you care about updating. This is more than just convenience; it makes it possible for multiple updaters to operate on the same object without worrying that they clobber each other.

For example, suppose Alice was updating the ACL for the `application_logs` dataset. She executes a `Datasets.read()` operation to get the current state, applies her ACL changes, and then calls `Datasets.update()` to commit her changes. At the same time, however, Bob wants to update the dataset's friendly name to Bob's Dataset. If he reads the dataset before Alice's changes have been made but writes his update after her changes have finished, the ACL updates will be wiped out. The `patch` command gives a way to avoid that problem, by only specifying the fields to update. Alice could patch the ACL while Bob is patching the friendly name, and both updates will complete successfully and produce the wanted outcome.

Here is a `curl` session showing a patch operation on the dataset to set the friendly name to "Bob's Dataset." Notice that you don't even have to specify the dataset reference fields:

```
$ curl -H "$(python auth.py)" \
    -H "Content-Type: application/json" \
    -X PATCH \
    --data-binary  "{'friendlyName': 'Bob\'s dataset'}" \
    "${DATASET_URL}"
{
  ...
  "datasetReference": {
   "datasetId": "scratch",
   "projectId": "bigquery-e2e"
  },
  "friendlyName": "Bob's dataset",
  "access": [ ... ],
  "creationTime": "1376367421192",
  "lastModifiedTime": "1376370888255"
}
```

Datasets.delete()

The final operation on a dataset (pun intended) is the `Datasets.delete()` method. To delete a dataset, you must be an owner of the dataset, and the dataset must be empty (i.e. there are no tables in the dataset). If you really want to delete the tables too, you can specify the `deleteContents` flag. It should go without saying that you should be careful when using this operation because there is no undelete operation available for datasets.

One thing that can be surprising is that delete operations do not return the standard HTTP `200` response on success; they return `204` instead. The `204` response code is defined as `No Content`. Because the delete operation doesn't return any content, you get a `204` instead of a `200`. Because this is still a response in the range 200–299, it is still a successful response code, but naïve code may assume that anything that isn't a `200` is a failure.

The following `curl` command deletes the `scratch` dataset:

```
$ curl -H "$(python auth.py)" \
    -X DELETE \
    -w "%{http_code}\\n" \
    "${DATASET_URL}"
204
```

That's it—bye-bye dataset!

Tables

The Tables collection contains metadata about BigQuery tables. Table data is not accessible via the Tables collection; if you want to access the contents of a table, use the TableData collection instead. Tables offer all the common REST operations: `insert()`, `get()`, `list()`, `update()`, `patch()`, and `delete()`. Just as datasets belong to a project, tables belong to a dataset. Tables do not have their own access control; all access control decisions are made via the containing dataset.

The URL for the Tables collection is nested underneath the datasets collection. For example, the URL to read the table `bigquery-e2e:application_logs.usage_log` is `https://www.googleapis.com/bigquery/v2/projects/bigquery-e2e/datasets/application_logs/tables/usage_logs`. Table 5.6 shows the available REST methods and their relative URLs. Several of the URLs are identical; the only difference is the HTTP verb used.

Table 5.6: Tables REST Collection

METHOD	URL	HTTP VERB
`Tables.insert()`	`. . . /datasets/<dataset_id>/tables/`	POST
`Tables.get()`	`. . . /datasets/<dataset_id>/tables/<table_id>`	GET
`Tables.list()`	`. . . /datasets/<dataset_id>/tables/`	GET

METHOD	URL	HTTP VERB
`Tables.update()`	`. . . /datasets/<dataset_id>/ tables/<table_id>`	`PUT`
`Tables.patch()`	`. . . /datasets/<dataset_id>/ tables/<table_id>`	`PATCH`
`Tables.delete()`	`. . . /datasets/<dataset_id>/ tables/<table_id>`	`DELETE`

Table Resource

The Table resource is similar to the Dataset resource. Table references contain an extra field, `tableId`, which uniquely identifies it within the dataset. Instead of an ACL, the primary distinguishing feature of a Table resource is a schema, which describes the format of each row in the table. Finally, there are some additional statistics fields, such as row and byte counts (`numRows` and `numBytes`, respectively). Tables also may have an expiration time (the `expirationTime` field), which is a way to create tables that are automatically deleted when they expire. The interesting fields of the Table resource are described in Table 5.7.

Table 5.7: Table Resource Fields

FIELD	TYPE	DESCRIPTION
`tableReference`	`object`	Components of the table name. Immutable after the table has been created.
`tableReference .tableId`	`string`	Name of the table, unique within the dataset.
`tableReference .datasetId`	`string`	Name of the dataset the table belongs to.
`tableReference .projectId`	`string`	Unique name or number identifying the project the dataset belongs to.
`creationTime`	`number`	Creation time of the table, in milliseconds since 1/1/1970. Set automatically.
`lastModifiedTime`	`number`	Last time the table was modified, in milliseconds since 1/1/1970. Is updated whenever the table metadata or underlying data is changed. Set automatically.

Continues

Table 5-7 (*continued*)

FIELD	TYPE	DESCRIPTION
numBytes	number	Number of bytes of data in all fields. If you run a SELECT * query on this table, this would be the number of bytes you'd be charged for accessing.
numRows	number	Number of rows in the table.
expirationTime	number	Time (in milliseconds since 1/1/1970) when the table will be deleted automatically. Settable by the user.
schema	object	Schema of the table. May be set by the user or implicitly via a job.
schema.fields	object array	Repeated list of fields, or columns, in the table.
schema.fields .name	string	Name of the field.
schema.fields .type	string	Type of the field. One of {INTEGER, FLOAT, BOOLEAN, TIMESTAMP, STRING, or RECORD}.
schema.fields .mode	string	Field mode. One of {NULLABLE, REQUIRED, or REPEATED}. Default is NULLABLE.
schema.fields .fields	object array	Nested schema field records, of the same type as schema.fields.
friendlyName	number	Friendly name for the table. Not unique.
description	string	Description of the table.

Tables.insert()

You can create a table via the Tables.insert() operation; although in practice, most tables are created as a side effect of a job. For example, a Load job can specify a create disposition of CREATE_IF_NEEDED, which means the target table will be created if it doesn't already exist. One reason you might want to create a table by hand is if you want to reserve the name and make sure it is available for querying (that is, it wouldn't cause an error) even before any data arrives. Alternatively, you might want to specify an expiration time so that the table will be automatically deleted when it expires.

Here is the output of using `curl` to create a simple table (after re-creating the dataset first with `bq`):

```
$ bq mk -d scratch
$ TABLES_URL=${DATASETS_URL}/scratch/tables
$ SCHEMA="{'fields': [{'name':'foo', 'type': 'STRING'}]}"
$ TABLE_REF="{'tableId': 'table1', \
    'datasetId': 'scratch', \
    'projectId': '${PROJECT_ID}'}"
$ curl -H "$(python auth.py)" \
    -H "Content-Type: application/json" \
    -X POST \
    --data-binary "{'tableReference': ${TABLE_REF}, \
        'schema': ${SCHEMA}}" \
    "${TABLES_URL}"
{
...
 "tableReference": {
  "projectId": "bigquery-e2e",
  "datasetId": "scratch",
  "tableId": "table1"
 },
 "schema": {
  "fields": [
   {
    "name": "foo",
    "type": "STRING"
   }
  ]
 },
 "creationTime": "1376533497018",
 "lastModifiedTime": "1376533497018"
}
```

Tables.get()

The `Tables.get()` method returns the current state of the table. You can use field projections to return only certain fields (useful because the schema can be very large), or use the `If-None-Match` header to return only the result if the table has changed. The `lastModifiedTime` on the table gets updated whenever any data in the table changes, not just when the table metadata changes, so looking at the `lastModifiedTime` can let you know whether you need to reread the table data. For instance, you might want to rerun a query every time a table changes. Following is an example that reads the table `scratch.table1` after running a Load job that added one row:

```
$ curl -H "$(python auth.py)" \
    -H "Content-Type: application/json" \
```

```
    -X GET \
    "${TABLES_URL}/table1"
{
  ...
  "tableReference": {
   "projectId": "bigquery-e2e",
   "datasetId": "scratch",
   "tableId": "table1"
  },
  "schema": {
   "fields": [
     {
       "name": "f1",
       "type": "STRING"
     }
   ]
  },
  "numRows": "1",
  "numBytes": "8",
  "creationTime": "1376533497018",
  "lastModifiedTime": "1376534761629"
}
```

Tables.list()

The `Tables.list()` method returns the list of tables in a dataset. If there are more results than can be comfortably returned in a single response, you can use the paging mechanisms described earlier in the chapter to page through the results. `Tables.list()`, like `Datasets.list()`, is eventually consistent with respect to recently added tables. That is, if you add a table and immediately call `Tables.list()`, you might not see it. If you call `Tables.get()`, however, you always see the table if it exists.

Unlike `Datasets.list()`, `Tables.list()` returns a count of the total number of tables in the dataset, even if fewer are returned in the list operation. If the list operation doesn't return all of the tables, this is due to paging, not access control, since all tables in a dataset share the same ACL.

To conserve response size (because table schemas can be very large), `Tables.list()` doesn't return the full Table resource; it includes only the table reference information. If you need to see the full Table resource, you should call `Tables.get()`.

Following is a `curl` transcript showing a `tables.list()` request:

```
$ curl -H "$(python auth.py)" \
    -H "Content-Type: application/json" \
    -X GET \
    "${TABLES_URL}?maxResults=1"
{
  ...
```

```
  "nextPageToken": "table1",
  "tables": [
   {
    "kind": "bigquery#table",
    "id": "bigquery-e2e:scratch.table1",
    "tableReference": {
     "projectId": "bigquery-e2e",
     "datasetId": "scratch",
     "tableId": "table1"
    }
   }
  ],
  "totalItems": 2
}
```

Tables.update()

The `Tables.update()` operation enables you to modify the mutable fields of a table. The freely modifiable fields are the expiration time, friendly name, and description (`expirationTime`, `friendlyName`, and `description`). The schema can also be modified in certain limited ways.

If a table doesn't have a schema, you always can add one. If a table already has a schema, you can't remove fields, and the only change you can make to a field is to change the mode from REQUIRED to NULLABLE. You can, however add fields, but again with restrictions. The fields you add must have the mode set to NULLABLE or REPEATED (or empty because NULLABLE is the default). This restriction makes sense because if you added a new required field, all previous data in the table wouldn't have had that field, so it wouldn't match the schema. You can also only add fields at the end of the schema.

Following is an example of a `curl` request adding a field to the table schema:

```
$ SCHEMA2="{'fields': [ \
    {'name':'foo', 'type': 'STRING'}, \
    {'name': 'bar', 'type': 'FLOAT'}]}"
$ TABLE_JSON="{'tableReference': ${TABLE_REF}, 'schema': ${SCHEMA2}}"
$ curl -H "$(python auth.py)" \
    -H "Content-Type: application/json" \
    -X PUT \
    --data-binary "${TABLE_JSON}" \
    "${TABLES_URL}/table1"
{
...
"tableReference": {
  "projectId": "bigquery-e2e",
  "datasetId": "scratch",
  "tableId": "table1"
 },
```

```json
    "schema": {
     "fields": [
       {
         "name": "foo",
         "type": "STRING"
       },
       {
         "name": "bar",
         "type": "FLOAT"
       }
     ]
    },
    "numBytes": "0",
    "numRows": "0",
    "creationTime": "1376537757773",
    "lastModifiedTime": "1376537882648"
}
```

Tables.patch()

Patch enables you update a table without specifying all the fields on the table. This is especially nice if you want to leave the schema as-is and just want to update a single field such as expirationTime. Here is a curl command showing how you can update the expiration time with a simple request without affecting the schema:

```
$ EXPIRATION_TIME=$(($(date +"%s")+24*60*60))000
$ curl -H "$(python auth.py)" \
    -H "Content-Type: application/json" \
    -X PATCH \
    --data-binary "{'expirationTime': '${EXPIRATION_TIME}'}" \
    "${TABLES_URL}/table1"
{
...
"tableReference": {
. "projectId": "bigquery-e2e",
  "datasetId": "scratch",
  "tableId": "table1"
 },
 "schema": {
  "fields": [
    {
      "name": "foo",
      "type": "STRING"
    },
    {
      "name": "bar",
      "type": "FLOAT"
```

```
      }
    ]
  },
  "numBytes": "0",
  "numRows": "0",
  "creationTime": "1376537757773",
  "expirationTime": "1376624670453",
  "lastModifiedTime": "1376538270453"
}
```

Tables.delete()

Deleting a table is simple and irrevocable. Just call `Tables.delete()` or send the HTTP DELETE verb to the table name, and poof! Your table is gone! Note that like `Datasets.delete()`, `Tables.delete()` returns the HTTP response code 204 on success.

```
$ curl -H "$(python auth.py)" \
    -X DELETE \
    -w "%{http_code}\\n" \
    "${TABLES_URL}/table1"
204
```

TableData

The TableData collection is one of the ways you can access the data in your tables. The collection's resource is a table row, which contains a single row of data from the table. There are only two operations available on table data: `list()` and `insertAll()`. Only `list()` is a true REST operation; `insertAll()` is an RPC method that inserts multiple rows into the table.

Because table data belongs to a table, it is nested under the table URL. A full `TableData.list()` URL for the `bigquery-e2e:application_logs.usage_log` table is `https://www.googleapis.com/bigquery/v2/projects/bigquery-e2e/datasets/application_logs/tables/usage_logs/data`. Table 5.8 shows the available REST methods in the table data collection and their relative URLs.

Table 5.8: TableData REST Collection

METHOD	URL	HTTP VERB
TableData.list()	. . . /tables/<table_id>/data/	GET
TableData .insertAll()	. . . /tables/<table_id>/data/ insertAll	POST

TableData Resource

The TableData resource is the TableRow, which, at first, looks like an odd collection of f and v lists. After you get familiar with it, it still looks like an odd
collection of f and v lists, but at least they make a little bit more sense.

Each row is a structure with one field f, containing a list of structures that also
have a single field, this time called v. The TableData rows use the same format as
query results that are returned by Jobs.query() and Jobs.getQueryResults()
and are modeled after the Google GViz format.

So what's with the f and v? Why not have more idiomatic JSON with lists
of {"fieldName": "fieldValue"}? The primary reason is compactness. If you
request a million rows and each row has the same field names, it is highly
redundant to specify the field names in each row. The names f and v were also
chosen to be as compact as possible, rather than something more verbose like
fields and value.

Schemas in BigQuery can be recursive. In the nested case, there will be a
nested f inside of a v.

The table data row format is described in Table 5.9.

Table 5.9: TableData Resource Fields

FIELD	TYPE	DESCRIPTION
f	object array	List of fields in the row.
f.v	any	Value of the field. Although the field can be of any type, it will always be rendered as a string.
f.v.f	object array	Nested field representation.

TableData.list()

The TableData.list() method reads data from a table. The TableData.list()
method supports both index-based pagination and page-token-based pagination.
Although token-based pagination is usually preferred, sometimes the actual
index of the row is important.

When using index-based pagination, if the table is changing while you page
through it, you always see the latest data, which may not be what you expect.
Token-based pagination always gives you a stable view of the table, so if you
ask for the next page, you get the next page of results as of the time you started
paging through the table. Because this may require extra storage to keep around
old versions of the table, page tokens have a limited lifetime—if you try to use
them after seven days you'll get an error.

In order to see how TableData.list() works on nested data, let's first load
some nested data via the bq tool.

```
$ bq load \
    --source_format=NEWLINE_DELIMITED_JSON \
    scratch.nested nested.json \
    nested.schema.json
```

Here is a `curl` command that reads data from a small nested table. You can see all of the funny `f`s and `v`s:

```
$ curl -H "$(python auth.py)" \
    -H "Content-Type: application/json" \
    -X GET \
    "${TABLES_URL}/nested/data?prettyPrint=false"
{"kind":"bigquery#tableDataList", ... "totalRows":"3",
"rows":[
  {"f":[{"v":"1"}, {"v":{"f":[{"v":"2.0"}, {"v":[{"v":"foo"}]}]}}]},
  {"f":[{"v":"2"},{"v":{"f":[{"v":"4.0"}, {"v":[{"v":"bar"}]}]}}]},
  {"f":[{"v":"3"},{"v":{"f":[{"v":"8.0"},
    {"v":[{"v":"baz"},{"v":"qux"}]}]}}]}]}
```

TABLEDATA ORDERING

Loosely speaking, `TableData.list()` returns rows in order of oldest data to newest data. That is, if you have a table where you append new values daily and page through it using `TableData.list()`, you get the data from the first day first, then the next day, and so on.

There is a caveat to the ordering rules, however. BigQuery periodically runs a background operation to optimize table representation for querying. When you do a lot of small imports, the internal representation of the table is less efficient to query against. The table optimization process can reorder data, but does so only with older data in the table. Data that was added within the last seven days will never be reordered.

Reading data from tables in a dynamic programming language, such as Python, is quite convenient. Dynamic languages make it easy to handle cases in which you don't know the types ahead of time. In Python, you can parse the JSON response and turn it into a `dict` object and then access the fields as you would any `dict`. Here is the code in Python to iterate through query results and print them:

```python
def print_results(results):
  fields = results['schema']['fields']
  rows = results.get('rows', [])
  for row in rows:
    for i in xrange(0, len(fields)):
      cell = row['f'][i]
      field = fields[i]
      print "%s: %s " % (field['name'], cell['v']),
    print ''
```

Most of the Python examples in this book will look similar if translated into other programming languages. However, statically typed languages, such as Java, make it more difficult to write code where the types are not known ahead of time. Because the code is much different from the Python version, we show the Java code in Listing 5.2 to iterate through the rows in a `Tabledata.list()` response and print it as JSON with the fields labeled.

Listing 5.2: Parsing TableData list nested responses from Java (ResultReader.java)

```java
import com.google.api.client.util.Data;
import com.google.api.services.bigquery.model.GetQueryResultsResponse;
import com.google.api.services.bigquery.model.QueryResponse;
import com.google.api.services.bigquery.model.TableCell;
import com.google.api.services.bigquery.model.TableDataList;
import com.google.api.services.bigquery.model.TableFieldSchema;
import com.google.api.services.bigquery.model.TableRow;
import com.google.api.services.bigquery.model.TableSchema;

import java.io.PrintStream;
import java.util.List;
import java.util.Map;

/**
 * Translates f / v results from BigQuery table listing or query results
 * into {field1 : value1, field2 : value2, ...} JSON output.
 */
public class ResultReader {
  private final PrintStream printer;
  public ResultReader() {
    this(System.out);
  }
  public ResultReader(PrintStream stream) {
    this.printer = stream;
  }

  private <T extends Map<String, Object>> T fixup(T parent,
      Object obj) {
    // Because of the cell recursion, we have to do something slightly
    // goofy: We turn the cell/row into a map, then turn it back into a
    // cell/row. This works around some Java type inconsistencies
    // between neted calls and outer ones.
    @SuppressWarnings("unchecked")
    Map<String, Object> valueMap = (Map<String, Object>) obj;
    parent.putAll(valueMap);
    return parent;
  }

  private void printCellValue(TableFieldSchema field, TableCell cell) {
    if (Data.isNull(cell.getV())) {
      printer.append("null");
```

```java
        return;
    } else if (field.getType().toLowerCase().equals("record")) {
      TableRow tableRow = fixup(new TableRow(), cell.getV());
      printCells(field.getFields(), tableRow.getF());
    } else {
      // Everything that isn't a record can be printed as a string.
      printer.format("\"%s\"", cell.getV().toString());
    }
  }
}

private void printCell(TableFieldSchema field, TableCell cell) {
  printer.format("\"%s\": ", field.getName());
  String mode = field.getMode();
  if (mode != null && mode.toLowerCase().equals("repeated")) {
    // We've got a repeated field here. This is actually a list of
    // values.
    printer.append("[");
    if (!Data.isNull(cell)) {

      @SuppressWarnings("unchecked")
      List<Object> values = (List<Object>) cell.getV();

      for (int ii = 0; ii < values.size(); ii += 1) {
        if (ii != 0) {
          printer.append(", ");
        }
        TableCell innerCell = fixup(new TableCell(), values.get(ii));
        printCellValue(field, innerCell);
      }
    }
    printer.append("]");
  } else {
    printCellValue(field, cell);
  }
}

private void printCells(List<TableFieldSchema> fields,
    List<TableCell> cells) {
  printer.append("{");
  for (int ii = 0; ii < fields.size(); ii += 1) {
    if (ii != 0) {
      printer.append(", ");
    }
    TableFieldSchema field = fields.get(ii);
    TableCell cell = fixup(new TableCell(), cells.get(ii));
    printCell(field, cell);
  }
  printer.append("}");
```

Continues

Listing 5.2: *(continued)*

```
  }

  public void printRows(TableSchema schema, List<TableRow> rows) {
    for (TableRow row : rows) {
      printCells(schema.getFields(), row.getF());
    }
  }

  public void print(QueryResponse response) {
    printRows(response.getSchema(), response.getRows());
  }

  public void print(GetQueryResultsResponse response) {
    printRows(response.getSchema(), response.getRows());
  }

  public void print(TableSchema schema, TableDataList response) {
    printRows(schema, response.getRows());
  }
}
```

TableData.insertAll()

The `TableData.insertAll()` method is used for appending records to a table. It is described in much more detail in Chapter 6, "Loading Data," in the section on streaming imports. You may ask, why provide a nonstandard `insertAll()` RPC method but not a normal REST `insert()` call? The primary reason is efficiency; if you have Big Data but send individual POST requests to add each row to your table, you're going to incur a lot of network overhead to set up and tear down HTTP connections. Although you can call `TableData.insertAll()` to send records one at a time, the record list in the API signature encourages you to batch up your requests.

Jobs

The Jobs collection enables you to actually "do" things with BigQuery, such as add your data or query it. This chapter gives only a cursory introduction to the types of jobs you can run in BigQuery and some of their more common options. Later chapters go into more detail. For now, we just consider REST operations on jobs and the shared portions of the Job resource.

Jobs always belong to a single project—the project that will be responsible for paying for running the jobs. Job quotas are per-project as well. To reflect this relationship, the Jobs collection is nested under the Projects collection. A full `Jobs.list()` URL for the `bigquery-e2e` project is `https://www.googleapis.com/bigquery/v2/projects/bigquery-e2e/jobs`. Table 5.10 shows the available REST methods and their relative URLs.

Table 5.10: Jobs REST Collection

METHOD	URL	HTTP VERB
Jobs.insert()	... /projects/<project_id>/jobs/	POST
Jobs.get()	... /projects/<project_id>/jobs/<job_id>	GET
Jobs.list()	... /projects/<project_id>/jobs/	GET
Jobs.query()	... /projects/<project_id>/queries/	POST
Jobs.getQueryResults()	... /projects/<project_id>/queries/<job_id>	GET

Jobs Resource

The Job resource has four main parts: job reference, which uniquely identifies the job; configuration, which tells BigQuery what to run; statistics that describe how the job ran; and status to tell you the current state of the job. These components are described at a high level in Table 5.11.

Table 5.11: Job Resource Top-level Components

FIELD	TYPE	DESCRIPTION
jobReference	object	Components of the job name. Unique within the project. Immutable after the job has been created.
configuration	object	JobConfiguration object indicating what operation the job should run. For example, for a Query job, the configuration.query portion will be filled out with the query to run.
status	object	JobStatus object describing current job state and any errors that may have accumulated on the job.
statistics	object	JobStatistics object containing statistics about how the job was run, such as when the job started, when it completed, and how much data it processed.

JobReference

The job reference contains two fields: jobId and projectId, as shown in Table 5.12 The projectId is the project that "owns" the job. For example, if you run a query, the project specified in the project ID is responsible for paying for any charges incurred by the query. It doesn't matter which project the tables being queried belong to—just the project specified in the job.

The job ID must be unique within the project. If multiple users all run jobs in the same project, this can mean some coordination between users is required.

If you do not specify a job ID when you create the job, BigQuery will create one for you that is random and guaranteed to be unique. If you care about tracking the outcome of the job, however, you should specify your own ID. This way you can find out what happened with the job, even if the `Jobs.insert()` request returns an error.

Table 5.12: Job Reference Components

FIELD	TYPE	DESCRIPTION
jobId	string	ID of the job, unique within the project
projectId	string	ID of the project that will be billed for the job

JobConfiguration

The `JobConfiguration` object contains several subsections, one for each type of job that can be run. When creating a job, you should fill out only one of these sections—the one that corresponds to the type of job you want to run. Table 5.13 shows the top-level configurations. The details of per-job configurations will be described in later chapters.

Table 5.13: Job Configuration Components

FIELD	TYPE	DESCRIPTION
copy	object	Configuration for table Copy jobs. Table copy is a fast metadata-only operation. Described in Chapter 11, "Managing Data Stored in BigQuery."
extract	object	Configuration for Extract jobs, used to export an entire table out of BigQuery. Extract is described in Chapter 12, "External Data Processing."
load	object	Configuration for Load jobs, used to get bulk data into BigQuery. Load jobs are described in Chapter 6.
query	object	Configuration for Query jobs. Can be created directly, or indirectly via the `Jobs.query()` method. Query jobs are described in Chapter 7.
dryRun	boolean	When set, runs the job in dry-run mode, which means that the configuration is verified but the job is not actually run. This does not create an actual job. `dryRun` jobs are free.

JobStatus

The job status object, shown in Table 5.14, will let you know whether the job has started or whether it had any errors. The `state` field will always be either PENDING, RUNNING, or DONE. If the job failed, the reason for the failure will be in the `errorResult` field. The `error` field also contains a list of errors but does not necessarily indicate that the job failed. Instead, the errors in the `error` list should be thought of as warnings when the `errorResult` is not present.

Table 5.14: JobStatus Components

FIELD	TYPE	DESCRIPTION
state	string	Either PENDING, to indicate the job is still queued; RUNNING, to indicate the job is actively running; or DONE to indicate the job has completed and all side effects are committed.
errorResult	object	If present, the error that caused the job to fail.
errorResult .location	string	Optional location of the error.
errorResult .message	string	A user-readable description of the error.
errorResult .reason	string	A short error code describing the error, such as notFound. If you have code that handles errors, the reason should be used to make decisions about the type of error, rather than the message, which may change at any time.
errors	object array	All the errors that occurred on the job. Presence of errors in this field does not necessarily indicate job failure.

JobStatistics

The job statistics tell you information about the job that ran, such as how long it ran for and how much work it did. The `JobStatistics` object, described in Table 5.15, has a main section that has job timing data, in addition to per-job-type nested sections.

Table 5.15: JobStatistics Components

FIELD	TYPE	DESCRIPTION
creationTime	number	The time, in milliseconds since 1/1/1970 UTC that this job was created.
startTime	number	The time, in milliseconds since 1/1/1970 UTC that this job was started (that is, the state went from PENDING to RUNNING).
endTime	number	The time, in milliseconds since 1/1/1970 UTC that this job was completed (that is, the state transitioned to DONE).

Continues

Table 5.15 (continued)

FIELD	TYPE	DESCRIPTION
query	object	Statistics reported by Query jobs.
query.cacheHit	boolean	Whether the query result was found in the query cache.
query .totalBytesProcessed	number	Number of bytes scanned by the query. This is the value used for assessing billing charges for queries.
load	object	Statistics reported by Load jobs.
load.inputFileBytes	number	Number of bytes of read from source files that were imported.
load.inputFiles	number	Number of source files that were imported.
load.outputBytes	number	Number of bytes added to the table. This value will be used in computing billing for table storage.
load.outputRows	number	How many additional rows of data were added to the table.

Jobs.insert()

When you insert a job into the Jobs collection, this tells BigQuery to run a job to perform some asynchronous operation on your behalf. The only information you need to provide is the configuration section. That said, it is strongly recommended that you also provide a jobId in the jobReference section, so that it is easier to track what happened if something goes wrong. The following commands create a job ID from the current time and run a curl request to start a Query job.

```
$ JOB_ID=job_$(date +"%s")
$ JOB_REFERENCE="{'jobId': '${JOB_ID}', 'projectId': '${PROJECT_ID}'}"
$ JOB_CONFIG="{'query': {'query': 'select 17'}}"
$ JOB="{'jobReference': ${JOB_REF}, 'configuration': ${JOB_CONFIG}}"
$ curl -H "$(python auth.py)"  \
    -H "Content-Type: application/json" \
    -X POST \
   --data-binary "${JOB}" \
    "${JOBS_URL}"
{
...
 "jobReference": {
  "projectId": "bigquery-e2e",
  "jobId": " job_1394518034"
 },
```

```
 "configuration": {
  "query": {
   "query": "select 17",
   "destinationTable": {
    "projectId": "bigquery-e2e",
    "datasetId": "_0e32b38e1117b2fcea992287c138bd53acfff7cc",
    "tableId": "anon5c03da1f543a2486eca295f285b40eb87b01ea84"
   },
   "createDisposition": "CREATE_IF_NEEDED",
   "writeDisposition": "WRITE_TRUNCATE"
  }
 },
 "status": {
  "state": "RUNNING"
 },
 "statistics": {
  "creationTime": "1376685153301",
  "startTime": "1376685153396"
 }
```

Jobs.get()

After you create a job, it is common to poll until the job completes. (That is, wait until job['status']['state'] == 'DONE'.) You should wait a second or so between polling attempts, so your polling doesn't look like an attempted denial-of-service attack on Google.

If you hadn't specified the job ID, you could still know how to look up the job because the Jobs.insert() request returns the jobReference in the response. However, if Jobs.insert() returned an error (say your network was temporarily disabled), you'd have no way of knowing whether the job actually ran.

If it sounds like we're over-hyping the value of providing your own job ID , it is because it is something that is easy to do that can solve a lot of potential problems. We see a lot of support requests that are made more difficult by not having a job ID to use to investigate, and a lot of customers that end up accidentally rerunning jobs because they haven't provided a job ID. We just want to make sure that you're aware of the option.

Here is a curl request that shows getting job state for the same job_1394518034 previously created:

```
$ curl -H "$(python auth.py)" \
    -H "Content-Type: application/json" \
    "${JOBS_URL}/${JOB_ID}"
{
...
"jobReference": {
  "projectId": "bigquery-e2e",
  "jobId": " job_1394518034"
 },
```

```
  "configuration": {
   "query": {
    "query": "select 17",
    "destinationTable": {
     "projectId": "bigquery-e2e",
     "datasetId": "_0e32b38e1117b2fcea992287c138bd53acfff7cc",
     "tableId": "anon5c03da1f543a2486eca295f285b40eb87b01ea84"
    },
    "createDisposition": "CREATE_IF_NEEDED",
    "writeDisposition": "WRITE_TRUNCATE"
   }
  },
  "status": {
   "state": "DONE"
  },
  "statistics": {
   "creationTime": "1376685153301",
   "startTime": "1376685153396",
   "endTime": "1376685153696",
   "query": {
    "totalBytesProcessed": "0",
   }
  }
 }
```

Jobs.list()

The Jobs.list() method tells you which jobs are currently running or which jobs have run recently. You can specify a job state filter, so you can see just running jobs, or just pending jobs by using the stateFilter parameter. Jobs will be returned in reverse order of time; that is, the jobs that were created most recently will be returned first.

When you call Jobs.list(), you see only the jobs you have run yourself. If you want to see jobs run by others, you should set the allUsers flag to true, which will let you see all the jobs run by all users in the project. (You need to be an owner of the project, however.) The allUsers flag allows project owners to see the jobs that have been run that they will, ultimately, be paying for.

When listing jobs, you can also specify a projection. The default projection is "minimal," which doesn't include the configuration field, but if you'd like to see the full Job resource, you can specify projection=full.

Here is a curl command that shows you just the job IDs of recently completed jobs:

```
$ FIELDS="jobs(jobReference(jobId))"
$ PARAMS="stateFilter=DONE&fields=${FIELDS}&maxResults=2"
$ curl -H "$(python auth.py)" \
    -H "Content-Type: application/json" \
```

```
      -X GET \
      "${JOBS_URL}?${PARAMS}"
  {
    "jobs": [
      {
        "jobReference": {
          "jobId": "bqjob_r29016a1bfe5187c8_000001408ce3ffc5_1"
        }
      },
      {
        "jobReference": {
          "jobId": "bqjob_r239fa6e7bb78440_000001408ce3e8f2_1"
        }
      }
    ]
  }
```

Jobs.query() and Jobs.getQueryResults() RPCs

The `Jobs.query()` and `Jobs.getQueryResults()` APIs are used to run queries and get the results of queries, respectively. These APIs are covered in depth in Chapter 7, so we defer discussion of them until that chapter.

BigQuery API Tour

There is an old puzzle called the "knight's tour" in chess: How can you move a knight around a chessboard such that it hits every square exactly once? Listing 5.3 shows the "knight's tour" of the BigQuery API—it runs through each API method in each collection once, leaving the end state the same as when you started. This puts all the APIs in context, lets you see how they work, and shows how to call them from Python.

Listing 5.3: A Knight's tour of the BigQuery API (tour.py)

```python
# Python imports
import io
import json
import sys
import time

# Google APIs imports
from apiclient.discovery import build
from apiclient.errors import HttpError
from apiclient.http import MediaIoBaseUpload

# BigQuery e2e imports
```

Continues

Listing 5.3: *(continued)*

```python
import auth

## Runs through each BigQuery API request.
def run_tour(service, project_id):
  print 'Running BigQuery API tour'

  projects = service.projects()
  datasets = service.datasets()
  tables = service.tables()
  tabledata = service.tabledata()
  jobs = service.jobs()

  # Generate some IDs to use with the tour.
  tour = 'tour_%d' % (time.time())
  dataset_id = 'dataset_' + tour
  table_id = 'table_' + tour
  job_id = 'job_' + tour

  project_ref = {'projectId': project_id}
  dataset_ref = {'datasetId': dataset_id,
                 'projectId': project_id}
  table_ref = {'tableId': table_id,
               'datasetId': dataset_id,
               'projectId': project_id}
  job_ref = {'jobId': job_id,
             'projectId': project_id}

  # First, find the project and print out the friendly name.
  for project in projects.list().execute()['projects']:
    if (project['id'] == project_id):
      print 'Found %s: %s' % (project_id, project['friendlyName'])

  # Now create a dataset
  dataset = {'datasetReference': dataset_ref}
  dataset = datasets.insert(body=dataset, **project_ref).execute()

  # Patch the dataset to set a friendly name.
  update = {'friendlyName': 'Tour dataset'}
  dataset = datasets.patch(body=update, **dataset_ref).execute()

  # Print out the dataset for posterity
  print '%s' % (dataset,)

  # Find our dataset in the datasets list:
  dataset_list = datasets.list(**project_ref).execute()
  for current in dataset_list['datasets']:
    if current['id'] == dataset['id']:
      print 'found %s' % (dataset['id'])

  ### Now onto tables...
  table = {'tableReference': table_ref}
```

```
table = tables.insert(body=table, **dataset_ref).execute()

# Update the table to add a schema:
table['schema'] = {'fields': [{'name': 'a', 'type': 'string'}]}
table = tables.update(body=table, **table_ref).execute()

# Patch the table to add a friendly name
patch = {'friendlyName': 'Friendly table'}
table = tables.patch(body=patch, **table_ref).execute()

# Print table for posterity:
print table

# Find our table in the tables list:
table_list = tables.list(**dataset_ref).execute()
for current in table_list['tables']:
  if current['id'] == table['id']: print 'found %s' % (table['id'])

## And now for some jobs...
config = {'load': {'destinationTable': table_ref}}
load_text = 'first\nsecond\nthird'

# Remember to always name your jobs!
job = {'jobReference': job_ref, 'configuration': config}

media = MediaIoBaseUpload(io.BytesIO(load_text),
                          mimetype='application/octet-stream')
job = jobs.insert(body=job,
                  media_body=media,
                  **project_ref).execute()

# List our running or pending jobs:
job_list = jobs.list(
    stateFilter=['pending', 'running'],
    **project_ref).execute()
print job_list

while job['status']['state'] <> 'DONE':
  job = jobs.get(**job_ref).execute()

# Now run a query against that table.
query = 'select count(*) from [%s]' % (table['id'])
query_request = {'query': query, 'timeoutMs': 0, 'maxResults': 1}
results = jobs.query(body=query_request, **project_ref).execute()
while not results['jobComplete']:
  get_results_request = results['jobReference'].copy()
  get_results_request['timeoutMs'] = 10000
  get_results_request['maxResults'] = 10
  results = jobs.getQueryResults(
      **get_results_request).execute()
```

Continues

Listing 5.3: *(continued)*

```
    print results

    # Now let's read the data from our table.
    data = tabledata.list(**table_ref).execute()
    table = tables.get(**table_ref).execute()
    print 'Table %s\nData:%s' % (data, table)

    # Now we should clean up our toys.
    tables.delete(**table_ref).execute()
    datasets.delete(**dataset_ref).execute()

    # Now try reading the dataset after deleting it:
    try:
      datasets.get(**dataset_ref).execute()
      print "That's funny, we should never get here!"
    except HttpError as err:
      print 'Expected error:\n%s' % (err,)

    # Done!
def main(argv):

    service = auth.build_bq_client()
    project_id = 'bigquery-e2e' if len(argv) == 0 else argv[0]
    run_tour(service, project_id)

if __name__ == '__main__':
    main(sys.argv[1:])
```

Error Handling in BigQuery

In a perfect world, every BigQuery operation would succeed and there would be no need to debug or worry about errors. In practice, however, there are a number of different types of errors you'll encounter, and depending on how you use BigQuery, different ways to handle them.

HTTP Errors and Responses

All BigQuery API calls are HTTP requests; therefore in accordance with the HTTP 1.1 spec, they all return HTTP status codes. Codes between 200 and 299 are "success" codes, but nearly all requests will return 200 on success. The only other success code used by BigQuery is 204 No Content, which will be returned when deleting datasets or tables.

HTTP error codes are in the range 400–599. Unless there was some kind of severe network error or badly malformed request, BigQuery returns a standard JSON response on error, in addition to the raw status code, that can be used to make sense of what went wrong. Table 5.16 describes the field of that error response.

Table 5.16: HTTP Error Response Components

FIELD	TYPE	DESCRIPTION
code	number	HTTP status code that maps most closely to the response. Rather than using this to try to determine the issue, you should use the `errors.reason` value instead.
message	string	User-facing message describing the first error.
errors	object array	List of HTTP errors encountered. Will nearly always have exactly one error.
errors.domain	string	Nearly always `global`. Not very interesting.
errors.message	string	User-facing message describing the error.
errors.reason	string	Code categorizing the error. If you are handling errors in code, you should use this field rather than the message (which may change at any time) or the HTTP response code (which maps imperfectly onto the set of possible errors) to determine what went wrong.
errors.location	string (optional)	Describes where in the request the error occurred. May provide additional information about the error.
errors .locationType	string (optional)	Provides additional context for the `errors .location` field.

Following is an example error you'll get if you use an invalid `Authorization` header:

```
{
 "error": {
  "errors": [
   {
    "domain": "global",
    "reason": "authError",
    "message": "Invalid Credentials",
    "locationType": "header",
    "location": "Authorization"
   }
  ],
  "code": 401,
  "message": "Invalid Credentials"
 }
}
```

Here you can see that there is one error on the global domain (which 99.9 percent of error responses will share). The HTTP response code is 401. If you look that up in the HTTP 1.1 spec, you'll see that it is the code for `Unauthorized`. You shouldn't need to look it up because you can use the `reason` field `authError`, which means that there was an error authorizing the request.

If you forgot the `Authorization` header entirely, you'll still get an `HTTP 401` response, but you'll get the error `reason` of `required`, a `location` of `Authorization`, and a `locationType` of `header`. This enables you to know that your request was missing a required field: the `Authorization` header.

Table 5.17 provides a partial list of the HTTP errors that BigQuery can return.

Table 5.17: BigQuery HTTP Errors

CODE	REASON	DESCRIPTION
400	invalidParameter	One or more of the arguments you supplied in the request was invalid.
400	parseError	The JSON request you sent could not be parsed correctly.
400	invalidQuery	The BigQuery query you specified could not be parsed correctly.
400	required	Your request was missing a required field.
400	resourcesExceeded	Your query required too many resources to complete successfully. This can happen when doing an `ORDER BY` on a large query result, for example.
400	responseTooLarge	Your query response was larger than 128 MB and you did not specify `allowLargeResults`. Can also happen when an intermediate calculation was too large.
401	authError	Your `Authorization` header was invalid. This does *not* mean that you tried to access something you didn't have access to.
403	accessDenied	You tried to perform an operation on a resource that you weren't authorized to access. For example, you tried to run a job in a project without being a member of the project team.
403	billingNotEnabled	You tried to perform a BigQuery operation that requires billing to be enabled.
403	blacklisted	You tried to perform an operation that is on the blacklist. This can happen in rare instances when queries or types of queries are blacklisted to prevent the exploitation of bugs in the system. If you see this error, it should provide you contact information in the message so that you can find out what it is that has been blacklisted.
403	rateLimitExceeded	You're sending BigQuery requests too quickly; try slowing down.

CODE	REASON	DESCRIPTION
403	quotaExceeded	You've exceeded a long-term (most likely daily) quota limit.
404	notFound	You tried to access a resource that doesn't exist.
409	duplicate	You tried to create a resource that already exists.
500	internalError	Your response triggered an internal BigQuery error. This is always a BigQuery bug.
503	backendError	There was an error connecting to BigQuery, or BigQuery experienced an error contacting another required service. If you retry, this error will likely go away.

Job Errors and Responses

Most BigQuery errors are reported as an HTTP error of the type described in the previous section. However, when you run a BigQuery job, it gets run asynchronously. Errors that are encountered on the job may not happen in the context of an HTTP request. To report errors, jobs use the `status.errorResult` and `status.errors` fields. These are described in more detail in the more detail in the "Jobs" section in this chapter.

Job errors are reported using the same data structure as the HTTP response errors. The only difference is that they do not have an HTTP response code because they aren't HTTP errors. But they look virtually identical to the HTTP responses.

For example, when you try to read a dataset that doesn't exist, you get the following error in the `errors` field of the response:

```
{
  "domain": "global",
  "reason": "notFound",
  "message": "Not Found: Dataset bigquery-e2e:nonexistent"
}
```

When you run a query against a nonexistent dataset, which creates a job, you get a nearly identical error in the `job.errorResult` field:

```
"errorResult": {
  "reason": "notFound",
  "message": "Not Found: Dataset bigquery-e2e:nonexistent"
}
```

Error Reporting for Jobs.query() and Jobs.getQueryResults()

The lines between a job error and an HTTP error get murkier when you consider the `Jobs.query()` and `Jobs.getQueryResults()` APIs. These APIs wait for a query to complete and return the results. The `Jobs.query()` API is designed to be callable in a synchronous fashion—having to distinguish between errors in the request and network errors, and errors in the job would be too onerous. For this reason, the `Jobs.query()` and `Jobs.getQueryResults()` methods that hit a fatal error (that is, the Query job has a `status.errorResult`) return those errors as HTTP errors. For example, the same query that previously generated the `notFound` `errorResult` would return the following HTTP response code if executed via the `jobs.query()` API:

```
{
 "error": {
  "errors": [
   {
    "domain": "global",
    "reason": "notFound",
    "message": "Not Found: Dataset bigquery-e2e:nonexistent"
   }
  ],
  "code": 404,
  "message": "Not Found: Dataset bigquery-e2e:nonexistent"
 }
}
```

Summary

In this chapter we discussed how Google APIs in general and BigQuery in particular fit in with the REST model. You saw some of the raw HTTP-level features of Google APIs and how they can be invoked from higher-level languages. You also walked through the BigQuery REST collections: Projects, Datasets, Tables, TableData, and Jobs, and saw the operations that are valid on those collections.

Also of note in the chapter were the coding samples: the code to get an up-to-date OAuth2 token and Python code exercising every method in the BigQuery API. You also saw how to read table data from both Java and Python.

Finally, you went through the types of errors you're likely to see, what they mean, and what to do when you see them.

Loading Data

Before you can begin to slice, dice, and roll up your data in BigQuery, first you have to get the data into the service. In Chapter 3, "Getting Started with BigQuery," you worked through a simplified example of loading data to verify that billing was correctly enabled on your account. Unfortunately, loading data is not usually quite so simple. For that example a file hosted in Google Cloud Storage was available in a format understood by BigQuery, and you were supplied with a schema that matched the data. When you need to load your own data into the service, you need to tackle each of these steps. This is not to imply that loading data is super challenging; rather it is to emphasize that it is an important part of using the service that is at times overlooked.

There are two distinct pieces to the process of loading data into BigQuery:

- Formatting your data appropriately
- Transferring the data to BigQuery

In most scenarios the data you need to analyze lives in a system you control: files on your computer, records in a database, or logs from hosted servers, to name a few. The first task is to extract the data from the systems in a form that BigQuery can accept. In some cases this is trivial because the data happens to be in a suitable format such as a CSV file on your machine, but in other cases it might require some massaging or an extraction (the E in Extract-Transform-Load) from a database. With installed software you might be done at this point because the application and data usually reside on the same machine or network. With cloud services there is an additional step; the data needs to be shipped to the service. With ever-increasing bandwidth this is becoming less of an issue, but there are still data volumes at which it becomes important to plan how you move bytes around.

The aim of this chapter is to give you an in-depth understanding of BigQuery's capabilities for ingesting data. The material is organized around the two tasks described above. It may be that your use case allows for straightforward loading that does not rely on any of the advanced options. But if this is not the case, you will be equipped to select and implement an appropriate solution for your data pipeline into BigQuery.

NOTE   To try the examples in this chapter, you need access to a project with billing enabled because BigQuery does not allow loading data into projects without billing. Billing setup is covered in Chapter 3.

Bulk Loads

Broadly, BigQuery has two modes for loading data:

- Batch or bulk loads of a *large* number of records
- Single record insertions

In practice, a batch could contain a single record, and a single insert request can contain multiple records. The more meaningful difference is that the bulk mode is designed to provide *high throughput,* and the single record mode is designed for *low latency.* This is reflected in their performance and in the costs and quotas associated with these modes. This is covered in detail in the sections on quotas, but the main point is that bulk loads are the mode best suited to getting a large amount of data into BigQuery quickly.

In addition to enabling high throughput data transfers into BigQuery, bulk uploads have an important property; in database terminology they have Atomic, Consistent, Isolated, and Durable (ACID) semantics. In simple terms it means that a bulk load operation modifies a table in BigQuery so that:

- The records loaded become visible in queries at the same time. Another way of saying the same thing is that a query sees all the records from a load operation or none of them. (*Atomic*)
- Either the operation succeeds and the table is modified appropriately or the operation fails and the table is left unperturbed. (*Consistent*)

▪ When the operation is reported as successful, all future queries are guaranteed to observe the data added by the job. (*Durable*)

Isolation is not particularly relevant in this case because load jobs are not read-modify-write operations, so they are not dependent on the existing contents of a table. This makes them trivially isolated. These properties of bulk loads are often crucial when loading data because they make it simple to ensure that queries operate on valid data.

So far we have been qualifying load with the term "bulk." In the BigQuery API this corresponds to a *job* with *load* configuration and *bulk* is implied. For simplicity, from here, the operation of loading a batch of records is referred to as a *load* job. It is this job that has ACID semantics in BigQuery, particularly for other jobs in the system. As described in Chapter 5, "Talking to the BigQuery API," a load job like every BigQuery job goes through the same life cycle of pending, running, and done.

NOTE The code in this chapter assumes a dataset named ch06 exists in the project you use for trying the sample code. You can create this dataset by running:

```
bq mk ch06
```

And when you finish this chapter, you can clean up by running:

```
bq rm -f -r ch06
```

Listing 6.1 (a and b) is the skeleton Python code for executing a load job in BigQuery and monitoring it over its life cycle. This involves a job insertion, polling to detect completion, and inspecting the final status of the job. The main feature to note is the polling loop. It is not generally necessary to poll load jobs frequently because they usually take at least 30 seconds. The code provided uses a 10-second wait between `Jobs.get()` operations and this is a reasonable value. You may want to tune the wait depending on the nature of the load jobs you need to run—if you run large loads, a longer wait time would be more appropriate. Also observe that the code Listing 6.1b has comments indicating where you would add code to control the configuration of the job and manage the transfer of data to the service. The following sections contain code snippets to place in these locations to enable a particular configuration.

The configuration of a load job has three distinct components:

▪ **Source:** Location from which bytes will be read

▪ **Destination:** Table that will be modified on success

▪ **Format:** Instructions on how to turn the bytes into valid records

The reason it is useful to consider these separately is that they can, for the most part, be varied independently. In addition, the settings you select for each of these is driven by different considerations. *Source* is dictated by where your data currently exists, *destination* by how you would like to structure your data in the service, and *format* by what you can most conveniently generate or the schema of your table. Now dive into each of these sections to understand what BigQuery supports.

Listing 6.1a: (run_load.py)

```python
'''Common functions used to execute load jobs.'''

import json
import time

def start_and_wait(jobs, project_id, load, media_body=None):
  '''Run a load job with the given specification.

    jobs: client for the jobs collection in the service.
    project_id: project ID under which the job will run.
    load: the load job configuration.
    media_body: optional media object, ie file, to upload.
  '''
  start = time.time()
  job_id = 'ch06_%d' % start
  # Create the job.
  result = jobs.insert(
    projectId=project_id,
    body={
      'jobReference': {
        'jobId': job_id
      },
      'configuration': {
        'load': load
      }
    },
    media_body=media_body).execute()
  print json.dumps(result, indent=2)
  # Wait for completion.
  done = False
  while not done:
    time.sleep(10)
    result = jobs.get(projectId=project_id, jobId=job_id).execute()
    print "%s %ds" % (result['status']['state'], time.time() - start)
    done = result['status']['state'] == 'DONE'
  # Print all errors and warnings.
  for err in result['status'].get('errors', []):
    print json.dumps(err, indent=2)
  # Check for failure.
  if 'errorResult' in result['status']:
    print 'FAILED'
    print json.dumps(result['status']['errorResult'], indent=2)
  else:
    print 'SUCCESS'
```

Listing 6.1b: (load.py)

```python
# Sample code authorization support.
import auth
# Functions to help run a load job.
import run_load

def main():
  service = auth.build_bq_client()

  # Load configuration with the destination specified.
  load_config = {
    'destinationTable': {
      'projectId': auth.PROJECT_ID,
      'datasetId': 'ch06',
      # You can update this for each example.
      'tableId': 'example_basic'
    }
  }
  # Setup the job here.
  # load[property] = value
  load_config['schema'] = {
    'fields': [
      {'name':'string_f', 'type':'STRING'},
      {'name':'boolean_f', 'type':'BOOLEAN'},
      {'name':'integer_f', 'type':'INTEGER'},
      {'name':'float_f', 'type':'FLOAT'},
      {'name':'timestamp_f', 'type':'TIMESTAMP'}
    ]
  }
  load_config['sourceUris'] = [
    'gs://bigquery-e2e/chapters/06/sample.csv',
  ]
  # End of job configuration.

  run_load.start_and_wait(service.jobs(),
                          auth.PROJECT_ID,
                          load_config)

if __name__ == '__main__':
  main()
```

Moving Bytes

Fundamentally, the task of loading data involves shipping your data encoded as bytes to BigQuery and having the service interpret those bytes and turn them into records that faithfully represent the data you want to analyze. We start by describing how to transfer your data into the service. BigQuery has a few different mechanisms for receiving your data:

■ Google Cloud Storage

■ Resumable uploads

■ Multipart HTTP requests

The following sections describe the strengths and limitations of each mechanism and how to use them.

Google Cloud Storage

A useful way to think about the role of Google Cloud Storage is to compare it to the file system on your personal machine. Effectively, GCS is the file system for the Google Cloud Platform. Every component of the platform, including BigQuery, supports reading files stored in GCS. Unless you use GCS as part of your application platform, your data will not be hosted in the service. However, there are a couple of compelling reasons to use GCS for transferring data to BigQuery.

■ Robust tools and APIs for uploading data

■ Simple BigQuery integration

■ Cost effective data archival and backup solution

The drawback is that you have to pay for storing the data in GCS until you load it into BigQuery, which can be wasteful if you already store your data in a different location.

With GCS you have already completed the heavy lifting of moving the bytes representing your data into the Google Cloud Platform even before initiating the API call to BigQuery. This is accomplished via the GCS API (`https://developers.google.com/storage/docs/overview`) or more simply using one of the client tools (`gsutil`, browser application). GCS objects are arranged according to a two-level naming scheme: a top-level bucket name and an object name. *Bucket names* are globally unique in the service, and *object names* are unique within a bucket. When using the gsutil command-line tool to access a file stored in GCS, you will use a URI of the form:

```
gs://<bucket>/<object>
```

BigQuery expects URIs in the same format when referencing GCS files in a load job. Here is the code snippet to configure GCS locations in a load job:

```
loadConfig['sourceUris'] = [
    'gs://bigquery-e2e/chapters/06/sample.csv',
    'gs://bigquery-e2e/chapters/06/sample_*',
]
```

You can see that a single load job can specify multiple GCS URIs and that URIs can be *wildcards*. Following the terminology commonly used in shells, a URI with a wildcard is called a *glob*. Note that wildcard characters are only valid in the object name portion of the GCS URI. The glob features shown in Table 6-1 are supported:

Table 6-1: Glob Patterns

PATTERN	MATCHES
?	Any single character except for /
*	Any sequence of characters except for /
[*characters*]	Set of characters, which can include ranges, for example [a–z]
[!*characters*]	Characters *not* in the list

Even though GCS does not support explicit directories, the wildcards still do not match the "/" character so globs match files like they would in a regular file system. For example, `gs://bucket/f*` will match `gs://bucket/file` and exclude `gs://bucket/f/other`. There is an upper limit of 1000 files per load job, *after* glob expansion. Additional limits apply to the number of bytes in a single file and the total number of bytes, which are covered when discussing the limits and quotas that apply to load jobs.

Access control works as you would expect; the creator of the job must have reader access for all the files you enumerate in the `sourceUris` list. If you include a glob in the list, you must also have reader access on the bucket, which grants permission to list the contents of a bucket.

Because GCS and BigQuery are both a part of the Google Cloud Platform, it is easy to forget that loading data from GCS into BigQuery creates an additional copy of your data. The data stored in GCS is unchanged by the BigQuery load job, and after the job has completed, deleting the GCS files will have no effect on the data in BigQuery. Again it is useful to consider the analogy to your local file system. If you restore the contents of a database from a backup file, the database ends up storing a copy of the data in a manner suitable for its operation. The backup remains unchanged. GCS and BigQuery operate in a similar manner.

Resumable Uploads

When using GCS as the data source, you need to have transferred the bytes before issuing the load job creation request. BigQuery also supports issuing the load job creation *before* moving the bytes to the service and moving the bytes in the same HTTP request that creates the load job. There are a couple of advantages to passing the job in the initial HTTP request and then transmitting the data over multiple requests.

■ Some types of request errors can be caught early, so that you are notified before actually transferring all the bytes. Currently the validation is limited, but over time it is likely to become more comprehensive.

- When you do not require a copy of the data in GCS, a direct upload to BigQuery avoids explicit management of the files in GCS and associated charges.

- The transfer is accomplished via a protocol that allows interrupted uploads to be resumed rather than restarted.

Defining the load job before moving the bytes to BigQuery sounds like it requires time travel; fortunately nothing so advanced is involved. This mode of operation is achieved by having the job insertion HTTP request return a URL that you use to upload the data to be loaded. BigQuery does not start processing the request until you start pushing the data into the service. Error conditions that can be detected by just inspecting the job creation request are reported before the upload location is returned. Of course, the operation can still fail after you start uploading the data if there is an error parsing the bytes supplied, but this should not be surprising.

The details of the protocol are neatly wrapped up when you use the Google-supplied API client libraries. The following code sample shows how it is done in the Python client library.

```
from apiclient.http import MediaFileUpload
upload = MediaFileUpload('sample.csv',
                         mimetype='application/octet-stream',
                         # This enables resumable uploads.
                         resumable=True)
result = jobs.insert(projectId=PROJECT_ID,
                     body=body,
                     media_body=upload).execute()
```

There is no need to set sourceUris in the load configuration because BigQuery is going to use the uploaded data as the source. Using the client libraries hides the details of how the data is transferred, but it is useful to understand what is happening under the covers.

Like every REST (as covered in Chapter 4, "Understanding the BigQuery Object Model," and Chapter 5) creation operation, the initial insert request is an HTTP POST request specifying the full configuration of the job in the body of the request with one crucial difference. Instead of posting to:

```
https://www.googleapis.com/\
bigquery/v2/projects/${PROJECT_ID}/jobs
```

the following variant is used:

```
https://www.googleapis.com/upload/bigquery/v2\
/projects/${PROJECT_ID}/jobs?uploadType=resumable
```

When this alternative URL is used, the request is handled a little differently. Initial error checking is performed, but instead of fully processing the request (strictly it cannot complete processing because the bytes have not yet been supplied), a location to upload the data is returned as an HTTP header in the response. Here is an example initial request:

```
$ BASE_URL=https://www.googleapis.com/upload/bigquery/v2
$ PROJECT_ID=317752944021
$ PROJECT_URL=${BASE_URL}/projects/${PROJECT_ID}
$ curl -D - -H "$(python auth.py)" \
    -H 'Content-Type: application/json' \
    -H 'X-Upload-Content-Type: application/octet-stream' \
    -H 'X-Upload-Content-Length: 2000000' \
    --data-binary '{}' \
    ${PROJECT_URL}/jobs?uploadType=resumable
HTTP/1.1 200 OK
Location: https://www.googleapis.com/upload/bigquery/v2/projects\...
Cache-Control: no-cache, no-store, max-age=0, must-revalidate
Pragma: no-cache
Expires: Fri, 01 Jan 1990 00:00:00 GMT
Date: Wed, 12 Mar 2014 04:35:01 GMT
Server: HTTP Upload Server Built on Mar 3 2014 15:12:04 (1393888324)
Content-Length: 0
Content-Type: text/html; charset=UTF-8
Alternate-Protocol: 443:quic
```

Notice the X-Upload-* headers used to supply information about the bytes to be uploaded. The X-Upload-Content-Length header is optional and can be left out if the size is not known. The URL returned in the Location header should be used to perform the upload. It is referred to as the session_url in the snippets that follow. At this point the service is ready to accept the data to import using the Resumable Upload protocol at the supplied URL. You can find a detailed description of this protocol at https://developers.google.com/drive/web/manage-uploads#resumable that you should refer to if you write your own client implementation. The main features are support for a range header in PUT requests, which allows you to specify the piece of the upload being supplied in the request, and the ability to interrogate how much of the data has been received. A partial upload is achieved by including the Content-Range header as shown here:

```
PUT {session_url} HTTP/1.1

Authorization: your_auth_token
Content-Length: 524288
Content-Type: application/octet-stream
Content-Range: bytes 0-524287/2000000
```

This allows a large file to be uploaded in chunks rather than a single large HTTP request, which can be unreliable. If the final size is unknown, you can use "*" instead of a number. To discover how much of the upload has been received, you PUT a 0 byte range and the server responds with a Range header indicating the range that has been received.

```
PUT {session_uri} HTTP/1.1
Authorization: your_auth_token
Content-Length: 0
Content-Range: bytes */*

HTTP/1.1 308 Resume Incomplete
Content-Length: 0
Range: 0-42
```

The response indicates that the client needs to resume uploading from byte 43 (0-indexed). Uploading a range that has already been accepted leads to undefined behavior, so don't do that. Also, if the upload is never completed, it simply times out and the request is deemed incomplete. The upload and request are considered complete when the last byte of the range is supplied. If the size was not specified upfront, the final request must contain the total size rather than "*" so that the server can determine that the upload is complete. Completing the upload triggers the final request processing, so the response to the PUT request that completes the upload contains the response to the initial insert request. Because this was a job insert request, it contains the load job that was inserted. All other operations on the job proceed via the standard request path.

As mentioned earlier when using the Python or Java client, all these details are hidden from the programmer. All that needs to be supplied is the file (or file-like) object to be uploaded and a flag indicating that the Resumable Upload protocol should be employed. If all you need to do is load data into BigQuery for analysis, most of the time the Resumable Upload protocol is the appropriate way to move your data.

Multipart Upload

You have now covered uploading data before creating a load job and uploading data after creating one. BigQuery also supports uploading data in the *same* request that creates the load job. This approach is not well suited for large data transfers because it relies on moving all the data in a single HTTP request, which becomes less reliable with increasing upload sizes. If at all feasible it is preferable to use the Resumable Upload method. However, in some scenarios it is not convenient to implement the resumable protocol because it requires multiple HTTP operations. In this case you can use *multipart* uploads, which are based on the widely used MIME multipart standard (http://www.w3.org/Protocols/rfc1341/7_2_Multipart.html). The standard is a scheme for packing multiple objects into a single stream of bytes. It is used to transfer attachments in an e-mail message and for file uploads from browsers as part of web forms. The Content-Type header specifies a string (chosen so that it does not collide with the content) that is used as a separator between sections of the stream. Each section within the stream contains headers describing the content in the section followed by the body of the section containing the actual data.

When using this method to upload data to BigQuery, you construct the request body to contain two MIME multipart sections. One section contains the body of the job insert request specifying the details of the job. The second section contains the bytes to be loaded by job. As was the case with Resumable Upload, you do not specify `sourceUris`, and you use a different URL to indicate that the request is a multipart request rather than a regular request:

```
https://www.googleapis.com/upload/bigquery/v2\
/projects/${PROJECT_ID}/jobs?uploadType=multipart
```

Here is a skeleton request highlighting the key features of the multipart standard:

```
POST /upload/bigquery/v2/projects/999/jobs?uploadType=multipart HTTP/1.1
Authentication: your_auth_token
Content-Length: 67342
Content-Type: multipart/related; boundary=gc0p4Jq0M2Yt08jU534c0p

--gc0p4Jq0M2Yt08jU534c0p
Content-Type: application/json; charset=UTF-8

{
  'configuration': {
    'load': {    …
    }
  }
}
--gc0p4Jq0M2Yt08jU534c0p
Content-Type: application/octet-stream
Content-Transfer-Encoding: base64

<your data base64 encoded>
--gc0p4Jq0M2Yt08jU534c0p--
```

And that is about all there is to say about this method, which is its main advantage: simplicity. The response to this request will be an error if the job could not be created (in which case the work done to transfer the bytes is lost); otherwise, it will contain the job created. Notice that in the example we have base64-encoded the data in the request body and added the `Content-Transfer-Encoding` header. This is not strictly necessary but it can help mitigate issues with problematic HTTP proxies.

When using the client library, you select this mode of operation by simply leaving out `resumable=True` or setting it explicitly to `False`. However, there is no good reason to use this mode when working through the client libraries. The `resumable` flag defaults to `False` to maintain backward compatibility with earlier versions of the client library and APIs that do not support the Resumable Upload protocol. If for some reason you cannot use the client library in your application, it is reasonable to implement this multipart method rather than implement the full Resumable Upload protocol, which requires more complicated code. Just be aware that you may encounter issues with failed HTTP requests trying to upload large amounts of data with this approach. The problem is that the likelihood of a random failure affecting a request increases with the size of a request. So a very large request can fail frequently due to intermittent network failures.

That covers the different options you have for moving your data into BigQuery. If you primarily work with installed software, it may seem odd to move the data rather than move the software. On the other hand, if you are familiar with cloud-based services, the process of moving your data into the cloud will feel natural. This section has covered three separate methods for transferring data. Google Cloud Storage is ideal if you would like to retain a backup copy of your data outside of BigQuery. Once the data is uploaded to GCS, importing it into BigQuery is simply a matter of referencing the files. If you only need the data to be stored in BigQuery, the Resumable Upload protocol is the best choice because it allows for large amounts of data to be transferred robustly. Finally, if simplicity or minimizing the number of HTTP requests is the most important consideration, you can use multipart requests, but be aware that this method may not scale well to large data sizes.

Destination Table

Now you need to control where the data you are loading ends up inside BigQuery. The load job configuration specifies a single destination table and optionally includes a schema for the table. The destination table can live in any project or dataset as long as the job creator (the identity used to insert the job into the service) has write permissions on the dataset containing the table. This was explained in Chapter 4 in the section on access controls. If the job creator does not have suitable permissions, the job will still be created but will end up in the done state and include an error indicating that access was denied. Here is the code snippet specifying a destination for a load job:

```
load_config = {
  'destinationTable': {
    'projectId': auth.PROJECT_ID,
    'datasetId': 'ch06',
    'tableId': 'example_basic'
  }
}
load_config['schema'] = {
  'fields': [
    # ...
  ]
}
```

The schema is optional if the specified destination table already exists and has a schema. In this case the load job uses the schema on the table to interpret the data uploaded. When there is no existing schema or the table does not exist, the job must specify a schema. If the table has a schema and the job specifies a schema, the schemas must be compatible. Compatibility here means that every field present in the existing table schema must be present with the same type in the job schema. This effectively implies that new columns can be added to tables by load jobs, but columns can never be removed. The previous snippet shows you where the schema is specified in the job configuration.

Multiple load jobs running concurrently and attempting to modify the schema of a table can fail in unpredictable ways. Frankly, if you are in this situation, you probably should rethink your loading strategy. However, it is worth understanding the nature of the problem. Before spelling out the problematic issue, it is worth recalling the discussion of the ACID properties of jobs. (A)tomic, (C)onsistent, and (D)urable were covered but we indicated that (I)solated was not relevant because load jobs do not depend on the existing contents of a table. This was something of a white lie. It is true that they have no access to the data already present in a table. However, they do depend on the existing schema of the table and as mentioned can modify the existing schema by adding columns. In this respect isolation is relevant and load jobs are isolated from other load jobs because they capture a copy of the destination table's schema at the time they are created and do not observe changes to the schema that may occur while they are running. This can lead to the job eventually failing because the schema of the table changes while it is in progress.

If all this seems too complicated, follow this simple rule of thumb: Do not modify the schema of an existing table by specifying a schema on a job. Instead modify the schema by updating the table, and do this only when there are no pending or running jobs. However, if you are interested in how this unpredictable behavior can arise, here is a concrete example. Assume that the table being updated has columns A and B. Load job 1 adds column C, and load job 2 adds columns C and D. Both jobs can be legally started at the same time because they are both performing compatible (with the existing table) schema updates. If job 1 completes before job 2, both jobs can succeed because the schema update of job 2 is adding a column (D) in addition to the column (C) added by job 1. However, if job 2 completes before job 1, job 1 will fail because the schema it specified removes a column (D) with respect to the schema specified in job 2. Because the completion order of concurrently executing jobs is not guaranteed, this implies that job 1 may fail randomly, which is unwanted. Also after job 2 succeeds it will be impossible to retry job 1.

In addition to specifying where the load job should put the data, you can also tune how the load job behaves if the existing destination table does or does not exist, and what it does with any data that might already be present in the destination table. This behavior is tuned by controlling the create and write dispositions of the job. These properties were briefly described in Chapter 4 in the overview of the Jobs collection. You can control the dispositions by modifying the job configuration:

```
load['createDisposition'] = 'CREATE_IF_NEEDED'
load['writeDisposition'] = 'WRITE_TRUNCATE'
```

Table 6-2 shows the supported dispositions and how they affect the operation of the job:

Table 6-2: Create and Write Dispositions

CREATE DISPOSITION	
CREATE_IF_NEEDED	Creates the table if it does not exist
CREATE_NEVER	Fails if the table does not already exist
WRITE DISPOSITION	
WRITE_EMPTY	Fails if the table is not empty
WRITE_TRUNCATE	Replaces any existing contents with the new data
WRITE_APPEND	Adds the new data to the existing data

You could argue that actually all that is required is WRITE_APPEND because manually deleting and re-creating the table as required could simulate all the other modes. However, these properties are useful when there are concurrent query jobs and load jobs operating on the same table. It allows for well-defined behavior without additional coordination at the application level to ensure that a query job is not run while a table is being deleted and re-created. A simple example is a daily job that creates a table containing data for the previous day. By using the WRITE_EMPTY write disposition, you can guarantee that the data will be loaded exactly once, even if for some reason your daily loading script is invoked twice. Because both instances of the script will be writing to the same table with the WRITE_EMPTY disposition, only one of them will be allowed to succeed and actually add data to the table. If WRITE_APPEND were the only supported mode, it is possible that the data could be duplicated unless care was taken in the script to ensure that a second attempt did not run unless it was certain that the first attempt failed prior to initiating the load job. Because concurrent updates and queries are common, the API supports these modes to ensure that table modifications happen in a predictable fashion.

When the job API was described in Chapter 5, you saw that specifying an ID when inserting a job was optional. If no ID is specified as part of the job insert, the server assigns a random unique ID. For query jobs that are not modifying an existing table, it is reasonable to rely on this automatic assignment. However, when working with load jobs that modify the contents of a table it is important for the client to select an ID, so we are going to revisit that discussion.

Client selected job IDs prevent the creation of duplicate instances of a job due to retries in the client or communication layer. The reason for avoiding duplication is easy to see in the context of WRITE_APPEND jobs. If you insert two jobs that are configured to append the same data to a given destination table, the table will end up with two copies of the data, which is almost certainly not what you want. Of course, you would not intentionally insert duplicate jobs, but it is easy for error handling code to inadvertently generate duplicate requests.

When a Jobs.insert() request fails due to a network error, it is possible that BigQuery actually performed the insert operation but the client failed to receive the success response. Without a client selected job ID, the only way to detect this condition is to list all the jobs and see if a job exists with the configuration you were trying to submit. However, if you selected a job ID before issuing the request, you could simply retry inserting the job with the same ID. If BigQuery has already accepted the job, it responds with an already exists error; otherwise, the retried insert succeeds. This way you can guarantee that an append operation happens exactly once.

The bq command-line client supports explicitly specifying the job ID for any operation that creates a job:

```
bq --job_id=<job id> load ...
```

To use this correctly you need to select an ID that corresponds to the specific data you are trying to load so that multiple instances of the same command do not duplicate the job. For example, if the data were collected on a particular day, you could use an ID of the form my_data_YYYYMMDD. The client also supports a flag that computes the ID as a function of the job configuration it constructs:

```
bq --fingerprint_job_id load ...
```

This way you do not have to come up with an ID generation scheme but retain the important property of not doing the same work more than once. Because the ID is a hash of the configuration, its value will not be meaningful, but if you do not need to look up specific jobs at a later time, this is not an issue.

In some situations with multiple writers, it is not always convenient to coordinate the writers to select a suitable job ID. If the operation they are performing is *idempotent* (repeated application does not affect the state) or it is acceptable that only one of them succeeds, it is possible to avoid explicit coordination for ID selection and instead rely on write dispositions to produce the desired behavior. Previously you saw an example with WRITE_EMPTY, which ensures that only one job ends up modifying the table. Another example is the use of CREATE_NEVER with jobs that create the table. Again only one job can successfully create the table. If WRITE_TRUNCATE is used by multiple jobs updating the same table, the table usually contains the data loaded by the most recent job. BigQuery does not guarantee the order of completion for concurrently running jobs, but generally they complete in the order they were submitted if they are doing a similar amount of processing. Creative use of these dispositions is covered in more detail in Chapter 11, "Managing Data Stored in BigQuery," which deals with strategies for managing data in BigQuery.

Data Formats

You learned how to transfer your data to BigQuery and how to control where the data ends up. This section describes how the service interprets the data you transfer. Currently BigQuery supports three different data formats: CSV, newline-delimited JSON, and AppEngine Datastore backups. CSV is more like a family of related formats, whereas the other two formats are more strictly specified.

Generally, the choice of format is determined by the application that is producing your data or where you have it stored. However, not all the formats support the full range of types and modes available in BigQuery schemas. In this case the schema imposes an additional constraint on suitable formats.

CSV

It is a bit generous to say the CSV format was designed. There is a specification of the format available (`http://tools.ietf.org/html/rfc4180`) but in practice a lot of CSV encountered in the wild is actually some variant of this basic standard. However, for better or worse it is the de facto standard for data interchange and is supported by almost every data processing tool. BigQuery supports the basic format and has a number of flags to adjust parsing so that it can support common variants.

BigQuery tables support fields that are arrays and fields that are nested within other fields. When a table contains such fields, it is not possible to represent a record in the table as a simple list of values. The CSV family of formats was designed to represent tabular data, so each record or line of data is a simple list of values. As a result this input format is not compatible with BigQuery schemas that contain fields that are arrays or have type RECORD. If you are constrained to using CSV as an input format, you should not employ a schema that includes these features.

To understand how CSV formatted data is turned into a BigQuery record, consider the following concrete schema:

```
load_config['schema'] = {
  'fields': [
    {'name':'string_f', 'type':'STRING'},
```

```
        {'name':'boolean_f', 'type':'BOOLEAN'},
        {'name':'integer_f', 'type':'INTEGER'},
        {'name':'float_f', 'type':'FLOAT'},
        {'name':'timestamp_f', 'type':'TIMESTAMP'}
    ]
}
```

Because the default mode for a field is NULLABLE, all the fields in this schema are optional. Now look at a couple of lines of CSV to see how they can be transformed into records.

```
"one",true,1,1.0,2011-11-11 11:11:11
,,,,
"",false,,3.14e-1,1380378423
bare string ,"TRUE","0","0.000","2013-01-03 09:15:02.478 -05:00"
"quoted , and "" in a string",,,,
```

All the preceding lines import correctly into the table. The fields mapping is a simple positional mapping, so the order of the fields in the schema is significant, and the order of the values in the CSV data must line up. The first line illustrates the basic formatting of values. An unquoted empty string is interpreted as a missing or null value, so the second line generates a record with null values for every field. In the fourth line you can see that quoting is optional for strings that do not contain the field separating character (comma by default). It is legal to quote any field even if the quotes are not required. Floating point values can use either a decimal representation or scientific notation. Boolean values can be any of true, false, t, and f, and the case is not significant.

Whitespace handling is easy to overlook in CSV. Leading and trailing whitespace characters in fields are ignored. So on the fourth line, the first field is parsed as "bare string" with the trailing space dropped. If you need to preserve whitespace in a string field use quotes.

Timestamp values can be represented as a calendar date and time or as seconds since the UNIX epoch (1970-01-01 00:00:00 UTC). The first and fourth lines use the string format, and the third line uses seconds since the epoch. The string format for timestamps is:

```
YYYY-MM-DD HH:MM:SS[.ssssss] [±00:00]
```

The fractional seconds and time zone offset are optional. If the offset is not present, the UTC time zone is assumed. Time zone offset codes (e.g. UTC, EST, PDT) are not supported.

The line (record) separators are not easy to see in the previous sample. Each line must be terminated by a newline (\n), carriage return (\r), or a carriage return followed by a new newline (\r\n). By default the service assumes that these characters do not appear within fields, even if the field is quoted. The reasons for this is explained in a separate section, but the main thing to note is that these characters serve as the record separators in the CSV format.

This covers the basics of the CSV format. If you can directly generate the CSV to be loaded into BigQuery, this is all you need. However, in many scenarios you cannot control the details of how the CSV is generated, so it is necessary to adjust how the data is parsed. The next few sections are organized by parsing options specific to the CSV format.

fieldDelimiter

A common variant of the CSV format is Tab-Separated-Values where the tab (\t) character is used to separate fields rather than a comma. This is convenient when the fields are text and frequently contain commas. With tab as the separator, commas can appear in fields without quoting. More generally, it is useful to choose an arbitrary character as the field separator depending on the characters that are common in the field data. BigQuery supports a field delimiter option that allows the overriding comma as the separator.

```
load_config['fieldDelimiter'] = '\011'
```

This code sets the delimiter to the tab character, which corresponds to octal code 011. We used the octal code instead of the C escape code '\t' to emphasize that the delimiter has to be set to a single byte in the range 0–255. Setting a byte using the octal code escape only works for bytes in the range 0-127. If you are sending a byte in the range 128–255 it needs to be encoded as a multi-byte UTF-8 character in the request. The service converts the UTF-8 string back to ISO-8859-1, almost the same as Latin1, encoding and uses the first byte in the converted string. To get a feel for what is happening on the wire, try the following commands on the Python interactive prompt:

```
separator = b'\246'.decode('latin1')
separator
u'\xa6'
print separator
¦
separator.encode('utf8')
'\xc2\xa6'
```

If you want to use the byte with decimal value 166 (octal value 246), which corresponds to the broken bar (¦) in Latin1 encoding, as the separator for field values you would need to send the bytes '\xc2\xa6' on the wire, which is the UTF-8 encoding of this character.

quote

Just like you can customize the field delimiter, you can change the default quoting character (") to be any single byte character. The setting is interpreted like `fieldDelimiter`, the first byte of the string after conversion to Latin1 encoding. For example, this is how you would set it to the single quote character:

```
load['quote'] = "'"
```

Modifying the delimiter and quote is useful when fields contain sentences and paragraphs that usually have punctuation. You still need to be careful about the handling of newlines and carriage returns and may need to come up with a scheme for escaping them or transforming them in your data.

encoding

You just got a taste for the complications that character encoding brings to the table. If you work with UTF-8, you can basically ignore encoding because UTF-8 is the encoding used natively by BigQuery and is the encoding used in the HTTP-based API. If at all possible you want to stick with UTF-8 because it avoids any difficulty associated with encoding conversions.

Note that even if you use UTF-8 for the values of the field, the lines of data will not be valid UTF-8 data if you use a field delimiter in the range 128–255. When BigQuery parses your data; it first splits the data into rows based on the record delimiter (limited to "\n," "\r," and "\r\n"). Then it splits rows into fields based on the customizable field delimiter and then checks the encoding of each individual field. The only alternative encoding supported is ISO-8859-1, which is a superset of Latin1. To request that your values be treated as Latin1 strings and converted to UTF-8, use the following setting:

```
load['encoding'] = 'ISO-8859-1'
```

It is also legal to set this field to UTF-8, but that has no effect because it is the default encoding. If you set the input encoding to ISO-8859-1, single-byte characters in the range 128–255 will be converted to the corresponding multi-byte UTF-8 characters.

skipLeadingRows

Many tools that produce CSV include one or more header rows describing the fields present in the data. It is tedious to have to strip this header because in practice it means regenerating the entire file to just remove the first few lines. Instead you can set a parameter in the configuration to indicate to the parser that it should ignore some number of lines at the start of the file. If your configuration specified multiple source files (on GCS), the lines at the start of *each* of the files will be skipped.

```
load['skipLeadingRows'] = 6
```

This code causes the first six lines of every file to be ignored.

allowJaggedRows

When encoding records with a lot of fields (columns) that are frequently null-valued, some tools choose to leave out trailing fields that are null. When reading this data all columns after the last column present in a row must be treated as null or absent. Making this data conform to the requirements of the basic CSV format would mean padding each row with trailing commas (the field delimiter) to represent the null columns. Again BigQuery has a feature that can handle this data.

```
load['allowJaggedRows'] = True
```

In this mode BigQuery will accept a row with fewer columns than the number of fields in the schema as long as all the fields in the schema that are missing are marked as NULLABLE. Note that any null column that appears *before* a non-null column must still be explicitly encoded as a blank field in the row.

allowQuotedNewlines

This option deserves careful explanation because it affects the one aspect of CSV parsing in which BigQuery's default behavior differs from the specification of the format. The CSV format enables the newline character to appear within quoted fields. This is necessary to let the format encode values that contain the line separator. However, it turns out that this feature makes it impossible to safely process chunks of a CSV file in parallel. In any chunk other than the first chunk, it is impossible to tell if a newline occurs inside a quoted string or outside a quoted string. This means that the file can be processed only from beginning to end by a single process keeping track of whether it is in the middle of a quoted value. However, the majority of CSV associated with data processing does not contain quoted newlines, so it would be a shame if the default behavior were to use the slow, but specification-compatible, serial processing strategy instead of the faster parallel processing strategy. As a result, BigQuery defaults to behavior that assumes that no quoted newlines are present in the input data, and it can be safely divided up for parallel processing. If your data does have quoted newlines, you can set the allowQuotedNewlines property:

```
load['allowQuotedNewlines'] = True
```

This makes it process each input file serially (separate files are still processed in parallel) so that it can correctly handle the values. Beware that this can be *much* slower than processing your data in parallel. If each individual load is small (say, <100MB) this is not a significant issue, but if your loads are much larger, you should consider alternatives. One simple workaround is to substitute newlines in strings with some other sequence, for example, the C escape sequence \n. The exact choice of replacement characters depends on how you intend to query the field.

Compression

The last option to cover is not quite an option but rather a property of the data. BigQuery supports GZIP-compressed CSV data. It automatically detects if the data is compressed in a recognized format, and if so it decompresses the data before processing it. GZIP compression has the same property as quoted newlines for distributed processing. Decompressing a file requires that a single process decompress the entire file because it is not possible to resume decompression in the middle of file. However, compression can be critical for transferring data, especially with formats such as CSV, which compress quite well, so it may still be necessary to employ compression. Most HTTP client implementations can transparently compress the request so that both ends deal only with uncompressed data. If you are instead relying on explicit compression prior to transmitting your data to BigQuery (or GCS), it is a good idea to generate multiple compressed files with sizes between 10MB–100MB rather than a single, large compressed file. Because the processing can still be parallelized over files, you can benefit from distributed processing.

This completes the discussion of CSV, which has the most options for processing because it is such a loosely implemented format. There is a good chance that you will use it as an input format because it is so widely adopted. It is a good idea to be familiar with all the options covered in this section because they might end up saving you the trouble of reformatting your data.

JSON

The other textual format that BigQuery supports is JSON (http://www.json .org), which has established itself as the standard for data exchange between web applications. This is the only textual format that BigQuery supports that can represent schemas with array and RECORD type fields, so if you use those features in your tables, you have to use this format to load data into your tables. The JSON format has a detailed specification with fully defined lexical analysis rules that produce strongly typed values. The most natural way to encode a list of records with JSON encoding would be to use the JSON list type, which is basically a comma-delimited series of JSON values enclosed in square brackets ([]). This encoding, like quoted newlines in CSV, would make it impossible to process a large JSON encoded file in parallel. To overcome this data processing, frameworks (for example, Hive, http://hive.apache.org) have introduced a variant of JSON that is referred to here as newline delimited JSON. In regular

JSON the newline character (\n) is treated as whitespace and is allowed to appear anywhere that whitespace is allowed. However, it is not allowed to appear in strings. Instead it must be escaped in strings as "\n". (This would be a JSON string representing a single newline character.) Newline delimited JSON takes advantage of this and promotes it to a record separating character that must appear only at record boundaries. It is not permitted to appear anywhere within a single record. The advantage of this format is that it is trivial to detect record boundaries (simply scan for a newline) making it convenient for parallel processing. This is the variant of JSON that is accepted by BigQuery load jobs.

To illustrate how the list and record types are encoded, use a schema that includes these features:

```
load_config['schema'] = {
  'fields': [
    {'name':'string_f', 'type':'STRING'},
    {'name':'boolean_f', 'type':'BOOLEAN', 'mode':'REPEATED'},
    {'name':'record_f', 'type':'RECORD',
     'fields': [
       {'name':'integer_f', 'type':'INTEGER'},
       {'name':'float_f', 'type':'FLOAT'}
     ]
    },
    {'name':'timestamp_f', 'type':'TIMESTAMP'}
  ]
}
# Select the JSON input format.
load_config['sourceFormat'] = 'NEWLINE_DELIMITED_JSON'
```

The last line of the previous snippet configures the job to treat the input as JSON. The following sample illustrates the newline-delimited format. To emphasize the role of newlines, they are explicitly rendered as \n. Ignore the actual line breaks because they are present only to improve legibility.

```
{
  "string_f": "one",
  "boolean_f": [true, false],
  "record_f": {
    "integer_f": 1,
    "float_f": 1.1
  },
  "timestamp_f": "2013-09-18 13:21:03 -07:00"
}\n
{
  "string_f": null,
  "boolean_f": []
}\n
```

```
{
  "timestamp_f":1379897943.51
}\n
{
  "boolean_f": ["true"],
  "record_f": {
    "integer_f":"3",
    "float_f":"1"
  }
}
```

The top-level record is represented as a JSON object with field names of the object corresponding to the columns or top-level fields of the table. Repeated fields are represented as JSON lists and nested records as nested JSON objects. This mapping is natural and probably obvious. The first line of input in the sample illustrates these features. Note that a JSON null value is equivalent to the absence of the JSON field and is interpreted as a NULL value for the corresponding field in the table. So in the second line of the sample, nothing would change if you simply left out the string_f entry from the JSON object.

JSON supports just three primitive types: string, Boolean, and number. Because BigQuery supports more types, a one-to-one mapping between primitive types does not exist. BigQuery can accept a JSON string value for any primitive field if it can parse the string value as the type declared in the schema. For example, on line 4 of the sample, you can see that the boolean and integer values are present as strings. These will be converted because they can be parsed as the respective types. Note that the float_f field happens to have an integer value. However, this does not affect how it ends up being stored in BigQuery, namely the value 1.0. Finally, timestamp fields are interpreted as they are in the CSV format. You can pass a JSON number value that represents (integer or fractional) seconds since the UNIX epoch or a human readable string with the format described in the CSV section. Here, too, if you are passing seconds since the epoch, it is acceptable to pass it as a string containing the number.

It is plain to see that JSON is a verbose format because the field names appear in every record. In web applications it has replaced XML, which is even more verbose, so it is generally seen as an improvement over that format. However, for large data transfers the repetition of field names imposes a significant byte cost. Fortunately, it turns out that GZIP is effective at bringing this cost down. CSV and JSON representations of the same data end up being about the same size after GZIP compression. BigQuery supports GZIP compressed JSON, so you should definitely consider compressing the data but bear in mind the constraint of keeping each individual compressed file a reasonable size. The same guideline given for CSV, 10–100 MB post compression is also reasonable for JSON.

AppEngine Datastore Backup

Datastore is the scalable NoSQL store that is part of the Google AppEngine platform (http://appengine.google.com/). It is available within the platform and is also accessible through a standalone HTTP API (https://developers .google.com/datastore/). Datastore supports efficient single-record updates, lookup, and index-based scans. However, scanning a large Datastore table is an expensive operation that is significantly slower than running a query in BigQuery over a similar sized table. The two services complement each other in their performance characteristics, and in many cases it is useful to load your Datastore table into BigQuery to perform analytics and reporting. The bridge between these two services is based on the AppEngine facility to generate backups of Datastore tables (Kinds, in Datastore parlance) stored in GCS. BigQuery can import these backups from GCS and enable queries over the data. Because the data in BigQuery corresponds to a snapshot of the Datastore table at the time of the backup, the queries are not executing over the live data. This limitation poses a problem for real-time use cases, but for many reporting and analytics use cases, this is generally acceptable.

When you perform a Datastore backup to GCS, it produces a manifest file describing the contents of the backup that is stored in GCS along with the actual data files containing your data. Importing this into BigQuery is simply a matter of specifying the right format and the location of the manifest file in GCS:

```
load_config['sourceFormat'] = 'DATASTORE_BACKUP'
load_config['sourceUris'] = ['gs://<backup bucket>/<backup manifest>']
```

Running this load job is simple enough and is much like a CSV or JSON load from GCS. However, there is a lot going on behind the scenes. The most important part is that the schema for the destination table is derived from the entities in your backup. A good understanding of the Datastore data model is required to follow the schema generation algorithm and appreciate its limitations. This discussion is beyond the scope of this chapter on loading data into BigQuery. Instead, check out the full details of this integration in Chapter 11, which covers this topic and the relevant concepts in Datastore.

Errors

The beginning of the chapter mentioned that one of the challenges with moving data is that often the producer and consumer have minor disagreements about how the data should be represented. BigQuery is no different and despite your best intentions, it is possible that the data you ship to the service will be considered invalid. Common issues include:

- Incorrectly formatted fields, for example, an invalid timestamp representation

- Mismatches between the declared schema and supplied data
- Data corruption at some point in the pipeline
- Bad data in fields such as invalid UTF-8 characters

These errors fit the label of data errors. In addition a load operation can fail due to a configuration error or a quota error. Possible configuration errors are:

- Permission errors
- Quota limits
- Data size limits
- Non-existent sources or destination table

Data errors are somewhat different from the other types of errors because a load job can have many data errors and can be configured to succeed even if data errors are present. The other types of errors always cause the job to fail. As covered in Chapter 5, the jobs resource in the API has a status section, which contains two fields related to errors. The `errorResult` field is present if the job is done and has failed. The `errors` field is a list of objects with the same structure as `errorResult` and may be present even if the job completed successfully. As such, the `errors` field is better interpreted as a list of warnings and errors. Most job types in the service do not generate warnings that appear in this field. Load jobs, however, use this field to report data errors. It is often the case that the input data has multiple data errors, and it would be inconvenient if each run of a load job reported only a single error. So assuming the absence of configuration and quota errors, a load job reports zero or more errors in the `errors` field, and if the job failed, one of the entries in the list also appears in the `errorResult` field.

Unlike data errors, configuration errors can show up in two different locations. A configuration or quota error that causes the job creation request to fail results in a top-level error (HTTP error codes 40x) being returned in the response to the creation request. Configuration errors that occur after the job has been created have the error reported in the `errorResult` field and included in the `errors` list.

To see all this in action, here are sample jobs that generate errors of all sorts. These examples do not bother with errors that cause the job creation to fail because that is covered in Chapter 5 and is not specific to load jobs. Instead, start with a job that has an invalid configuration due to missing permissions. For example, attempt to load some data into the BigQuery public samples dataset:

```
load_config['destinationTable'] = {
    'projectId': 'publicdata',
    'datasetId': 'samples',
    'tableId': 'mypersonaltable'
}
```

Unless you have somehow gotten write access to the BigQuery samples dataset, you should see the script report that the job failed. The code listing you have been using for all the examples in this chapter supports reporting the errors and checking the overall success status of the job.

```
for err in result['status'].get('errors', []):
  print json.dumps(err, indent=2)

if 'errorResult' in result['status']:
  print 'FAILED'
  print json.dumps(result['status']['errorResult'], indent=2)
else:
  print 'SUCCESS'
```

In this snippet the for-loop prints out the contents of the errors (and warnings) list. The conditional is checking for the presence of the errorResult field to report whether the job succeeded or failed. The job you just ran ended up in the done state with errorResult present, so the final lines of output indicate the job failed.

```
FAILED
{
 "reason": "accessDenied",
 "message": "Access Denied: Table publicdata:samples.mypersonaltable:
  CREATE_TABLE"
}
```

In this case you can see that the job failed because you lack sufficient permissions to create a table in the specified dataset.

To see what kind of data errors can be generated, there's an input file that is riddled with errors. The following job configuration loads this file:

```
load_config['schema'] = {
  'fields': [
    {'name':'string_f', 'type':'STRING'},
    {'name':'boolean_f', 'type':'BOOLEAN'},
    {'name':'integer_f', 'type':'INTEGER',
     'mode':'REQUIRED'},
    {'name':'float_f', 'type':'FLOAT'},
    {'name':'timestamp_f', 'type':'TIMESTAMP'}
  ]
}
load_config['sourceUris'] = [
  'gs://bigquery-e2e/chapters/06/sample_bad.csv',
]
```

The example also changes the schema to include a field that is declared a REQUIRED field to illustrate that an error is reported when no value is supplied for a required field. When you run the sample that loads this data, you can observe seven errors that look like this:

```
{
  "reason": "invalid",
  "message": "Could not interpret bool from string.",
  "location": "File: 0 / " "Line:2 / Field:2"
}
```

The errors are reporting bad records that were rejected. The `reason` code is always `invalid` and the `message` field describes the problem. In this case you passed the value "nottrue" for a boolean field, which was not recognized. These errors also contain a location entry describing where the error was encountered. The location may refer to a specific field but in some cases—for example, too many or too few columns—it just refers to the line or position at which the error occurred. When the input file is processed in parallel, the location will be reported as the byte offset of the start of the line rather than a line number. This is more convenient when dealing with large files because it does not require reading the file from the beginning to count lines.

The most interesting error is the one that appears in the `errorResult` field. It does not correspond to any of the errors that were encountered while parsing the data.

```
{
  "reason": "invalid",
  "message": "Too many errors encountered. Limit is: 0."
}
```

The job did not fail due to the individual parse errors that resulted in bad records. Rather the job failed because the number of bad records encountered exceeded a threshold. The default limit for the number of bad records allowed in a load job is zero. This limit can be modified, but first you should discuss why you might want to change its value. Generally, when loading data into the service, users expect that all the data will be loaded without any errors. If errors are present it usually indicates a serious error in how the data is being supplied, which needs to be corrected before retrying the load operation. However, in some cases users are dealing with imperfect data; for example, the collection process corrupts a small number of records. If the data is still useful with these corrupt records dropped, it is reasonable to have the service ignore some number of faulty records. To support this load jobs accept a `maxBadRecords` parameter. For example, modifying the load job you just ran to set this parameter can make the job succeed:

```
loadConfig['maxBadRecords'] = 7
```

The job still reports the bad records encountered, but if they are fewer than the value specified in this parameter, the job still succeeds and all the good records are added to the destination table. If there are a large number of bad records, only a sample of them will be reported in the `errors` list; however, all the bad records are counted for the purpose of enforcing the `maxBadRecords` test.

This completes the review of the errors commonly encountered by load jobs. One class of errors mentioned but not discussed in detail is quota errors. The next section discusses the limits that apply to load jobs and also covers the related errors raised when these limits are exceeded.

Limits and Quotas

Load jobs are subject to two types of limits by the service:

- Limits on the total amount of data processed by a single job
- The rate at which import jobs can be submitted to the service

The limits on a single job are rarely encountered in practice because they are large enough that network transfer is usually the bottleneck. The second set of limits requires more attention because a large number of tables requiring regular updates or a single table being updated concurrently can run into these limits. The values specified in this section are subject to change. You should refer to the service documentation for up-to-date information (`https://developers` `.google.com/bigquery/quota-policy#import`).

Start by looking at the limits on a single job because they are simple to describe. An individual load job is restricted to a maximum of:

- 10,000 input files, only relevant when loading multiple files from GCS
- 1 TB total input bytes

In addition, there are limits on each file to ensure that processing can be sufficiently parallelized. As discussed in the section on formats, some formats can be split up for parallel processing and others cannot, so these limits vary by format. GZIP compressed input is limited to a maximum of 1 GB per file. For uncompressed data the following limits apply:

- 4 GB for CSV data that may contain quoted newlines
- 1 TB for CSV data that does not contain quoted newlines
- 1 TB for newline delimited JSON

Although each compressed file is limited to 1 GB, the total job can still reference up to 1 TB of input data. It is common to achieve compression ratios greater than 10x on CSV, so the limit of 1 GB of input data per file can translate to more than 10 GB of uncompressed CSV per file or 10 TB for the entire job, which is a substantial volume of data. So if your primary requirement is loading a large volume of data, the most effective choice is generating compressed files between 100 MB and 1 GB in GCS.

Now consider the second set of limits, or quotas, that apply to the rate of load job creation and execution:

- 20 load jobs per project in RUNNING state
- 10,000 load jobs per project per day
- 1,000 load jobs per destination table per day

To understand the first limit, remember that every job proceeds through the states PENDING, RUNNING, and DONE. When your job is PENDING, it is queued but no processing is actually occurring. The actually work is performed in RUNNING state. The system limits the number of load jobs concurrently in RUNNING state. If additional load jobs are submitted after there are 20 running jobs, they remain in the PENDING state until some of the running jobs are completed. This effectively caps the maximum load throughput available to a single project. There is a nontrivial amount of overhead associated with a load job, so to access the full throughput available to a project, you need to issue load jobs larger than 10 GB of uncompressed data. This is only a rough guideline because it is perfectly reasonable to initiate load jobs with smaller input sizes, but be aware that after you drop below 1 MB, a significant fraction of the running time will be spent setting up and tearing down the job. This means your effective throughput of bytes loaded will be lower.

The next two limits on total load jobs per day are self-explanatory, but they have significant ramifications. Consider the following scenarios:

- 1,000 separate tables that each need to be updated once per hour
- A single table that needs to be updated by 10 independent processes every 5 minutes

Both these load requirements run up against the quota limits before one-half of the day is over. The first case exhausts the project level quota and the second exhausts the per table quota. When you attempt to create a load job that violates these limits, the job creation request fails with an error that has reason code quotaExceeded. Retrying the job cannot help until the quota resets. These limits are an indication that load jobs are not intended for small frequent table updates. If you run up against these limits, it is likely that restructuring your tables or load operation can address the issue. For example, in the 1,000 table scenario described, it may be feasible to combine the 1,000 tables into a single table with an additional field to distinguish between records that were in separate tables. In the single table case, it is likely possible to collect the updates from all 10 independent processes and combine them into a single load operation. In both cases this would work around the quota constraint without sacrificing the frequency of updates.

Another point to note is that small load jobs are wasteful of the per table quota. If you load only a handful of records per load job, at the end of the day, your table will contain only a few thousand records, not exactly Big Data. The usual reason for issuing small frequent updates is to keep the table fresh for some real-time data source. Considering that even a small load job can take anywhere from tens of seconds to a couple of minutes, this is not an effective way to keep data fresh or utilize your daily quota. This issue sets you up nicely for the next major section of this chapter. As previously mentioned, BigQuery supports a throughput optimized load operation and a latency optimized load operation. When you run into the daily table or project limits, it may be a signal that you should use the latency optimized operation. The next section covers this alternative way of loading data into the service.

Streaming Inserts

If you are familiar with traditional databases, you may wonder why so much machinery is required to load a couple of records into a table. As discussed in Chapter 2, "BigQuery Fundamentals," aspects of the service resemble a relational database, but at its core BigQuery is a distributed processing framework optimized for dealing with large amounts of data. As a result, its primary loading mechanism is geared toward ingesting large quantities of data rather than individual records. Nevertheless, the service does provide a simple operation for inserting individual records, referred to here as a streaming insert. Even though it bears a strong resemblance to the SQL insert statement, do not be fooled; there are substantial differences. The API gains it simplicity and low latency by foregoing the strong guarantees offered by the job-based load operation. Perhaps in contrast to the ACID properties of load jobs, you can describe this operation as Eventual-At-least-Once. This means one or more copies of a record inserted via the streaming API are guaranteed to eventually appear in queries over the destination table. This may seem like an alarmingly weak promise, but it is sufficient for a variety of applications. In practice, records inserted via this API are available immediately and exactly once in queries, which means that it enables real-time analytics. You just have to be careful not to rely on this behavior for the correctness of your application because it is not guaranteed. Chapter 11 discusses patterns for working around this weaker guarantee. Here you dive into the details of using this API.

Before you can insert a row into a table, you must first create the table with a schema compatible with the rows you will be inserting. You can use the bq tool to create the table and then insert a row into the table using curl:

```
$ bq mk -t ch06.streamed ts:timestamp,label:string,count:integer

$ BASE_URL=https://www.googleapis.com/bigquery/v2
$ PROJECT_ID=317752944021
$ PROJECT_URL=${BASE_URL}/projects/${PROJECT_ID}
```

```
$ DATASET_URL=${PROJECT_URL}/datasets/ch06
$ table_url() {
>     echo -n ${DATASET_URL}/tables/${1}
> }
$ curl -H "$(python auth.py)" \
>     -H 'Content-Type: application/json' \
>     --data-binary '{
> "rows": [
>    {"json": {"ts":1381186891,"label":"test","count":42}}
> ]
}' $(table_url streamed)/insertAll
{
 "kind": "bigquery#tableDataInsertAllResponse"
}

$ bq head ch06.streamed
+---------------------+-------+-------+
|         ts          | label | count |
+---------------------+-------+-------+
| 2013-10-07 23:01:11 | test  |    42 |
+---------------------+-------+-------+
```

It may take a minute or so for the row to appear when you list the table or query it. This delay is only present the first time you insert a row into a table. Once a streamed row appears in the table, additional rows inserted are available immediately. If you do not stream any data to a table for an extended duration (a couple of hours or so), this initial delay may recur.

Looking at the insert request you can see that the actual data inserted is nested within a JSON object. The top-level object must contain a list-valued field named rows. Each entry in the list is an object with a field named json whose value is the record being inserted. The JSON value that appears at this field is identical to the row that you would use in JSON formatted input to load jobs. The only difference is that new lines are not significant and are treated the same as any other whitespace that appears between JSON values. Here is the full specification for the insert request:

```
{
  "kind": "bigquery#tableDataInsertAllRequest",
  "rows": [
    {
      "insertId": string,
      "json": {record data}
    }
  ]
}
```

The only additional field that was not part of the example request is insertId. This field is actually important and requires the most explanation.

Just as job ID protects you from inserting the same job multiple times, the insert ID prevents the same record from being inserted multiple times if a request is retried. Because the client might receive a failure response even if the server has successfully handled the request, the client might attempt to reinsert a record that has already been received by the service. If you set the `insertId` to the same value across multiple insert requests, the service uses it to de-duplicate records. You should always insert the same record for a given ID because the service does not guarantee which record (first, last, or any in between) will be saved for a given ID. But there is an important caveat: This deduplication works only for a finite amount of time. The exact duration may change but it is currently around 5 minutes. Beyond that, the service discards the state associated with the `insertId`. After this time the service treats an insert with the same ID as a new distinct record. In most scenarios in which a client has to retry an operation, this time window is sufficient to avoid duplication. However, it is not a strong guarantee, which is why this API has at-least-once semantics. To summarize, using a unique `insertId` for each record inserted reduces the chance of duplication but does not eliminate all duplication.

WARNING   The insert operation implemented in the `bq` tool does not supply insert IDs to the API. This makes in unsuitable for production usage, but it is convenient to use during development and testing.

Now turn to the response returned by the insert request. The response is used to report the errors that occurred while processing the insert. As you saw, when the request succeeds, the response is basically empty. Errors that cause the entire request to fail return an HTTP error status code and the body contains additional details. Otherwise, a 200 status is returned, and the response contains information about individual rows that failed. This is analogous to how load job errors are handled. You can see the error reporting in action by issuing a couple of bad requests. To give you a better sense of the actual HTTP requests and responses, use `curl` to manually construct the requests.

```
$ curl -H "$(python auth.py)" \
    -H 'Content-Type: application/json' \
    --data-binary '{
  "rows": [
    {"json": {"count": "4.2", "ts": 123, "label": "bad"}}
  ]
}' $(table_url foo)/insertAll
{
 "error": {
  "errors": [
   {
    "domain": "global",
    "reason": "notFound",
    "message": "Not Found: Table 317752944021:ch06.foo"
   }
```

```
    ],
    "code": 404,
    "message": "Not Found: Table 317752944021:ch06.foo"
  }
}
```

Because the request attempts to insert data into a table that does not exist, the request fails and returns a 404 response code indicating that the table does not exist. Now try to insert the same request using the table you created.

```
$ curl -H "$(python auth.py)" \
    -H 'Content-Type: application/json' \
    --data-binary '{
    "rows": [
      {"json": {"count": "4.2", "ts": 123, "label": "bad"}}
    ]
}' $(table_url streamed)/insertAll
{
  "kind": "bigquery#tableDataInsertAllResponse",
  "insertErrors": [
    {
      "index": 0,
      "errors": [
        {
          "reason": "invalid",
          "message": "Could not convert value to integer."
        }
      ]
    }
  ]
}
```

When individual records fail the `insertErrors` list is returned, which contains an entry for every failed record. Each entry contains an `index` (0-based) field that links the errors in the entry to a corresponding record in the request. Invalid records generate errors similar to the data errors reported by JSON load jobs. There is no point retrying invalid inserts, but connection and other transient errors should be retried. If the request contains only a couple of records, and includes the `insertId` fields, it is reasonable to retry the entire request, but if the request has a large number of records, it is more efficient to retry only the failed records.

Just as with load jobs, there is a size limit on an individual request and rate limits on the total number of requests.

- **Maximum record size:** 100 KB
- **Maximum bytes per request:** 1 MB
- **Table rate limit:** 10,000 rows/second (enforced over 10 seconds)
- **Project rate limit:** 100,000 rows/second

Record size and bytes refers to the size computed based on the data in the records and not the JSON encoded size.

To complete this section now look at how to perform inserts using the Python client API. Listing 6.2 is a script that accepts a filename as an argument. It tails (polls for data appearing at the end) the given file and parses each line, turns it into a record, and then performs an insert. Notice that it uses the filename and position of the record as the `insertId`, which ensures that if the script is restarted on the file, the records will not be duplicated. This is not perfect because if the script is restarted after the deduplication window has passed, the records will end up duplicated. Fixing this behavior is left as an exercise to the reader. Another feature to note is that the script builds batches of up to 10 records before submitting the request, but only if the records are immediately available. This usually increases throughput without delaying the delivery of records.

Listing 6.2 : (stream.py)

```
def tail_and_insert(infile,
                    tabledata,
                    project_id,
                    dataset_id,
                    table_id):
  '''Tail a file and stream its lines to a BigQuery table.

    infile: file object to be tailed.
    tabledata: tabledata collection client
    project_id: project ID of the destination table.
    dataset_id: dataset ID of the destination table.
    table_id: table ID of the destination table.
  '''
  pos = 0
  rows = []
  while True:
    # If the file has additional data available and there are less than
    # 10 buffered rows then fetch the next available line.
    line = infile.readline() if len(rows) < 10 else None
    # If the line is a complete line buffer it.
    if line and line[-1] == '\n':
      # Record the end of the last full line.
      pos = infile.tell()
      ts, label, count = line.split(',')
      rows.append({
          'insertId': '%s%d' % (sys.argv[1], pos),
          'json': {
            'ts': int(ts.strip()),
            'label': label.strip(),
            'count': int(count.strip())
          }
```

```
          })
    # 10 buffered rows or no new data so flush buffer by positing it.
    else:
      if rows:
        tabledata.insertAll(
          projectId=project_id,
          datasetId=dataset_id,
          tableId=table_id,
          body={'rows': rows}).execute()
        del rows[:]
      else:
        # No new data so sleep briefly.
        time.sleep(0.1)
      # Re-position the file at the end of the last full record.
      infile.seek(pos)

def main():
  service = auth.build_bq_client()

  with open(sys.argv[1], 'a+') as infile:
    tail_and_insert(infile,
                    service.tabledata(),
                    auth.PROJECT_ID,
                    'ch06',
                    'streamed')

if __name__ == '__main__':
  main()
```

It is worth calling attention once again to the key feature of the streaming insert API—records appear in the table as soon as the request completes. Usually records are available within 100 ms of the request being initiated. This enables a number of real-time use cases in applications; so building a pipeline that utilizes the API is a good investment.

Summary

Data storage is a big part of the BigQuery service, so it has a lot of features related to loading data. This chapter covered all the methods for moving your data into the service and highlighted common pitfalls. It discussed using Google Cloud Storage, the Resumable Upload protocol, and multipart requests as mechanisms to transfer data into the service. Next, the formats, CSV, JSON, and Datastore backups that the service currently supports were covered. Finally, how to use the low latency streaming API for inserting individual records was explained.

It is useful to be aware of the full range of options because often you are constrained by the current location of your data and may be able to avoid complicated transformations if you can use the right combination of features. In cases in which you build a custom data pipeline, this information can help you design an effective solution. Hopefully, the task of getting your data into BigQuery will be simple in relation to the overall challenge of collecting data that can deliver useful insights.

Running Queries

This chapter describes how to run queries in BigQuery—from how to send the API requests to how to construct valid queries in the BigQuery variant of SQL. The chapter is divided into two sections: query API and query language.

The query API section describes the mechanics of how to run queries. If you do not intend to write code to interact with the BigQuery API, you might want to skim this section rather than skip it completely; it has information about what is possible via the underlying API, which might come in handy even if you're going to use only a web interface or command-line client to interact with BigQuery.

The query language section describes the features of BigQuery SQL. It assumes some familiarity with writing SQL queries and does not attempt to be an in-depth query reference. It does, however, walk through simple query creation and focus on differences between BigQuery and standard SQL.

After reading this chapter you should know everything you need to know to construct and run simple queries in BigQuery. Understanding how the query engine works at a high level is key to getting the most out of BigQuery queries. For this reason, more advanced query topics are deferred until Chapter 10, "Advanced Queries," after the query architecture has been explained.

BigQuery Query API

As discussed in Chapter 5, "Talking to the BigQuery API," all BigQuery queries are jobs. Because they are jobs, they execute asynchronously; you can decouple the act of starting a query from fetching results. You can also see which queries you've already run and fetch the results in multiple pages.

Another salient feature of query jobs helps with reading query results: All query results are saved in a BigQuery table. This enables you to interact with query results the same way you would read any other table. You can copy the query result table, export it to Google Cloud Storage, and run queries against the query results themselves. Query result tables are discussed more thoroughly in the "Query Result Tables" section later in this chapter.

Query API Methods

There are two ways to run queries using the BigQuery HTTP API: You can call `Jobs.insert()` to add a Query job to the Jobs REST collection, or you can use the `Jobs.query()` and `Jobs.getQueryResults()` RPC methods. The former method is a bit more complex; you need to insert the Query job, poll for completion, and then read the results. The latter can be simpler when you want to do simple things; you can run a query and get results back in a single API call. That said, by the time you account for large query results, queries that take more than a few seconds, or error handling, the two methods may involve the same amount of code.

WHEN SHOULD YOU USE JOBS.QUERY() VERSUS JOBS.INSERT() TO RUN QUERIES?

The difference between the `Jobs.query()` and the `Jobs.insert()` method is sometimes referred to as "porcelain" versus "plumbing." The `Jobs.insert()` "plumbing" API enables you do anything the `Jobs.query()` API does and more but may have fewer conveniences; the `Jobs.query()` "porcelain" method is simpler and easier to use.

The `Jobs.query()` method should generally be preferred whenever it can be used, for example, when you won't need to save the results in a named destination table, when you won't need large (> 128 MB) query results, and when you expect the query to run quickly. One advantage of `Jobs.query()` is that it waits for results before returning. This saves you from having to poll for query completion.

The `Jobs.insert()` method, conversely, should be used whenever you need to control your destination table, query priority, or when you need large query results. It is also useful when you're writing code that needs to work with all kinds of jobs, rather than just query jobs.

The following Python command shows running a simple query via the `Jobs`
`.query()` API:

```
$ python
>>> import auth
>>> import pprint
>>> project_id = 'bigquery-e2e'
>>> service = auth.build_bq_client()
>>> response = service.jobs().query(
...     projectId=project_id,
...     body={'query': 'SELECT 17'}).execute()
>>> pprint.pprint(response)
{u'cacheHit': True,
 u'jobComplete': True,
 u'jobReference': {u'jobId': u'job_86V_-s5k_EyN3Fuk8ym03nItDrM',
                   u'projectId': u'bigquery-e2e'},
 u'kind': u'bigquery#queryResponse',
 u'rows': [{u'f': [{u'v': u'17'}]}],
 u'schema': {u'fields': [{u'mode': u'NULLABLE',
                          u'name': u'f0_',
                          u'type': u'INTEGER'}]},
 u'totalBytesProcessed': u'0',
 u'totalRows': u'1'}
```

The corresponding commands to just start the query using `Jobs.insert()`
is not much more complex:

```
>>> import time
>>> job_id = 'job_%d' % int(time.time() * 1000)
>>> response = service.jobs().insert(
...     projectId=project_id,
...     body={'configuration': {'query': {'query': 'SELECT 17'}},
...           'jobReference': {'jobId': job_id,
...                            'projectId': project_id}}
...     ).execute()
>>> pprint.pprint(response)
{u'configuration': {
    u'query': {
        u'createDisposition': u'CREATE_IF_NEEDED',
        u'destinationTable': {
            u'datasetId': u'_0e32b38e1117b2fcea992287c138bd53acfff7cc',
            u'projectId': u'bigquery-e2e',
            u'tableId': u'anon5c03da1f543a2486eca295f285b40eb87b01ea84'
            },
        u'query': u'SELECT 17',
        u'writeDisposition': u'WRITE_TRUNCATE'}},
 u'etag': u'"Ny_MVtklP3Cn04wt1Sr9PinHZEI/jqd_3fxcej4s3YkUyZl--c8JK88"',
 u'id': u'bigquery-e2e:job_1394904041084',
```

```
u'jobReference': {u'jobId': u'job_1394904041084',
                  u'projectId': u'bigquery-e2e'},
u'kind': u'bigquery#job',
u'selfLink': u'https://www.googleapis.com/bigquery/...',
u'statistics': {u'creationTime': u'1394904325715',
                u'startTime': u'1394904326024'},
u'status': {u'state': u'RUNNING'}}
```

However, if you look at the output of `Jobs.insert()`, you can notice two things: You don't get any query results, and the job is still in the RUNNING state. Before you can get query results, you need to wait for the job to complete. You can do this by calling `Jobs.get()` with the job ID from the original request:

```
>>> response = service.jobs().get(projectId=project_id,
...                               jobId=job_id).execute()
```

You can use a Python trick to avoid having to pass parameters individually, by using the `**` operator to turn a Python `dict` into named parameters. The following command is identical to the previous one, but saves some typing:

```
>>> response = service.jobs().get(**response['jobReference']).execute()
```

Here is what the resulting Job resource looks like:

```
>>> pprint.pprint(response)
{u'configuration': {
    u'query': {
        u'createDisposition': u'CREATE_IF_NEEDED',
        u'destinationTable': {
            u'datasetId': u'_0e32b38e1117b2fcea992287c138bd53acfff7cc',
            u'projectId': u'bigquery-e2e',
            u'tableId': u'anon5c03da1f543a2486eca295f285b40eb87b01ea84'
            },
        u'query': u'SELECT 17',
        u'writeDisposition': u'WRITE_TRUNCATE'}},
u'etag': u'"Ny_MVtklP3Cn04wt1Sr9PinHZEI/jqd_3fxcej4s3YkUyZl--c8JK88"',
u'id': u'bigquery-e2e:job_1394904041084',
u'jobReference': {u'jobId': u'job_1394904041084',
                  u'projectId': u'bigquery-e2e'},
u'kind': u'bigquery#job',
u'selfLink': u'https://www.googleapis.com/bigquery/...',
u'statistics': {u'creationTime': u'1394904325715',
                u'endTime': u'1394904326418',
                u'query': {u'cacheHit': True,
                           u'totalBytesProcessed': u'0'},
                u'startTime': u'1394904326024',
                u'totalBytesProcessed': u'0'},
u'status': {u'state': u'DONE'}}
```

The job looks similar, but is now in state DONE, and has a couple of extra statistics values. You'll note that the table and dataset IDs are long unintelligible strings; these values describe an automatically created table to hold the query results. Now that the job is complete, you can read the results by calling `TableData` `.list()` with the table ID returned by the job:

```
>>> table_ref = response['configuration']['query']['destinationTable']
>>> results = service.tabledata().list(**table_ref).execute()
>>> pprint.pprint(results)
{u'etag': u'"Ny_MVtklP3Cn04wt1Sr9PinHZEI/dXCj1HevhJ0HiCBv_gB0LRPFaDE"',
 u'kind': u'bigquery#tableDataList',
 u'rows': [{u'f': [{u'v': u'17'}]}],
 u'totalRows': u'1'}
```

Using `Jobs.insert()` you got the same result: "17," but with two more API calls. You might also notice that the results of `Jobs.query()` contained the schema of the result table but the `TableData.list()` response did not. Sometimes you might already know the resulting schema. If you wrote the query yourself, you may know exactly what the schema should look like. Most of the time, however, you likely won't know the result schema in advance. To get the table schema requires another API call, this time to the `Tables.get()` API.

```
>>> schema = service.tables().get(**table_ref).execute()['schema']
>>> pprint.pprint(schema)
{u'fields': [{u'mode': u'NULLABLE', u'name': u'f0_',
              u'type': u'INTEGER'}]}
```

Jobs.query() RPC

As previously mentioned, `Jobs.query()` is the simpler query API. It lacks some of the configuration options controlling how to run your query that `Jobs` `.insert()` has but is usually the easiest way to run a query and get the results.

Running `Jobs.query()` is equivalent to calling `Jobs.insert()` to start the job, `Jobs.get()` to poll for job completion, and `TableData.list()` to get the first page of results. Query results get stored in a temporary table that lives for 24 hours. If you need your query results to stick around longer, you can copy them to a permanent table with a copy job, or you can use the more fully featured `Jobs.insert()` method to run your query and specify a destination table.

The most important parameter (other than the query string, of course) is `timeoutMs`, which controls how long the query request waits before returning. The default timeout is 10 seconds; it is set so short because many contexts where you may be issuing the query (such as AppEngine) automatically cancel any

HTTP request that takes too long. The maximum `timeoutMs` is 200 seconds; you can set it to something larger, but BigQuery treats it as if you set it to the maximum value.

More than 98 percent of BigQuery queries return in less than 3 seconds (obviously this is highly dependent on the query being run); if you set the `timeoutMs` value to a large value, you're almost certain to get a response without a timeout. Queries that take longer than a few seconds are generally complicated with lots of `JOIN` or `GROUP BY` operations; simpler queries should always complete within a reasonable timeout, unless they are operating over truly massive amounts of data.

When `Jobs.query()` times out, it doesn't return an HTTP response error. Instead, it returns a normal query response, but the `jobComplete` flag will be set to `false`. It also returns a `jobId` for the Query job. You can use this `jobId` to call `Jobs.getQueryResults()` to both wait for the job to complete and return the results.

You might wonder why the `Jobs.query()` request is a POST request and not a GET request. After all, a number of systems that you might want to use to run queries support only GET requests, and there is a convenient standard "q=<url encoded query>" syntax that you could use. One technical issue is that GET requests require passing all the data in the URL, and many web-capable systems have a limit on the length of URL they can use in a GET request. Internet Explorer has a hard-limit for URLs at approximately 2048 characters; Microsoft Excel limits URL query strings to 256 characters. Many SQL queries in BigQuery are several kilobytes long; any system with a URL length limit would be unable to issue a considerable proportion of BigQuery queries.

SET MAXRESULTS ON YOUR QUERIES

If you set the `maxResults` flag on a query to a value that isn't too large (say, 1000 results), you reduce the chances of hitting a connection error. Large HTTP responses can fail in many different places and many different ways; if you request smaller results you can always go back and fetch more. Most of the time, you actually are only interested in the first few results; requesting more is just going to take longer to download.

It is easy to confuse the `maxResults` field with the `LIMIT` keyword in the query. The `LIMIT` keyword controls how many results are computed by the query engine and stored in the result table. The `maxResults` field controls only how many results are returned in the first page of results. Your query might return many more rows, which would be stored in the query result temporary table in BigQuery. For example, if your query returned a million rows and you set `maxResults` to 10, `Jobs.query()` would return only the first 10 rows. You can page through the rest, however, by calling `Jobs.getQueryResults()`.

There is also an API design-related reason that `Jobs.query()` is a POST operation instead of a GET. HTTP GET requests are not supposed to make any state changes. They can be crawled, pre-fetched, cached, are susceptible to double-dispatch, and so on. However, running a query can cost you money. It would not seem right to have an HTTP GET run up a bill, so the `Jobs.query()` method is exposed as a POST operation, not a GET.

Table 7.1 shows the fields that are returned in the `Jobs.query()` method:

Table 7.1: Jobs.query() Response Fields

FIELD	TYPE	DESCRIPTION
cacheHit	boolean	Whether the query results were found in the cache. When true, the query did not actually need to run (and you weren't charged).
jobComplete	boolean	Whether the job is actually finished. If this is False or absent, there was a timeout, and you need to call `Jobs.getQueryResults()` to wait for and fetch the results.
jobReference	object	JobReference describing the query job. You can use this to look up the job information with `Jobs.get()` or look up query results via `Jobs.getQueryResults()`.
jobReference.projectId	string	ID of the project in which you ran the job. This is the project that will get billed for query processing.
jobReference.jobId	string	A job ID that was generated by BigQuery
pageToken	string	An opaque value that you can use to fetch subsequent pages of results. This will be present only if there are more results to return.
rows	object array	TableRow list of results in f / v format. (See the `TableData.list()` API description in Chapter 5 for more information on this format.)
schema	object	TableSchema of the results. (See the Table resource description in Chapter 5 for more information.)
totalBytesProcessed	number	Total number of bytes processed in the query. This is the amount that you will be billed for running the query (or in the case of a dry run, the amount that you would have been billed).
totalRows	number	The total number of rows in the result table

Here is an example Python command to send a simple query request with a large timeout value:

```
>>> response = service.jobs().query(
...        projectId=project_id,
...        body={'query': 'SELECT 17', 'timeoutMs': 1000000}).execute()
>>> pprint.pprint(response)
{u'cacheHit': True,
 u'jobComplete': True,
 u'jobReference': {u'jobId': u'job_85QYWMD7jBuqPOtIEgk1BaheODE',
                   u'projectId': u'bigquery-e2e'},
 u'kind': u'bigquery#queryResponse',
 u'rows': [{u'f': [{u'v': u'17'}]}],
 u'schema': {u'fields': [{u'mode': u'NULLABLE',
                          u'name': u'f0_',
                          u'type': u'INTEGER'}]},
 u'totalBytesProcessed': u'0',
 u'totalRows': u'1'}
```

Jobs.getQueryResults() RPC

There are two limitations to the Jobs.query() API: Sometimes queries run longer than the timeout you specify, and sometimes queries return more data than you can read in a single page of results. The Jobs.getQueryResults() API addresses both of these issues by giving you a mechanism to pick up where Jobs.query() left off.

When you run the original Jobs.query(), it returns three important pieces of data: a jobId that can be used to look up information about the Query job, a jobComplete flag that tells you whether the query completed within the timeout value, and a pageToken that can let you page through additional results (if there are any).

After you have the jobId from the Jobs.query() result, you can use it to call Jobs.getQueryResults(). The result format of Jobs.getQueryResults() is identical to Jobs.query(). If the query still isn't done, the jobComplete flag will still be false. If the query does complete within the timeout, the first page of results will be returned, along with a pageToken that lets you read more results.

You can call Jobs.getQueryResults() on any query job, not just one that was run via Jobs.query(). This can be useful because the waiting is done on the server side, so you'll get a response as soon as the query has completed. That is, since the Jobs.getQueryResults() API waits for the query to finish (or timeout), you don't need to add a sleep operation in your code; all of the waiting occurs during the API call. It also does one fewer API call because you don't have to wait for the query to complete before reading the results—the results are returned as soon as they are ready.

Listing 7.1 demonstrates the use of `Jobs.query()` and `Jobs.getQueryResults()` to run a query and fetch all the results.

Listing 7.1: Running a query via Jobs.query() and polling for results with Jobs .getQueryResults() (query.py)

```python
import auth
import pprint
import sys

def print_results(schema, rows):
  ''' Prints query results, given a schema. '''
  for row in rows:
    line = []
    for i in xrange(0, len(schema)):
      cell = row['f'][i]
      field = schema[i]
      line.append({field['name']: cell['v']})
    pprint.pprint(line)

class QueryRpc:
  def __init__(self, service, project_id):
    self.service = service
    self.project_id = project_id

  def run(self, query, response_handler=print_results,
          timeout_ms=30*1000, max_results=1024):
    '''Run a query RPC and print the results.

      query: text of query to run.
      response_handler: function that is used to process results.
      timeout_ms: timeout of each RPC call.
      max_results: maximum number of results to process.
    '''
    query_request = {
        'query': query,
        # Use a timeout of 0, which means we'll always need
        # to get results via getQueryResults().
        'timeoutMs': 0,
        'maxResults': max_results
    }

    # Start the query.
    response = self.service.jobs().query(
        projectId=self.project_id,
        body=query_request).execute()
    job_ref = response['jobReference']

    while True:
      page_token = response.get('pageToken', None)
```

continues

Listing 7.1: *(continued)*

```
        query_complete = response.get('jobComplete', False)
        if query_complete:
          fields = response.get('schema', {}).get('fields', [])
          rows = response.get('rows', [])
          response_handler(fields, rows)
          if page_token is None:
            # The query is done and there are no more results
            # to read.
            break
        response = self.service.jobs().getQueryResults(
            projectId = self.project_id,
            jobId = job_ref['jobId'],
            timeoutMs = timeout_ms,
            pageToken = page_token,
            maxResults = max_results).execute()

def main(argv):
  if len(argv) == 0:
    print 'Usage: query.py <project_id> [query]'
    return
  service = auth.build_bq_client()
  project_id = argv[0]
  query = QueryRpc(service, project_id)
  if len(argv) < 2:
    query_text = 'SELECT 17'
  else:
    # The entire rest of the command line is the query.
    query_text = ' '.join(argv[1:])

  query.run(query_text)

if __name__ == "__main__":
    main(sys.argv[1:])
```

Querying via Jobs.insert()

As previously mentioned, `Jobs.insert()` is the most flexible way to run a query job. To indicate that the job is a query, you need to fill out the `query` subsection of the job configuration. When using `Jobs.insert()`, you can run your query at a lower priority, abort the query if the result isn't already cached, append results to a destination table, or specify your own job ID.

If you're not familiar with using the Jobs REST Collection, check out Chapter 5, which describes the Jobs resource in detail. Table 7.2 shows the options available in the query configuration.

Table 7.2: JobConfigurationQuery Request Fields

FIELD	TYPE	DESCRIPTION
allowLargeResults	boolean	Whether the results of the query can be larger than 128 MB. (The default is False.)
createDisposition	btring	A create disposition value (CREATE_NEVER or CREATE_IF_NEEDED) describing under which conditions to create the output table. (Note that CREATE_NEVER doesn't mean that the query won't write its output to a table; it means that the destination table must already exist.)
defaultDataset	object	DatasetReference to use to qualify table names in the query text that don't have a dataset or project specified. Note you can specify only the projectId, only the datasetId, or both.
destinationTable	object	TableReference of the table where destination results will be written. If not specified, a unique temporary table will be created by BigQuery.
priority	string	The priority of the query. The default and highest priority is INTERACTIVE. Alternatively, specify BATCH priority to run your query in the batch queue.
query	string	Query string, in BigQuery SQL format
useQueryCache	boolean	Whether the query is allowed to get results from the query cache. The default is True. Set this to False if you want to rerun the query even if it is already cached.
writeDisposition	string	Write disposition value describing how to write out the results. Options are WRITE_APPEND to append results to an existing table, WRITE_EMPTY to fail the job if the destination table is not empty, and WRITE_TRUNCATE to replace the table contents with the query results.

Listing 7.1 showed how to query via Jobs.query() and Jobs.getQueryResults(). Listing 7.2 shows a similar mechanism to query via the Jobs.insert() method. Note that this requires more code; you need to call Jobs.get() to wait for the job to complete, Tables.get() if you want the table schema, and TableData.list() to read the results. There are also some additional options shown in the code, such as specifying a destination table, specifying a job ID, allowing large result sizes, and running the query at batch priority.

Listing 7.2: Alternative way to run queries: Jobs.insert() and TableData.list() (query_job.py)

```python
import sys
import pprint
import time

def print_results(schema, rows):
  ''' Prints query results, given a schema. '''
  for row in rows:
    line = []
    for i in xrange(0, len(schema)):
      cell = row['f'][i]
      field = schema[i]
      line.append({field['name']: cell['v']})
    pprint.pprint(line)

class QueryJob:
  def __init__(self, service, project_id):
    self.service = service
    self.project_id = project_id

  def run(self, query, response_handler=print_results,
          job_id=None, destination_table=None,
          allow_large_results=False,
          batch_priority=False):
    '''Run a Query Job and print the results.

    query: text of query to run.
    response_handler: function that is used to process results.
    job_id: optional job id to provide to BigQuery.

allow_large_results: whether to allow query results larger than
        128 MB.
    destination_table: if present, the destination table to write
        the query results to.
    batch_priority: whether to run the query at batch priority
    '''

    query_config = {
        'query': query,
        'allowLargeResults': allow_large_results
    }
    if not job_id:
      # If the caller did not specify a job id, generate one
      # based on the current time.
      job_id = 'job_%d' % int(time.time() * 1000)

    if destination_table:
      # If this is run multiple times, truncate the table and
      # replace it with the new results.
```

```
        query_config['writeDisposition'] = 'WRITE_TRUNCATE'
        query_config['destinationTable'] = destination_table
        query_config['allowLargeResults'] = allow_large_results

    if batch_priority:
        query_config['priority'] = 'BATCH'

    job_ref = {'projectId': self.project_id}
    if job_id:
        job_ref['jobId'] = job_id

    job = {
        'configuration': {'query': query_config},
        'jobReference': job_ref
    }

    print 'Starting query job "%s"' % (job,)
    job = self.service.jobs().insert(projectId=self.project_id,
        body=job).execute()
    # Fetch the job ID from the running job, in case one wasn't
    # already specified above.
    job_ref = job['jobReference']

    # Wait for the job to complete.
    while job['status']['state'] != 'DONE':
        print 'Waiting for job %s to complete: %s' % (
            job_ref, job['status']['state'])
        time.sleep(1.0)
        job = self.service.jobs().get(
            jobId = job_ref['jobId'],
            projectId = job_ref['projectId']).execute()

    if 'errorResult' in job['status']:
        print 'Error %s' % (job['status']['errorResult'],)
        return

    # Read the results using TableData.list(). Note that we could
    # also read the results using jobs.getQueryResults(), but for the
    # purposes of this sample, we wanted to show the TableData
    # equivalent.

    qery_config = job['configuration']['query']
    destination_table_ref = query_config['destinationTable']
    schema = self.service.tables().get(
        tableId=destination_table_ref['tableId'],
        datasetId=destination_table_ref['datasetId'],
        projectId=destination_table_ref['projectId']
        ).execute()['schema']
```

continues

Listing 7.2: *(continued)*

```
        page_token = None
        while True:
          response = self.service.tabledata().list(
              pageToken=page_token,
              tableId=destination_table_ref['tableId'],
              datasetId=destination_table_ref['datasetId'],
              projectId=destination_table_ref['projectId']).execute()
          page_token = response.get('pageToken', None)
          fields = schema.get('fields', [])
          rows = response.get('rows', [])
          response_handler(fields, rows)
          if page_token is None:
            # The query is done and there are no more results
            # to read.
            break

  def main(argv):
    if len(argv) == 0:
      print('Usage: query_job.py <project_id> [query]')
      return
    service = auth.build_bq_client()
    project_id = argv[0]
    query_job = QueryJob(service, project_id)
    if len(argv) < 2:
      query = 'SELECT 17'
    else:
      # The entire rest of the command line is the query.
      query = ' '.join(argv[1:])
    destination = {
        'projectId': project_id,
        'datasetId': 'scratch',
        'tableId': 'results'}
    query_job.run(query, destination_table=destination)

  if __name__ == "__main__":
      main(sys.argv[1:])
```

After you start the job via `Jobs.insert()`, you can still call `Jobs .getQueryResults()` to read the results. This listing shows the lower-level methods that demonstrate what `Jobs.getQueryResults()` actually does behind the scenes.

Query API Features

Now that you have seen the basic mechanics of the query API, consider some of the more advanced features available. You can access these features, for the most part, in the BigQuery web interface or via the `bq` command-line tool. We show the Python code in order to demonstrate the raw API settings.

Query Result Tables

All query results are first-class tables in BigQuery; whether you use the `Jobs` `.query()` or the `Jobs.insert()` method to run a query, your query results are always tables. This means you can list them, copy them, get their schema, and run queries against them. Query result tables have some special properties, which are described in this section.

Anonymous Tables

When you don't explicitly provide a name for the destination table, BigQuery generates a unique table name for the result. These unique tables are called *anonymous tables* because their names are unimportant. The name of the table is added to the job configuration in the job resource; you can find it by calling `Jobs.get()`. Here is an example of using the `Jobs.query()` method to run a query and then `Jobs.get()` to find the anonymous table name:

```
>>> response = service.jobs().query(
...     projectId=project_id,
...     body={'query': 'SELECT 42'}).execute()
>>> job = service.jobs().get(**response['jobReference']).execute()
>>> destination_table=job['configuration']['query']['destinationTable']
>>> pprint.pprint(destination_table)
{u'datasetId': u'_0e32b38e1117b2fcea992287c138bd53acfff7cc',
 u'projectId': u'bigquery-e2e',
 u'tableId': u'anonde3fd1ade53226f48a842c7518bb9b0fe911e606'}
}
```

One interesting thing about the anonymous table is the dataset ID: `"_0e32b38e1117b2fcea992287c138bd53acfff7cc"`. This dataset doesn't show up when you list your datasets, either via the API or in the web UI. Datasets that start with an underscore are hidden; they can be listed only if you pass the `all` flag to `Datasets.list()`. BigQuery creates hidden datasets as needed to hold query results on a per-user-per-project basis. All the queries you run in a particular project use the same dataset to hold your query results; if different users run the same query, their results would go in a different dataset. If you inspect the ACL of the hidden dataset created to hold query results, you can see that it is restricted to a single user:

```
>>> dataset = service.datasets().get(
...     projectId=destination_table['projectId'],
...     datasetId=destination_table['datasetId']).execute()
>>> pprint.pprint(dataset)
{u'access': [{u'role': u'OWNER', u'userByEmail': u'jtigani@gmail.com'}],
 u'creationTime': u'1374444606886',
 u'datasetReference': {
     u'datasetId': u'_0e32b38e1117b2fcea992287c138bd53acfff7cc',
             u'projectId': u'bigquery-e2e'},
```

```
u'etag': u'"Ny_MVtklP3Cn04wt1Sr9PinHZEI/T9T-JJCytvKVcXb9FoswD2KVexo"',
u'id': u'bigquery-e2e:_0e32b38e1117b2fcea992287c138bd53acfff7cc',
u'kind': u'bigquery#dataset',
u'lastModifiedTime': u'1374444606886',
u'selfLink': u'https://www.googleapis.com/bigquery/v2/..."}
```

Anonymous tables have some special properties; they are immutable, meaning you cannot append to them. (Although you can rewrite them, as you see in the section on caching.) You also do not pay for their storage. Because BigQuery doesn't charge for anonymous tables, they have a limited lifespan—they expire in 24 hours. This lifespan of an anonymous table cannot be directly changed, although running a query that returns the same table from the query cache can renew the table so that it will be valid for another 24 hours.

Here is a Python command that shows the anonymous table created by the previous query:

```
>>> table = service.tables().get(
...        projectId=destination_table['projectId'],
...        datasetId=destination_table['datasetId'],
...        tableId=destination_table['tableId']).execute()
>>> pprint.pprint(table)
{u'creationTime': u'1394986053339',
 u'etag': u'...',
 u'expirationTime': u'1395072453345',
 u'id': u'...,
 u'kind': u'bigquery#table',
 u'lastModifiedTime': u'1394986053339',
 u'numBytes': u'8',
 u'numRows': u'1',
 u'schema': {u'fields': [{u'mode': u'NULLABLE',
                          u'name': u'f0_',
                          u'type': u'INTEGER'}]},
 u'selfLink': u'...',
 u'tableReference': {
    u'datasetId': u'_0e32b38e1117b2fcea992287c138bd53acfff7cc',
    u'projectId': u'bigquery-e2e',
    u'tableId': u'anonde3fd1ade53226f48a842c7518bb9b0fe911e606'},
 u'type': u'TABLE'}
```

Specifying Where to Write Query Results

Sometimes, you want to keep query results around longer than 24 hours. You can do this by specifying the name of a destination table for the query rather than letting BigQuery pick the destination. To specify the destination table, you must use the `Jobs.insert()` method (not `Jobs.query()`), and you should fill out the `destinationTable` parameter in the query configuration. Note that when you use a named destination table, you must pay for any storage the table uses, and the table never expires unless you explicitly set an expiration time on the table.

The `writeDisposition` flag may come in handy when specifying the destination table. Specifying `WRITE_APPEND` lets you append the results to an existing table. If you want to overwrite an existing table completely, you can specify `WRITE_TRUNCATE` instead. These operations happen atomically; you can either see the table as it was before the query results get written or you see all the results added to the table. If the query fails, the table will not be modified at all.

Query Cache

BigQuery attempts to cache query results and returns results from the cache whenever possible. If you run `SELECT COUNT(*) FROM [publicdata:samples.wikipedia]`, the result is added to the cache. If you run the same query a second time, you get the cached result. As a user this is nice because you don't get charged for queries that hit the cache. You also can get a result faster if you don't actually have to run the query. Cached queries live for 24 hours after the last access.

Queries are cached per-user, so if you run a query and your coworker runs the same query, she can't use your cached result. Having per-user caches helps prevent both security and privacy issues.

Some types of queries cannot be cached. For example, if you run the query `SELECT NOW() + RAND()`, the query won't be cached because the result is non-deterministic. Likewise, if you write the query results to a named destination table, the results won't be cached because the results live in the destination table rather than the cache. Finally, if the tables you query against change, the cache will be purged.

If you don't want to allow your results to be cached, you can set `useQueryCache` to `false` when you run the query (either via `Jobs.insert()` or `Jobs.query()`). For the most part, you won't need this flag; however, you might be explicitly trying to test performance without using the cache, and you'll actually want to see how long the query takes to run and how much data it processes. Queries that return cached results will have the `cacheHit` flag set to `true`, and the `totalBytesProcessed` will be set to `0`, indicating you aren't charged for any processing.

The following Python commands show the cache in operation. First, a unique query is generated, so it will be guaranteed not to be in the cache. Then the same query is run twice, back to back. The first time it will not be in the cache, the second time it will be:

```
>>> query = 'SELECT COUNT(word), %f FROM [%s]' % (
...     time.time(), 'publicdata:samples.shakespeare')
>>> response1 = service.jobs().query(
...     projectId=project_id,
...     body={'query': query}).execute()
>>> response2 = service.jobs().query(
...     projectId=project_id,
...     body={'query': query}).execute()
```

```
>>> pprint.pprint(response1)
{u'cacheHit': False,
 u'jobComplete': True,
 u'jobReference': {u'jobId': u'job_ruB2mvCJliNKHeERhsPzxhZJtSs',
                   u'projectId': u'bigquery-e2e'},
 u'kind': u'bigquery#queryResponse',
 u'rows': [{u'f': [{u'v': u'164656'}, {u'v': u'1.394988017942355E9'}]}],
 u'schema': {u'fields': [{u'mode': u'NULLABLE',
                          u'name': u'f0_',
                          u'type': u'INTEGER'},
                         {u'mode': u'NULLABLE',
                          u'name': u'f1_',
                          u'type': u'FLOAT'}]},
 u'totalBytesProcessed': u'1332943',
 u'totalRows': u'1'}
>>> pprint.pprint(response2)
{u'cacheHit': True,
 u'jobComplete': True,
 u'jobReference': {u'jobId': u'job_5mIaUK-wRS477BZoYTBipN18Qd8',
                   u'projectId': u'bigquery-e2e'},
 u'kind': u'bigquery#queryResponse',
 u'rows': [{u'f': [{u'v': u'164656'}, {u'v': u'1.394988017942355E9'}]}],
 u'schema': {u'fields': [{u'mode': u'NULLABLE',
                          u'name': u'f0_',
                          u'type': u'INTEGER'},
                         {u'mode': u'NULLABLE',
                          u'name': u'f1_',
                          u'type': u'FLOAT'}]},
 u'totalBytesProcessed': u'0',
 u'totalRows': u'1'}
```

Note that the number of bytes processed is 1332943 in the first query, but goes down to 0 in the second query. The `cacheHit` flag also goes from `False` to `True`.

The operation of the cache relies on the anonymous tables described in a previous section. Because BigQuery is free to give these tables any names that it wants, it generates a deterministic name from the query. To create this name, it takes a parsed version of the query that you're running and the last modified times of all of the tables involved in the query, and computes a cryptographic hash. It then uses this cryptographic hash as the name of the table. The next time the query is run, BigQuery checks for the existence of a table with this name, and if it already exists, just uses that in the response. You can see this in action by checking the destination table names of back-to-back query jobs that run the same query—they will be the same table.

Sometimes, you might want to run a query only if it is already cached. Maybe you want to avoid running up any more charges, or maybe the query takes a long time and you don't want to wait for the query to execute. If you set the `cre-ateDisposition` in the query configuration to CREATE_NEVER, this tells BigQuery that if the cached table doesn't exist, don't create it.

Returning Large Results

By default, BigQuery query responses are limited to 128 MB. There are some architectural reasons for this limitation, which are discussed in Chapter 9, "Understanding Query Execution," but there is also a common-sense justification as well: When you're dealing with Big Data, it is easy to generate giant results. Much of the time, however, you don't actually care about those giant results. For example, you might want to read some of the data from the table, so you run a "SELECT *" query on the table. If that table is 100 TB, you've just filled up the equivalent of dozens of hard drives just to read a few rows.

Sometimes, however, you really do want to run a query that generates a lot of output data. The way to tell BigQuery you're serious about wanting all that data is to set allowLargeResults to true in the query configuration. Note that because you're going to be writing out a lot of data, BigQuery wants to make sure you know in advance where that data is supposed to go. As a consequence, allowLargeResults requires the destinationTable parameter to be set on the job.

Query Priorities

By default, queries run at an INTERACTIVE priority, which is the highest priority level. However, sometimes you might not need the results of a query immediately. Maybe you're building a dashboard or computing some intermediate tables that will be queried later. In this case, you can specify BATCH as the query priority.

The advantage to running your query at BATCH priority is that you will not be subject to the same query limitations as when you run interactive queries. When you run a query at INTERACTIVE priority, BigQuery assumes there is someone waiting for the answer who will be grumpy if he doesn't get it soon, so if it can't process the query quickly, it will return an error. When running at BATCH priority, BigQuery tries to run the query if at all possible, even if it is going to take a long time.

There are a number of query quotas, described in the next section, designed to keep one user from taking too many compute resources at once. Batch queries are not subject to concurrent query quotas; however, if BigQuery can't run your query quickly or soon, it will just queue it up and run it when there is available space. This makes it easy to create a lot of batch queries at once without having to worry about rate limits.

Query Billing and Quotas

When you run a BigQuery query, you may be using several thousand machines and hundreds of thousands of disks. That hardware is expensive to buy, run, and maintain. Moreover, the cluster of machines you're using to run your query needs to be shared across multiple users who may be running queries at the same time. If someone at Company A is running giant queries, he shouldn't affect your ability to run queries. These factors are what drive the quota and billing policies for BigQuery.

What Does It Cost to Run My Query?

As of the time of publication, BigQuery queries cost $5 per TB scanned, whether they're for interactive or batch queries. These numbers are likely to change in the future; if they do change, they will probably go down. (This is based on assumptions made about costs of processing over time, not on any inside information about pricing plans.) If you care about how much your queries cost, you should check out the BigQuery pricing page here: `https://developers.google.com/bigquery/pricing`. Google also offers reserved instances for users who expect to run a lot of queries.

If the query cost is measured in dollars per byte scanned, how do you know how many bytes are going to be scanned? Every query in BigQuery does a full-table scan. That is, if the query requires reading even a single row from a table, BigQuery reads all the rows. Even if you add a `LIMIT` clause to a query, it still requires reading all the rows because `LIMIT` limits only the results, not the amount of data read in the first place. This behavior is different from traditional databases, which use indexes to avoid having to read portions of a table.

Although you do need to read all the rows of the table, you won't necessarily read all the columns. In practice, most queries actually read only a few columns from a table. Because BigQuery stores data in columnar format, it needs to read only the columns used in the query, and the other columns can be left alone. This is, again, different from a traditional relational database, where rows are stored together; so if you need to read part of a row, the database would need to read the whole thing.

BigQuery enables users to take advantage of the column-store format; you get charged for reading only the columns that are used in your query. Although the columns are stored compressed, the amount charged is based on the uncompressed size. One rationale behind charging for uncompressed data rather than compressed data size is that it makes it easier for people to understand how much they are being charged.

If you have two tables with the same number of rows and columns but different data but you are charged different amounts for querying them, this could lead to confusion. Moreover, if you went from highly compressible data to less-compressible data, you'd likely be surprised if you started getting charged more. Furthermore, because compression ratios can be influenced by ordering, if BigQuery moves data around and gets better or worse compression, you'd likely be surprised if the cost for querying the same data changed over time.

The byte cost of the data is related to the type of the data. Table 7.3 shows the column data type and the number of bytes that are charged:

Table 7.3: Bytes Charged by Column Type

TYPE	NUMBER OF BYTES
INTEGER	8
FLOAT	8
TIMESTAMP	8
BOOLEAN	1
STRING	Length of the string encoded as UTF-8 + 2 bytes
RECORD	0 (see RECORD fields in the following list)

In addition to the type-based byte count, following are some other rules for the byte cost calculation:

- NULL fields are considered size 0. That is, any NULL value in any field is "free."

- RECORD fields—that is, fields that have nested data—do not add to the cost. However, any field referenced inside the record counts normally toward the query cost.

- Repeated fields are billed as the sum of the cost of each of the repeated values. That is, if you have an integer that is repeated 10 times, you are charged for 80 bytes. If the repeated value count is 0, you are not charged for any bytes consumed.

The byte count used for query billing calculation is the same as the byte count used for storage; that is, you will be billed for storing all the columns in the table based on the same type-based byte count that is used for queries.

SELECT * CONSIDERED HARMFUL

When BigQuery was initially released, it didn't support `SELECT *`. This wasn't an oversight; it was intended to prevent users from unintentionally incurring unnecessary charges. If you consider how BigQuery works, you'll realize that `SELECT *` is going to tell BigQuery to read every byte in the table as fast as possible; that is going to be an expensive operation. If you have a terabyte of data in your table, `SELECT *` is going to cost you $5 (at current prices). Because `SELECT *` doesn't actually change your data, you could have just read it via `TableData.list()` for free.

The initial assumption was that if you wanted to read all the columns in the table, you would be willing to list all those columns to indicate that you're serious about it. However, several customers complained, so `SELECT *` was added. That said, most of the time, there are better ways to get the data you want than using `SELECT *`.

In the relational database world, it is common to run a `SELECT *` query to check out a table and try to understand the data in it. Maybe one column is always `NULL`, or you want to find out whether the `State` column uses abbreviations. If you're just trying to get a feel for your data, you can read the rows directly from the table (for free!) rather than running a query. If you have access to the `bq` command-line client, you can use the "`bq head tablename`" command. If you use the BigQuery Web UI, you can select the table and click the Details button, which shows you the first few rows. Both of these mechanisms use the underlying `TableData.list()` API, which is free, instead of running a query.

Sometimes people who run `SELECT *` actually do want to read all the data in the table. Maybe they want to make a copy of the table or want to download the table. If you use `SELECT *` for either of these reasons, there are better, less expensive ways to accomplish your goals.

If you want to download the table, consider an Export job, which can write out the table as CSV or JSON to a Google Cloud Storage location of your choosing. If you want to make a copy of the table, you can run a Copy job. Both these options are available from the command line or the web UI.

There are valid use cases in which you still want to use `SELECT *`. For example, maybe you want to filter your table and you want to create a smaller temporary table (as in `SELECT * FROM . . . WHERE . . .`). Using `SELECT *` in an inner query (as in `SELECT foo FROM (SELECT * from tablename)`, which will read only the `foo` column) is efficient because only the columns that are used in the outer query actually need to be read.

The bottom line is this: If you use `SELECT *` in your query, you should pause a moment and consider whether there is a better option.

Determining Query Cost

You can tell how much a query costs by reading the `totalBytesProcesed` field in the response to `Jobs.query()` or in the `statistics` field in the Job resource returned by `Jobs.get()`. Consider the following query, which counts the number of active ZIP codes with nonzero populations in each state:

```
>>> query = """
...     SELECT state, COUNT(*) AS cnt
...     FROM [bigquery-e2e:reference.zip_codes]
...     WHERE population > 0 AND decommissioned = false
...     GROUP BY state, ORDER BY cnt DESC
... """
```

This query reads three fields from the table `bigquery-e2e:reference.zip_codes`: `state`, `decommissioned`, and `population`. Here is a Python command that runs the query and returns only the number of bytes processed:

```
>>> service.jobs().query(
...         projectId=project_id,
...         body={'query': query, 'useQueryCache': False}
...         ).execute()['totalBytesProcessed']
u'552786'
```

With the `Tables.get()` method, you can see that the table has 42,522 rows:

```
>>> service.tables().get(
...         projectId=project_id,
...         datasetId='reference',
...         tableId='zip_codes').execute()['numRows']
u'42522'
```

If there were no `STRING` fields read by the query, the number of rows would be enough to determine the number of bytes processed. However, the `state` field has a variable length (it will be different in every row). The number of bytes processed per row should be the length of the `state` field plus 2 bytes, 8 bytes for the `population` field, and 1 byte for the `decommissioned` field. The following query computes the cost by adding up the field sizes:

```
>>> cost_query = """
... SELECT state_len + pop_len + decommissioned_len FROM (
...     SELECT SUM(LENGTH(state) + 2) AS state_len,
...     8 * COUNT(population) AS pop_len,
...     COUNT(decommissioned) AS decommissioned_len
...     FROM [bigquery-e2e:reference.zip_codes])
... """
>>> service.jobs().query(
...         projectId=project_id,
...         body={'query': cost_query}
...         ).execute()['rows'][0]['f'][0]['v']
u'552786'
```

This query returns the same value as the previous `totalBytesProcessed`: 552,876—or just over one-half a megabyte. Of course, running a query to compute how much a query costs is not particularly efficient because that query will cost you money, too. What if you want to find out how much a query will cost *before* actually running it? You can do this by running a query command that sets the `dryRun flag` to `true` in the query configuration, which tells BigQuery to not actually run the query.

```
>>> service.jobs().query(
...     projectId=project_id,
...     body={'query': query, 'dryRun': True}
...     ).execute()['totalBytesProcessed']
u'552786'
```

The same options for determining query cost are also available in the UI. If you click the green query validation icon under the query, you can see how many bytes would be processed if you ran the query. Likewise, after you run the query, it tells you how many bytes were processed when the query was run. Figure 7.1 shows both of these indicators.

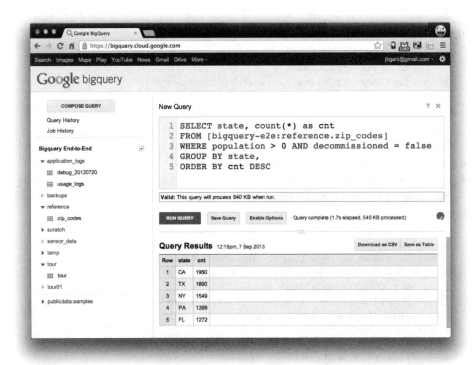

Figure 7.1: Query byte estimation

How Many Queries Can You Run?

BigQuery imposes two different types of limits on queries: quotas and rate limits. The quotas are the easiest to understand; you can run up to 20,000 queries a day that process up to 100 TB of data. (Note that although these numbers are subject to change, it is extremely unlikely that the quotas will be reduced.) If you're running lots of huge queries and those amounts aren't enough for you, don't worry—these caps (unlike some other quotas that BigQuery exposes) can be raised —they are put in place to prevent people from unintentionally running up a large bill quickly. That said, 100 TB of data processed is $500 (at current prices), so you can still spend a lot of money in a 24-hour period. If you want to run more queries, contact Google Cloud Support. They will likely want some more information about how you use BigQuery to make sure you get the most for your money and aren't abusing the system.

Query rate limits are designed to encourage users to spread their queries out throughout the day to smooth out load on the query clusters responsible for executing queries. These clusters, although large, are not infinite. To make sure that they remain responsive even when one customer performs a lot of queries, BigQuery imposes rate limits on how many queries a single customer can send at once. These rate limits are somewhat complex; they're designed to let users run giant queries if they want but also to more strongly limit queries that process a lot of data.

The simplest rate limit is the concurrent query rate limit. You can run up to 20 queries at once. The other rate limit is a bit more confusing: You can run 1 query of any size and up to 19 other queries that add up to 1 TB of simultaneous processing. The 1 TB portion of the limit can be thought of as a pipe with fixed capacity. When the pipe is full, you cannot start new queries. When one query completes, it opens up space in the pipe that you can fill with another query. The number of bytes processed by a query determines the amount of space the query takes in the pipe.

If the pipe was the only mechanism used, you could never run queries that processed more than 1 TB of data. To make sure customers can run larger queries, any query that doesn't fit in the 1 TB pipe fills the "large" query slot. This slot doesn't need to be taken up by an actual large query; if the pipe is full with two 500 GB queries and you run another query that processes only 1 MB that will go in the "large" query slot. That said, the "large" query slot is most useful when you run queries that are actually large. These limits do mean, however, that you can never run more than one large query at once.

If your query has already been cached, it won't need to actually be executed by the compute cluster, so it won't count against any of the rate limits. It *will* however, count toward your daily limit. This is to prevent people from abusing the cache. If you need to access the same data over and over again, you should use `TableData.list()` to read the data directly without running the query or caching the data locally.

Batch Query Limits

When you hit a rate limit in a query run at normal (INTERACTIVE) priority, your query will fail, and you will need to try again later. The reasoning is that INTERACTIVE queries are intended to be, well, interactive. The assumption is that if the queries were queued, people would experience degraded query performance and think the queries were just running slowly rather than realize that their queries are stuck in the queue.

Sometimes, however, you aren't actively waiting for the query to return; maybe you're updating a dashboard that runs a large number of queries once an hour. In these cases, it would be nice to just "fire and forget" your queries; that is, start all your queries at once and not have to worry about query pipes and large query sizes. Batch queries can help with this issue. When you run a query at BATCH priority, it is not subject to any of the rate limits discussed in the previous section. The only limitation is the total number of allowed batch queries per day, which is set at 10,000.

That said, when you run BATCH queries, BigQuery runs them at a lower priority. They are queued and execute when the system has spare capacity. To make sure that your queries make forward progress, if a batch query hasn't executed within 3 hours, it gets promoted to INTERACTIVE priority and will run as soon as it can be scheduled.

Other Query Limitations

BigQuery works on Big Data, so there should be no limitations, right? Well, not exactly. BigQuery can perform many operations faster than a relational database because of its architecture (which is described in more detail in Chapter 9). That said, there are some trade-offs—things that insert it may seem like it should do, but it doesn't do well.

Query Result Size Limitations

When you run a normal query in BigQuery, the response size is limited to 128 MB of compressed data. Sometimes, it is hard to know what 128 MB of compressed data means. Does it get compressed 2x? 10x? The results are compressed within their respective columns, which means the compression ratio tends to be very good. For example, if you have one column that is the name of a country, there will likely be only a few different values. When you have only a few distinct values, this means that there isn't a lot of unique information, and the column will generally compress well. If you return encrypted blobs of data, they will likely not compress well because they will be mostly random.

Often it is easy to write a query that returns large results without intending to; maybe you just ran a SELECT * query when you just wanted to see the first few rows of data. Or maybe you just wanted to see the top few rows from the query results. To prevent these types of queries from having to do a lot more work writing out massive query results, BigQuery defaults to failing when you run a query with massive results sets. If you don't need all the results, it is easy to just add a LIMIT 1000 to the end of the query, and you'll just get the first 1000 rows.

Although the rationale behind the query result size limitation is closely tied to the BigQuery architecture, at a high level it is because the entire query result must be returned from a single worker in the compute cluster. When an operation must be done on a single worker, it means that it doesn't scale out. For this reason, the size is limited.

Sometimes, however, you want to see results larger than 128 MB. You can work around this limitation by setting the `allowLargeResults` flag on the query. This causes each of the BigQuery workers to write their results out individually. Because the query results can be written in parallel for `allowLargeResults` queries, there are no limits to their size. The only limit is that you must specify a destination table for the query, so you will know where to refer to it afterward, and you can manage its lifetime. Even though results are written in parallel, writing large results can be significantly slower than writing out small ones.

Query Length and Table Limits

The maximum-allowed length of a query is 100,000 characters. It is unlikely that hand-written queries will ever get this long—usually the ones that bump up against the limit are machine-generated, often with certain sections repeated over and over again. If you find yourself wanting to write a query that is longer than 100 k, you might break it up into multiple subqueries.

There is also a 1000-table limit to the number of tables you can reference in a query. If you hit this limit, it is usually because your data is sharded too finely. You can read more about sharding strategies in Chapter 11, "Managing Data Stored in BigQuery." Moreover, the more tables you use in your query, the slower your query will run. For small numbers of tables (up to a few dozen) the slowdown will likely be imperceptible. But if you run queries against hundreds of tables, you'll likely be adding a couple of seconds to the query that are spent looking up information about the tables you've referenced.

BigQuery Query Language

The query language used by BigQuery is a variant of SQL. This section assumes some familiarity with SQL, but the concepts should be straightforward enough that you can write basic queries even if you've never seen a SELECT statement before. More advanced queries are covered in Chapter 9, after you have had a chance to digest the BigQuery query architecture.

If you're a SQL guru, you may see some of these examples and exclaim, "But that's not how it is done in the SQL-92 standard!" The last part of this section walks you through the differences between BigQuery SQL and standard SQL to shine some light on why certain syntax decisions were made. You'll also see some features, such as querying over nested and repeated fields, for which there is no standard.

BigQuery SQL in Five Queries

If it were done, when 'tis done, then 'twere well it were done quickly

—Macbeth

Rather than try to exhaustively define the BigQuery SQL language, we take a simpler approach: considering five simple queries that show off interesting BigQuery features and functionality. These queries build upon each other to compute word usage analysis for Shakespeare's plays. If you understand these five queries, you can use the same techniques to answer questions about your data.

Source Table Introduction

The queries in this section reference the public Shakespeare sample table (`publicdata:samples.shakespeare`). Although it is not a "big data" table—it weighs in at only 6.1 MB—it is useful for trying out queries because it is almost free to query it. You can run more than 170,000 queries against it and still be under your monthly "free query" quota.

The Shakespeare table contains the breakdown of word usage in Shakespeare plays and sonnets. The fields are described in Table 7.4.

Table 7.4: Shakespeare Table Schema

FIELD	TYPE	DESCRIPTION
word	STRING	Word used in a play. If the same word is used in multiple plays, it will have an entry for each play it appears in.
word_count	INTEGER	Number of times the word appears in the play
corpus	STRING	Name of the play, with spaces removed and in all lowercase. The sonnets get a single entry ("sonnets"), as do Shakespeare's other writings ("various").
corpus_date	INTEGER	Year the play was written, or 0 for "sonnets" and "various" because they were written across multiple years.

Query #1: Field Projection with Filter

```
SELECT LOWER(word) AS word, word_count AS frequency, corpus
FROM [publicdata:samples.shakespeare]
WHERE corpus CONTAINS 'king' AND LENGTH(word) > 5
ORDER BY frequency DESC
LIMIT 10
```

This query returns the most commonly used words (lowercased) longer than five letters, the count, and the corpus in which they appear, in any of Shakespeare's plays with "king" in the title. It doesn't, however, count frequency across plays; it just returns the count of the word per-play. Here are the results:

```
+------------+-----------+----------------+
|    word    | frequency |     corpus     |
+------------+-----------+----------------+
| falstaff   |       199 | 2kinghenryiv   |
| prince     |       192 | 1kinghenryiv   |
| richard    |       188 | kingrichardiii |
| gloucester |       182 | kingrichardiii |
| edward     |       181 | 3kinghenryvi   |
| falstaff   |       168 | 1kinghenryiv   |
| gloucester |       141 | kinglear       |
| richard    |       134 | kingrichardii  |
| warwick    |       122 | 3kinghenryvi   |
| cardinal   |       121 | kinghenryviii  |
+------------+-----------+----------------+
```

Now let's walk through the query, line by line:

```
SELECT LOWER(word) AS word, word_count AS frequency, corpus
```

All SQL queries that return data (and thus all BigQuery queries) start with the word SELECT, indicating that you're selecting data out of a table. After SELECT, you have comma-delimited field projections. These can be the raw fields (like word_count), computed values (like LOWER(word), which transforms word to lowercase), or aggregation functions (see the next query). You can also decide what you want the name of the field to be by using the AS keyword. For example, word_count AS frequency renames word_count to frequency in the output. Fields with computed values get assigned a unique field name, like f0_, which you may have seen in query results earlier in this chapter. In this query when we lowercased the word field, we also assigned an alias, so that it would get a user-friendly name, rather than f0_.

The next line is:

```
FROM [publicdata:samples.shakespeare]
```

After the selected field list comes the FROM clause, which instructs the query engine where to find the data. Fully specified BigQuery table names are designated by project_id_or_number:dataset_name.table_name. That said, you often don't need to use the fully specified name. The project ID defaults to the project that runs the query. If you don't like specifying the dataset name either and are using the API (as opposed to the query UI), you can set a default dataset in the job query configuration.

You may have noticed the funny brackets around the table name that aren't there in standard SQL. These are generally optional, but some table names require these quote characters to parse correctly. For example, if the table name was `shakespeare-plays` rather than `shakespeare`, the query parser would have a difficult time telling whether this was a subtraction operation (`shakespeare` minus `plays`) or a table name. To prevent parsing ambiguities, it is usually safest to just include the brackets.

Moving to the next line in the query, you have:

```
WHERE corpus CONTAINS 'king' AND LENGTH(word) > 5
```

This line contains the `WHERE` clause, which enables you to filter which rows are returned. In this case, the filter returns only rows where the `corpus` field contains "king" and the `word` field is longer than five letters. You can also call most functions here; the test for words longer than five letters in the name could have been written as `REGEXP_MATCH(word, '\\w{5}\\w+')`.

One of the last pieces of a query is the optional `ORDER BY` clause, which enables you to choose the sort order of the query results:

```
ORDER BY frequency DESC
```

One trick that can come in handy is to order by the index of the field in the `SELECT` clause. In this case, `frequency` is the second field mentioned, so this could have been written as `ORDER BY 2 DESC`.

`ORDER BY` has some limitations, however. At this time, it is the only non-parallelizable operation in BigQuery. That means that the entire sort operation must occur in a single query worker. To prevent that single worker from getting bogged down, there are limits on the size of result that an `ORDER BY` can process. If you get a Response Too Large error that you didn't expect, the `ORDER BY` clause may be the culprit.

Finally, you have a limit on the number of rows that are returned:

```
LIMIT 10
```

It is generally a good idea to add a limit to your query to prevent the dreaded Response Too Large error that is returned whenever the query result size is larger than 128 MB (unless, of course, you have set the `allow_large_results` option on your query).

If you're interested in why the Response Too Large error exists, Chapter 9 describes how query execution works and why result sizes for most queries are limited. For the most part, however, the maximum result size is not an issue because you usually care about only the first few results of your query. In addition, much of the time when the query returns too many results, it means that there was something wrong with the query—a filter condition was missing, or something about the data was unexpected.

Query #2: Aggregation

```
SELECT word, COUNT(*) AS corpora, SUM(word_count) AS total
FROM [publicdata:samples.shakespeare]
WHERE LENGTH(word) > 5
GROUP BY word
HAVING corpora >= 2 AND corpora <> total
ORDER BY corpora DESC, total DESC
LIMIT 20
```

Although it is interesting to see the word frequency in a single Shakespeare play, it may be more interesting to see how the word frequencies look across all the plays that Shakespeare wrote. Query #2 returns the words that Shakespeare uses in more than two plays and appear more than once in some play, and ranks them by how many plays they appear in and the number of total occurrences. It also includes a count of how many plays use the word and the total number of times the word is used across all Shakespeare's plays. The top results are displayed here:

```
+----------+---------+-------+
|   word   | corpora | total |
+----------+---------+-------+
| should   |      42 |  1505 |
| heaven   |      42 |   585 |
| myself   |      42 |   564 |
| himself  |      42 |   471 |
| though   |      42 |   445 |
| tongue   |      42 |   436 |
| thought  |      42 |   400 |
| thousand |      42 |   343 |
| things   |      42 |   321 |
| without  |      42 |   301 |
| reason   |      42 |   290 |
| cannot   |      41 |   745 |
| before   |      41 |   658 |
| honour   |      41 |   641 |
| better   |      41 |   587 |
| nothing  |      41 |   567 |
| little   |      41 |   503 |
| friends  |      41 |   480 |
| friend   |      41 |   440 |
| indeed   |      41 |   369 |
+----------+---------+-------+
```

The top result is "should," appearing a total of 1,505 times in all 42 corpora. Perhaps this means that Shakespeare enjoyed telling people what to do.

The `SELECT` statement, at first, doesn't look too different from query #1. You now have `SELECT word, COUNT(*) AS corpora, SUM(word_count) AS total` instead of `SELECT LOWER(word) AS word, word_count as frequency, corpus`.

However, the operations performed by these two lines are different; the key is in the functions that are called. In Query #1, the function called in the `SELECT` statement was `LOWER()`, which translates the field value to lower-case. The `LOWER()` function operates only on a single row at a time. In Query #2, however, you have `COUNT()` and `SUM()`. These are aggregation functions, which operate over a field in multiple rows at once.

If you take a query without a `GROUP BY` and add an aggregation function to the `SELECT` line, you'll get only a single result; that result will be the value of the aggregation function applied over the entire table. Note there are rules on mixing aggregation functions with nonaggregations: You either need aggregations everywhere or nowhere. If you think about this, it makes sense: If you compute the sum over a particular field, you want one result, but if you return the field as well, you want multiple results. Because you can't satisfy both of these constraints at once, this situation is disallowed.

You may notice, however, that we did have a mixture of aggregation functions and raw fields in the query; we are selecting `word` as well as `SUM()` and `COUNT()`. Why is this legal? You can legally perform this operation because of the `GROUP BY` clause: `GROUP BY word`. This causes the query engine to partition the table into buckets—one for each value of the `word` field. The aggregation functions then get applied to each of the buckets, outputting one row per distinct `word` value.

To give a concrete example, consider the word "bagpipe," which occurs twice in *Merchant of Venice*, once in *King Henry IV part 1* and once in *Winter's Tale*. When you group by `word`, you get a single bucket for "bagpipe." The `COUNT()` operation returns "3" because there are three plays in which it appears. The `SUM(word_count)` operation returns 4 since it appears four times across the three plays. In the query results, then, you'd get one row for "bagpipe" in the results: `{word: bagpipe, corpora: 3, total: 4}`.

There is one more line we haven't mentioned yet and doesn't look familiar from query #1:

```
HAVING corpora >= 2 AND corpora <> total
```

A `HAVING` clause is a lot like a `WHERE` clause; this one filters out any word that appears only in one corpus or once per corpus. The difference between a `WHERE` and `HAVING` clause is when the filtering is applied. A `WHERE` clause filters values in the original table; it gets applied before any aggregation is done. However, a `HAVING` clause applies filters after any aggregation, so you can use the aggregated fields. This HAVING clause uses the corpora and total fields, which are not fields on the original table—they were computed via aggregating row values.

Query #3: Joins

```
SELECT shakespeare.word AS word,
  SUM(shakespeare.word_count / english.count) AS rel_freq,
FROM [publicdata:samples.shakespeare] AS shakespeare
JOIN [bigquery-e2e:reference.word_frequency] AS english
ON shakespeare.word = english.word
GROUP BY word
ORDER BY rel_freq DESC
LIMIT 10
```

For the third query, we combine Shakespeare data with another data set— one that tells you overall frequency of words in the English language. This other data set contains two fields: word, which is the word in question, and word_frequency, which is the total number of times the word appeared when scanning a large corpus of English-language documents. This data came from a free word-frequency list compiled here: http://invokeit.wordpress.com/ frequency-word-lists/. We have downloaded the list and saved it in a table named bigquery-e2e:reference.word_frequency.

Armed with a list of overall English word frequency, you can now see how the word frequencies in Shakespeare compare to overall English-language usage. Query #3 computes the relative frequency between Shakespeare's usage and English-language usage.

We no longer have to filter based on word length because (we assume) the high-frequency words in the Shakespeare corpus like "the" will also be high-frequency in the English-language corpus and won't show up in the top of the results. If they do, that might be someone's doctoral thesis waiting to happen: "An analysis of the preponderance of definite article usage in Shakespeare. What does usage of the word 'the' in the Bard's early plays tell us about socio-economic conflict in Elizabethan England?"

The way to combine multiple data sets in this way in SQL is to use a JOIN operation. A JOIN takes two tables and matches every row in the first table against every row in the second table. The ON clause (required in BigQuery SQL) is a kind of filter that keeps only those rows where fields in the first table match fields in the second. BigQuery supports only equijoins, which is a fancy way of saying that you can perform a JOIN only when the values on the first table exactly match the values on the second. If the fields require coercion, you can usually use a nested SELECT, which is introduced in query #4, to make the values match up correctly.

When performing a JOIN, the JOIN clause follows the FROM clause:

```
FROM [publicdata:samples.shakespeare] AS shakespeare
JOIN [bigquery-e2e:reference.word_frequency] AS english
ON shakespeare.word = english.word
```

The FROM clause looks slightly different too—we've added a table alias. Because you now have more than one table involved in your query, you need to have a way to tell which table you're talking about when you reference a field. To do this, you can qualify the field name with the table name. For example, this query uses english.count to refer to the field count in the table with the alias english.

The JOIN clause is a lot like a FROM clause; you provide the name of the table you are joining against (or a nested SELECT statement, which is described in the next query). BigQuery supports both INNER and OUTER joins, but the description of these is deferred to chapter 10.

A feature that can come in handy when you join two large tables is the EACH keyword (which is not standard SQL). You can think of EACH as a hint to the BigQuery query optimizer that tells it you have two large tables. Chapter 9 gives more background on how this optimization works, but for now just remember that JOIN EACH can be useful for joining two large tables.

The results of this query are here:

```
+-----------+----------+
|   word    | rel_freq |
+-----------+----------+
| villany   |     49.0 |
| pass'd    |     34.0 |
| wrong'd   |     31.0 |
| learn'd   |     30.0 |
| begg'd    |     25.0 |
| offer'd   |     22.0 |
| mock'd    |     21.0 |
| prevail'd |     20.0 |
| wash'd    |     20.0 |
| he'll     |    19.75 |
+-----------+----------+
```

The highest relative frequency ratio between words in a Shakespeare play and words in modern English is the word "villainy." In fact, "villainy" is the only word in the top 10 that isn't a contraction (for example, "wrong'd"). The Ph.D. dissertation on this subject is left as an exercise for the reader.

Query #4: Subselects

```
SELECT shakespeare.word AS word,
  SUM(shakespeare.word_count / english.cnt) AS rel_freq,
```

```
FROM (
  SELECT LOWER(word) AS word,
    word_count / 945845 as word_count
  FROM [publicdata:samples.shakespeare]
  WHERE NOT REGEXP_MATCH(word, '[A-Z]+')
    AND NOT word CONTAINS "'"
  ) AS shakespeare
JOIN (
  SELECT LOWER(word) AS word,
    count / 121464569 AS cnt
  FROM [bigquery-e2e:reference.word_frequency]
  ) AS english
ON shakespeare.word = english.word
GROUP BY word
ORDER BY rel_freq DESC
LIMIT 100
```

One problem with query #3 is that the words in the Shakespeare table have inconsistent capitalization. That is, if the word appeared at the beginning of a sentence, its first letter is capitalized, but if it appears elsewhere in the sentence, it is in lowercase. We'd like to correct for this, so "Falchion" and "falchion" show up as the same word. To do this, we can just convert the word to lowercase. Unfortunately, we need to do this conversion before the JOIN operation takes place, which means we need to use a subselect.

We change our original FROM clause into a nested select statement that computes the lowercase word. We make one other change: We filter out words that are all caps. In our Shakespeare dataset, names of characters display in all caps, such as "HAMLET." Because names of characters are going to show up in the plays more often than in a wider dataset, to prevent these from distorting the results, we filter them out. We also filter out anything with an apostrophe—Shakespeare made up a lot of contractions that don't exist in modern spelling—"wrong'd," for example—and these aren't particularly interesting to report.

As a bonus, we've also applied the same lowercase conversion to the word_ frequency corpus. In this case, it wasn't necessary, but we've added it here to show that you can also perform subselects in the JOIN clause too. We've also divided the counts by the number of rows in each table, so that neither table is weighted more heavily than the other.

Query #4 starts to look complicated. But if you compare it to query #3, it isn't that different. This is a common pattern to use in BigQuery, maybe more so than in other dialects of SQL. You start with a simple SQL query, and start nesting subselects when you need to convert or aggregate values. It can make it harder to read the query, but can allow you get a lot done in a single query without creating temporary tables.

For those playing along at home, you'll notice that "villainy" is still in the #1 spot, but some other interesting words show up near the top: "trencher," "falchion," "tapster," "fitly," and "spritely"—these all sound like good names for startups.

```
+----------------+--------------------+
|      word      |      rel_freq      |
+----------------+--------------------+
| villany        |  6292.536177703534 |
| amain          | 1926.2865850112858 |
| severally      |  1797.867479343867 |
| trencher       | 1412.6101623416098 |
| beseeming      | 1284.1910566741906 |
| clamours       | 1284.1910566741906 |
| falchion       | 1027.3528453393526 |
| swinged        | 1027.3528453393526 |
| strucken       |  898.9337396719336 |
| bewray         |  898.9337396719335 |
| wooers         |  898.9337396719335 |
| cozen          |  770.5146340045145 |
| fitly          |  770.5146340045145 |
...
| tapster        |  770.5146340045144 |
...
| spritely       |  642.0955283370954 |
...
```

Query #5: Table Unions

```sql
SELECT shakespeare.word AS word,
  (shakespeare.word_count / english.freq) AS rel_freq,
FROM (
  SELECT LOWER(word) AS word, SUM(word_count) AS word_count
  FROM [publicdata:samples.shakespeare]
  WHERE NOT REGEXP_MATCH(word, '[A-Z]+')
  AND NOT word CONTAINS "'"
  GROUP BY word
  ) AS shakespeare
JOIN (
  SELECT word, SUM(freq) AS freq
  FROM (
    SELECT LOWER(word) AS word, FLOAT(count) AS freq
    FROM [bigquery-e2e:reference.word_frequency]
  ), (
    SELECT LOWER(first) AS word, sum(cell.match_count)/1583 AS freq
    FROM [publicdata:samples.trigrams]
    GROUP BY word)
  GROUP BY word
  ) AS english
ON shakespeare.word = english.word
ORDER BY rel_freq DESC
LIMIT 100
```

WARNING   This query processes 54 GB of data, which would cost $0.27 at current BigQuery prices. This might not break the bank, but you also might want to think twice before running it too often.

This query looks a bit intimidating—five SELECT statements, one JOIN, three GROUP BYS, and a lot of parentheses. But if you look at it carefully, you've already seen just about everything used in this query, with a single exception: We combine two SELECT statements together with a comma. This is addressed in a minute, but first consider what this query does and why you'd want to use it.

If you look at the actual numbers returned from query #4, you'll notice something surprising: The ratio between the number of times "villainy" appears in Shakespeare to the total number of times it appears in a wider English-language corpus is 49:1. That is 49 times more total, not 49 times more frequently. This means that "villainy" probably appeared only one or two times in the word_frequency corpus, but it appeared a lot more often in Shakespeare. Clearly, the Shakespeare texts weren't part of the corpus used.

This problem can be fixed by adding another data source that contains the Shakespeare texts. The trigrams table in the BigQuery public sample dataset contains every three-word combination in the English language that was found during the Google Books book-scanning project. There are 68 billion rows in the table, representing 192 billion scanned words. BigQuery is supposed to work on Big Data, but so far we've mostly used toy tables; this query should test BigQuery's handling of a real Big Data table.

The first step, as you can see in the added inner query, is rolling up the trigrams to individual words. The table has three fields representing the word in the trigram: first, second, and third. We're going to consider only the first element in the trigram, and sum up how many times it appears throughout the corpus. The subquery follows:

```
SELECT LOWER(first) AS word, sum(cell.match_count)/1583 AS freq
FROM [publicdata:samples.trigrams]
GROUP BY word)
```

This should look very familiar, although the appearance of the constant 1583 may be surprising. This number is the ratio of the number of total elements in the trigrams corpus to the number of elements in the word_count corpus. We scale the frequencies this way so that the trigrams dataset doesn't dwarf the importance of the word_count corpus; we'd like to treat them as equals, despite one having vastly more data.

The next step is combining the two tables, word_count and trigrams. Query #5 shows how to combine these tables using a table union. The syntax for a table union is simple: concatenate two or more tables together with a comma (for example, FROM table1, table2, . . .).

If you're a SQL guru, you're probably more than a little bit surprised by this—there is already an accepted standard interpretation of tables separated by commas—an implicit JOIN. BigQuery, perhaps unfortunately, changes this convention to mean UNION ALL. This nonstandard behavior is discussed in the next section.

In this query, we want to combine the data from the two tables but they have different column names. To get the column names to match up, we use a sub-select to lowercase the words and change the column names. Then we group by word and sum the word counts to get a single effective table that has the combined frequency data.

There is another change in this query, related to a potential problem with numerical precision when summing the ratios. To fix this, we changed the first subselect to compute the total word frequency across all plays, so there will be a single row per word. We moved the GROUP BY inside that sub-select, so the ratio computation is done only once per word and not as an aggregation.

If you look at these results, you'll find that Shakespeare uses some strange words, indeed:

```
+-------------+---------------------+
|    word     |       rel_freq      |
+-------------+---------------------+
| holp        |   207.0076923076923 |
| pricket     |   79.81512605042016 |
| unpeople    |   57.56363636363636 |
| burgonet    |   55.54385964912281 |
| therewithal | 55.435797665369655  |
| nonino      |              50.656 |
| extemporal  |   46.10679611650485 |
| hungerly    |   45.66346153846154 |
| prains      |   42.78378378378378 |
| vizards     |  40.851612903225806 |
+-------------+---------------------+
```

According to the Internet, "holp" is an archaic form of the past tense of "to help," as in "My colleague was hungerly trying to learn BigQuery, so I donned my burgonet, and thus equipped with my vizards, by extemporal query editing, I *holp* him therewithal." This sentence would probably make more sense to someone living in Elizabethan England.

Differences from Standard SQL

There are a number of differences between BigQuery SQL and standard SQL. The reasons for these differences primarily fall into three buckets: things that were more difficult to implement in a parallel query engine (for example, an exact COUNT DISTINCT), syntax shortcuts for expected usage patterns (for example, comma as UNION ALL rather than JOIN), and extra features that aren't available in standard SQL (for example, handling of nested and repeated fields). Some of the principal differences from standard SQL are listed in this section.

Comma as UNION ALL

This is perhaps the most confusing quirk of BigQuery for people with a background in SQL. In most variants of SQL, if you specify "... FROM table1, table2," this is actually an implicit JOIN operation. However, in BigQuery, the previous operation is UNION ALL; that is, BigQuery performs the query as if there was one large table with all the data from both table1 and table2.

You may be wondering why this behavior was chosen. When Dremel (the query engine behind BigQuery) was first developed, JOIN operations were not supported. However, there were a lot of users who had tables broken up by day; they often wanted to query across several of them. To make the syntax for querying across multiple tables as simple as possible, the Dremel SQL designers used a comma-separated list of tables to concatenate tables. This syntax wasn't ambiguous because JOIN didn't exist. Now that JOIN is supported, however, the syntax creates confusion. However, because there are now a lot of users who rely on the comma-separated list to mean UNION ALL, it would be difficult to change.

JOIN EACH and GROUP EACH

If you run a query that has a GROUP BY operation where the number of resulting rows is high, the query may fail with a Resources Exceeded error. Likewise, if you try to do a JOIN operation on two large tables, you may get the same error. In both of these cases, the EACH keyword can come to the rescue.

EACH is a hint to the BigQuery query optimizer that instructs it to perform a *shuffle operation*. Shuffle is described in detail in Chapter 9, but for now it can be described as sorting the data to process more of the data in parallel. At some time in the future, BigQuery may be smart enough to infer the table size so that you won't need to use a qualifier, but as of this writing, the EACH keyword is required when performing "big" JOINs or certain GROUP BYs.

It isn't recommended to just add EACH to all your queries; for many types of queries (JOIN of one large table against a smaller one, or GROUP BY with only a few distinct values), using EACH may be significantly slower. A reasonable rule of thumb is that if the smaller table in the JOIN is more than 1 million rows, or the GROUP BY has more than a million distinct values, you're probably better off using EACH.

Approximate Values: COUNT DISTINCT

Another BigQuery deviation from standard SQL is the behavior of COUNT DISTINCT, which returns only an approximate value. This is often surprising to users who want to get an exact count of the number of distinct values in a column. The fewer the number of distinct values, the better the approximation will be; if less than 1000, the number will be exact.

BigQuery doesn't provide an exact value by default because the exact value is surprisingly difficult to calculate for a large table. To know whether you've seen a value before, you have to keep track of all values that you've seen; this is expensive and difficult to do unless you first sort the data.

If you're not content with the approximate value, you have two options: Supply a bucket count as an optional argument to COUNT(DISTINCT field, [buckets]), or rewrite your query to perform a GROUP EACH BY and count the results.

For example, say your original query is:

```
SELECT COUNT(DISTINCT word)
FROM [publicdata:samples.shakespeare]
```

The exact value is 32,786, but the value returned by the preceding query is 31,719. One option for rewriting the query is just to specify a bucket count larger than the expected value. There are only approximately 50,000 words in the English language, so a bucket count of 50,000 should be reasonable.

```
SELECT COUNT(DISTINCT word, 50000)
FROM [publicdata:samples.shakespeare]
```

This gives the exact value. Specifying a higher bucket count has limitations; however, each bucket takes up memory, and too many buckets can cause a Resources Exceeded error. If you want to remove any uncertainty, you can perform a GROUP BY operation:

```
SELECT COUNT(*)
FROM (
  SELECT word
  FROM [publicdata:samples.shakespeare]
  GROUP BY word)
```

The downside to the GROUP BY approach is that it may make it more difficult to compute multiple values in a single query; that is, if you were also trying to compute the sum of the word_count field as well, you'd have to make sure that count would propagate through the GROUP BY, as in:

```
SELECT COUNT(word), SUM(word_count)
FROM (
  SELECT word, SUM(word_count) AS word_count
  FROM [publicdata:samples.shakespeare]
  GROUP BY word)
```

Size Limitations in Ordered Results

In most SQL databases, you can add an ORDER BY X clause to the end of your query, and no matter what, your results will come back in a prescribed order. When you have large data, however, sorting is expensive.

If you run an ORDER BY operation on too many values, BigQuery returns a Too Many Results error. This error often confuses people because ORDER BY is often combined with a LIMIT clause limiting the number of results. How can there be too many results if you limit it to 10? The problem is that the ORDER BY must be done over the entire result set before the limit is applied—the query engine can't just take 10 random results and return those in order.

There is only a partial workaround for the size limitation in the ORDER BY operation. Much of the time when you run a query that has an ORDER BY operation, you're interested only in the first few results. You want to find the highest value, or the most frequent, and so on. If you run queries that have this pattern but have a large number of potential results, you can use the TOP function. Following is an example of rewriting a query with an ORDER BY into a TOP query:

```
SELECT corpus, COUNT(*) AS total
FROM [publicdata:samples.shakespeare]
GROUP BY corpus
ORDER BY total DESC
LIMIT 20
```

You can rewrite as
```
SELECT TOP(corpus, 20), COUNT(*) AS total
FROM [publicdata:samples.shakespeare]
```

Note that TOP() is only approximate; however if you are just looking for the most common values, it will virtually always give you the ones you want.

Nested and Repeated Fields

The BigQuery data model supports nested and repeated fields; neither of these are part of standard SQL. Nested fields are simply fields that are nested into records; for the most part they are indistinguishable from fields with "." in the name. Repeated fields are a bit funkier, however. They allow you to have a single field contain multiple values of the same type. Fields can be both nested and repeated; this means that a single field can have an array of records.

Because there wasn't a standard syntax for SQL queries over nested and repeated data, the BigQuery team opted for query simplicity rather than language rigor. That means that BigQuery tries to "do the right thing" with respect to your query and often makes queries over nested and repeated data convenient. For example, when you use a repeated field in a GROUP BY clause in a query, the repeated field is automatically flattened. (That is, for each repeated value, the entire row is repeated.) However, sometimes nested and repeated data can be awkward or surprising. For instance, seemingly trivial changes to the query can cause an automatic flattening. Multiple repeated fields can also be difficult to manage in a single query.

That said, having the ability to query over nested and repeated fields is extremely powerful and can be a way to write much more convenient queries than if you had to store your data in a less natural format. You can read about how to query over your nested and repeated data in Chapter 10.

Summary

This chapter showed you how to run queries via the BigQuery API and how to write queries in the BigQuery SQL language. You should now be comfortable with the various options for executing queries; you should know how to set destination tables and priorities; and you should know how to get query results larger than 128 MB. This chapter also discussed the quotas and limits imposed by BigQuery. Forthcoming chapters delve into the architecture, which hopefully can provide some rationale behind those limits.

The BigQuery SQL language should be more familiar; you went through several example queries that were similar to queries you might want to run on your own, and differences between BigQuery SQL and SQL dialects you may be more familiar with were highlighted.

By this point in the book, you've walked through all the major pieces of BigQuery, and you should be ready to start developing applications that leverage the service. The next chapter ties together the pieces and builds a log-processing application with what you've learned so far.

Putting It Together

The first one-half of the book describes the mechanics of how you interact with BigQuery at different layers of the programming stack; covering the low level HTTP transport all the way up to the command-line and web client. The following chapters cover more advanced uses of BigQuery by exploring the query language and how to assemble basic operations into useful solutions. This chapter in the middle of the book is a bit of a diversion. It covers the construction of a toy application involving Android, App Engine, and a few JavaScript frameworks—all of which are quite independent of BigQuery. The point of building an application involving these pieces and BigQuery is to concretely demonstrate how the service can be leveraged in a real application.

One important caveat is that the application code is not actually production code. Production code with all the requirements of testability and comprehensive error handling tends to obscure the core functionality. The code samples that accompany this chapter provide a complete application while allowing you to quickly see how the various pieces fit together. Even the discussion in the chapter focuses on the parts where the different components integrate with each other because those tend to be the most interesting. Also, no attempt has been made to strictly adhere to the best practices of any of the platforms other than BigQuery. After all, this is a book about BigQuery, and a number of excellent books and online resources for working with Android and App Engine are available. To summarize, this chapter can be a source of ideas for how you can incorporate BigQuery into your applications to enable easy data analyses rather than source code to be incorporated directly. Portions of the code are also called out that can be made more robust as a useful exercise.

This chapter appears in the middle of the book rather than at the end because it presents concrete use cases for the solutions described in the following chapters that cover advanced BigQuery features. If you are not interested in the details of the application, you may want to at least read the first section explaining its functionality because it provides some context for the material in later chapters.

A Quick Tour

The introduction to the book discussed the question of what qualifies as *Big Data*. One possible criterion was data volumes that exceed the capacity of a single machine to process in an acceptable amount of time and hence require some distributed processing scheme. One way to generate this volume would be to have a single machine generating data for a long time. The more common way you might end up in this situation is when the data generation is distributed. Now that connected devices are ubiquitous, it is common for applications to have a million or more clients. Even if each client generates only a couple records per day, with these kinds of numbers, it is easy for the data volumes to quickly exceed the bounds of a single machine. As homage to the wild rise of mobile devices, the sample application involves a mobile app that periodically records the state of the phone and pushes it into the cloud for analyses.

The mobile component of the application is an Android app. The app has a simple management panel that handles registering the device for log collection, manages the state of log collection, and selects an interval for logging, as shown in Figure 8.1. When logging is enabled, a background task is scheduled to periodically sample the state of the phone and ship it to the cloud component of the application.

You can inspect the logs being recorded by selecting the Last Log menu item, which brings up a panel containing the last record that was posted as a JSON value. Before you can proceed with registration, you need to visit the web application.

The Google App Engine hosted web application implements the registration service that maintains a list of registered devices for each user. You can find this at `https://bigquery-sensors.appspot.com/manage`.

You may download and install the mobile app by selecting the Google Playstore link. The device management page requires that you are logged in to the website (using Google managed sign on). The page, as shown in Figure 8.2, lists the set of devices you have registered with the application and a registration code to add a new device. You need to enter this code into the mobile app to register it with the service before you can enable monitoring on your phone. Deleting a device from the list causes the application to stop accepting data from the device. The descriptions that follow do not require you to have the application installed or your device registered, so feel free to skip these steps.

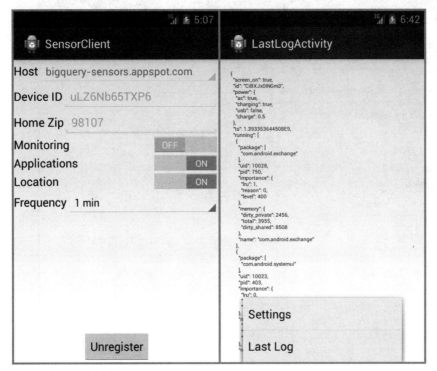

Figure 8.1: Mobile client

This is a good time to describe the type of information that will be transferred to the service. The logs include the following information about your phone:

- Device ID
- Screen status
- Battery and power
- System memory usage
- Location information
- Running applications

The version of the application available on the site records only the *coarse* location information, whereas the version built from the sample code records *fine* location information. This is a fair amount of information, but the app does allow you to disable recording location and application information. Still, if you have concerns, you should definitely consider building your own version of the application and logging to your private instance for experimenting with this sample application.

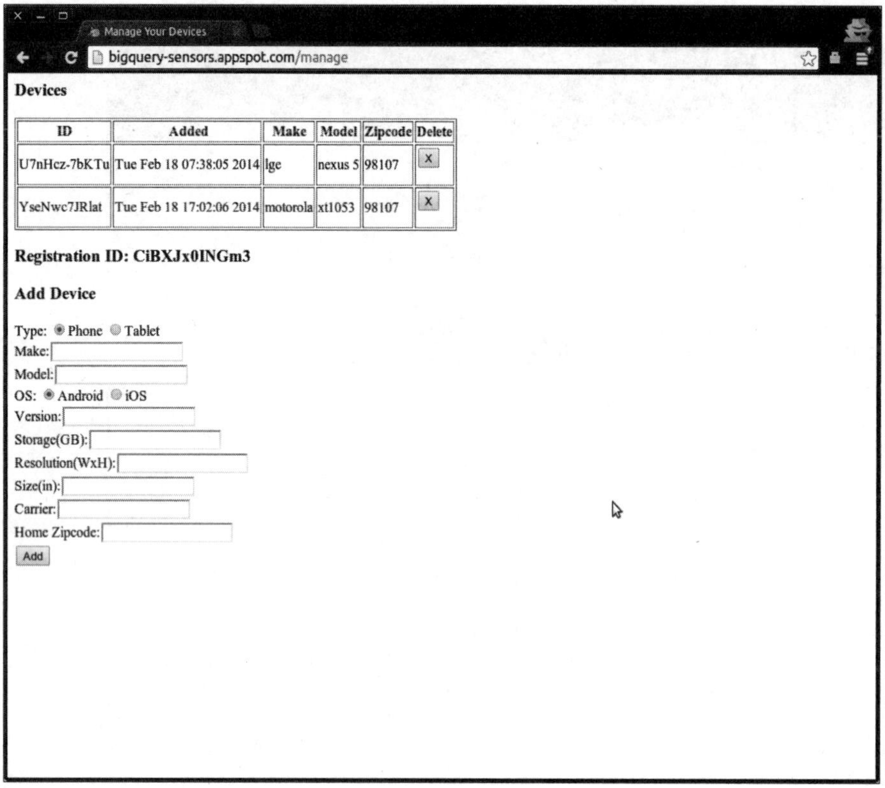

Figure 8.2: Device registration

The last part of the application is a dashboard that summarizes the logs being received by the application. Although the first two parts described dealt with getting data into BigQuery, this part deals with extracting and rendering a useful summary of the data. The dashboard is again built on Google App Engine and is available at: https://bigquery-sensors.appspot.com/console.

The page consists of a collection of graphs and tables that provide an aggregated view of the state of the phones registered with the service. Of course, aggregated information is interesting, but a key strength of BigQuery is the capability to perform interactive queries over a large number of records without any pre-aggregation. To highlight this capability, the application generates reports for individual phones registered under your account. You can navigate to these records from the device management page previously mentioned by clicking the device ID for the registered device. This takes you to a page with a summary of the records associated with that device.

GIT REPOSITORY

The source for the sample application is included in the download for this chapter. However, we expect it to evolve over time, so we have also made it available as an online repository at `https://code.google.com/p/bigquery-e2e/`.

You can download the latest version from the site as a zip file, or if you have git installed, you can check out the source code.

```
$ GOOGLE_USER='<your Google username>'
$ git clone https:/${GOOGLE_USER}@code.google.com/p/bigquery-e2e/
```

We would be happy to receive patches!

In the process of building the sample application, we were frequently reminded that interesting data is often sensitive data. Whenever a large amount of detailed information is collected, it must be carefully managed. We have ensured that the top-level dashboard, shown in Figure 8.3, contains only aggregated data and that only the owners of devices have access to device level dashboards. Also, the datasets containing the logs are not publicly shared because it is hard to predict what kind of information can be extracted by running queries. We encourage you to deploy your own instance of the application if you want to try it in depth.

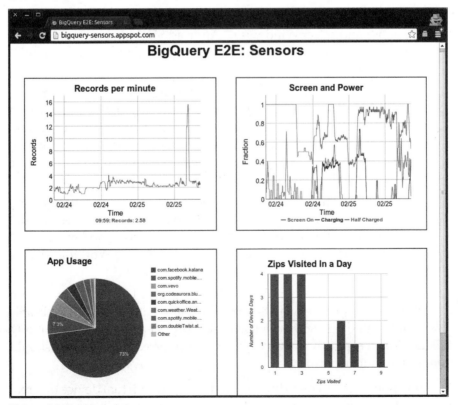

Figure 8.3: Dashboard

Now that you have some idea of what the application does, you can peel back the covers and see how the individual components are put together. The next few sections are organized to roughly correspond with the description of the parts given in this section. Other than a few points of integration, the individual pieces are fairly independent, so you can focus on the ones that are most interesting to you.

Mobile Client

The Android platform was chosen for the sample, so you need to install the developer tools for building Android applications. The current Android Development Kit is a tool chain that integrates with the Eclipse IDE. A version is also available for IntelliJ, referred to as Android Studio, which is available as an early access preview at this time. For the sample in this book we have supplied an Eclipse project that you can import to build the code and experiment with the application. If you do not already have Eclipse installed, first you need to download and install the IDE from `http://www.eclipse.org`. You can download and install the development kit from `http://developer.android.com/sdk/`. Detailed installation instructions are available on the site, which we will not bother reproducing here. The sample application targets version 17 of the Android runtime.

1. Start Eclipse and select Windows ➪ Android SDK Manager and ensure that version 17 of the SDK is installed. It is fine if more than one SDK version is installed.

2. After you have the SDK installed, create a new Eclipse project that imports the sample application code. The recommended practice for Android projects is to include the Eclipse project settings in your source code (and revision control system), so it is included in the download for this chapter. After unpacking the download for the chapter, you can find the source code for the mobile client under `ch08/sensors/client`.

3. To create the project in Eclipse, select File ➪ Import ➪ Android/Existing Android Code into Workspace. In the dialog that appears, set the root directory to the full path to the client source directory, and ensure that both Copy Projects into Workspace and Add Project to Working Sets are unchecked.

4. Clicking Finish creates a project called SensorsClient in your Eclipse workspace. The project defaults to building automatically. You can disable automatic building and instead select the project and then use Project ➪ Build Project explicitly. If everything is set up correctly, the project should build without any errors.

The built application needs to be deployed either to a virtual device or a real phone. A virtual device is convenient for testing and is straightforward to set up. Selecting Window ⇨ Android Virtual Device Manager brings up a dialog listing configured devices and controls to edit them and create new ones. You can find instructions on managing virtual devices at `http://developer.android.com/tools/devices/`.

The sample application targets SDK version 14 as the minimum supported version, so the main setting to pay attention to when creating the device is to select a target with a SDK version equal to or higher than 14. For reference, the app was developed using a Nexus 4 virtual device with Android 4.2.2 (API version 17). It is also fairly simple to test the application on a real device. Detailed instructions are available at `http://developer.android.com/tools/device.html`.

These online resources are part of the Android developer website, which is a useful destination if you are interested in experimenting with the sample mobile client. With the SDK set up you can start exploring the source code.

Monitoring Service

The source code for the project is spread across four Java source files and a handful of XML files that contain UI resources. The core part of the application is a background service that periodically wakes up, captures the state of the phone, and ships it to the cloud component of the application by performing an HTTP POST operation. This functionality is implemented in the files:

- `MonitoringService.java`
- `CommandRunner.java`

The rest of the files implement the user interface for the application and handle the registration of the device. In the context of BigQuery and analytics, this background service, shown in Listing 8.1, is the most interesting part of the application and demonstrates a design you may end up reusing in your clients.

Listing 8.1: MonitoringService.java

```java
public class MonitoringService extends IntentService {
  // ELIDED
  private String deviceId;
  private CommandRunner commandRunner;
  private PendingIntent pendingIntent;
  private JSONObject lastRecord;
  // ELIDED

  public void start(String deviceId, int intervalMillis,
      CommandRunner commandRunner) {
    stop();
    this.deviceId = deviceId;
    this.commandRunner = commandRunner;
    // ELIDED
    pendingIntent = PendingIntent.getService(this, 0, logIntent, 0);
```

continues

Listing 8.1 *(continued)*

```java
        AlarmManager alarm =
            (AlarmManager) getSystemService(Context.ALARM_SERVICE);
        alarm.setRepeating(AlarmManager.RTC_WAKEUP, Calendar.getInstance()
                .getTimeInMillis(), intervalMillis, pendingIntent);
    }

    public void stop() {
        if (pendingIntent != null) {
            AlarmManager alarm =
                (AlarmManager) getSystemService(Context.ALARM_SERVICE);
            alarm.cancel(pendingIntent);
            pendingIntent = null;
        }
        deviceId = null;
    }


    @Override
    protected void onHandleIntent(Intent intent) {
        if (intent.filterEquals(logIntent)) {
            try {
                JSONObject newRecord = buildRecord();
                appendToLog(newRecord);
                lastRecord = newRecord;
                Intent update = new Intent(LOG_UPDATE);
                sendBroadcast(update);
                transmit(newRecord);
            } catch (JSONException ex) {
                Log.e(TAG, "Failed to build JSON record.", ex);
            } catch (IOException ex) {
                Log.e(TAG, "Could not save record.", ex);
            }
        }
    }

    private void transmit(final JSONObject record) {
        AsyncTask<Void, Void, Void> task =
            new AsyncTask<Void, Void, Void>() {
            @Override
            protected Void doInBackground(Void... params) {
                try {
                    // Performs the HTTP operation to transmit the record.
                    commandRunner.run("record", record);
                } catch (ErrorResult e) {
                    Log.e(TAG, e.getError() + ": " + e.getMessage());
                }
                return null;
            }
        };
```

```
      task.execute();
  }

  private JSONObject buildRecord() throws JSONException {
    SharedPreferences prefs =
        getSharedPreferences(ManageActivity.PREFS, MODE_PRIVATE);
    JSONObject newRecord = new JSONObject();
    newRecord.put("id", deviceId);
    newRecord.put("ts",
      ((double) Calendar.getInstance().getTimeInMillis()) / 1000.0);
    newRecord.put("screen_on",
      ((PowerManager)
       getSystemService(Context.POWER_SERVICE)).isScreenOn());
    newRecord.put("power", getPowerStatus());
    ActivityManager activityManager =
        (ActivityManager) getSystemService(ACTIVITY_SERVICE);
    newRecord.put("memory", getMemory(activityManager));
    if (prefs.getBoolean(ManageActivity.LOCATION_STATE, true) &&
        lastLocation != null) {
      newRecord.put("location", getLocation(lastLocation));
    }
    if (prefs.getBoolean(ManageActivity.APPLICATIONS_STATE, true)) {
      newRecord.put("running", getRunning(activityManager));
    }
    return newRecord;
  }
  // ELIDED

  private void appendToLog(JSONObject record) throws IOException {
    File currentLog = new File(getCacheDir(), CURRENT_LOG);
    if (currentLog.exists() && currentLog.length() > MAX_LOG_SIZE) {
      File lastLog = new File(getCacheDir(), LAST_LOG);
      if (lastLog.exists()) {
        if (!lastLog.delete()) {
          Log.e(TAG, "Could not delete old log file: "
              + lastLog.getPath());
          return;
        }
      }
      if (!currentLog.renameTo(lastLog)) {
        Log.e(TAG, "Could not rotate: " + currentLog.getPath());
        return;
      }
    }
    FileOutputStream log = new FileOutputStream(currentLog, true);
    log.write(record.toString().getBytes());
    log.write('\n');
    log.close();
  }
}
```

When users interact with an application, there is often a stream of interesting events developers would like to capture. Shipping these events from the client to a backend service needs to be done with some care. Performing blocking network operations on user interface threads is entirely taboo because it can cause the user interface to become unresponsive. Even issuing individual asynchronous I/O operations is usually not optimal because it leads to small, frequent, and concurrent network operations that each have fixed HTTP and network overheads that can lead to inefficient usage of network bandwidth.

In Android you can instead implement a background logging service for your application, as done in the sample application. This allows you to optimize the transmission of the logs, for example, by batching them into larger requests, ensuring only a single request is outstanding at any given time and controlling the rate at which requests are initiated.

In Listing 8.1 you can see the main methods that control the life cycle of the service. The `start(...)` method registers periodic alarms with the operating system that cause the `onHandleIntent(...)` method to be invoked periodically. The `stop()` method cancels the alarm using the handle saved when the alarm was registered. The log is captured and sent in the `onHandleIntent(...)` method, but notice that the actual transmission of the record that occurs in the `transmit(...)` method is wrapped in an `AsyncTask`. The reason for this additional complexity is that `onHandleIntent(...)` is invoked on the event handling thread, and we want to avoid stalling the event handling thread. Even for a background service, it is important to avoid blocking on the event handling thread because that would make the service appear to be unresponsive to the OS.

This background logging service is not complex because the data is generated in the background service and on a fixed schedule. A useful exercise would be to modify the implementation so that it can batch records rather than transmit each one independently.

Next turn your attention to the `buildRecord()` method that collects the data to be logged. Observe that we use the Android JSON library to construct a `JSONObject` with the data. This is convenient because it ends up in a format that is directly compatible with what the BigQuery API expects. The table schema we are targeting is shown in Listing 8.2. In the `appendToLog(JSONObject record)` method, we append the records to a log file on the device. This is convenient for testing because the resulting file can be extracted from the virtual device and loaded into BigQuery using the load operation because the log file is correctly formatted as newline-delimited JSON. If the load job succeeds, you know that you are generating records with the correct fields for the table you are aiming to fill.

Listing 8.2: Log table schema

```
[
  {"name": "id", "type": "string", "mode": "required"},
  {"name": "ts", "type": "timestamp", "mode": "required"},
```

```
    {"name": "screen_on", "type": "boolean"},
    {"name": "power", "type": "record", "fields": [
      {"name": "charging", "type": "boolean"},
      {"name": "usb", "type": "boolean"},
      {"name": "ac", "type": "boolean"},
      {"name": "charge", "type": "float"}
    ]},
    {"name": "memory", "type": "record", "fields": [
      {"name": "available", "type": "integer"},
      {"name": "used", "type": "integer"},
      {"name": "low", "type": "boolean"}
    ]},
    {"name": "location", "type": "record", "fields": [
      {"name": "ts", "type": "timestamp"},
      {"name": "accuracy", "type": "float"},
      {"name": "provider", "type": "string"},
      {"name": "lat", "type": "float"},
      {"name": "lng", "type": "float"},
      {"name": "altitude", "type": "float"},
      {"name": "bearing", "type": "float"},
      {"name": "speed", "type": "float"},
      {"name": "country", "type": "string"},
      {"name": "state", "type": "string"},
      {"name": "zip", "type": "string"}
    ]},
    {"name": "running", "type": "record", "mode": "repeated", "fields": [
      {"name": "name", "type": "string"},
      {"name": "pid", "type": "integer"},
      {"name": "uid", "type": "integer"},
      {"name": "memory_trim", "type": "integer"},
      {"name": "importance", "type": "record", "fields": [
        {"name": "level", "type": "integer"},
        {"name": "reason", "type": "integer"},
        {"name": "lru", "type": "integer"},
        {"name": "pid", "type": "integer"},
        {"name": "component", "type": "string"}
      ]},
      {"name": "package", "type": "string", "mode": "repeated"},
      {"name": "memory", "type": "record", "fields": [
        {"name": "total", "type": "integer"},
        {"name": "dirty_private", "type": "integer"},
        {"name": "dirty_shared", "type": "integer"}
      ]}
    ]}
  ]}
]
```

Client Server Protocol

Generally, when implementing client/server communication, you would use a full-featured framework that enables you to concentrate on the higher level details of the messages being communicated rather than the details of the wire protocol. A nice option for the Google Android/App Engine (iOS is also supported) platform is the Google Cloud Endpoints framework. This is available at `https://cloud.google.com/products/cloud-endpoints/`.

This is a well-rounded framework for implementing web services with support for generating strongly typed server and client libraries that simplify building the application. However, for our sample such a framework adds a lot of machinery that tends to obscure the core functions performed. Also, implementing a simple client/server protocol is a good way to appreciate what these frameworks are trying to solve and why you would want to use them in a production application. This section describes the code that implements the client side of the simple protocol used in the application.

CLIENT/SERVER FRAMEWORKS

The Google Cloud Endpoints framework is only one of many frameworks suitable for production client/server communication. Following are a few other libraries that you may want to consider if you are looking for a solution for client/server communication.

- GSON: Automatic Java object to JSON conversion (`https://code.google.com/p/google-gson/`)

- Volley: Framework for asynchronous HTTP requests (`https://developers.google.com/events/io/sessions/325304728`)

- Retrofit: Java annotation-based framework for generating REST API bindings (`http://square.github.io/retrofit/`)

The protocol the application uses is based on passing JSON encoded data in HTTP POST requests and responses. For each message to be sent, the client initiates a separate POST request with the data encoded in the body of the request, and the server responds with a JSON object. If no errors occur the client can go ahead and use the response object from the server. Because this is a monitoring application, the server never has to return data to the client, so when a request succeeds, the client simply receives an empty JSON object. The client has to deal with three types of errors:

- Errors at the HTTP transport layer and below

- Request encoding errors

- Application level errors

You cannot control how the first class of errors is reported but the latter two classes of errors are detected by the code, so you can decide how to signal the issue. We chose to report request-encoding errors using the appropriate HTTP client error (4xx) status codes. When the request is well formed but the server encounters an error while processing it, we chose to return HTTP status code 200 (which indicates success at the HTTP layer) but return a JSON object containing the keys `error` and `message` to indicate why the request failed. Finally, the client specifies the action to be performed with the request object using the appropriate URL on the server (`/command/<action>`). The client side implementation of the protocol is shown in Listing 8.3.

Listing 8.3: CommandRunner.java

```java
class CommandRunner {
  private final URI host;

  static class ErrorResult extends Exception {
    private static final long serialVersionUID = 1L;
    private final String error;

    ErrorResult(JSONObject error) {
      super(error.optString("message"));
      this.error = error.optString("error", "Unknown");
    }

    ErrorResult(Throwable ex) {
      super(ex);
      this.error = ex.getClass().getSimpleName();
    }

    String getError() {
      return error;
    }
  }

  CommandRunner(String host) {
    try {
      this.host = new URI("http://" + host);
    } catch (URISyntaxException ex) {
      throw new RuntimeException(ex);
    }
  }

  // Handles transmitting a command and decoding the response.
  JSONObject run(String command, JSONObject arg) throws ErrorResult {
    JSONObject result = new JSONObject();
    HttpURLConnection conn = createConnection(command);
    try {
      byte body[] = arg.toString().getBytes();
      int responseCode = sendRequest(conn, body);
      String response = readResponse(conn);
      try {
        result = responseCode == 200 ?
            new JSONObject(response) :
```

continues

Listing 8.3: *(continued)*

```
            connectionError(responseCode, response);
    } catch (JSONException ex) {
      throw new ErrorResult(ex);
    }
  } finally {
    conn.disconnect();
  }
  if (result.has("error")) {
    throw new ErrorResult(result);
  }
  return result;
}


// Sets up an HTTP connection to the command URL.
private HttpURLConnection createConnection(String command)
    throws ErrorResult {
  String path = "/command/" + command;
  try {
    URL url = host.getPort() == -1 ?
        new URL(host.getScheme(), host.getHost(), path) :
        new URL(host.getScheme(), host.getHost(),
            host.getPort(), path);
    HttpURLConnection conn = (HttpURLConnection) url.openConnection();
    conn.setConnectTimeout(60 * 1000);
    conn.setReadTimeout(60 * 1000);
    conn.setRequestProperty(
      "User-Agent", CommandRunner.class.getCanonicalName());
    conn.setDoInput(true);
    conn.setDoOutput(true);
    return conn;
  } catch (IOException ex) {
    throw new ErrorResult(ex);
  }
}


// Opens the connection and performs the HTTP POST operation.
private int sendRequest(HttpURLConnection conn, byte[] body)
    throws ErrorResult {
  conn.setRequestProperty("Content-Type", "application/json");
  conn.setFixedLengthStreamingMode(body.length);
  try {
    conn.setRequestMethod("POST");
    conn.connect();
    OutputStream os = conn.getOutputStream();
    try {
      os.write(body);
    } finally {
      os.close();
    }
    return conn.getResponseCode();
```

```
    } catch (IOException ex) {
      throw new ErrorResult(ex);
    }
  }


  // Reads the response body from the HTTP connection.
  private String readResponse(HttpURLConnection conn)
      throws ErrorResult {
    int contentLength = conn.getContentLength();
    try {
      InputStreamReader is =
          new InputStreamReader(conn.getInputStream(), "UTF-8");
      try {
        StringBuilder builder = new StringBuilder();
        char buffer[];
        if (contentLength > 0) {
          buffer = new char[contentLength];
        } else {
          buffer = new char[512];
        }
        int charsRead;
        while ((charsRead = is.read(buffer)) > 0) {
          builder.append(buffer, 0, charsRead);
        }
        return builder.toString();
      } finally {
        is.close();
      }
    } catch (IOException ex) {
      throw new ErrorResult(ex);
    }
  }

  // Wraps a HTTP error code and response body in an ErrorResult object.
  private JSONObject connectionError(int code, String body) {
    JSONObject result = new JSONObject();
    try {
      result.put("error", "ConnectionError");
      result.put("message", String.format("Code = %d: %s", code, body));
    } catch (JSONException e) {
      throw new RuntimeException(e);
    }
    return result;
  }
}
```

The application performs two types of requests, a registration request and a log request. The registration request is initiated by the settings UI component (ManageActivity.java), and you can see in Listing 8.1 that the monitoring service initiates the logging request in transmit(...). Both classes use the CommandRunner class, shown in Listing 8.3, that implements the protocol described. This class is initialized with a host that it will direct the requests to and provides a method that accepts a command and JSON object pair and returns a JSON object result. It handles all the details of turning this into a suitable request and decoding a suitable response. Note how it also unifies all error handling across the three types of errors discussed previously so that the caller needs to deal only with a single uniform type of exception. This class provides a good transition to the server side of the application because the two pieces integrate based on this protocol, so the next section covers the server side implementation of this protocol.

Log Collection Service

The Google App Engine was chosen for the implementation of the web component of the service. This platform is particularly well suited to building custom user interfaces over data hosted in BigQuery. Communication between the services is simple and efficient; and the GAE framework provides a number of support services, like scheduled tasks and task queues, to build data management solutions on top of BigQuery. Chapter 11, "Managing Data Stored in BigQuery," and Chapter 12, "External Data Processing," discuss how to move data, in both directions, between Datastore, the App Engine scalable transactional store, and BigQuery. In the sample application, App Engine is used to manage the registry of devices, relay logs from the devices into BigQuery, and serve the dashboard pages. The source code for the application is available in the chapter download at:

```
ch08/sensors/cloud
```

To work with this code you need the App Engine Python SDK, which is available at `https://developers.google.com/appengine/downloads`.

If you are entirely new to App Engine you should take a look at the Python tutorial on the App Engine documentation site. It covers the initial setup and the basics of using App Engine for developing web applications. It is available at `https://developers.google.com/appengine/docs/python/`.

There are plug-ins that can help with development if you use Eclipse as your IDE, but it is not necessary for working with the code for this chapter. You can test the application locally without actually provisioning an App Engine application, but if you want to test it with real devices, you need to deploy the code to a live instance.

USING YOUR OWN INSTANCE

To use the source code with your own BigQuery project and application instance, you need to modify constants in three files.

`sensors/cloud/src/app.yaml`

```
application: <your application id>
```

`sensors/cloud/src/config.py`

```
PROJECT_ID = '<your project id>'
```

`sensors/client/res/values/strings.xml`

```
<your application id>.appspot.com
```

After you modify the code, you can upload the application to your instance using the App Engine SDK.

```
appcfg.py update --oauth2 sensors/cloud/src
```

Since the App Engine application will be invoking the BigQuery API, you need to configure API access for your application. In the Developer Console, you need to enable the BigQuery API for the project associated with your App Engine application. Then you need to add the application service account, available from Administration ➤ Application Settings, to your BigQuery project as an editor. This setup can be reused for the App Engine examples discussed in Chapters 11 and 12.

Log Trampoline

Start by looking at how the client communicates with the web application to implement registration and logging. Just like the client had a single class, `_JSONHandler`, encapsulate the details of the client server protocol in the mobile client, there is a class in the server code that deals with the detail of unpacking requests and packing responses. Subclasses implement the `handle(self, arg)` method and perform the actual operation and return a result as a JSON object, which in Python is any dictionary-like object that the JSON library can serialize. The method can optionally raise an exception, which the base class catches and transforms into an error as specified by the simple communication protocol used in this application. Listing 8.4 contains the source code for the base class and the two handlers implemented in the application.

Listing 8.4: Command handlers (main.py)

```
class _JsonHandler(webapp2.RequestHandler):
  '''Generic JSON command handler.'''
```

continues

Listing 8.4: *(continued)*

```python
MAX_PAYLOAD_SIZE = 16 * 1024

  def post(self):
    if self.request.headers.get('Content-Type') != 'application/json':
      self.response.set_status(
          httplib.UNSUPPORTED_MEDIA_TYPE,
          message='Expected Content-Type: application/json')
      return
    if len(self.request.body) > self.MAX_PAYLOAD_SIZE:
      self.response.set_status(
          httplib.REQUEST_ENTITY_TOO_LARGE,
          message=('Max payload size (%d) exceeded' %
                   self.MAX_PAYLOAD_SIZE))
      return
    try:
      arg = json.loads(self.request.body)
    except ValueError, e:
      self.response.set_status(
          httplib.BAD_REQUEST,
          message='Could not parse body as json: ' + str(e))
      return
    self.response.headers['Content-Type'] = 'application/json'
    try:
      result = json.dumps(self.handle(arg))
    except Exception, e:
      result = self.json_error(e)
    self.response.out.write(result)

  def json_error(self, e):
    logging.warn('Handler Error: %s' % unicode(e))
    return json.dumps({'error': e.__class__.__name__,
                       'message': e.message})

  def handle(self, arg):
    raise NotImplementedError

class RegisterHandler(_JsonHandler):
  '''Handle the registration command.'''
  def handle(self, arg):
    device_id = arg.get('id', None)
    if not device_id:
      raise ValueError('id entry missing from argument')
    candidate = models.Candidate.get_by_device_id(device_id)
    if not candidate:
      raise KeyError('Id %s not valid' % device_id)
    candidate.register(arg)
    return {}

class RecordHandler(_JsonHandler):
```

```
  '''Handle the logging command.'''
  def handle(self, arg):
    device_id = arg.get('id', None)
    if not device_id:
      raise ValueError('id entry missing from argument')
    device = models.Device.get_by_device_id(device_id)
    if not device:
      raise KeyError('id %s not valid' % device_id)
    # Extract the UTC day from the timestamp in the record.
    ts = int(arg.get('ts', 0.0))
    day = datetime.utcfromtimestamp(ts)
    # Save the record using the streaming API.
    result = bigquery.tabledata().insertAll(
        projectId=PROJECT_ID,
        datasetId='logs',
        tableId='device_' + day.strftime("%Y%m%d"),
        body=dict(rows=[
            # Generate a suitable insert id.
            {'insertId': ('%s:%d' % (device_id, ts)),
             'json': arg}])).execute()
    if 'error' in result or result.get('insertErrors'):
      logging.error('Insert failed: ' + unicode(result))
    return {}

app = webapp2.WSGIApplication([
    # ELIDED
    webapp2.Route(r'/command/register',
        handler=RegisterHandler, name='register'),
    webapp2.Route(r'/command/record',
        handler=RecordHandler, name='record'),
], debug=True)
```

The registration handler looks up the supplied registration ID in Datastore, and if it finds it, the handler adds a new device record with the data supplied by the client. Chapter 11 looks at this device registration information in more detail and explains how to pull it into BigQuery for analytics. Here you focus on the handler, which handles the logs sent by the clients, particularly because this method directly integrates with BigQuery via the streaming insert API.

The server receives a log record as a JSON object, which is handled by RecordHandler.handle(...). The one bit of logic that the code applies is to direct the record to the daily table corresponding to the timestamp in the record. It is significant that the code uses data from the record to deterministically compute the destination table. If instead it used the system time or some other value that could change independently of the record, then it is possible for a given record to be inserted into different tables if the client happened to retry the request due to an unexpected error receiving the acknowledgment from the server. To protect against similar duplication between the handler and BigQuery, it generates a globally unique `insertId`, assuming at most one record per second from each device, by concatenating the device ID and timestamp.

Since the client is shipping a JSON object that conforms to the schema of the BigQuery table, it can directly be added as the `json` field of the insert record. The server is a trampoline for the mobile logs because it bounces the record from the client with no transformations into a BigQuery operation. This implementation tends to be straightforward but suffers from the drawback that you will be paying for the App Engine resources required to process these records. If you have a large volume of data flowing to BigQuery, the resources required can be substantial. In the next section on how authentication works on App Engine, you look at a scheme to avoid passing the data through App Engine.

Before wrapping up this section on saving the logs, consider how these daily tables are created. After all, the streaming insert operation requires that the tables already exist. The function to create a set of daily tables for upcoming days is fairly simple and shown in Listing 8.5. It attempts to create 3 tables between 2 and 4 days ahead of the current time. The advantage of creating multiple consecutive tables is that it automatically incorporates retries on failures. If you run this handler every day, then it attempts to create a given table 5 times before it is required. Of course, creating a table for a given day on that same day is too late since insertions will already be failing. However, it is convenient for initial setup. Also take a look at how the expiry time is set up on the table. Note that the expiry time is calculated relative to the time it will start to receive records rather than its creation time. Keeping the expiry aligned with the UTC day boundary also makes the lifetime more predictable. Tables vanishing at arbitrary times within a day would be confusing. The mechanism to run this handler every day is discussed in detail later in the chapter.

Listing 8.5: Table Creation Handler (dashboard.py)

```
class _CreateTableHandler(webapp2.RequestHandler):
  # The get call schedules the post call to create tables.
  def get(self):
    taskqueue.add(url=self.request.route.build(
        self.request, [], {}))
    self.response.headers['Content-Type'] = 'text/plain'
    self.response.write('ok')

  # Performs the actual creation.
  def post(self):
    # First create required datasets.
    for dataset in ['logs', 'dashboard']:
      try:
        bigquery.datasets().insert(
          projectId=PROJECT_ID,
          body={
```

```
            'datasetReference': {
              'datasetId': dataset
            }
          }).execute()
      except HttpError, e:
        if e.resp.status == httplib.CONFLICT:
          logging.info('Dataset %s exists' % dataset)
        else:
          logging.error('Error: ' + str(e))

      # Create daily tables for the next few days.
      with open('bq/schema_log.json', 'r') as schema_file:
        schema = json.load(schema_file)
      today = datetime.datetime.utcnow()
      for delta in xrange(2, 5):
        day = today + datetime.timedelta(days=delta)
        exp = calendar.timegm(
          (day + datetime.timedelta(days=15)).replace(
              hour=0, minute=0, second=0, microsecond=0)
          .utctimetuple()) * 1000
        request = bigquery.tables().insert(
          projectId=PROJECT_ID,
          datasetId='logs',
          body={
            'tableReference': {
              'tableId': day.strftime('device_%Y%m%d')
            },
            'expirationTime': exp,
            'schema': {
              'fields': schema
            }
          })
        try:
          result = request.execute()
          logging.info('Created table ' + result['id'])
        except HttpError, e:
          if e.resp.status == httplib.CONFLICT:
            logging.info('Table for %s exists' % day)
          else:
            logging.error('Error: ' + str(e))
```

Authentication

There are three separate types of credentials used in this application:

- The end user's Google credentials
- The application service account's Google credentials
- Application-specific device registration IDs

This section describes how these three credentials related to each other and in particular how a device is bound to an end user account.

The Manage Devices page of the application is annotated using a Python decorator, @login_required, to indicate it requires authenticated access. The user proves their identity by presenting a cookie issued by Google's login service. If users visit the page without the appropriate cookie, they are redirected to the login page to obtain one. Based on the user's identity, the page fetches and renders the set of phones associated with the account and a registration ID, also bound to the user's identity, which can be used to add a new phone. When the user enters this ID in the mobile client, the client passes the ID to the web application to verify that it is valid, and if it is, the client uses it to start logging records. This completes the association of a device to a user account.

Each time a log record is received from the mobile client, the web application validates that the device ID in the record is still associated with some user account. Because there is no user identity involved at this point, it is assumed that the ID is globally unique. This is achieved, with an infinitesimal chance of collision, by generating a 9-byte (9 bytes fit in a 12 byte Base64 encoded string) random number as the registration ID for a user. If the ID in the record is successfully located, then the application writes the record to BigQuery under its *service account identity*. This completes the chain of custody that ensures only users with registered devices can get their logs into the project's BigQuery tables.

The mechanism used to prove the application's service account identity to BigQuery is OAuth, which is covered in detail in Chapter 5, "Talking to the BigQuery API." However, there is a simple API for obtaining the OAuth token for this special identity when running under App Engine. Because App Engine runs the application code, it can vouch for the identity of the application. It does this by essentially injecting a token into the application. An App Engine-specific module in the Google OAuth library can access this injected token.

```
import httplib2
from oauth2client.appengine import AppAssertionCredentials
from apiclient import discovery
from google.appengine.api import memcache

credentials = AppAssertionCredentials(
  scope='https://www.googleapis.com/auth/bigquery')
bigquery = discovery.build('bigquery', 'v2',
  http=credentials.authorize(httplib2.Http(memcache)))
```

When the BigQuery client is constructed this way under App Engine, the framework supplied token is added as an authentication header by the OAuth library to the client HTTP requests. Of course, this authenticates only the requests. There is still the question of authorization, which depends on suitable ACLs being present on the objects accessed. You need to add the service account identity to the BigQuery projects and datasets that will be accessed from App Engine. The identity is referenced using a handle that looks like an e-mail address:

```
<app id>@appspot.gserviceaccount.com
```

You can add this handle to an ACL just like you would a regular user account. This information is always available under the Application Settings section of the App Engine administration console for your application.

SERVICE ACCOUNT AND LOCAL TESTING

Service account credentials are easy to obtain when your application is actually running in App Engine. However, during development, the local development server cannot generate the credential for the service account associated with your application. This is inconvenient because all the code that interacts with BigQuery will fail. Fortunately, the `dev_appserver.py` supports passing it a different service account and private key on the command line and then simulates the production behavior but generates credentials for the supplied service account instead. Chapter 3, "Getting Started with BigQuery," covers the provisioning of service accounts in a project.

The private key downloaded from the Google Developer Console is not in the right format for use with the development server, so it needs to be converted before it can be used. The following instructions require that you have OpenSSL installed.

```
$ SERVICE_ACCOUNT='<account email>'
$ DOWNLOADED_KEY='downloaded-privatekey.p12'
$ DEVAPPSERVER_KEY='/tmp/key-rsa.pem'
$ openssl pkcs12 -in ${DOWNLOADED_KEY} \
    -nodes -nocerts -passin pass:notasecret |
    openssl rsa -out ${DEVAPPSERVER_KEY}
$ dev_appserver.py \
    --appidentity_email_address ${SERVICE_ACCOUNT} \
    --appidentity_private_key_path ${DEVAPPSERVER_KEY} \
    sensors/cloud/src/app.yaml
```

This runs the development server locally on port 8080 and an administration console on port 8000. The application depends on certain datasets and tables existing in your BigQuery project. To create them, visit the administration console at `http://localhost:8000/` and navigate to the Cron Jobs section. Run each of the jobs listed starting with `/dashboard/create`. Once this is done you can visit `http://localhost:8080/`. You will be greeted with a very empty dashboard until you actually record some data.

The authentication and authorization scheme described here is the simplest approach supported by the App Engine framework. Most of the time it should be sufficient. However, as was pointed out in the previous section, it suffers from the drawback that it requires all BigQuery bound requests to pass through App Engine. It turns out that the OAuth protocol allows you to avoid this pass-through without compromising the security of your data. Remember, from Chapter 5 "Talking to BigQuery API," that an OAuth credential consists of two pieces: a short-lived access token passed in API requests to service providers such as BigQuery, and a refresh token passed to authentication providers such as the Google login service to obtain fresh access tokens. Instead of requests passing through the application, just let the application return the access token to clients and have them directly communicate with BigQuery.

To do this safely, a service account with limited access should be provisioned, and the OAuth credential should be constructed only with the scopes required by the client operation. For example, for logs written by the clients, the account needs to have write access to the dataset containing the log tables and only the streaming scope is required.

```
https://www.googleapis.com/auth/bigquery.insertdata
```

Like the scopes introduced previously, this is not really a URL. It is just the string used to identify the scope when authenticating. It is important to create a separate account solely for this purpose and limit its access to just the datasets that will receive the records. This will avoid inadvertently leaking additional privileges to clients that have the access token.

Because the access token is only valid for a short time, its capabilities will be fairly limited. Although such an approach is definitely valuable in scenarios in which the traffic volume is substantial, significant drawbacks exist. The most obvious one is that you can no longer rely on server-side validation. If there are rogue or broken clients, they might corrupt tables by writing bad data, so pay attention to these scenarios when considering this approach.

You can encounter the same issue of passing data through the App Engine application when building the dashboard component discussed next. Reading data can also bypass the web application if the access token is shipped to a JavaScript client running in the browser. Locking down the capabilities for this type of access can be quite challenging and is often not justified because the resources required are not that much greater than what is required to serve the dashboard itself.

Dashboard

The goal of the dashboard page is to provide a summary of the data collected by the application so that viewers can quickly identify the main trends. Most of the effort in putting together a useful dashboard goes toward finding the right queries and selecting the appropriate visualizations. However, there are aspects of using BigQuery that require special attention when it is used to drive a dashboard or reporting application. Chapter 11 covers these patterns in detail. This section highlights where they appear in the sample application so that you can see them in action.

Data Caching

Because a dashboard page is often viewed frequently, requires multiple queries to construct, and users expect it to appear with little delay, it is not a good idea to issue new queries for every dashboard page request. Queries that involve large tables are especially problematic because the costs for these will be substantial and the latency high enough that it will stall the rendering of the page. Instead, you can cache the data that needs to be rendered periodically so that the resources used to compute the data can be shared across multiple views of the dashboard. In App Engine it is easy to coordinate this caching using its task-scheduling feature. The application defines a `cron.yaml` file containing a list of tasks and their scheduling information.

```
cron:
- description: create daily tables
  url: /dashboard/create
  schedule: every day 01:00
- description: 10m dashboard refresh
  url: /dashboard/trigger/10m
  schedule: every 10 minutes
- description: hourly dashboard refresh
  url: /dashboard/trigger/12h
  schedule: every 12 hours
```

App Engine invokes the configured URLs at the appropriate time to kick off the operation. You can see that we also included an entry for the table creation task shown in Listing 8.5. Keep in mind that these URLs need to be locked down because we would not want end users to trigger these operations. The simplest way to do this is in the dispatch configuration in `app.yaml`.

```
- url: /dashboard/.*
  script: dashboard.app
  login: admin
```

Note that the development server does not run these automatically, but you can use the administration console to trigger them for testing as described in the "Service Account and Local Testing" feature above.

To avoid running expensive and slow queries each time the dashboard page is requested, we have chosen to maintain a cache of results required by the page in the `dashboard` dataset. The contents of this dataset are updated periodically by using the scheduled task facility of AppEngine to run query jobs that write their results to tables in this dataset. The page itself only uses tables in this dataset to present a visual summary to the viewer.

The way we have chosen to organize updating our tables for the dashboard is to define a list containing BackgroundQuery objects. Each object specifies the query job configuration to be executed and a refresh interval. The handler for the scheduled task scans the list for entries with a refresh interval matching the interval specified as a request parameter to the task and launches the job for each match.

For simplicity, the scheduled task does not bother to check the status of these jobs because it does not need the result. Of course, there is the possibility of transient failures. For cached results that are updated frequently this may not matter because the job will be re-executed in a little while. However, for longer intervals this may lead to unacceptable staleness, so in a production application you would ideally wait for completion and, if a transient error is detected, retry the query. It is important that the destination tables for these jobs be in a specific location, as opposed to being anonymous, because they are going to be read or queried while rendering the dashboard, as shown in Listing 8.6.

Listing 8.6: Dashboard cache management (dashboard.py)

```python
# Structure representing a query to be cached.
BackgroundQuery = namedtuple('BackgroundQuery', [
 'query_job',
 'max_age',
 ])



# Scheduled task to trigger dashboard refreshes.
class _Trigger(webapp2.RequestHandler):
 # max_age is the interval be handled.
 def get(self, max_age):
   logging.info("Triggering: " + max_age)
   for index in xrange(len(BACKGROUND_QUERIES)):
     cached = BACKGROUND_QUERIES[int(index)]
     # Only trigger if it is the special value 'all' or if the
     # configuration specifies an interval matching the input interval.
     if (max_age == 'all' or cached.max_age == max_age):
       taskqueue.add(url='/dashboard/update', params={'index': index})
   self.response.headers['Content-Type'] = 'text/plain'
   self.response.write('ok')



# Handles a dashboard cache update for a given configuration.
class _Update(webapp2.RequestHandler):
 # max_age is the interval be handled.
 def post(self):
   index = self.request.get('index')
   logging.info("Dashboard update: " + index)
   cached = BACKGROUND_QUERIES[int(index)]
   result = bigquery.jobs().insert(
```

```python
      projectId=PROJECT_ID,
      body=cached.query_job).execute()
    logging.info(str(result))
    self.response.headers['Content-Type'] = 'text/plain'
    self.response.write('ok')


# Helper function to construct query job configurations.
def _dashboard_query_job(
  query,
  table,
  # Results cached for rendering go in the dashboard dataset.
  dataset='dashboard'):
  return {
      'configuration': {
        'query': {
          'query': query,
          'destinationTable': {
            'projectId': PROJECT_ID,
            'datasetId': dataset,
            'tableId': table
          },
          'writeDisposition': 'WRITE_TRUNCATE'
        }
      }
    }


# List of queries that need to be cached in the dasboard dataset.
BACKGROUND_QUERIES = [
  BackgroundQuery(
    _dashboard_query_job(
      '''SELECT
        SEC_TO_TIMESTAMP(INTEGER(TIMESTAMP_TO_SEC(ts)/60) * 60)
          [Minute],
        COUNT(ts) [Records],
        SUM(IF(screen_on, 1, 0)) / COUNT(ts) [FracScreenOn],
        SUM(IF(power.charging, 1, 0)) / COUNT(ts) [FracCharging],
        SUM(IF(power.charge > 0.5, 1, 0)) / COUNT(ts) [FracHalfCharged]
      FROM TABLE_DATE_RANGE(logs.device_,
                            DATE_ADD(CURRENT_TIMESTAMP(), -1, 'DAY'),
                            CURRENT_TIMESTAMP())
      WHERE TIMESTAMP_TO_USEC(ts) > (NOW() - 24 * 60 * 60 * 1000 * 1000)
      GROUP BY 1
      ORDER BY 1''',
      'records_per_minute'
    ),
    max_age='10m'
  ),
  BackgroundQuery(
    _dashboard_query_job(
      '''SELECT running.name, COUNT(id)
```

continues

Listing 8.6: *(continued)*

```
    FROM TABLE_DATE_RANGE(logs.device_,
                        DATE_ADD(CURRENT_TIMESTAMP(), -6, 'DAY'),
                        CURRENT_TIMESTAMP())
    WHERE LEFT(running.name, LENGTH('com.android.')) != 'com.android.'
    AND LEFT(running.name, LENGTH('android.')) != 'android.'
    AND LEFT(running.name, LENGTH('com.google.')) != 'com.google.'
    AND LEFT(running.name, LENGTH('com.motorola.')) != 'com.motorola.'
    AND LEFT(running.name, LENGTH('com.qualcomm.')) != 'com.qualcomm.'
    AND running.name NOT IN (
        'system',
        'com.googlecode.bigquery_e2e.sensors.client',
        'com.redbend.vdmc')
    AND running.importance.level >= 100
    AND running.importance.level < 400
    GROUP BY 1
    ORDER BY 2 DESC''',
    'top_apps'
  ),
  max_age='12h'
),
BackgroundQuery(
  _dashboard_query_job(
    '''SELECT ZipsInDay, COUNT(1) FROM (
      SELECT D, id, COUNT(zip) ZipsInDay FROM (
        SELECT
          DATE(ts) D, id, location.zip [zip]
        FROM TABLE_DATE_RANGE(logs.device_,
                            DATE_ADD(CURRENT_TIMESTAMP(),
                                    -6, 'DAY'),
                            CURRENT_TIMESTAMP())
        GROUP EACH BY 1, 2, 3)
      GROUP EACH BY 1, 2)
    GROUP BY 1 ORDER BY 1''',
    'zips_in_day'
  ),
  max_age='12h'
),
]
```

This simple application has only a couple of tables that need to be updated, so you could just initiate the query jobs from the scheduled task. However, if there are a large number of tables and especially if you want to monitor the outcome of the operation, it is not practical to issue them sequentially in a single scheduled task handler. The sample code is designed to scale up by leveraging the Task Queue framework available in App Engine (https://developers.google.com/appengine/docs/python/taskqueue/). The scheduled task adds tasks to a queue rather than performing the actual work. Besides ensuring that the scheduled task completes in a bounded amount of time, the use of queues also allows the application to manage the concurrency of operations to ensure you stay under BigQuery rate limits. Here we simply use the default queue configuration, but App Engine allows custom queue configurations that rate limit task execution.

Data Transformation

You now have data cached in the dashboard dataset, ready for delivery to the user for rendering in the UI. In the sample application you have the JavaScript client fetch the data from the web application rather than directly from BigQuery so that you can control the access to the data. Also, you want to make it simple for the JavaScript application to render the data, so you want to supply it in a format that is convenient for your rendering framework. To support this you can implement a handler in the web application that enables you to transform the data returned by BigQuery into different formats. This code is a little complex because it needs to be flexible in input and output. Chapter 5 describes two different methods for reading data. The data from a table can be read via the `bigquery.tabledata().list()` operation, and data that is the result of a query job can be read via the `bigquery.jobs().query()` and `bigquery.jobs().getQueryResults()` methods. The former can read data from any table. The latter which is limited to tables generated by query jobs has the advantage that you can issue a query and read its result in a single call for queries that run quickly and return a modest amount of data. We have implemented the data handler in the application so that it supports both methods as shown in Listing 8.7. If an existing table is requested, the `bigquery.tabledata()` API is used, and if the request requires running a new query, the `bigquery.jobs()` API is invoked.

Listing 8.7: Data formatting handler (dashboard.py)

```python
class _Formatter(object):
  '''Base class for formatting rows.'''

  def mime_type(self):
    '''Returns the mime type that the format conforms to.'''
    return 'text/plain'

  def start(self, out):
    '''Called before the first row is output.'''
    pass

  def format(self, out):
    '''Called for each batch of rows to be formatted.'''
    pass

  def finish(self, out):
    '''Called after all rows have been written.'''
```

continues

Listing 8.7: *(continued)*

```python
    pass

class _CSV(_Formatter):
  '''Format rows as CSV.'''
  def format(self, rows, out):
    out.write('\n'.join([
      ','.join([cell.get('v') for cell in row.get('f')])
      for row in rows]))

class _Datatable(_Formatter):
  '''Format data for consumption by the google visualization library.'''
  def __init__(self, config):
    self._columns = json.dumps(config.columns)
    # Need to cast values because the Datatable will treat strings
    # as 0 rather than casting to a number.
    self._converters = [
        float if c['type'] == 'number' else str
        for c in config.columns
      ]
    self._add_comma = False

  def _cast(self, cols):
    return [
        {"v":self._converters[i](cols[i]['v'])}
        for i in xrange(len(cols))
      ]

  def mime_type(self):
    return 'application/json'

  def start(self, out):
    out.write('{"cols":' + self._columns + ',\n "rows":[\n')

  def format(self, rows, out):
    if rows:
      if self._add_comma:
        out.write(',\n')
      else:
        self._add_comma = True
      out.write(',\n'.join([
          ('{"c":[' +
          (','.join([json.dumps(cell) for cell in
                  self._cast(row.get('f'))])) +
          ']}')
          for row in rows]))

  def finish(self, out):
    out.write(']}')
class _NextPage(object):
```

```python
    '''Abstract class for paginating over data.'''
    def fetch(self, token=None, num=10000):
      return self._make_request(token, num).execute()

  def _make_request(self, token, num):
    pass

class _TableData(_NextPage):
  '''Implements paginating with tabledata().list().'''
  def __init__(self, project, dataset, table):
    self._kwargs = dict(
      projectId=project,
      datasetId=dataset,
      tableId=table)

  def _make_request(self, token, num):
    return bigquery.tabledata().list(
      pageToken=token,
      maxResults=num,
      **self._kwargs)

class _QueryResults(_NextPage):
  '''Implements paginating with jobs().getQueryResults().'''
  def __init__(self, project, job):
    self._kwargs = dict(
      projectId=project,
      jobId=job)

  def _make_request(self, token, num):
    return bigquery.jobs().getQueryResults(
      pageToken=token,
      maxResults=num,
      **self._kwargs)

class _DataHandler(webapp2.RequestHandler):
  def _init_formatter(self, config):
    if self.request.get('format') == 'datatable':
      return _Datatable(config)
    return _CSV()

  def get(self, console_id):
    self.response.headers['Cache-Control'] = 'max-age=300'
    console = CONSOLES[int(console_id)]
    formatter = self._init_formatter(console)
    self.response.headers['Content-Type'] = formatter.mime_type()
    if console.table:
      dataset, table = console.table
      next_page = _TableData(PROJECT_ID, dataset, table)
      result = next_page.fetch()
    else:
      result = bigquery.jobs().query(
```

continues

Listing 8.7: *(continued)*

```python
            projectId=PROJECT_ID,
            body={'query': console.query, 'maxResults': 10000}).execute()
        if 'jobReference' in result:
            job_id = result['jobReference']['jobId']
            next_page = _QueryResults(PROJECT_ID, job_id)
            while 'jobComplete' in result and not result['jobComplete']:
                result = next_page.fetch()
        formatter.start(self.response)
        while result.get('rows'):
          formatter.format(result['rows'], self.response)
          result = (next_page.fetch(result['pageToken'])
            if 'pageToken' in result else {})
        if result.get('code', 200) != 200:
          self.response.set_status(
            500, message=('Could not fetch data for %s\n%s' %
                (str(console.table or console.query), json.dumps(result))))
          return
        formatter.finish(self.response)


CONSOLES = [
  ConsoleData(
    [
      {'label': 'Minute', 'type': 'number'},
      {'label': 'Records', 'type': 'number'},
    ],
    query=(
      '''SELECT Minute, Records
      FROM dashboard.records_per_minute
      ORDER BY 1''')),
  ConsoleData(
    [
      {'label': 'Minute', 'type': 'number'},
      {'label': 'Screen On', 'type': 'number'},
      {'label': 'Charging', 'type': 'number'},
      {'label': 'Half Charged', 'type': 'number'},
    ],
    query=(
      '''SELECT Minute, FracScreenOn, FracCharging, FracHalfCharged
      FROM dashboard.records_per_minute
      ORDER BY 1''')),
  ConsoleData(
    [
      {'label': 'Application', 'type': 'string'},
      {'label': 'Users', 'type': 'number'},
    ],
    table=('dashboard', 'top_apps')),
  ConsoleData(
    [
      {'label': 'Zips In One Day', 'type': 'number'},
```

```
        {'label': 'Num Device Days', 'type': 'number'},
      ],
      table=('dashboard', 'zips_in_day')),
  ]
```

Note that the handler does not actually accept a table name or query in the request. Instead it expects an index into a list defined in the file that explicitly defines specific tables and queries. This avoids the issue of SQL injection exploits or inadvertently exposing tables because the client is not allowed to directly specify a query or table name. The list is constructed a bit like our cached table definitions with a structure describing the data to be supplied to the web client. One aspect that may seem a little odd is that we use queries in this list despite having the ability to cache data. The reason is that the queries in this list are designed to take advantage of the BigQuery internal cache, so they do not add any overhead. This technique is covered in Chapter 11.

Web Client

Turning data into useful visualizations is a vast topic. The main goal of the sample application is to demonstrate the pattern for integrating with a suitable framework. There are a bewildering number of visualization libraries spanning the dimensions of sophistication and ease of use. The right choice greatly depends on the application and other components being employed. For the sample application we use two separate visualization frameworks:

- http://dygraphs.com/
- https://developers.google.com/chart/

Honestly, we could have just made do with the second, Google Charts, framework. However, we chose to use two fairly different frameworks to better illustrate what it takes to integrate with a given framework. When you look at the code, you see that most of the machinery that moves and manipulates the data is independent of the visualization layer. There is a little bit of plumbing that varies that needs to be switched. In fact, we have already covered the most complex piece, the formatting of the data. The previous section introduced the CSV and Datatable formatters. We use CSV to populate Dygraph time series visualizations and the Datatable format to populate Google Charts visualizations. In the JavaScript code, this results in a minor change to the URL from which the data is loaded, as shown in Listing 8.8.

Listing 8.8: Dygraph and Google Charts (dashboard.js)

```
(function() {
  var g = new Dygraph(
    document.getElementById("g1"),
```

continues

Listing 8.8: *(continued)*

```
      "/data/1?format=csv",
      {
        title: "Screen and Power",
        xlabel: "Time",
        ylabel: "Fraction",
        labels: ["Time", "Screen On", "Charging", "Half Charged"],
        legend: "always",
        labelsDiv: document.getElementById("g1-legend"),
        xValueParser: function(x) { return 1000 * parseFloat(x); },
        axes: {
          x: {
            valueFormatter: function(ms) {
              return new Date(ms).strftime('%H:%M');
            },
            axisLabelFormatter: function(d) {
              return d.strftime('%m/%d');
            },
            ticker: Dygraph.dateTicker,
            pixelsPerLabel: 100
          }
        },
        rollPeriod: 12
      });
})();

$.ajax({
    url: "/data/2?format=datatable",
    dataType:"json",
}).done(function (data) {
  (new google.visualization.PieChart(document.getElementById('g2')))
      .draw(new google.visualization.DataTable(data),
          {
            title: "App Usage",
            titleTextStyle: { fontSize: 20 },
            chartArea:{left:"10%", top:"10%",
                       width:"90%", height:"90%"},
            sliceVisibilityThreshold: 1.0/120
          });
})
```

This code is simple, assuming some familiarity with Javascript and HTML, because all the heavy lifting has been done on the server. If you are not familiar with Javascript or JQuery, in particular, the key point is that this code is mostly configuration specifying labels and visual options for the graphs. Beyond that the only information needed to fetch and render the data is a URL where the server returns results in the appropriate format. With this done you have finally completed the dashboard application. If you want to experiment with the visualization code and integration with BigQuery, you do not have to limit yourself to these mobile logs. It is easy to modify the code to use tables from the public dataset or any other dataset your service account can access.

Beyond the Dashboard

One of the key features of BigQuery is that the raw data is always easily accessible for exploration as shown in Figure 8.4. As part of the sample project, we have made some of the data we collected from our personal phones available for queries, so you can get a sense of ad-hoc exploration. This feature was used heavily during development to select and refine suitable queries. In later chapters you also see how to use third-party tools to build dashboards or visualize this data.

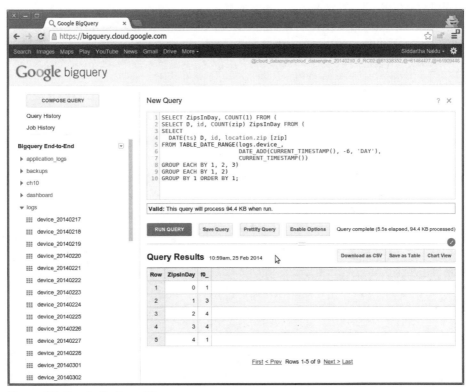

Figure 8.4: Data in BigQuery UI

Summary

This chapter demonstrated how the whole platform can be stitched together to build rich applications for recording and analyzing data. This sample code might be a useful starting point for exploring various features of the Google Cloud Platform. There are certainly areas in which the integration is challenging, but we demonstrated that in a lot of cases the pieces fit together quite naturally. If there is an aspect of the application that does not seem clear at this point, read on, because detailed explanation of the techniques used in this application appear in the following chapters.

Lastly, you should also check out the sample applications released by the BigQuery team. You can see one example at `https://demobigquery.appspot.com/`.

Generally, the source code for these applications is also made available so that you can adapt it to your application. Because the product is adding features regularly, these examples evolve over time to reflect the best way to implement solutions using the service.

Advanced BigQuery

In This Part

Understanding Query Execution

The SQL query language defines *what* data should be returned by a query, not *how* the results should be obtained. For the past 40 years or so, the primary engine for performing SQL queries has been the relational database. People are familiar with how a relational database works. They've developed an intuition for what will run quickly, what will be inefficient, and what kinds of things to avoid. Their intuition is based on knowledge about how a relational database will execute their queries.

Although BigQuery runs the same types of SQL queries that you can run on a relational database, it executes them in a different way. Because of this, intuition that you may have about query execution is likely to lead you astray. For example, in a relational database, there may be a performance advantage to storing some computed value so that it can be indexed. In BigQuery, because of the parallel architecture, you can do complex manipulation inline in the query without a significant change in query execution time.

This chapter describes the architecture of the underlying Dremel query engine used by BigQuery. The aim is to help you develop an intuition about how BigQuery queries will execute. It also should shine a light on some of the quirks of execution, such as why you may get a Response Too Large error even if you've specified that you want only 10 rows in the response.

There are three main sections in this chapter. The first part describes the ColumnIO storage format and Dremel query execution architecture. The second part discusses how various queries are processed, and some of the tricks that are used to process queries in parallel. Finally, Dremel is compared to other familiar execution environments, such as a traditional relational database (for example, MySQL) and MapReduce (for example, Hadoop or Hive).

After reading this chapter, you should be able to write queries that run efficiently and take advantage of the power of the Dremel query engine. Moreover, you should understand why some queries fail and what to do to fix them. The next chapter, which describes some advanced query techniques, draws heavily from the concepts described here.

Background

A large portion of the effort that goes into database research and engineering development deals with improving query performance. Much of that work is predicated on the knowledge that some things are slow and others are fast— reading from disk is slow, whereas reading memory is fast; seeking to a new spot on the disk is slow, but a sequential scan is fast. Processors can compute values quickly, but it is even better to precompute values that you're going to need.

One of the cardinal sins of database design is the table scan, which is what you resort to when the query optimizer gives up and can't figure out a fast way to execute your query. A table scan does exactly what it sounds like; it scans the entire table by reading it one row at a time. On many database systems, not only are table scans slow, but also they risk slowing down other operations because they keep the disk busy. A significant portion of the complexity in a modern database system is designed to avoid table scans, at all costs.

The designers of Dremel thought, "Why does a table scan have to be slow?" "What would it take to make a table scan fast?" and "If we do make a table scan fast, does that make other things easier?" They set a goal of performing a table scan over a 1 TB table in less than 1 second.

Achieving a processing rate of a terabyte per second is tough. A standard hard disk can read approximately 100 MB per second. (That is probably a bit on the high side, but it is in the right ballpark.) If you have a hard disk and want to read a terabyte from it, it is going to take you 10,000 seconds, or approximately 3 hours.

Moreover, if you're going to do interesting queries, but don't have indexes, you're going to need a lot of processing capacity. If your 1 TB table has 256 bytes per row, you can process 1 million rows per second per CPU. To process the whole table in one second would take 4,000 CPUs.

The combination of innovative software design, scale-out architecture, and Google's massive hardware infrastructure enabled the Dremel team to achieve its goal of taming the table scan. The architecture sections in this chapter describe how they did it. If you prefer to read the technical writeup, a research paper introducing Dremel is available from the Google Research website here: `http://research.google.com/pubs/pub36632.html`.

The technology described in this chapter is not necessarily what will be running when you use BigQuery. The individual components, from the ColumnIO storage format to the Colossus File System to the Dremel servers, are all undergoing constant improvement and innovation. Description of some components in this chapter are simplified in order to prevent disclosing confidential information. The important part is that the high-level concepts are likely to remain the same in the future, even if the underlying technology stack changes over time.

Storage Architecture

The most expensive part of any operation over Big Data is almost always I/O. As previously mentioned, the disk I/O involved to read a 1 TB table will take hours. If your goal is to interactively query a 1 TB table, you need to figure out ways to bring the time you spend reading data down by 5 orders of magnitude.

There are two technologies that Dremel uses to achieve (and at times far surpass) the 1 TB per second goal. The first is called Colossus: a large, parallel, distributed filesystem, developed at Google as a successor for the Google File System (GFS). The second is the storage format, called ColumnIO, which arranges the data in a manner that makes it easier to query.

Colossus File System (CFS)

Although Google described the architecture of its predecessor GFS in a public research paper (`http://static.googleusercontent.com/media/research.google.com/en/us/archive/gfs-sosp2003.pdf`), it has kept Colossus largely under wraps. Details about Colossus are generally confidential; it is a refinement of GFS that fixes a number of scalability problems. For now just focus on the features of CFS that enable Dremel's super-fast query performance, which for the most part, are the same as GFS (or the open source clone, HDFS).

Colossus is a distributed filesystem, which means that the storage is not physically attached to the machines requesting the data, and that data is distributed across the network. All of the data in Colossus is stored on commodity disks. Expensive storage hardware solutions can be fast, but they are a single point of failure and often don't scale well. Storing the data on standard server hard drives means that you can afford a lot more of them—you just need to be prepared when some of them inevitably fail.

The machines that contain the disks and serve up the data are called *chunk servers*. The term "chunk" refers to portions of the files; a large file will be split into multiple chunks, and each will be stored on different physical disks. This partitioning means that you can get higher effective read bandwidth because you can read from many of these disks in parallel. Dremel takes advantage of this; when you run a query, it can read your data from thousands of disks at once.

Splitting the data into multiple partitions that can be read in parallel is a powerful way to make reads fast, but it isn't sufficient for the performance required by Dremel. There are a lot of reasons that reading a particular chunk could be slow; the machine serving it could be overloaded, it could have crashed, there could be network congestion, or the disk could be going bad. Although the probability of each of these problems is small, when you read from thousands of disks, the chances that at least one has a problem gets much higher.

The term for having a laggard or two among a lot of samples is called *tail latency*. A query is only as fast as the slowest disk; a problem in the "tail" of the latency distribution can significantly affect query performance. One way that Colossus handles tail latency is via replication. That is, multiple copies of the same data are stored in different locations. So if one chunk server is slow, the data can be fetched from somewhere else.

The published Dremel paper mentioned another way of limiting tail latency— ignoring data that takes too long to read, as long as enough of it can be read. Internal Google services use this option, usually requiring only 98 percent of the data to be read before calling a query successful. BigQuery, however, does *not* use this option; for a BigQuery query to succeed, every last byte of data must be read.

ColumnIO

ColumnIO is the primary file format used to store data in BigQuery. In a traditional database, data is laid out on disk in order to ensure access is as fast as possible for typical workloads. The ColumnIO data format is laid out to ensure fast access for Dremel workloads. Traditional databases rely on indexes so that they can skip to the data they need for the query. Dremel takes a more brute force approach, reading every single row for each query. While a database such as MySQL can skip rows it doesn't need, Dremel takes an alternative approach; it can avoid reading columns it doesn't need.

Traditional databases store data in row-order. That is, they store all the fields in the first row, then all the fields in the second row, and so on. ColumnIO stores the data in column-order. Each column gets its own file. To read from multiple columns at once, you need to open all the files you need and iterate through each one in parallel. This read operation must be synchronized, but because each column is coming from a different chunk server, the I/O requests can all be performed in parallel.

Note that in a traditional storage system, reading from column-based storage will likely be slow because the disk would have to constantly seek for each of the column files instead of just reading sequentially. Because BigQuery stores the data in CFS, however, each column is going to come from a different disk in the storage cluster. This means that reading from multiple files at once will not involve any additional seek operations.

Figure 9.1 shows a columnar layout and compares it to a record-based one. Nested fields are treated as completely separate fields. Repeated fields are packed within the parent field, with a special marker that indicates the start of the next row. This makes seeking in a repeated field somewhat more expensive than seeking in a singular field because you have to scan through all the repeated values to get to the next row.

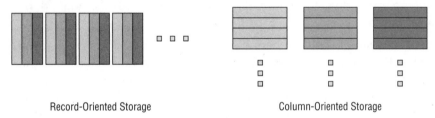

Record-Oriented Storage   Column-Oriented Storage

Figure 9.1: Record-oriented versus column-oriented storage

There are two factors that make reading from column-oriented storage faster than record-oriented storage: selectivity and compression. *Selectivity* is the ability to select only the columns needed in the query. Many tables have a wide schema, but most queries just reference a few fields. The ability to read only the columns needed by the query is a key feature of ColumnIO, which can often reduce the amount of data needed to read by an order of magnitude or more.

Each column in ColumnIO is compressed separately. Dremel reads back the compressed data and decompresses it on-the-fly as needed. Because I/O bandwidth is by far the biggest bottleneck in the system, you can improve your overall throughput by a factor of 10 or more by operating over compressed data.

At first, you might not expect a column store to compress so well because it isn't immediately apparent why it would compress much better than a record store—after all, they're both storing the same data. You're probably used to seeing data compress at 2 or 3 to 1 when you compress a file, so 10x sounds unreasonable.

To see why column stores compress so well, think about what a compression algorithm does: It searches for redundant information and re-encodes it in a smaller way. For example, if you have the string QQQrrQQQ, you could compress it to aba, and store the mapping of a to QQQ and b to rr. Although this is a contrived example, it is how most compression algorithms work, in some form. First, the algorithm scans the input and looks for repeated strings. Then it saves the repeated data in a dictionary. Finally, it can then replace the redundant input with an optimal encoding.

Now think back to the ColumnIO disk format, which has one file per column. What do the individual fields look like? They're not usually random text. They often fall into one of the following categories:

- **IDs:** These could be a customer ID or an e-mail address. They usually have a decent amount of redundancy (or to be technical, low entropy). An e-mail address, for example, probably ends in ".com." In addition, there are probably a lot of e-mail addresses from the same domain, like "user@hotmail.com."

- **Small numbers:** Most numbers are small and don't use all their allotted 8 bytes. For example, an age column will be unlikely to have more than 100 distinct values. Even when they're larger, numbers often follow patterns; numbers in nature have a lot more 1s than 9s, whereas prices have a lot more 9s than anything else.

- **Enumerated data:** Enumerations are the kings of redundancy. Often in a database table, you have a column for Item Code or Language. These fields may have only a few distinct values but may take up a lot of space writing out those values in full for each row.

- **Regular strings:** Many string-valued fields compress extremely well. A URL, for example, nearly always starts with http://, and the rest of the URL could be mostly redundant. A user-agent string is another example, which tends to be a long string describing a browser but with a high degree of regularity.

It is also usually more efficient to compress values of the same type than it is to compress records containing multiple types. Floating point values have numerical similarities, as do UTF-8 encoded characters in a string; these similarities can be exploited by the compression algorithm to come up with a more compact representation.

Of course, not all fields compress well. But in practice, the compression ratio within a column is much higher than for raw text. By trading off the time spent decompressing the data for time spent reading the data from the network, you can scan the data even faster.

IF COLUMNIO COMPRESSES SO WELL, WHY DOES BIGQUERY CHARGE PER BYTE INSTEAD OF PER COMPRESSED BYTE?

BigQuery charges for storage based on the number of bytes stored in the table without accounting for compression. As previously described, BigQuery stores data as compressed and relies on this compression for performance. If your data in BigQuery is highly compressible, shouldn't you be rewarded with smaller storage costs?

There are two reasons you're charged full-freight for your stored data. The first is that just because the data compresses well doesn't mean that it is much less difficult to query. For example, if you compare long strings via a WHERE clause, the query engine has to read the whole string to determine if there is a match, even if that string compressed well on disk. And although BigQuery could compute one size for queries and another for storage, that adds significant complexity without much additional benefit.

The second rationale behind the pricing is just predictability. Say you upload a column containing 1,000 integers today and get charged for 2,000 bytes because those integers compressed at a 4-to-1 compression ratio. If then you upload another 1,000 integers tomorrow, you might get a completely different compression ratio. Moreover, BigQuery periodically reshuffles data as needed by the service. Sometimes, that might change how the data is split between files, which can change the compression ratio for better or worse. It would be highly surprising if the storage costs for a table changed from day to day just because BigQuery moved the underlying data.

The compromise that was chosen was to charge only for uncompressed bytes, but to charge perhaps a lower rate than might have been otherwise picked.

Durability and Availability

This section describes the current implementation of how your data is stored in BigQuery. While BigQuery does not have official data reliability guarantees, every table in BigQuery is replicated several times. Data in a CFS cell is replicated in three ways to provide durability and reduce tail latency. BigQuery also asynchronously replicates all tables to multiple geographically distributed datacenters. If there is a power failure in one datacenter, it should not affect your ability to get to your data.

When you initially load data into BigQuery, it is added only to a single datacenter, so there is a small window where the data is singly homed (even though it is still replicated three ways within the datacenter). When the load completes, a synchronization process copies that data to other remote datacenters. When you query your table, you should always get the most recent version of your data, even if it has not finished replicating everywhere.

When you have distributed a filesystem with a large number of disks (at least 10s of thousands), replication is essential because some of those disks fail every day. Disks can fail in a lot of different ways: They can develop errors due to cosmic rays, their motors can burn out slowly, the machine that hosts them can have a bad power supply, or the magnetic disks can lose their sensitivity. Having multiple choices of where to read data from comes in handy when you read from a lot of disks because the odds that at least one is healthy are high.

Durability is a measure of the persistence of data. Data that is replicated nine ways and has adequate failure replacement policies (that is, when a disk fails it isn't just removed, but the copy of the data is replaced on a fresh disk) has an expected lifetime on the order of 1 million years (see `http://cseweb.ucsd.edu/users/pasquale/Papers/ipdps10.pdf`). That said, Google BigQuery does not at this time publish a durability guarantee for its data. As with all data, if it is critical, make a backup. BigQuery enables you to easily copy a table to back it up, or you can export it to Google Cloud Storage for safekeeping.

Availability is a measure of your ability to get to your data when you want it. BigQuery does publish a guarantee that the service will be available 99.9% of the time. This guarantee includes the ability to get to your data. The most likely data non-availability scenario would be if the BigQuery servers had a global outage.

Of course, this section describes a snapshot in time; BigQuery may increase or decrease the replication factor. Durability and availability of data are and will continue to be top priorities of Google and BigQuery. For more reading on the subject, check out this blog post on disaster data recovery for Google enterprise data: `http://googleenterprise.blogspot.com/2010/03/disaster-recovery-by-google.html`. Although this article was not specifically written with BigQuery in mind, the policies described are similar.

Query Processing

SQL is a declarative language rather than an imperative one. This is a fancy way of saying that you declare *what* you want to happen, rather than describe *how* you want it to happen. Without this property, the switch from a standard, sequentially processed relational database to a parallel query engine like Dremel would not be nearly as easy. Imagine if, instead of a WHERE clause, you had to describe how to look up the data in a B-Tree (an on disk data structure that backs most relational databases). If this was the case, you'd be stuck with databases that use B-Trees (and, most likely, only programmers would be able to figure out how to run queries).

With SQL, however, the query describes precisely which data you want to be returned in the query and leaves up to the database implementation how it wants to get that data. You might have an Oracle database responding to your queries, or you might have an overworked graduate student typing all the responses by hand.

In the last section, you saw that between the Colossus distributed filesystem and ColumnIO, you can easily meet the goal of reading the data for a 1 TB table in less than 1 second. Of course, just because you can get all of that data off a disk quickly doesn't mean it is going to be fast to run the query. For instance, you're not going to be able to process it all on a single machine—even if you have a magical 10 terabit Ethernet; the fastest memory bandwidth is something like 25 GB per second, which means you'd need 40 seconds just to read the data out of memory. And then if you were able to only spend one processor cycle per row, it would take almost a minute to process a terabyte table.

From these rough calculations, it should be apparent that you need to scale out the query processing so that it can be done on multiple machines in parallel, especially if you don't want to invest in absurdly expensive custom hardware. In general, Google prefers to buy a lot of off-the-shelf hardware and figure out ways to make algorithms scale out. Any query processing solution, therefore, should run on commodity hardware.

This section describes the Dremel query engine, which is Google's solution for scaling out SQL queries by processing them in parallel.

Dremel Serving Trees

If you were going to construct a parallel SQL engine, how would you do it? You'd likely want to have a number of independent workers, each operating over a small subset of the data. For some simple queries, this might be all you need. Take, for example, the query SELECT field1 FROM table1 WHERE field2 > 0. This query is trivially parallelizable. Each worker, operating over a portion of the data, can read the two required fields, and return the `field1` values whenever `field2` matches the filter condition.

You may suspect that not all queries will be this easy, and if so, you are right. Now take a similar query: SELECT COUNT(`field1`) FROM table1 WHERE `field2` > 0. This seems like it should be easy too, but instead of just returning the `field1` values, you need to count values. Because you need to return a single total count, you can't just have each parallel worker operate independently. However, you can have another worker aggregate the results and compute the total sum. Let's call the aggregator the "mixer," since it mixes data from multiple workers, and the workers that are reading the data directly "shards."

After partitioning the query workers into a mixer and shards, to compute the query results you can send the filter portion of the query (SELECT `field1` WHERE `field2` > 0) to each of the shards and have them send the filtered results to the mixer. The mixer would then count the results and report the final sum.

Alternatively, you could pre-aggregate the count in the shards. That is, compute the local count in the shards, and the mixer would just have to sum up the partial counts. This way of running the query means that a lot more of the work can be done in the shards, since the mixer only has to compute the sum of a few values (one value per shard). Performing more work in the shards means that the query can scale out efficiently.

This mechanism just described—shards reading the raw table data and performing filters and partial aggregation, and then passing results up to a mixer that does further aggregation—is the basis of how Dremel works. Each aggregation method, from COUNT() to SUM() to STDDEV(), and so on, can be partitioned into parallel operations that can be combined into a final result or results. Operations like GROUP BY, as well, can be partially performed in the shards and subsequently combined in the mixer.

In a typical Dremel tree, there are hundreds or thousands of shards. Because aggregating the results from all these shards is more work than a single mixer could handle, the mixers are arranged in a tree. At the root of the tree is the root mixer, which is responsible for responding back to the caller with the result data. Figure 9.2 shows a Dremel tree with two levels of mixers.

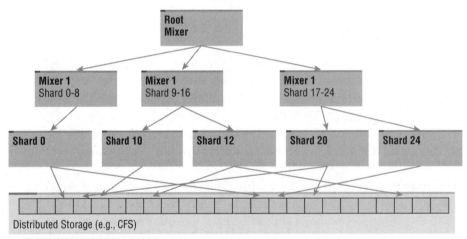

Figure 9.2: Dremel serving tree

Basic Queries

To help you understand how Dremel works, this section looks at a few queries and walks you through how they are executed. For clarity in these examples, we only describe the operations of a single mixer. When there are multiple levels of mixers, they just repeat the same operations, so if you understand how one works, you understand how a tree of them works. These queries all use the `publicdata:samples.shakespeare` table which contains counts for each word used in each Shakespeare play.

The first query performs a filter and a sort:

```
SELECT word, corpus, word_count
FROM [publicdata:samples.shakespeare]
WHERE LENGTH(word) > 4 AND NOT REGEXP_MATCH(word, "^[A-Z]+")
ORDER BY word_count DESC
LIMIT 5
```

This query computes the top five words in any Shakespeare play by frequency, returning the word, the play in which it appears, and the word count. It filters out any word less than four letters and anything that is all caps (in order to ignore character names). If you run the query, you find that the top value is "shall," which appears in both *Merry Wives of Windsor* and *Henry VI, Part 2* 119 times each.

Query Execution

When you run this query, Dremel performs the following steps:

1. The mixer receives the query. Its job is to parallelize the query so that it can be sent to the shards for execution. The first thing that it does is translate the query into a form that can be handled by the shards—in many cases, this means simplifying the query. In this case, however, the entire query is meaningful to the shard. The mixer then looks up the table name and translates it into its underlying file names.

    Each shard gets a subset of the files to operate over. The number of files may limit the amount of parallelism possible in the query. If there are 1,000 shards available but only 10 files, only 10 shards will be involved in the query. For small tables like the Shakespeare sample table, only a few shards may be used. For other large tables, there may be more files than shards, and each shard will be responsible for processing multiple files. In general, BigQuery manages the file count to balance performance with shard efficiency. (That is, too many files can be just as bad as too few because you'll end up with shards that spend most of their time opening files.)

2. The shards receive the customized query. They open the underlying files that they were assigned and start reading. Because each field in ColumnIO is stored in a separate file, this means opening one file per column referenced in the query. As it scans the table, the shard walks through the opened column files in parallel, one row at a time.

    The first portion of the query to be applied is the WHERE clause, which filters out rows that aren't interesting. In this case, all rows where the word length is less than 4 are dropped, and the regular expression is applied to remove words in all caps.

The shards can apply an optimization here—they need to return only the top five values ordered by word count. To find the top five values, they use a data structure called a *priority queue*, which is an efficient way of keeping track of the top values without having to sort them all in place.

3. Each shard returns its top 5 results to the mixer. The mixer can also use a priority queue to keep track of the top five results from the shards, and after all the shards have completed, it can return results back to the caller. The mixer doesn't have to worry about the WHERE clause because all the values it handles should be valid responses to the query.

If there was no ORDER BY operation, the mixer could perform another optimization; it could return immediately after it had received five valid results from the shards. But in this case it has to wait until all the shards have finished because the top five values might be returned only in the last shard.

GROUP BY Queries

You saw how a simple query that just does a filter and a sort operates. Now look at a slightly more complex query that does aggregation:

```
SELECT corpus, SUM(word_count) AS total_words
FROM [publicdata:samples.shakespeare]
WHERE LENGTH(word) > 4
GROUP BY corpus
ORDER BY total_words DESC
LIMIT 5
```

This query computes the top five Shakespeare plays in terms of total word count, excluding words shorter than five characters, and returns them in reverse order. For example, the top result is *Richard III*, which has 11,514 words, followed by *Hamlet* at 11,439 words.

Query Execution

The steps necessary to execute this query are:

1. The mixer receives the query. In this case, the shards don't need to know about the ORDER BY operation because they'll have to return all of their data. The mixer strips the ORDER BY clause and the LIMIT, and sends the query to the shards.

2. The shard receives the query and starts reading the corpus and word_count fields. The shard applies the WHERE clause and computes the aggregations needed for the GROUP BY. After the shard has totaled all the word_count values for each corpus, it returns those results to the mixer.

The amounts of resources used in this step are proportional to cardinality of the `corpus` field—that is, the number of unique values. In a large table, there might be billions of individual values. The shard needs to keep all of them in memory so that it can perform the aggregation (the sum of the `word_count` field for each `corpus`). If there are too many values, it will run out of memory and return an error complaining that resources have been exceeded. There are ways around this error—see the section entitled "Shuffled Queries" later in this chapter.

You might think, at first, that each shard could collect corpus names and word counts and would have to return only the top five to the mixer. However, this isn't the case; the shard has to return all the results. Imagine a case in which a certain corpus didn't score highly when its word count was computed by any individual shard, but after all the shards aggregated their results together, the corpus would end up with the highest word count. In other words, because the data may be unevenly distributed, all the results need to be aggregated in the mixer.

3. The mixer receives the results from the shards. It then needs to merge the aggregates. That is, if shard 1 finds 1,500 words in *Hamlet* and shard 2 finds 1,000 words in *Hamlet*, the mixer needs to compute the running total. After all the shards have returned, the mixer takes the top five values (it needs to sort all the values this time—it can't use the priority queue trick you saw in the last query, for the same reason that the shards had to return all of their data) and returns them to the caller.

The mixer is another place where too many unique values can cause memory exhaustion and lead to queries failing. Like memory exhaustion in the shards, a shuffle operation is usually the solution to the problem.

JOIN Queries

Although most aggregation functions and query clauses follow the same patterns as described in the previous sections, JOIN queries operate significantly differently. BigQuery has two types of JOIN operation: "small" JOIN and "big" JOIN. A "small" JOIN is any JOIN operation where at least one of the tables is less than 8 MB, compressed. The underlying table doesn't necessarily have to be small; you could do a small JOIN where you JOIN on the outcome of a subquery that filters a large table down to a smaller one. A "big" JOIN is any JOIN where both sides of the JOIN are larger than 8 MB and requires a different technique to execute it. This technique is discussed in the "Shuffled Queries" section.

JOIN Relational Operator

Before discussing how JOIN queries work, it may be useful to review what a JOIN query does. Every JOIN operation has two tables, which are usually denoted

LEFT and RIGHT. The LEFT table is the one that is mentioned first in the query, the RIGHT table is the one mentioned after the JOIN keyword. Both the LEFT and RIGHT need not be physical tables; they could be the results of subqueries instead.

JOIN is an operator in the relational algebra that says to take every row in the LEFT table and match it with every row in the RIGHT table and generate a new row that has the contents of the row in the LEFT table along with the contents of the row in the RIGHT table. A CROSS JOIN is the simplest form of JOIN, which actually does generate one row for every possible combination of rows in the source tables. Other JOIN types can be thought of as applying a CROSS JOIN but filtering the results based on some condition.

Most JOINS are either INNER or OUTER JOINS instead of CROSS JOINS. INNER and OUTER JOIN operations specify a filter via an ON clause (for example, ON table1 .foo = table2.bar). The filter says to generate all the rows that would be in the CROSS JOIN, but only keep rows where a field in the LEFT table matches a field in the RIGHT table. Some other SQL systems allow the filter to be specified in a WHERE clause (for example, WHERE table1.foo = table2.bar), but in BigQuery, only the ON clause version is supported.

The difference between INNER and OUTER is how they handle cases when there are no matches between the value in the LEFT table and the value in the RIGHT. An INNER JOIN drops any rows where there is not a match, whereas an OUTER JOIN keeps the row and fills the side that doesn't match with null values. The difference between LEFT OUTER and RIGHT OUTER JOIN is which table gets precedence—the LEFT or the RIGHT. It isn't important to understand all the possible JOIN options now, but some familiarity with JOIN semantics helps to understand the BigQuery JOIN implementation.

Broadcast JOIN

A "small" JOIN is often called a "broadcast" JOIN because it relies on broadcasting the smaller table to all the nodes in the computation tree. A JOIN operation needs to generate all combinations of rows where the fields specified in the ON clause match. To process the JOIN operation, you can walk all the rows in the LEFT table and figure out whether there is a matching row in the RIGHT table. If the RIGHT table is small, you can just put all the values into a hash table. The hash table has keys that are the JOIN keys from the ON clause, and the values are the rest of the row (or the fields needed from the row in the query). Then, for each row on the left, you can do a quick lookup by key to find the matching row from the RIGHT table.

This algorithm is parallelizable, as long as you replicate the hash table to each parallel worker. This, in essence, is how the broadcast JOIN works. The smaller table is required to be on the RIGHT side of the query, and it is broadcast to each worker node. Then the worker can perform the JOIN operation by doing a simple key lookup. Figure 9.3 shows how a broadcast JOIN operation works in practice.

The small boxes to the left of the shards and mixers are the RIGHT table from the query, which gets distributed to every node in the tree.

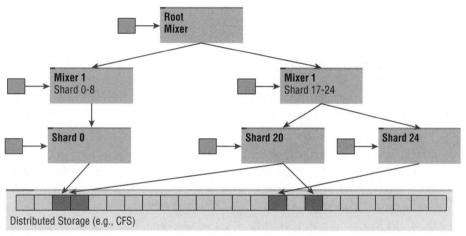

Figure 9.3: Broadcast JOIN

You may see why there is a size limit for broadcast JOIN. First, the entire hash table needs to fit in memory, so it is constrained by memory limitations on the worker. Furthermore, the hash table also needs to be broadcast to every shard in the Dremel cluster. If there are 5,000 shards and you have an 8 MB table, you've just sent 40 GB of traffic across the network.

Now that you've seen how broadcast JOIN works, we can walk through an example:

```
SELECT wiki.title
FROM [publicdata:samples.wikipedia] AS wiki
JOIN (
  SELECT word
  FROM [publicdata:samples.shakespeare]
  GROUP BY word
  ) AS shakes
ON wiki.title = shakes.word
```

This query joins the Wikipedia sample table with the Shakespeare sample table. The Wikipedia table has one row for every update made to any Wikipedia page. The only field we use in this query is title, which is the title of the page that was edited. The query returns one row per revision to each Wikipedia entry whose title is a word in a Shakespeare play.

The Wikipedia table is "large," so it must go on the LEFT side of the JOIN. The Shakespeare table is small, but it is made even smaller by performing GROUP BY word. The reason to do this is because there are many rows in the Shakespeare table for each word—one for each corpus that used that word.

There are also multiple rows in the Wikipedia table for each title—one for each revision to the entry.

If you had just done the JOIN without a GROUP BY, you'd get one row for each corpus containing the word multiplied by the number of revisions. The word "Peace" is in 33 of Shakespeare's plays and the "Peace" Wikipedia entry has 2741 revisions, so joining just those two keys would generate 33 x 2741= 90,453 rows in the result—just for that one word. Because this isn't what you want, you should do the GROUP BY on the Shakespeare table so that you collapse the *Hamlet* entries down to one row, and you end up with only 2 million rows in the result.

Here is how this query executes:

1. The mixer receives the query. This is a two-stage query; you have to compute the results of the subquery on the Shakespeare table in order to find and prepare the RIGHT table of the JOIN. To kick off the first stage, the mixer extracts the subquery SELECT word FROM [publicdata:samples .shakespeare] GROUP BY word and sends it to the shards.

2. Each shard receives the subquery, reads the Shakespeare table, and performs the GROUP BY aggregation. Each shard then returns one row per Shakespeare corpus.

3. The mixer completes the aggregation from the shards' responses, and ends up with an in-memory table containing one row per corpus. It names that result table [__inline_table] so that it can be referred to later.

4. Once the results of the subquery have been computed, the mixer sends the following query to the shards: SELECT wiki.title FROM [wiki_table_path] AS wiki JOIN [__inline_table] AS shakes ON wiki.title = shakes .word. It also sends the inline result table along with the query.

5. Each shard gets this query and the inline table computed in the subquery. It takes the inline table and generates a lookup table from it. The keys of the lookup table are the Shakespearean words and the values of the lookup table are the same as the keys (because word is the only field needed by the query).

   After the lookup table has been created, the shard iterates through each row of its portion of the Wikipedia table. For each row, it takes the title field and looks for it in the lookup table. If it does not exist, it skips the row. If it does exist, it adds a row to the results. The only field needed in the results in this example is the title, but in other cases there could be fields from the RIGHT table or other computed fields that would go in the results.

6. All of the work to compute the JOIN can be done in the shards, so all the mixer has to do is collect the results and return them to the caller.

Shuffled Queries

As previously described, both the GROUP BY and the JOIN operations have some limitations; GROUP BY cannot handle cases in which there are large numbers of distinct values, and JOIN can't handle cases in which one of the tables is larger than 8 MB. The good news is that there is a mechanism that works around both of these problems; the bad news is that this mechanism requires a slight syntax change.

In both the GROUP BY case and the JOIN case, you need to aggregate data in the mixer because the shards don't have enough information to compute the results. For example, if you were grouping by corpus, multiple shards might see rows for the corpus Hamlet, so the partial result has to be passed back to the mixer. What if, however, the underlying data were sorted by corpus, and a single shard processed all the Hamlet entries? If this was the case, you could perform the GROUP BY operation in the shards, and it wouldn't matter how many distinct corpus values you had because you wouldn't have a bottleneck at the mixer.

When you use GROUP EACH BY instead of GROUP BY, this tells Dremel to perform a *shuffle* operation. If you've used Hadoop or another MapReduce system, the shuffle step may look familiar; the hidden step in a MapReduce is shuffle, which sorts all the data before passing it to the reducer.

Dremel's shuffle is a little bit different from Hadoop's shuffle; the latter performs a merge sort of all the keys in the dataset. Dremel doesn't care about the ordering, however; it performs a hash partitioning of the data. The goal of these two approaches is the same, but a hash partitioning is less work than a sort.

The way the hash partitioning works is that each value is assigned a key. A hash function is applied in a source shard to the key to turn it into a number. That number, the hash code, is used to assign the entire row to a destination shard. The source shard then sends the row over to the network to the assigned destination shard. Because the workers are assigned stable ranges of the hash key space, a single worker gets all the values that have the same key.

For GROUP EACH BY operations, the shuffle key is the field or fields used for the grouping. That is, if you do a GROUP EACH BY corpus on the Shakespeare table, all the rows that have Hamlet as the corpus hash to the same value and are sent to the same shard. All the rows that have the corpus of Macbeth will hash to a different value, so they will be sent to a different shard than the Hamlet rows. Figure 9.4 shows how the shuffle operation works. Each shard first reads the data from storage, then forwards that data on to a diferent shard depending on the value of the shuffle key.

This same trick also works for JOIN, but both sides of the JOIN need to be shuffled. To specify a shuffled JOIN, you can use the syntax JOIN EACH where you would otherwise have used JOIN, as in LEFT OUTER JOIN EACH. The shuffle key is the field or fields used in the ON clause. That is, if your query looks like JOIN EACH . . . ON left.key1 = right.key2, the left table is shuffled by the key1 field, and the right table is shuffled by the key2 field. Since the same hash function is used on both, all of the rows with matching values from either table will end up in the same shard. This enables the JOIN operation to proceed in the shards and in parallel, in a method similar to the broadcast JOIN.

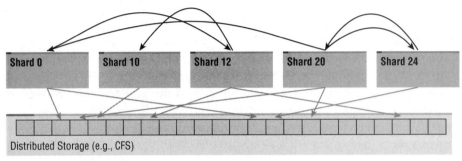

Figure 9.4: Shuffle operation

Now that we've discussed the basic operation, we can consider an example, using the same query as in the broadcast JOIN example, but with JOIN EACH instead of JOIN. Note that this query doesn't *need* to use a shuffled JOIN, but it is useful to do so to compare its execution with the broadcast JOIN version. Here is the query:

```
SELECT wiki.title
FROM [publicdata:samples.wikipedia] as wiki
JOIN EACH(
  SELECT word
  FROM [publicdata:samples.shakespeare]
  GROUP EACH BY word) as shakes
ON wiki.title = shakes.word
```

The steps involved to execute this query are:

1. The mixer receives the query and plans the execution. This query requires five phases:

   a. The Shakespeare table on the right must be shuffled prior to the GROUP BY.

    b. The GROUP BY subquery on the right must be run to compute the distinct Shakespeare words.

    c. The right table must be shuffled prior to the JOIN.

    d. The left table must be shuffled prior to the JOIN.

    e. Finally, the JOIN results can be computed in the shards.

To start things off, the mixer dispatches the first part of the query (the shuffle of the Shakespeare table) to the shards.

2. The shards receive the request to shuffle the publicdata:samples .shakespeare table into 100 partitions based on the word field. Each shard computes a hash key for each word value and sends the hashed row to a different shard indicated by the hash. For the word "peace" for example, the hash function returns the value 7146922576. This would get sent to shard 76, because there are 100 shuffle partitions and 7146922576 % 100 = 76. After the shuffle is complete, the shards return to the mixer indicating they are finished. (Note that they do not return any results at this point.) The temporary table with the results is given the name __table1.

3. Once the Shakespeare table rows have been sorted by word value into distinct partitions, the GROUP BY operation from the RIGHT subquery can be done entirely in the shards. The shards receive the query SELECT word FROM [__table1] GROUP BY word. The results of this subuery are stored in table __table2.

4. The mixer now kicks off a new shuffle on the left table by instructing the shards to shuffle the [publicdata:samples.wikipedia] table into 500 partitions based on the title field. The results are saved in a temporary table called __table3.

5. Now that all the preparatory work is done, the two temporary tables can be joined. Because the LEFT and RIGHT tables have been sorted by the field they are being joined by, the work of the JOIN can be done in parallel on the shards. The mixer sends SELECT wiki.title FROM __ table3 AS wiki JOIN __table2 AS shakes ON wiki.title = shakes . word to the shards. The __table2 and __table3 tables are the outputs of the shuffle phases that have been patiently waiting to be joined. After computing the JOIN, the results are returned to the mixer.

6. The mixer doesn't need to do any aggregation in this query, so it just returns all the results to the caller.

WHEN TO USE SHUFFLED QUERIES

GROUP EACH BY and JOIN EACH BY queries are extremely powerful because they enable you to operate over larger and more complex data sets than you otherwise would be able to process. It is tempting, therefore, to use the keyword everywhere. However, there are some disadvantages to using the EACH keyword. Most obvious, using EACH adds a lot of extra processing to the query, which can slow down performance significantly. Although it is difficult to estimate how long a shuffle operation will take, you can count on anywhere from 2 seconds to 60 seconds added time, depending on table sizes.

What might not be obvious is that there are other cases in which a shuffle query is slower—when too many results all hash to the same shard. Because a single shard must process every row that hashes to a particular value, if a single value is too common, this can overload the shard and end up taking much longer to process.

A simple example of this would be if you imagine a huge customer table with a Country field. If 99 percent of your customers are in the United States, if you do a GROUP EACH BY Country, a single shard needs to process 99 percent of the rows. This process can take a long time and can even lead to your queries being canceled.

It is likely that future versions of BigQuery will be smarter about picking whether to do a shuffle, so you won't have to worry about it. For now, however, you should probably default to *not* using the EACH keyword unless you need it.

Materialize Queries

When you run a normal query in BigQuery, you're limited to results that are less than 128 MB. If you think about how the query runs in the Dremel serving tree, you can see why this limit exists—because everything has to be returned through the root mixer. If you had 100 GB of results, this would be a lot of data to return from a single server, with a lot of data to aggregate in one place.

Dremel supports an alternative query mode called *materialize* where the shards write out the results directly and in parallel. This, of course, means that the entire query must be parallelizable. Top-level ORDER BY operations may be slow (because a sort must be computed globally), and queries may end up taking substantially longer to complete because writing data to permanent storage is slower than returning it over the network. Despite these limitations, materialize queries are extremely powerful—they can write out hundreds of gigabytes in only a few seconds.

For most queries, however, the user who issued them cares only about the first few results. In the BigQuery Web UI, for example, few people fetch the second page of results, let alone the last one. If you run a SELECT * query to look at the first few rows of a table and you write out 10 TB and wait 5 minutes, you'll be wasting a lot of your time and Google's processing resources.

To prevent you from accidentally generating massive results, materialize queries are not the default. If you want a massive result set, you need to set the flag `allowLargeResults` in the query *and* specify a destination table. The destination table is required because of how large results tend to be used; because they are too large to be processed by a human, they are usually going to be processed by a machine. Often you want to run another query against your large result table, or maybe you want to export the results to Google Cloud Storage so that you can process them on an external system. In these cases, it is useful to have a table with a name to refer to as the source of those subsequent operations.

Finally, writing out large results is expensive. Although BigQuery doesn't charge you for normal query results, it does charge you for the storage used for anything with a destination table. If you write out a 1 TB table, you have pay the cost of storing that table.

Architecture Comparisons

To understand BigQuery, it can be helpful to put it in context with other architectures you may already be familiar with. If you're coming from a background where you've used a lot of relational databases, or you use Hadoop to process your data, you might have certain assumptions about what is going to be fast, what is going to be slow, or what is going to be impossible. BigQuery's architecture creates a different set of things that are fast, slow, or impossible; understanding the difference in the architectures can help you generate an intuition about when to use one tool versus another.

Relational Databases

If you're doing any kind of analytics, you almost certainly have experience using a relational database. Relational databases exist in many forms—from Open Source examples such as MySQL and Postgres to commercial juggernauts such as Microsoft SQL Server and Oracle.

In addition, if you've used a relational database, you've probably even thought about optimizing one—adding indexes, normalizing data, adding additional disk spindles, and so on. Relational database architecture tends to be almost hard-wired into how most people think about querying their data, whether they realize it or not.

This section outlines the architecture of a typical relational database, focusing on the parts that contribute most to its performance. You also see when to use it and how it compares to BigQuery.

Relational Database Design

Relational databases have been around since the early 1970s—they have had a lot of time to be refined and improved upon. That said, the fundamentals haven't changed in that time: They still rely on the same underlying data structures and apply the same types of optimization tricks as they have for the past several decades.

Data Storage Architecture

The fundamental data structure in a relational database is the B-Tree. A B-Tree is a specialized tree, usually stored on disk, with a relatively high branching factor (unlike a binary tree, which has a branching factor of two). Each node can point to a number of children, up to the branching factor, which is often on the order of 1000 elements. This means that a tree of depth 3 could contain up to a billion nodes (1000^3). Figure 9.5 shows a 3-level B-Tree. The diagram may look similar to a Dremel serving tree; the principal difference is that the boxes here represent metadata on disk, not independent services.

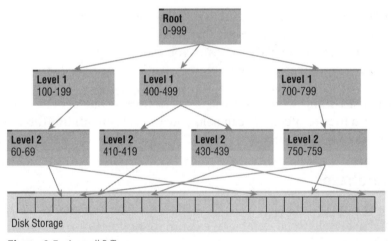

Figure 9.5: A small B-Tree

B-Trees take advantage of the fact that disk I/O is much slower than memory access. A single disk read operation can read an entire B-Tree node into memory, after which time the contents of node can be scanned quickly. A 3-level B-Tree requires at most three disk reads to find any element. The processor has to do more work, scanning three entire nodes (which may be composed of thousands of elements), but the time spent by the CPU is much smaller than the disk time.

Filesystem cache behavior can also help; the root node of the B-Tree will almost always be cached in memory. The second level nodes also have a high cache hit rate because there are only 1000 of them. This means that most searches have to do only a single disk seek and read to find the element they are looking for.

B-trees are also convenient data structures for inserting and deleting data. If you add a new node, most of the time you can do it by just adding the relevant pointer from the parent node. Only one out of every 1000 times will you have to rebalance. Of course, rebalancing can be tricky, but there have been decades of database improvements to work on perfecting this operation. A delete operation is even easier; just delete the pointer to the data. When an entire node is empty, you can reclaim the storage.

When doing analytics queries, you're not usually just looking up data—you're often scanning for data within certain parameters. B-trees make these types of scans easy; because they are stored in sorted order, scanning for values within a range is just a sequential in-order traversal of the tree.

Relational Database Optimization

Relational databases generally have primary and secondary indexes. Both of these are B-Trees. The only difference is that the primary index also generally stores the data within the B-Tree, which is a performance optimization to save additional disk I/O. Secondary indexes are additional B-trees that point to the data in the primary key.

In addition to the B-Tree, relational databases often store extra information about the table that can help when planning the best way to run the query. This information can be stored inside the B-Tree or in additional table metadata. For example, a database often stores the number of rows in a table and an approximation of the cardinality, or number of distinct values in each field. This metadata can be useful to avoid reading unnecessary data or deciding which index to use.

When a query is run, the query planner module makes an educated guess about the fastest way to find the data needed in the query. For instance, if there is a WHERE clause restricting the data on column foo, the query planner first tries to find an index on column foo. If there is no suitable index, the query has to do a full table scan, which can be extremely slow. This means that all the data in the table has to be read, even if the WHERE restriction picked out only a single row. This is why DBAs get paid a lot of money; they look at which types of queries get run and make sure there are indexes on the right columns.

Comparative Analysis

You may have noticed that a B-Tree in a relational database looks a lot like the computational tree in BigQuery; that isn't a coincidence. BigQuery's computation tree can be thought of as a B-tree that is computed on-the-fly. Whereas in a relational database, a table scan is punishment for not having an index, BigQuery always does the table scan and builds the index in parallel. The benefit of BigQuery is that table scans are optimized and ad-hoc queries just work, with no indexes or optimization required.

There are some things that a relational database does better. Lookups of single rows from the primary key or secondary keys are extremely fast. When data is changing, not just being appended to, a relational database can make more sense because BigQuery doesn't currently support updates or deletes. Finally, if you are doing a huge numbers of queries, you'll likely run up against the BigQuery quota policy.

There are drawbacks to a relational database, too. If you are running ad-hoc queries, and don't have a lot of time and energy to spend optimizing your data layout, you may end up spending a lot of time waiting for your queries to run. If you have large tables, the database software you're using may not scale well. This last point is why a number of new "no-SQL" databases exist and was the rationale for creating BigQuery in the first place.

MapReduce

MapReduce, as a Big Data processing architecture, has only been around for approximately 10 years. It was developed at Google by Jeff Dean and Sanjay Ghemawat as a mechanism to perform computations over large data sets by applying principles from functional programming (the Map and Reduce operations). The primary idea is that you decompose your computation into two phases: Map, which transforms the data, and Reduce, which combines the results.

After Google published the principles of MapReduce in a research paper, Doug Cutting picked up the concept and began building an open source version that he called Hadoop, after his son's toy elephant. In the past couple of years, Hadoop has gained rapid popularity because of companies such as Yahoo! that productized it and startups such as Cloudera and MapR that pushed the boundaries of what it could do. Most people who use MapReduce now use it via Hadoop.

Comparisons of BigQuery to MapReduce are included because many people who consider using BigQuery also wonder why they shouldn't just use something such as Hive on top of Hadoop. This section shows the architecture of MapReduce and why it is generally more suited toward batch workloads than interactive exploration of your data.

MapReduce Design

Despite the name, MapReduce isn't just Map and Reduce—it is actually Map, Combine, Shuffle, and Reduce. And actually, what you usually think of as MapReduce encompasses not just the actual computation, but also a number of other technologies that enable it such as a distributed filesystem.

Map Phase

The Map phase is modeled after the Map operation in functional programming. In functional programming, Map applies a function of one argument to each element in a collection and creates a new collection with all the results. An example would be taking a function `ToUpperCase()` and applying it to each element in a string of characters. The result would be another string of characters that were all capitalized. In functional programming, functions are "pure," which means that they do not have any external side effects.

This lack of side effects may sound like a technicality, but it is actually a key factor in a MapReduce. When you call Map on a collection, because the function called on each element doesn't have any inputs other than the element it is operating on and doesn't change any external state, the order in which elements are processed doesn't matter. The Map operation might process the collection in order, in reverse order, or in parallel. The operation might even run in another process or another machine.

In MapReduce, the Map phase is slightly more general. It runs a Mapper function over each element in the source data. The Mapper function takes one element and emits a list of 0 or more key-value pairs. The key is an address used by the Reduce phase, and the value is the value to be processed in the Reduce phase. For example, if your MapReduce was going to compute the number of times each word in the source data appeared, the Mapper function would take a single line, break it up into words, and emit each word paired with the number of times it appeared in that line. The Reduce phase is responsible for collecting the results.

Combine Phase

After the Map phase has started producing values, the Combine phase can start, if needed. Combine is merely an optimization to save the amount of I/O that has to be done in the next phases. A Combiner function can take multiple outputs within the same Map worker and combine them, so less data needs to be written out to disk before the Shuffle can operate on it.

Shuffle Phase

The Shuffle phase, like the shuffle operation in BigQuery, is just a big sort. In practice, it tends to be a merge sort because that can be done in parallel. The key used for the sort is the key emitted during the Map phase—so each key used is sorted to the same place.

Although Shuffle serves to only move data around and is actually a null operation from a computation standpoint, Shuffle is often the slowest part of the MapReduce operation. If you think about what has to happen, you have a lot of data—terabytes, potentially—and you need to compute a global ordering. In practice, Shuffle needs to only hash partition the data. That is, you need to make sure only that all data with the same key ends up in the same place, rather than requiring that keys actually get sorted. However, Hadoop does a complete merge sort to make it easier for Reducers that rely on ordering.

Reduce Phase

The Reduce phase is what enables MapReduce to aggregate data across the entire data set. It is based on the functional programming Reduce operation which, like Map, applies a function to each element in a collection and returns a collection of results. The Reducer function is a bit different, however—it takes two arguments—a key and a collection of inputs. Remember that the Mapper function returned key-value pairs and Shuffle sorted those pairs by key. Reduce calls the Reducer function once with each unique key returned by a Mapper along with all the values that were produced with that key.

To see how this can work, think about the previous word count example. The Mapper returns pairs of words with the number of times they appear in an input line. Shuffle then sorts these results by key. The Reduce phase calls the Reducer with each word as a key and a list of the counts from each line. The reducer can then just compute the sum of this list and emit the word and the total count to compute the word count.

MapReduce Example

The canonical MapReduce example is counting word frequencies in a data set. Consider a MapReduce operation that will count the word frequencies in the following three lines of text:

```
1: "Tomorrow, and tomorrow, and tomorrow"
2: "Creeps in this petty pace from day to day"
3: "To the last syllable of recorded time"
```

The Mapper function gets called once with each of these lines. It doesn't matter in which order they get called, or even whether the three calls are performed on the same machine. The output of the three Mapper calls look like:

```
1: [{tomorrow, 3}, {and, 2}]
2: [{creeps, 1}, {in, 1}, {this, 1}, {petty, 1}, {pace, 1},
   {from, 1}, {day, 2}, {to, 1}]
3: [{to, 1}, {the, 1}, {last, 1}, {syllable, 1}, {of, 1},
   {recorded, 1}, {time, 1}]
```

Next, the Shuffle phase goes to work on the Mapper's output and produces the following:

```
{and, [2]}
{creeps, [1]}
{day, [2]}
{from, [1]}
{in, [1]}
{last, [1]}
```

```
{of, [1]}
{pace, [1]}
{petty, [1]}
{recorded, [1]}
{syllable, [1]}
{the, [1]}
{this, [1]}
{time, [1]}
{to, [1, 1]}
{tomorrow, [3]}
```

The shuffler output is mostly uninteresting except for `to`, which is the only word to appear on more than one line. The `to` entry contains a list of two elements, one for each time it appeared in the Mapper's output.

Finally, this data is passed to the Reducer, which takes each word and sums up the totals and produces a count for each word. The results follow:

```
{and, 2}
{creeps, 1}
{day, 2}
{from, 1}
{in, 1}
{last, 1}
{of, 1}
{pace, 1}
{petty, 1}
{recorded, 1}
{syllable, 1}
{the, 1}
{this, 1}
{time, 1}
{to, 2}
{tomorrow, 3}
```

At first, it might seem a bit awkward to decompose your computation into a Map and Reduce phase. However, a very wide range of problems can be broken into a series of Map and Reduce operations, and there are a number of tools built on top of Hadoop that can help.

Storage System

MapReduce doesn't rely on a particular storage system or storage format the way relational databases do. However, in practice, a standard filesystem is not well suited for performing MapReduce operations. If you're just reading from a single disk, you are likely going to be limited by the disk speed, and processing the data in parallel isn't actually going to help.

Apache Hadoop uses a custom distributed filesystem called HDFS that is in many ways similar to the Google File System (GFS) or the Colossus File System used by BigQuery. Because HDFS is distributed among many nodes, it can read in parallel and hopefully keep up with the Map and Reduce workers.

Worker Management

The final key piece of MapReduce architecture is the worker manager, called the Controller in Google MapReduce or the Name Node in Hadoop. When dealing with large numbers of workers (many MapReduces use hundreds or thousands of nodes), individual workers often fail for some reason. If that causes the entire MapReduce operation to fail, it might cause you to lose a lot of work and have to restart the operation. Because the Mapper and Reducer functions are free of side effects, they should be idempotent—that is, you can rerun them and get the same results.

When a worker crashes, or even is particularly slow, the MapReduce Controller assigns a new worker to operate over the same data. If the initial worker completes, that should be fine because the operation was idempotent. The Controller also needs to distinguish between a worker that fails because of a hardware problem or a network hiccup and a worker that fails because there is something wrong with the Mapper or Reducer functions that causes it to crash on certain input data.

Comparative Analysis

The primary advantages of MapReduce are scalability and flexibility. Unlike a relational database, where if you want it to be faster you need to change how it is stored or buy faster hardware (which is often orders of magnitude more expensive), you can scale a MapReduce by just buying more of the same hardware. That is another way of saying that MapReduce scales out linearly.

MapReduce is extremely flexible. Because the Mapper and Reducer functions can be anything you want them to be, you can perform arbitrary computations over your data. You're not locked into a language such as SQL where you can perform only certain aggregations.

There are downsides, however. MapReduce is designed for batch workloads, not actually interactive ones. MapReduce frameworks usually take a long time to spin up the requisite number of workers, and the Shuffle operation often adds long delays. Most MapReduce operations take minutes or hours to run, rather than the seconds you'd hope for if you were performing exploratory analysis on your data.

Another drawback of MapReduce is that it forces you to divide up your operation into a Map and Reduce phase, which is not usually the way you'd think about your data analysis task. What's more, many computations can't be expressed in a single MapReduce, so they may require multiple passes through the data. It can be tricky to keep track of workflow for jobs that do more than one MapReduce.

There are various tools and programming paradigms that help with many of these drawbacks. Cascading provides a way of expressing your computation via stream operations that can turn into multiple MapReduce rounds. Hive and Pig are both mechanisms that enable you to write SQL or SQL-style queries that get turned into MapReduces.

MapReduce also is a lower-level tool than BigQuery or a relational database. That is, it requires you to know how many mappers and reducers you need, requires you to set up HDFS and monitoring software, and in general, requires a lot of knowledge about the system to run it.

At Google, MapReduce is still extremely popular and is used as a complement to Dremel. MapReduce is usually not run directly, however—there are higher-level tools, like FlumeJava (described here: `http://pages.cs.wisc .edu/~akella/CS838/F12/838-CloudPapers/FlumeJava.pdf`) that enable you to coordinate your MapReduces. For big, batch data transformations, MapReduce is usually preferred. For data investigation Dremel is a better tool.

Summary

This chapter described how the technologies that underlie BigQuery actually work—from the Dremel query engine to the Colossus File System. Hopefully, the next time you run a query that takes longer than you expect, or returns a ResponseToo Large error, you'll know a bit more about why it happened, and what you can do to improve it.

It also discussed how the architecture of BigQuery differs from architecture of other technologies such as Hadoop and MySQL. None of these is appropriate for all situations, and after reading this chapter, you should know more about when to use each of them. Hopefully, you'll find ample reasons to use BigQuery.

The next chapter shows a number of scenarios using a wide range of advanced BigQuery features. Understanding the underlying architecture should be helpful in developing an intuition about how these queries work and how to push the limits of what BigQuery can do.

Advanced Queries

At this point, you should be familiar with BigQuery SQL (Chapter 7, "Running Queries") and how BigQuery SQL is executed (Chapter 9, "Understanding Query Execution"). This chapter builds on those two topics, shows some additional things you can do with BigQuery, and demonstrates how they relate to the underlying architecture.

The chapter is divided into four portions:

- **Advanced SQL:** Describes how to use more advanced SQL constructs (variants of JOIN, windowing functions, and so on) that are part of standard SQL.

- **BigQuery SQL extensions:** Describes features in BigQuery, such as queries over nested and repeated fields that do not exist in standard SQL. It also relates these features to the BigQuery architecture.

- **Query Troubleshooting:** Gives some common errors encountered when writing queries and some tricks to avoid those errors. There are some cases where queries that seem like they should work actually fail; this section describes why they fail and how to fix them.

- **Query Recipes:** Contains a number of recipes for answering common questions in SQL, such as how to compute a trailing 3-day average and how to perform cohort analysis.

You can read this chapter through directly, but it may also be a useful reference guide. For example, the troubleshooting section can be helpful when debugging a query that you think should run successfully but BigQuery doesn't agree. The recipes section can be useful to refer to if you're struggling with how to phrase your question in SQL. If you have never worked with SQL before, you may want to look through a basic SQL tutorial before reading this chapter because it assumes familiarity with the basics of SQL.

Advanced SQL

This section describes some more advanced SQL features that are available in BigQuery. If you're a SQL guru, you might just want to skim and note "ah... feature X is available!" For others, this may be the first time you've encountered these features, and you might want to pay attention to the examples more closely.

The advanced SQL features described here include subqueries; join variants (inner, outer, semi-join and anti-join), and window functions (RANK, CUME_DIST, and so on). Depending on your background, these may seem like basic features or they may appear exotic. Either way, they are useful in BigQuery and are described here.

A NOTE ON "STANDARD" SQL

Many people refer to the SQL standard as if it was a single, uncontroversial document. As a comparison, the HTTP protocol, which is used whenever you navigate to a web page, is defined in RFC 2616. It has been implemented dozens of times by web severs and web browsers. The fact that you can usually switch from Firefox to Safari without much hassle is a testament to the clarity and widespread implementation of the HTTP standard.

The SQL standard, however, can mean a lot of different things. For example, there are SQL-92, SQL-99, SQL-2003, SQL-2006, and more. Moreover, most database implementations pick and choose from the various SQL standards and may lack basic features from any standard version. For example, Oracle doesn't have a TIME type, and few people care about the XML-based features that were added in the XML-mad days when the SQL-2003 specification was defined.

One of the biggest difficulties with the specification of SQL is that all vendors had ways that they wanted to extend what was possible to do in SQL. They may have proceeded with an implementation before there was a specification. Another vendor may have added a similar feature a different way. That feature, then, becomes difficult to standardize because there are competing implementations, and backward compatibility can become problematic.

BigQuery has a number of features for which no standards exist, such as support for nested and repeated fields. In these cases, BigQuery diverges from the standard SQL because the features aren't in the standard but were considered important to the product.

> There are also a number of potentially painful cases where BigQuery diverges from the SQL standard. The syntax for table union is an example of this: To make it easy to query multiple tables at once, the comma operator was used to indicate UNION ALL. This decision confuses many people because a comma-separated list of tables usually indicates a JOIN operation.
>
> Work is being done to make BigQuery SQL look more like Standard SQL. Most of the changes are in expanded support for the features described in the standard. For example, until recently, BigQuery required that all fields in an ORDER BY be listed in the SELECT field list; this is non-standard and inconvenient, so the limitation was quietly eliminated.

Changes that are not backward compatible will eventually arise. However, during the deprecation period following breaking changes, the new syntax will be opt-in, and the old syntax will likely be supported for an additional period after the default is changed.

Subqueries

A subquery is a query inside of another query. For instance, in SELECT foo FROM (SELECT field1 AS foo FROM table1), the SELECT field1 AS foo FROM table1 query in parentheses is a subquery. The SQL-92 specification says that you can use a subquery almost anywhere—in a FROM clause, in a SELECT field list, or in a WHERE clause.

In many SQL environments, such as MySQL, subqueries are somewhat rare and can have poor performance. (The two statements are often related; if subqueries are slow, people won't use them often.) In BigQuery, however, subqueries are used extensively in certain clauses and generally run quite fast.

Preventing Duplicate Computation

One of the reasons to use subqueries is that BigQuery doesn't do much in the way of query optimization. If you need to use a value multiple places in the query, you may be better off using a subquery and computing the value only once. Performance issues aside, this can often lead to a more readable query. For example, if you want to translate a timestamp to a particular time zone and use the same value in both the SELECT clause and a WHERE clause, you could write:

```
SELECT DATE_ADD(ts, -8, "HOUR") AS pst
FROM [bigquery-e2e:ch10.sample_data]
WHERE DATE_ADD(ts, -8, "HOUR") > TIMESTAMP("2013-12-13")
LIMIT 10
```

This query does the same date computation twice; moreover, if you want to change it, you have to remember to keep it in sync in both places. A cleaner way to write the query would be with a subquery:

```
SELECT pst
FROM (
  SELECT DATE_ADD(ts, -8, "HOUR") AS pst
  FROM [bigquery-e2e:ch10.sample_data])
WHERE pst > TIMESTAMP("2013-12-13")
LIMIT 10
```

This formulation of the query will likely run faster but also will be easier to maintain.

Working around Quirks in the Query Language

There are, admittedly, a couple of cases where BigQuery doesn't allow certain standard query formulations and requires you to revise your query accordingly. Usually, a good error message is given that can help you rewrite your query. For example, JOIN queries require the fields in the ON clause to be the same type, so if you have an integer value and a string value, the join will fail. For example, consider the following query:

```
SELECT t1.vInt
FROM (SELECT 17 AS vInt) AS t1
JOIN (SELECT "17" AS vString) AS t2
ON t1.vInt = t2.vString
```

If you run this, you'll get the error Cannot compare fields as join attributes (Incompatible types. 'vInt' : TYPE_INT32 'vString' : TYPE_STRING). This error message is a bit cryptic and exposes internal names for data types, but it should suffice to let you figure out that you need to coerce the values before comparing them. To fix the query, you can use a subquery again:

```
SELECT t1.vString
FROM (SELECT STRING(vInt) as vString
      FROM (SELECT 17 as vInt)) as t1
JOIN (SELECT "17" as vString) as t2
ON t1.vString = t2.vString
```

Note the only change necessary is to wrap one of the tables in a subquery that applies the necessary type coercion.

Many of the cases where subqueries were required to work around quirks in the BigQuery version of SQL have been fixed. As mentioned in the previous section, ORDER BY columns used to be required to be in the SELECT list; this often required a subquery if the field you wanted to sort by wasn't a field you wanted to have in your output. Many of these limitations are being quietly eliminated, and if you try again, one day they might just work. By the time you read this book, the JOIN coercion example in this section may no longer require a subquery.

IN and NOT IN Clauses

A common use of a subquery is in an IN or a NOT IN clause. The following query returns all the words in a play that match the title of a different Shakespeare play:

```
SELECT corpus, word FROM [publicdata:samples.shakespeare]
WHERE word <> corpus AND word IN (
    SELECT corpus
    FROM [publicdata:samples.shakespeare]
    GROUP BY corpus)
```

Queries that use the IN keyword together with a subquery are called semi-joins, and queries that use NOT IN however are called anti-joins. Both of these types of queries are discussed more in the "Semi-JOIN and Anti-JOIN" section later in this chapter.

Nested Computation

Often you'll want to run a subquery because that is the best way to compute your data. For instance, you need to do a GROUP BY before you do a JOIN, or you want to coerce fields in one table to look like another one. This query, for example, computes the largest update size for the top 100 most edited Wikipedia entries. It uses a subquery to figure out which titles have been edited most often:

```
SELECT
  a.title AS title,
  edit_count,
  MAX(num_characters) AS max_entry_size
FROM [publicdata:samples.wikipedia] b
JOIN (
  SELECT
    TOP(title, 100) AS title,
    COUNT(*) AS edit_count
  FROM [publicdata:samples.wikipedia]) a
ON a.title = b.title
GROUP BY
  title,
  edit_count
```

A common technique for composing queries in BigQuery is to start at the inside of the query and work your way out. That is, if you have complex queries with multiple joins and nested queries, you start by getting the inner queries to work and then wrap them with layers of outer queries like an onion. This way, each of the inner queries is something that you can run on its own and hopefully test. If you try to compose the query outside in, it is easy to get lost while you're composing the query. Strategies to speed up and reduce the cost of experimentation are described in the "Data Sampling" section later in this chapter.

Combining Tables: Implicit UNION and JOIN

In SQL, there are only two ways to combine data from multiple tables: UNION and JOIN. UNION takes the rows from multiple tables and appends them into a single logical table. JOIN, however, takes the columns from multiple tables and combines them into a single logical table. UNION is fairly straightforward, but JOINs come in many variants that control how the table rows are matched when the columns are appended.

Implicit UNION ALL

Standard SQL defines two types of UNION: UNION and UNION ALL. UNION (without ALL) combines two tables but ignores duplicates. If table A has 10 rows and table B has 7 rows, but two of the rows in table B are identical to rows in table A, the UNION of those two tables will have 15 rows—all the rows in A and B with the duplicates removed. As you can probably imagine, this is a computationally expensive operation.

UNION ALL, however, performs blind concatenation. If table A has 10 rows and table B has 7 rows, when you UNION ALL them together, you'll get all 17 rows of A and B together. UNION ALL is a much less computationally expensive operation because it doesn't have to find the duplicate values.

Currently, neither UNION nor UNION ALL is directly supported in BigQuery. So why is it discussed here? BigQuery does support UNION ALL via a nonstandard syntax: a comma-separated list of tables in the FROM clause. This is mentioned in the same section with JOIN operations because standard SQL uses this notation to mean JOIN.

WHY DOES COMMA MEAN UNION ALL AND NOT JOIN?

If we had to come up with the one deviation from the standard in BigQuery SQL that caused the most confusion, the choice of comma to mean UNION ALL and not JOIN would likely be it. This book mentions it several times because we wanted to make sure that this nonstandard pattern doesn't surprise users.

In BigQuery, UNION is much more common than JOIN. Users often split their tables up by day or by customer. This partitioning can help them manage data lifetime (for example, they delete tables older than 90 days) or to save them money on queries (because query cost is proportional to number of bytes in the columns referenced). But by splitting up data into multiple pieces, it means that users often want to query against multiple tables at once. For instance, if you have daily tables and want to query against a month's worth of data, you need to UNION ALL 30 different tables together.

From a syntax perspective, `UNION ALL` is clumsy; you don't `UNION` together table names, you `UNION` together subqueries. So to `UNION` a week's worth of tables together, you'd need to write the same query over and over again:

```
(SELECT foo FROM table1)
UNION ALL
(SELECT foo FROM table2)
UNION ALL
(SELECT foo FROM table3)
. . .
```

The BigQuery syntax lets you list the tables separated by commas:

```
SELECT foo FROM table1, table2, table3. . .
```

This is much easier to write and to understand. Are there other syntaxes that would have been almost as compact but didn't violate SQL standards so thoroughly? Yes, of course. It is possible that in the future BigQuery will introduce a new syntax for table `UNION` (perhaps a table-valued function `TABLE_UNION()` that lets you list tables) that doesn't look like a `JOIN`.

Here is an example of a `UNION ALL` operation in BigQuery:

```
SELECT COUNT(ts), COUNT(DISTINCT id)
FROM [bigquery-e2e:public.device_20140218],
    [bigquery-e2e:public.device_20140219],
    [bigquery-e2e:public.device_20140220]
```

BigQuery limits table unions to 100 tables. If you want to query over more than this, you need to split your query up into multiple pieces. If you query over a lot of tables, you might consider using the table functions `TABLE_DATE_RANGE` and `TABLE_QUERY`, which allow you to specify a range of tables rather than listing them individually.

INNER JOIN

`INNER JOIN` is the most common type of join; it instructs the query engine to take the left table and match it with rows in the right table where both tables share a set of matching column values. One row containing all columns from both tables is generated for every pair of rows from the left and right table that satisfy the `ON` clause. In BigQuery the `ON` clause is restricted to testing equality between fields from the tables. More complicated conditions must be placed in the `WHERE` clause.

For example, say you wanted to look up GitHub repositories that are also the name of Shakespeare plays and also return the date the Shakespeare play was written for each one. You could run this query:

```
SELECT shakespeare.corpus AS name,
  github.repository_owner,
  shakespeare.corpus_date
FROM [publicdata:samples.github_timeline] github
INNER JOIN (
  SELECT corpus, max(corpus_date) AS corpus_date
  FROM [publicdata:samples.shakespeare]
  GROUP BY corpus) shakespeare
ON shakespeare.corpus = github.repository_name
LIMIT 5
```

With an INNER JOIN, if there are Shakespeare plays that aren't GitHub repositories, they won't be returned; likewise if there are GitHub repositories that aren't Shakespeare plays, those won't be returned either. The above statements may seem somewhat obvious, but they aren't true of OUTER JOINS.

Because INNER JOIN is so common, it is the default behavior when you use JOIN without any other modifiers.

OUTER JOIN

OUTER JOINS are used when you want to return all the rows in a particular table, regardless of whether they match a result in the table you're joining against. If there is no match, then the fields for the other table will be null in the result.

OUTER JOINS have three flavors:

- LEFT OUTER JOIN: Returns all the rows in the left table (the table mentioned in the FROM clause)

- RIGHT OUTER JOIN: Returns all the rows in the right table (the table mentioned after the JOIN keyword). All RIGHT OUTER JOINS can be rewritten as LEFT OUTER JOINS by swapping the order of the tables in the query.

- FULL OUTER JOIN: Returns all the rows in both the left and right tables

To come up with an example for an OUTER JOIN, suppose you want to return all GitHub repositories, regardless of whether they matched the name of a Shakespeare play. If they do match, however, you want to return the date of the Shakespeare play whose name they share. To construct this query, you can use the exact same query from the INNER JOIN section, but change the INNER JOIN to a LEFT OUTER JOIN. (Use LEFT because the table you want to read in full is the LEFT table.)

```
SELECT github.repository_name AS name,
  github.repository_owner,
```

```
    shakespeare.corpus_date
FROM [publicdata:samples.github_timeline] github
LEFT OUTER JOIN (
  SELECT corpus, max(corpus_date) as corpus_date
  FROM [publicdata:samples.shakespeare]
  GROUP BY corpus) shakespeare
ON shakespeare.corpus = github.repository_name
WHERE repository_language = "Python"
LIMIT 5;
```

Note that in this case, we've changed the name field in the SELECT list to the repository name field from the GitHub table rather than the corpus name from the Shakespeare table. In an INNER JOIN, these can be used interchangeably because they will always be identical. But in an OUTER JOIN, the field referenced in the ON clause may be null if there was no match on that side.

CROSS JOIN

CROSS JOIN is used relatively rarely, but it is arguably the most powerful type of JOIN operation. CROSS JOIN says to match each row in the left table with each row in the right table. If you don't filter the results, you end up with N x M results, where N is the number of rows in the left table and M is the number of rows in the right table. It is easy to see that the numbers can get large; if you have a billion rows in the left table and a million rows in the right, a naïve CROSS JOIN will generate a quadrillion rows. That is a lot of rows, and chances are that was not what you actually intended to do.

When combined with a judicious filter—a WHERE clause on either the left side or right side or both—CROSS JOINS can be extremely useful to push the boundaries of SQL. Whereas INNER and OUTER JOINS are used to combine tables that have columns that can be tested for simple equality, CROSS JOIN, however, is usually used to relate tables using a more complex condition. For example, this query computes the Wikipedia titles that contain the name of any Shakespeare play.

```
SELECT wikipedia.title
FROM [publicdata:samples.wikipedia] wikipedia
CROSS JOIN (
  SELECT corpus
  FROM [publicdata:samples.shakespeare]
  GROUP BY corpus) AS shakespeare
WHERE wikipedia.title CONTAINS shakespeare.corpus
GROUP BY wikipedia.title
IGNORE CASE
```

The reason this query needed to be a CROSS JOIN was because the effective JOIN condition was that one field contains another, ignoring case. There is no ON clause that could specify the containment condition because ON clauses must specify an exact match. Instead, the CROSS JOIN matched each Wikipedia title with each Shakespeare corpus and returned only the ones where the title contained the name of the Shakespeare play. If part of the condition includes equality between columns, you should use an INNER JOIN and move that condition to the ON clause since it will be executed more efficiently. A CROSS JOIN is only required when no such equality condition exists. In addition, if the JOIN clause appears in a subquery, you should push filters into the WHERE clause of the subquery whenever feasible.

Semi-JOIN and Anti-JOIN

Semi- and anti-JOIN are fancy words for JOIN operations that you may not have even recognized are JOINs. If you want to specify a filter from a list generated by a query, you can use a subquery with the IN clause. For example, consider the following query, which returns long words from the five largest works in the Shakespeare table.

```
SELECT word
FROM [publicdata:samples.shakespeare]
WHERE corpus IN (
  SELECT corpus FROM (
    SELECT corpus, SUM(word_count) total
    FROM [publicdata:samples.shakespeare]
    GROUP BY corpus ORDER BY total DESC LIMIT 5))
AND LENGTH(word) > 14
GROUP BY word
```

This is a semi-JOIN. An anti-JOIN is the opposite when you filter based on not having membership in a list. The anti- JOIN version of the previous query returns long words from all works except for the five largest:

```
SELECT word
FROM [publicdata:samples.shakespeare]
WHERE corpus NOT IN (
  SELECT corpus FROM (
    SELECT corpus, SUM(word_count) total
    FROM [publicdata:samples.shakespeare]
    GROUP BY corpus ORDER BY total DESC LIMIT 5))
AND LENGTH(word) > 14
GROUP BY word
```

You may wonder why this is considered a JOIN. It turns out that it is possible to rewrite the semi-JOIN form as an INNER JOIN query and the anti-JOIN as a LEFT OUTER JOIN. However, the query is a lot more cumbersome when it is written with the explicit JOIN syntax. The IN operator makes the query easier to follow and modify.

JOIN KEY CARTESIAN-PRODUCT EXPLOSION

One aspect of SQL JOINs that often confuses people who are relatively new to using them is what happens when there are multiple matches on the left and the right. For instance, the following query joins the GitHub and Shakespeare tables where the Shakespeare corpus name matches the GitHub repository name and the Shakespeare corpus is *The Tempest*:

```
SELECT shakespeare.corpus
FROM [publicdata:samples.github_timeline] github
JOIN [publicdata:samples.shakespeare] shakespeare
ON github.repository_name = shakespeare.corpus
WHERE shakespeare.corpus = "tempest"
```

There are 146 rows in the GitHub table where the repository name is "tempest" and 3636 rows in the Shakespeare table where the corpus name is the same. So when we join these two tables by matching the repository name with the corpus, we get 146 * 3636 which is more than one-half of a million rows.

It is easy to see that if you're not careful, when you run a JOIN operation, you can get unintended explosions in the results. Imagine joining a table of customers with a table of orders on the customer_id. If both tables have a significant number of frequently occurring values, the join could end up producing billions of results by matching the commonly occurring value in one table with each instance of the value in the other table. If you run a JOIN operation and BigQuery tells you the results are too large to return, JOIN key explosion may be the culprit.

Analytic and Windowing Functions

There are some data transformations that are awkward to express in SQL. A good example is computing the rank of a record within a given group of records. The basic problem is that the tuple relational calculus, the formal framework underlying SQL, does not actually support ordered sequences and expressing operations that rely on the order. In fact, even the ORDER BY clause is not supported by the calculus but is nevertheless present in SQL. As the use of relational databases for data analysis grew, it became necessary to support these kinds of operations. Initially developers implemented custom solutions using programming extensions available in individual databases. Eventually database providers added SQL extensions to support these types of operations, and these extensions were standardized as window functions in ANSI SQL 99. Arguably, their syntax and usage is fairly awkward because they do not fit neatly into the underlying framework. Nevertheless, they enable a range of useful operations. BigQuery supports these window functions, and this section discusses how to use them.

The main property of window function expressions is the capability to define a sequence (in some cases just a set) of values over which the function should operate.

```
window-function OVER ([PARTITION BY fields]
                      [ORDER BY fields])
```

When the OVER clause is empty, the window covers all the rows in the query result. The partition clause is optional and divides the rows into separate windows over which the function is applied; much like a grouping clause but it does not combine rows. Window functions that operate over an ordered sequence require the ORDER BY clause to specify the ordering within each window. The window function can appear only as a column in a SELECT clause; for example, it cannot be used in an arithmetic expression or in a WHERE clause. You can always use a subquery if you need to operate on the result of a window function.

We will start with the simplest possible window function clause and work toward more complex usage.

```
SELECT zip, RATIO_TO_REPORT(population) OVER() AS population_fraction
FROM [bigquery-e2e:reference.zip_codes]
WHERE primary_city = 'Seattle'
```

This query computes the fraction of the population that resides in a ZIP code associated with Seattle. The fraction is computed with respect to the sum of the population field across all rows returned by the query.

You can modify the query to generate results for multiple cities of interest by adjusting the filter condition.

```
SELECT * FROM (
  SELECT primary_city, zip,
         RATIO_TO_REPORT(population) OVER() AS fraction
  FROM [bigquery-e2e:reference.zip_codes]
  WHERE primary_city IN ('Bellevue', 'Kirkland', 'Seattle'))
ORDER BY primary_city, fraction DESC
```

Currently, the use of window functions is not compatible with a top-level ORDER BY clause, so you need to use a subquery to order the final result. However, this gives different results from the previous query for Seattle alone. This is because now the population is being normalized with respect to the total population of Bellevue, Kirkland, and Seattle. To instead normalize the population with respect to the population of the city corresponding to each row, you need the PARTITION BY clause.

```
SELECT * FROM (
  SELECT primary_city, zip,
         RATIO_TO_REPORT(population)
```

```
                OVER(PARTITION BY primary_city) AS city_fraction
    FROM [bigquery-e2e:reference.zip_codes]
    WHERE primary_city IN ('Bellevue', 'Kirkland', 'Seattle'))
  ORDER BY primary_city, city_fraction DESC
```

This will treat rows with the same primary city as a window and use the total population of each window to normalize rows in the window.

Next, turn your attention to finding the three most populated ZIP codes in each state. Because you are ranking ZIP codes by population, you need the ORDER BY clause.

```
SELECT state, zip, population FROM (
  SELECT
    state, zip, population,
    RANK() OVER (PARTITION BY state
                 ORDER BY population DESC) AS pop_rank
  FROM [bigquery-e2e:reference.zip_codes]
  WHERE population > 0)
WHERE pop_rank <= 3
ORDER BY state, population DESC
```

Without the outer ORDER BY clause, the ordering of the rows returned is undefined; therefore, you need to explicitly specify the order you would like rather than relying on the order specified in the OVER clause.

Queries can also use multiple window functions in a single SELECT clause. There is a restriction that all the window functions in the query use the same partitioning and ordering clause. This restriction is nonstandard, so it is likely to be lifted as the service enhances support for the feature.

```
SELECT state, zip, fraction FROM (
  SELECT state,
    zip,
    RATIO_TO_REPORT(population)
           OVER (PARTITION BY state
                 ORDER BY population DESC) AS fraction,
    RANK() OVER (PARTITION BY state
                 ORDER BY population DESC) AS pop_rank
  FROM [bigquery-e2e:reference.zip_codes]
  WHERE population > 0)
WHERE pop_rank <= 3
ORDER BY state, fraction DESC
```

This query would be challenging to write in SQL without the support for window functions.

If you need to perform an aggregation before applying the window function, you need to mix in an aggregation operation. However, the GROUP BY clause does not play well with window functions. Like with ORDER BY, the trick is to use a subquery, but this time as an inner query that feeds the window function query.

```
SELECT
  primary_city,
```

```
    RATIO_TO_REPORT(city_total) OVER() AS fraction
FROM (
  SELECT
    primary_city,
    SUM(population) AS city_total
  FROM [bigquery-e2e:reference.zip_codes]
  WHERE primary_city IN ('Bellevue', 'Kirkland', 'Seattle')
  GROUP BY primary_city)
```

Refer to the BigQuery documentation for the list of currently supported window functions. Over time this list is certainly going to grow and it is also likely that some of the restrictions around the use of these functions will be lifted. Even with their current limitations, they can greatly simplify many data analysis tasks.

BigQuery SQL Extensions

As mentioned at length elsewhere, BigQuery SQL, like most implementations, is not standard-compliant. Some of the differences between standard SQL and BigQuery SQL are omissions or semantic changes. However, other differences are extensions that BigQuery made to the language because no standard exists for them, but they provide significant power and expressivity to the query language. One such example is the capability to query nested and repeated fields; this allows users to store their data in a conceptually convenient way while also allowing the data to be queried. There is no standard SQL way to query a field that is itself a list of values. Other examples include special syntax for accessing a portion of a table or hints that tell the query engine how to parallelize the query.

The EACH Keyword

The EACH keyword is an optimization hint to the query engine that tells it to perform a shuffle operation. Chapter 9 has a detailed discussion of how shuffle works, but the effect is that it sorts data so that it can be processed in parallel. Note that this is only a hint: BigQuery may decide to shuffle data without an EACH keyword, and the presence of an EACH keyword doesn't guarantee that your data will be shuffled. In fact, at some point, we'd like to eliminate the need for EACH entirely.

Adding EACH to your queries can often enable a query that otherwise would have failed with an "insufficient resources" error to succeed. Whether EACH is needed isn't always a factor of table size, it is often a factor of cardinality. *Cardinality* is the number of distinct elements considered for the operation (JOIN, GROUP BY, or PARTITION BY). This number is difficult for BigQuery to estimate, so it relies on hints from the query writer.

GROUP EACH BY

If you perform a GROUP BY of a large number of distinct values, you might need to use GROUP EACH BY instead. For example, the following query fails with the error "resources exceeded during query execution":

```
SELECT title, count(*) as cnt
FROM [publicdata:samples.wikipedia]
GROUP BY title
ORDER BY cnt DESC
LIMIT 100
```

It may seem counter-intuitive that you still exceed the available resources when you have limited the results to only the first 100; however, note that it isn't just any 100 results; it is the top 100 by frequency. This means that the count of entries matching a title has to be computed for every title. (There are almost 20 million of them.) Because there isn't a way to avoid computing the count for each title, there aren't any easy shortcuts to take. What's more, the root of the execution tree has to aggregate all the results; this is the point at which the available resources are exceeded because one node has to sum up all the counts returned by the computation nodes.

The solution to getting this query to run successfully, as you may have guessed, is to use GROUP EACH BY. This causes the table to be partitioned by title before the query is run. After the fields needed in the query have been sorted, the per-title counts become much easier to compute because each node can compute local values and just report their top 100 to their parent. And the root doesn't have to keep around counts for each value, just the top counts that it has seen. Here is the version of the previous query that will run successfully:

```
SELECT title, COUNT(*) AS cnt
FROM [publicdata:samples.wikipedia]
GROUP EACH BY title
ORDER BY cnt DESC
LIMIT 100
```

JOIN EACH

If you don't specify EACH when you perform a JOIN operation, BigQuery requires that the table on the right side of the join be small enough to send the entire thing to every node of the computation tree. This means that if the table on the right side of the join doesn't fit into less than 8 MB when compressed, your query will fail. For example, if you take the query from the OUTER JOIN example and reverse the left and right tables and switch to an INNER JOIN, you get:

```
SELECT github.repository_name,
  github.repository_owner,
  shakespeare.corpus_date
```

```
FROM (
  SELECT corpus, max(corpus_date) AS corpus_date
  FROM [publicdata:samples.shakespeare]
  GROUP BY corpus) shakespeare
INNER JOIN [publicdata:samples.github_timeline] github
  ON shakespeare.corpus = github.repository_name
```

This query fails with the error "The JOIN operator's right-side table must be a small table." This isn't as big of a limitation as it sounds because many JOIN queries use a subselect to narrow down the table that is joined against; as long as the computed result is smaller than 8 MB, the JOIN will succeed. However, when that is not possible you can fix the query by adding the EACH keyword to the join:

```
SELECT github.repository_name,
  github.repository_owner,
  shakespeare.corpus_date
FROM (
  SELECT corpus, max(corpus_date) AS corpus_date
  FROM [publicdata:samples.shakespeare]
  GROUP BY corpus) shakespeare
INNER JOIN EACH [publicdata:samples.github_timeline] github
  ON shakespeare.corpus = github.repository_name
```

Data Sampling

Sometimes, it would be nice to operate on only a small portion of your data. Maybe you're testing out a query over a giant table and don't want to incur large costs while you're getting your query right. Or maybe you are running into "resources exceeded" errors, so you need to break up your table into pieces. In a BigQuery query, there are two commonly used ways to break up your data: HASH sampling and partition decorators. A word of caution, you may not want to try all the queries in this section because they will consume a fair amount of your quota.

HASH Sampling

HASH sampling is a mechanism for selecting a small portion of your table. It assigns a HASH value to each row in the table and filters out only those rows that match a certain pattern. This mechanism is similar to how BigQuery performs the shuffle operation.

For example, say you want to select 10 percent of the unique titles from the Wikipedia sample dataset. You could run the following query:

```
SELECT title, COUNT(*)
FROM [publicdata:samples.wikipedia]
WHERE HASH(title) % 10 == 0
GROUP BY title
```

This applies a HASH function to each title and keeps the rows where the hash value divides evenly into 10. The HASH function can be thought of as a kind of random number generator. However, it isn't completely random: HASH applies a complex function that makes the output for a given input as random as possible; however, if you run it with the same input multiple times, you'll always get the same answer. This has the nice property that all rows that have the same source value will HASH to the same result, so if you filter on the HASH value, you can filter out a portion of the distinct source data.

The next interesting part of the WHERE clause is the % 10 == 0 part. The % symbol is the modulo operator, which returns the remainder of the left side divided by the right side. So WHERE HASH(title) % 10 == 0 is just a fancy way of taking 1 out of every 10 distinct hash values.

Note that this is different than just taking 10 percent of the data; applying the HASH filter means you keep 10 percent of titles, not necessarily 10 percent of the underlying data. If you want to know the number of distinct titles, multiplying by 10 gives you a good estimate. If, however, you had just kept 10 percent of the underlying rows, you likely wouldn't know how that would affect the distinct title count.

The other advantage of having the HASH function return stable results is that you can use it to compute different slices of your underlying table. You already got the first 10 percent of the titles; you can get the second 10 percent by changing the value that you're comparing against:

```
SELECT title, COUNT(*)
FROM [publicdata:samples.wikipedia]
WHERE ABS(HASH(title) % 10) == 1
GROUP BY title
```

To get the next slice of the table, increment the value you're matching against; this is the remainder when divided by 10. You can get each of the 10 slices in turn by running once with each number from 0 up to 9. If you look closely at the query, however, you might notice that there was one additional change: the addition of an absolute value (ABS()) call to the hashed value.

The modulo operator doesn't behave predictably when given a negative number. Some programming languages define the modulo of a negative number to be negative. Others say it is always positive. Others say it is always the same sign as the right side (10 in this case). BigQuery SQL defines the output of the modulo operator as the same sign as the left side of the operation. Because HASH can return negative values, taking the modulo of the result can return a negative value. So if you filter by HASH values where the modulo is equal to 1, you'll miss out on the ones where the modulo is –1. This is fairly confusing, and it confuses a lot of people who are surprised when their HASH filters don't work the way they expect.

There is one drawback to using HASH filtering: You have to run your queries over the whole table. If you run queries against each of 10 slices, it means you have to run 10 queries against the whole table, which can get expensive.

Partition Decorators

Partition decorators allow you to run a query that runs only over a subset of the rows in your table. Unlike HASH partitioning, you are billed only for accessing the rows in one partition. Using partition decorators can be faster than using HASH partitioning as well because your query has to read only a small portion of the table.

To use a partition decorator, just add `$<index>-of-<count>` to the name of the table you use, where `<index>` is the index of the partition you use, starting with 0, and `<count>` is how many pieces you want to divide the table into. For example, to access the first 10th of the Wikipedia sample table, use the table name `[publicdata:samples.wikipedia$0-of-10]`.

Here's the query used for the HASH partitioning example but with partition decorators instead:

```
SELECT title, COUNT(*)
FROM [publicdata:samples.wikipedia$0-of-10]
GROUP BY title
```

Although the HASH partition example scanned 6.79 GB, this one scans only 690 MB—a much less expensive query. The results, however, are subtly different. Although the HASH partitioning example filtered by title, this is filtering by row; it will run over approximately 10 percent of rows, but that might not mean only 10 percent of titles are returned. This may sound somewhat confusing now, but it is generally obvious what you want from the context. In the case of the Wikipedia edits data, since each title is edited many times, it is possible that 90 percent of the titles appear in a 10 percent slice of the edit records.

Partition decorators have some limitations; you can't partition a table any further than its underlying granularity. Internally, BigQuery stores tables in shards; these are discrete chunks of data that can be processed in parallel. If you have a 100 GB table, it might be stored in 5000 shards, which allows it to be processed by up to 5000 workers in parallel. You shouldn't make any assumptions about the size of number of shards in a table. BigQuery will repartition data periodically to optimize the storage and query behavior.

If you try to partition your table into more pieces than BigQuery has shards for that table, you won't get an error, but you won't get an even balance. If the table has only a single shard and you ask for partition 0 of 100, you will likely get a partition that has all the data in the table; in this case partitions 1 through 99 would all be empty.

Like other decorator types, but unlike HASH partitioning, partition decorators can be used anywhere that a table is read from in BigQuery. This means you can use `tabledata.list()` to read from a table partition. Chapter 12, "External Data Processing," describes how this can be useful when performing a MapReduce over the table. Alternatively, you can copy a single partition or export a single partition. On the other hand, decorators cannot be used to sample the results of a subquery, whereas HASH partitioning can be applied to the results of subqueries.

Stable Partitioning with Snapshot Decorators

Whether you use HASH partitioning or partition decorators, you can run into trouble if you try to run queries over several non-overlapping portions of the table but the underlying table is changing. Say you're using HASH partitioning to query the table in three different chunks and append the results together:

```
-- 0
SELECT title, COUNT(*) FROM [publicdata:samples.wikipedia]
WHERE ABS(HASH(title) % 3) == 0 GROUP BY title
-- 1
SELECT title, COUNT(*) FROM [publicdata:samples.wikipedia]
WHERE ABS(HASH(title) % 3) == 1 GROUP BY title;
-- 2
SELECT title, COUNT(*) FROM [publicdata:samples.wikipedia]
WHERE ABS(HASH(title) % 3) == 2 GROUP BY title;
```

What if the table changes in between the first and second queries? You're going to end up with results that don't actually reflect the underlying table at any particular point in time. The issue is even more severe with partition decorators because the partition boundaries will change when data is added to the table, so you could miss some rows entirely.

If you use either HASH partitioning or partition decorators on tables that may be changing, it is recommended that you use a snapshot decorator as well. A *snapshot decorator* can be used to read the table of a particular timestamp. To use a snapshot decorator, just append @<timestamp> to the table name, where <timestamp> is the time of the snapshot in milliseconds since 1970. The snapshot time must be within the last 7 days; detailed table history is kept only for a week.

For example, to use partition decorators with snapshot decorators to read the first third of a stable snapshot of the Wikipedia sample table at timestamp 1390581599000, you can use:

```
SELECT title, COUNT(*)
FROM [publicdata:samples.wikipedia@1390581599000$0-of-3]
GROUP BY title
```

Note that the snapshot decorator must come before the partition decorator. Describing the table this way is equivalent to reading the table at the snapshot time and then partitioning it into thirds.

Snapshot decorators have some extra tricks and options. To find out more, check out the table decorators' section in Chapter 11, "Managing Data Stored in BigQuery," which discusses them in more detail.

Repeated Fields

Relational databases encourage us to think of data as flat records spread across different tables with suitable foreign key relations. In practice, it is often more natural to have records with a rich structure. For example, an order placed on a website consists of top-level information such as the time of the transaction and the customer together with additional details like the list of items along with their quantities. This is a natural unit of data and the ability to represent it as a single large record would be convenient. Similarly, the application described in Chapter 8, "Putting It Together," stores all the data coming from devices in a single table with a large number of fields. These types of complex schemas are well supported in BigQuery.

It has been previously discussed that BigQuery uses a columnar storage scheme to deliver better performance. It is clear how records with a simple schema consisting of only required or optional fields with primitive types could be laid out in storage so the data in a single column appears sequentially. Optional fields would require some care because you would need to have some way to indicate that a particular field was absent in a given record, for example, a reserved value that represented NULL. Even nested or record type fields without repetition are easy to handle because you could just treat all the fields as top-level fields using the fully qualified names. However, after you combine nested and repeated fields, the columnar representation becomes more interesting. The scheme used in BigQuery is explained in the Dremel paper, and variants have been adopted in related open source formats (Parquet). These formats are designed to support complex schemas without sacrificing the advantages of columnar storage for data analysis.

Storing these complex records is only half the story; it would be quite useless if we cannot also query over them effectively. Since standard SQL operates on flat relational tables, it is not always convenient for working with complex schemas. BigQuery SQL has added support for some non-standard extensions to simplify working with these schemas. This section explains how to use these features.

Pre-Joined Layout

The catch with respect to queries is that you need to operate over these structured records using SQL. However, relational databases don't encourage schemas with nested and repeated fields, and as a result, SQL is not well suited to manipulating these records with internal structure. Fortunately, repeated fields bear a striking resemblance to foreign key relationships between relational tables. When you recognize the similarities, it can feel quite natural to operate on repeated fields using SQL. An example from the sample application can illustrate this point.

Each log record in the sample application consists of fields with one value per record such as the timestamp and location information. It also has fields that are lists, such as the set of applications that have recently been used on the phone. The full schema was described Chapter 8; here the portion relevant to the examples is reproduced.

```
[
  {"name": "ts", "type": "timestamp", "mode": "required"},
  {"name": "location", "type": "record", "fields": [
    {"name": "zip", "type": "string"}
  ]},
  {"name": "running", "type": "record", "mode": "repeated", "fields": [
    {"name": "name", "type": "string"},
    {"name": "importance", "type": "record", "fields": [
      {"name": "level", "type": "integer"}
    ]},
    {"name": "memory", "type": "record", "fields": [
      {"name": "total", "type": "integer"},
    ]}
  ]}
]
```

The standard way to represent this data in a relational database would be to use two separate tables and establish a foreign key relationship between them.

```
CREATE TABLE PhoneLog (
  record_id CHAR(64),
  id CHAR(64),
  ts TIMESTAMP,
  location_zip CHAR(5),
  PRIMARY KEY (record_id)
);
CREATE TABLE Application (
  record_id CHAR(64),
  position TINYINT UNSIGNED,
  name VARCHAR(128),
  importance_level INT,
  memory_total INT,
  PRIMARY KEY (record_id, position),
  FOREIGN KEY (record_id) REFERENCES PhoneLog(record_id)
);
```

You can see that the second table declaration looks a lot like the nested record schema definition, but instead of placing it within an outer schema, a foreign key relationship is declared. Now look at a simple query over these two tables that fetches the importance level of a given application within a particular ZIP code.

```
SELECT MAX(running.importance_level)
FROM PhoneLog
NATURAL JOIN Application running
WHERE location_zip = '98107'
  AND running.name = 'com.googlecode.bigquery_e2e.sensors.client'
```

The NATURAL JOIN operator combines the two tables to generate one larger table that has the columns from both tables and the same number of rows as the Application table. Because one record from the PhoneLog matches zero or more rows in the Application table, its values are repeated for each matching row. Now perform the same operation with the nested schema.

```
SELECT MAX(running.importance.level)
FROM [bigquery-e2e:ch10.sample_data]
WHERE location.zip = '98107'
  AND running.name = 'com.googlecode.bigquery_e2e.sensors.client'
```

Because we were careful in choosing the aliases, the query looks almost identical to the query over the separate tables, but now the NATURAL JOIN is implicit. Just as NATURAL JOIN repeated the values for the fields from the left side (PhoneLog) table, the values in the top-level fields are repeated once for each value in the application ID field.

You have probably realized where this discussion is leading. The NATURAL JOIN operation and repeated fields are nearly equivalent. In fact, sophisticated database storage engines allow you to configure your tables so that the records of one table are interleaved between the records of the *parent* (the left side of the join) table. This is advantageous when most queries end up accessing both tables because it reduces the disk seeks. However, queries that scan just the parent table are degraded because all the records from the child table must be skipped over. With columnar storage, scans are not impacted; a query that references only fields in the outer record incurs no penalty from fields in the nested record. However, any join operation in a query is relatively costly in BigQuery because it does not maintain indexes. To avoid joins in your query, you should store nested records whenever possible. In effect, this data is *pre-joined*, which makes it more efficient to query. There are caveats, which are discussed next, but a good rule of thumb is that you can use your data collection process as a guide for how to structure records. Another clue is if you find you need to update two different tables consistently, for example, if you have an Orders table and an ItemsInOrder table and you need to insert entries in both tables atomically for each order processed. In a database you will likely use a transaction. In BigQuery you could achieve the same result by nesting ItemsInOrder in Orders because record insertions are atomic. In general, all the information that is recorded in a single operation or event should be packaged into a record with a suitable schema.

When working with nested and repeated schemas, special attention needs to be paid to the use of COUNT. Take for example this query that counts various fields in our logs.

```
SELECT COUNT(running.name) / COUNT(ts) AS apps_per_record
FROM [bigquery-e2e:ch10.sample_data]
```

Note the use of COUNT(ts) rather than COUNT(*). In BigQuery, COUNT(*) returns the total number of top-level records. It is a good practice to use COUNT(*field*) unless you are certain you want COUNT(*). For a repeated field, COUNT(*field*) returns the total repetitions of the field across all records. This behavior is in contrast to the behavior you would see in a relational database. Assuming no NULL values are present in the fields, then a COUNT of any field in a natural join query would return the identical value, matching the total number of rows generated by the join. This difference is an indication that our analogy between multiple relational tables and repeated fields, while useful, is only approximate.

All this is a round about way of saying that for the majority of queries, repeated fields work the way you would expect. For many applications they are the natural choice for modeling data and should be leveraged. The remainder of this section describes nonstandard extensions to support operations on repeated fields in the SQL variant supported by BigQuery. These extensions are provided because some common operations on repeated fields would be tedious to implement using standard SQL.

WITHIN

Consider the problem of finding the average memory used by the application consuming the most memory in each record collected. This requires computing the maximum memory over all apps in a single record. To do this with the two relational tables previously introduced, you would perform a nested GROUP BY query.

```
SELECT AVG(max_mem_usage) AS avg_of_max
FROM (
  SELECT MAX(mem_usage) AS max_mem_usage
  FROM Application GROUP BY record_Id)
```

This does not work with the nested schema because there is no explicit record_ id field that can be used in the inner query. To support these kinds of queries, BigQuery supports the WITHIN clause, which can be applied to aggregation expressions in the SELECT clause.

```
<aggregation> WITHIN <RECORD|record field>
```

The WITHIN clause is used to narrow the scope of aggregation operators. The default scope for an aggregation operator (COUNT, SUM, MAX, and so on) is the GROUP BY clause if one is present; otherwise, its scope is all the records that satisfy the WHERE clause. Instead of using the GROUP BY clause to create separate aggregation scopes, you can use the WITHIN clause to specify scopes that correspond to the top-level record, with the RECORD keyword, or any nested record field. Each column in the SELECT clause can specify a different aggregation scope using WITHIN or can be a non-aggregate expression. This is in contrast to GROUP BY queries where the only non-aggregate columns permitted are the fields present in the GROUP BY clause. The following query illustrates how to use the clause.

```
SELECT AVG(max_mem_usage) AS avg_of_max
FROM (
  SELECT MAX(running.memory.total) AS max_mem_usage WITHIN RECORD
  FROM [bigquery-e2e:ch10.sample_data])
```

When a field, rather than the top-level record, is specified in the clause, the aggregation operator generates one value for each occurrence of the specified field. You need to expand the schema a little further to illustrate how field level aggregation is used. When you record the list of processes, you also record the list of packages loaded by the process.

```
[
  . . .,
  {"name": "running", "type": "record", "mode": "repeated", "fields": [
    . . .,
    {"name": "package", "type": "string", "mode": "repeated"},
    . . .
  ]}
]
```

Using this data you can compute the average memory used per package loaded, broken down by application.

```
SELECT application_id,
       AVG(mem_used / (num_pkgs + 1)) AS mem_per_pkg
FROM (
  SELECT running.name AS application_id,
         running.memory.total AS mem_used,
         COUNT(running.package) WITHIN running AS num_pkgs
  FROM [bigquery-e2e:ch10.sample_data])
GROUP BY application_id
ORDER BY mem_per_pkg DESC
```

This query illustrates both field scoped aggregation and the mixing of non-aggregate columns and aggregate columns in a single select expression.

You can see that the WITHIN clause is more than just a replacement for the GROUP BY technique you would use in a regular SQL. It greatly simplifies working with repeated fields in queries and gives you an easy way to summarize them.

OMIT IF

BigQuery SQL supports a filter clause in addition to the WHERE clause that simplifies operating on repeated fields. This clause should follow the FROM clause and has the form:

```
OMIT <RECORD|field> IF <condition>
```

In contrast to the WHERE clause, elements are excluded if they satisfy the condition. More important, whereas the WHERE clause filters only the entire top-level record, the OMIT IF clause can exclude an individual element in a repeated field, and its condition can include aggregate functions of fields that appear below the element being omitted. In fact, all repeated fields referenced that are scoped below the filtered field must appear within an aggregate function.

Before considering an example, it is worth noting that OMIT IF is just a syntactic convenience. It can always be replaced by a subquery that computes the condition using the WITHIN clause. Nevertheless, it is useful because it makes for more readable queries when dealing with repeated fields.

For the first example, modify the per package memory usage query to exclude apps that use fewer than three packages.

```
SELECT application_id,
       AVG(mem_used / (num_pkgs + 1)) AS mem_per_pkg
FROM (
  SELECT running.name AS application_id,
         running.memory.total AS mem_used,
         COUNT(running.package) WITHIN running AS num_pkgs
  FROM [bigquery-e2e:ch10.sample_data]
  OMIT running IF COUNT(running.package) < 3)
GROUP BY application_id
ORDER BY mem_per_pkg DESC
```

The usage of the clause is self-explanatory. The key point to note is that the aggregate functions are scoped to the field being omitted. If you replaced running with RECORD, then COUNT(running.package) would have counted the total packages across all applications in the record.

Say you want to ignore a specific application in the calculation of memory usage. You could do this quite simply by modifying the scope.

```
OMIT running.package IF running.package = 'com.google.android.gms'
```

If instead, you want to exclude entire applications that use this package you need to modify the scope of the OMIT IF clause. The issue is that you want to omit the entire running element but that requires you only refer to the running .package field inside an aggregate function. Here is one simple way to achieve this result.

```
OMIT running IF SOME(running.package = 'com.google.android.gms')
```

SOME(<condition>) acts as a disjunction, evaluating to true if any of its inputs are true. Similarly, EVERY can be used as a conjunction that requires all its inputs to evaluate to true. These simple aggregation functions make the OMIT IF clause useful in a variety of queries involving repeated fields.

FLATTEN

As long as a query does not involve *independently* repeating fields, the semantics of querying repeated fields are faithful to inner join semantics as described earlier. When there are multiple independently repeating fields, the rules are more complicated. Before discussing how such fields can be mixed, you first need to understand what it means to be independently repeating. Intuitively, two fields repeat independently if there is no correspondence between the elements of one field and the elements of the other field. More precisely, a field may repeat because it is itself repeated or any record in the path to the field is repeated; two fields repeat independently if the set of repeated fields in the path to either field is not a subset of the repeated fields in the other path. A concrete schema can help clarify this definition.

```
[
    {"name": "a", "type": "string"},
    {"name": "b", "type": "string", mode: "repeated"},
    {"name": "c", "type": "string", mode: "repeated"},
    {"name": "d", "type": "record", mode: "repeated", "fields": [
        {"name": "a", "type": "string"},
        {"name": "b", "type": "string", mode:"repeated"}
    ]}
]
```

Given this schema, (b, c) and (c, d.a) are examples of independently repeating fields while (a, b), (a, d.b), and (d.a, d.b) are not independently repeating. Trivially, a leaf field that is repeated is independent with respect to any other field that repeats. Non-repeated leaf fields (but potentially contained within one or more repeated records) require inspection of the paths to the fields to determine independence. With this understanding of independent repetition, now look at why it is interesting for queries.

Now expand the relational tables so that you can continue the comparison to traditional databases. Each log record in the sample data also contains a list of visible wireless networks. These fields are not defined in the schema in Chapter 8 and the data is not collected. They are only included in the sample data for this chapter to support the examples.

```
[
    . . .
    {"name": "wireless", "type": "record", "mode": "repeated", "fields": [
        {"name": "ssid", "type": "string"},
        {"name": "bssid", "type": "string"},
        {"name": "connected", "type": "boolean"}
    ]},
]
```

In the relational database you would use an additional table, `WirelessNetwork`, with a foreign key. The foreign key relationships of `Application` and `WirelessNetwork` to `PhoneLog` are identical.

```
CREATE TABLE WirelessNetwork (
  record_id CHAR(64),
  position TINYINT UNSIGNED,
  ssid CHAR(32),
  bssid CHAR(32),
  connected BOOLEAN,
  PRIMARY KEY (record_id, position),
  FOREIGN KEY (record_id) REFERENCES PhoneLog(record_id)
);
```

Consider a query that determines the relationship between recent applications running and the currently connected wireless network for a given device.

```
SELECT
  wireless.ssid AS ssid,
  running.name AS app,
  COUNT(1) AS cnt
FROM PhoneLog
NATURAL JOIN Application running
NATURAL JOIN WirelessNetwork wireless
WHERE id = 'U7nHcz-7bKTu'
  AND wireless.connected
  AND running.importance_level > 300
GROUP BY ssid, app
ORDER BY ssid, cnt DESC
```

Simply dropping the NATURAL JOINs does not yield a valid BigQuery query. This is because of the restriction on the use of independently repeating fields. The reason this restriction exists is to avoid inadvertent data explosions. The double natural join generates the cartesian product of records with a given log ID from the `Application` table with a set of records with the same log ID in the `WirelessNetwork` table. The query explicitly requests the cartesian product by including multiple joins. If BigQuery implicitly generated a cartesian product for each independently repeating pair, it would be easy to inadvertently construct computationally expensive queries.

Just because an operation is expensive does not mean it isn't the right thing to do. So BigQuery supports a FLATTEN operator that allows you to explicitly specify that a cartesian product is required.

```
FLATTEN(<table value>, <field>)
```

This operation converts the specified repeated field to an optional field, generating a new record for each value in the list and copying all other fields through unchanged. Before you port your relational query to BigQuery using this operator, consider a simpler example. Here is a query counting separate fields in the table.

```
SELECT COUNT(ts) AS records, COUNT(running.name) AS apps
FROM [bigquery-e2e:ch10.sample_data]
```

As discussed earlier the counts are different because repeated fields are not quite handled like a join between two relational tables. If you insert the FLATTEN operator into the query, you get a different result.

```
SELECT COUNT(ts) AS records, COUNT(running.name) AS apps
FROM FLATTEN([bigquery-e2e:ch10.sample_data], running)
```

The two counts returned by this query will be identical and will match the application count column in the previous query. This result exactly matches what you would expect from a relational database, an indication that FLATTEN multiplies the number or records like a JOIN.

Now you can get back to the query comparing wireless networks and applications. You can choose to flatten either of the two repeated fields involved. It is preferable to choose the field that has lower average multiplicity, but in this case there is no obvious choice, so arbitrarily flatten the wireless field.

```
SELECT
  wireless.ssid AS ssid,
  running.name AS app,
  COUNT(1) AS cnt
FROM FLATTEN([bigquery-e2e:ch10.sample_data], wireless)
WHERE id = 'U7nHcz-7bKTu'
  AND wireless.connected
  AND running.importance.level > 300
GROUP BY ssid, app
ORDER BY ssid, cnt DESC
```

Again the JOIN clauses drop away, but this time you must add a FLATTEN invocation around the source table. What if the WHERE clause involved three independently repeating fields? The FLATTEN operator can be nested to generate the cartesian product over multiple fields.

```
FLATTEN(FLATTEN(table), field1), field2)
```

Note that the first argument to flatten can also be a subquery. For example, you could rewrite the query to a more efficient form that filters records before flattening.

```
SELECT
  wireless.ssid AS ssid,
  running.name AS app,
  COUNT(1) AS cnt
FROM FLATTEN(
  SELECT *
  FROM [bigquery-e2e:ch10.sample_data]
```

```
    WHERE id = 'U7nHcz-7bKTu',
    wireless)
  WHERE running.importance.level > 300
    AND wireless.connected
  GROUP BY ssid, app
  ORDER BY ssid, cnt DESC;
```

You may not observe an improvement in performance because the optimizer could be performing the same transformation. One subtle point to pay attention to is that it is OK to pass independently repeating fields through a subquery. This is not a problem because the subquery just preserves the repeated structure. Independently repeating fields are only a problem if they explicitly appear in the query. Currently BigQuery automatically flattens a single repeated field appearing in the outermost SELECT clause. As a consequence, query results never have repeated fields. If more than one independently repeating field appears in the outermost SELECT clause, BigQuery will reject the query rather than generate the cartesian product of the repeating fields. If this is what you require you can explicitly FLATTEN one of the repeating fields.

Repeated Field Functions

Almost all the functions in the query language operate the same way on singleton and repeated fields. However, a couple of functions provided specifically operate on or produce repeated fields.

- NEST(*field*)
- POSITION(*field*)
- NTH(index, *field*)
- LAST(*field*)

NEST is an aggregation function that is roughly the inverse of FLATTEN. It must be used as a column in the SELECT clause together with a GROUP BY clause. Currently, it is not particularly useful because BigQuery flattens all top-level query results, so it will undo the work of a top-level NEST expression. In addition, the ability to operate only on a single field significantly limits its usefulness. In subqueries you will likely want to use window functions instead of NEST, so we will not bother with an example of its usage.

The rest of the functions take repeated fields as inputs. Keep in mind that a field itself may not be repeated, but if any of the records in the path to the field are repeated, then the field is treated as repeated. The functions operate with respect to the scope specified by the WITHIN clause. For example, in our application device log, POSITION(running.name) WITHIN RECORD returns the index of the application in the list of applications. As you have probably guessed, POSITION returns the position of a value in a repeated field; NTH returns a value at a particular position in the repeated field; and LAST returns the last element in the repeated field. There is no FIRST because that is the same as NTH(1, *field*). All the functions use 1-based indexing; there is no 0th element. Here is a query that computes the difference in importance levels between the applications in the first and last position:

```
SELECT AVG(importance_delta) FROM (
  SELECT
    (NTH(1, running.importance.level)
      - LAST(running.importance.level)) WITHIN RECORD
      AS importance_delta
  FROM [bigquery-e2e:ch10.sample_data])
```

The Parallel Lists query recipe that describes how to zip together two parallel repeated fields demonstrates the use of POSITION. Note that it is illegal to use POSITION on a non-repeated field.

Query Errors

Errors associated with query jobs fall into three categories:

- Transient
- Invalid user input
- Execution failures

The first two classes of errors can occur on any of the API operations. Of course, because queries can be complicated and are susceptible to a variety of syntax and semantic errors, it is common to encounter the second class of errors. The error message is usually clear enough to determine the problematic parts. Unfortunately, there are times when the message is cryptic, and there is no simple prescription for dealing with these cases. The best you can do is report instances of unhelpful messages through the support channels described in the introduction. The last class covers cases where the query is well formed but cannot be computed due to limitations in the execution engine. These types of errors are the focus of this section because in some cases workarounds exist.

Result Too Large

When new users first try the service, it is common for them to start by trying the simplest possible query to get a feel for the web interface, command-line client, or API. The usual candidate is something along the lines of:

```
SELECT * FROM [publicdata:samples.wikipedia]
```

It is an unfortunate way to start because the service responds with a disappointing error message.

```
errorResult": {
  "reason": "responseTooLarge",
  "message": "Response too large to return."
}
```

Considering that the service is intended to operate on "Big Data," it is somewhat surprising that it is complaining that such a simple operation is too large.

In this particular scenario the underlying issue is that users are expecting the service to behave like traditional databases they are familiar with, but the service is not quite meeting their expectation. In a database, the result of a query is a *cursor*, which allows you to fetch rows incrementally. When the result can be trivially computed, the cursor can just be a fancy pointer into the source table. Most tools will fetch a small number of rows from the cursor and then discard it. BigQuery operates differently; a query is actually a job that transforms a set of source tables into a new table. As a result the simple SELECT * query is actually attempting to make a full copy of the Wikipedia sample table. Making a copy is definitely not what users had in mind. Fixing the query is simply a matter of appending a LIMIT with a reasonable value to the end. However, this error merits additional discussion.

ENCOURAGING A LIMIT

In the first release of the web application, the query template in the compose box did not include a trailing limit. We quickly discovered users were hitting this error, so the default template was modified to include a limit of 1,000 rows. Unfortunately, no such safety net exists in the command-line client, so users still hit this error when testing with that tool.

Arguably, the aim of most queries is to turn "Big Data" into "Small Data"—the loose definition of small data being something humans can usefully consume. Even if the data is feeding visualizations, this limit is usually not more than a couple of thousand rows. In many cases a "Response too large" error is an indication that a query is not sufficiently selective or requires further aggregation. The error is triggered when the size of the result exceeds approximately 128 MB. The specific value is not particularly useful because it is likely to change over time, and in any case it is not easy to estimate the size of your results before running the query. A simpler rule of thumb is to aim for query results that return less than 10,000 rows.

When developing complex queries that involve subqueries, it is often useful to look at the result of the subquery to ensure it is producing the results you intended. Often these subqueries generate large results, which the final outer query will summarize into a manageable number of rows. Simply slap a LIMIT clause at the end of the subquery to test it independently; just remember to drop the clause when pasting it into the final query. Further, if you have an ORDER BY clause and need only the top or bottom *N* results, then adding a LIMIT *N* clause will likely significantly speed up your query execution.

Finally, there are times when you do want to execute a query that is going to return a large result. Possible use cases include:

- The result will be used as a source in future queries.
- Data will be exported for external processing.
- The table is being updated to fix bad data.

For these use cases BigQuery does support generating large results, but it requires that the allowLargeResults flag be explicitly set to true in the query job configuration. If you are wondering why this flag does not default to true, the reason is that large result generation uses a different execution mode that is slower than the default mode that has the size restriction. Queries that generate small results are orders of magnitude more common than large result queries, so it would be a shame to slow all of them down by defaulting to the large result execution path. Because you will need to reference the results in queries or export jobs, you are required to supply a destination table to save the results when the flag is set to true. Note that, unlike with anonymous tables, you will begin to accrue storage costs for your query results when the query completes, and it will not be automatically garbage collected.

```
job['configuration'] = {
  'query': {
    'allowLargeResults': True,
    'destinationTable': {
      'projectId': 'myproject',
      'datasetId': 'mydataset',
      'tableId': 'my_big_result'
    }
    'query': 'SELECT . . .'
  }
}
```

You can also enable the flag when issuing queries using the command-line client.

```
$ bq query --allow_large_results \
  --destination_table foo.bar \
  'SELECT * FROM [some.table] WHERE . . .'
```

This feature is powerful and should certainly be utilized when appropriate, but it is not a good idea to always enable it because then all your queries will be slower.

Resources Exceeded

Considering that every computational system has its limitations, it should not come as a surprise that there are some queries that simply do not fit within the resource constraints of BigQuery. However, the mode of failure may be somewhat surprising. Many database systems will not by default fail a query because it is too expensive. Instead they will attempt to make progress given the existing resources even if it means consuming all the resources at the expense of other queries in the system, and they may take an unreasonably long time. BigQuery aims to execute every query within a time frame that is proportional to the data being scanned, so it fails the query relatively quickly rather than processing it indefinitely. This approach has merits, but you also have to cope with its drawbacks.

It is useful to understand at a high level why some queries fail to fit within the constraints of the system. Chapter 9 covers the execution model in detail, and it is useful to keep it in mind when considering resource errors. To achieve good performance, the system avoids using a disk once the data has been read from a disk. The intermediate results in each node are kept in volatile memory, and every query is subject to a limit on the memory it uses in a single node. When a query exceeds this limit on any single node, the query fails and reports a resources exceeded exception.

```
errorResult": {
  "reason": "resourcesExceeded",
  "message": "Resources exceeded."
}
```

Retrying the unit of work on a different node is not going to help matters because the limit is a static value, so any other node will encounter the same limit. For the same reason, retrying the query is not going to help matters.

There are a few different query features that have high memory requirements within a single execution node:

- GROUP BY clauses that generate a large number of distinct groups
- Aggregation functions that require memory proportional to the number of input values
- Join operations that generate a greater number of outputs than inputs

Earlier in the chapter you saw how to deal with queries that have the first property by using the EACH qualifier in the GROUP BY clause. Queries that have large memory requirements for each group handled can fail even when the EACH qualifier is used. In some cases it is possible to avoid this resource limit; for example, the "Exact Count Distinct" section in this chapter presents a scalable alternative to the COUNT(DISTINCT field) function, which often causes resource exhaustion errors. Unfortunately, there is no reliable procedure for fixing all queries that encounter this issue. Here we discuss the class of queries that generally encounter this issue and suggestions for how to modify them so that they succeed.

Most of the familiar aggregation functions have outputs that are independent of the number of values fed to them, for example COUNT, SUM, MIN, and MAX. However, the GROUP_CONCAT and NEST aggregation functions have outputs that are proportional to the size of their inputs. Other aggregation functions have theoretically constant output size, but the constant is large as in the case of COUNT(DISTINCT field, N) with a large value for N (the constant is proportional N). Finally, operations like QUANTILES have intermediate state that grows logarithmically with input values, but once again have a large constant factor that can be problematic. Because all these consume a substantial amount of memory per output record, they tend to cause memory limit violations as the results are collected up the execution tree. To avoid the error you need to modify the query to generate fewer total output rows by limiting the set of input values considered. This may require building up the final result by running multiple queries, all appending their results to the same final result table.

When a query does not involve a join, the number of output rows is strictly less than or equal to the number of input rows. When a join is present, then for each distinct value of the join key, the number of output rows is the product of the number of rows in the left and right table with the given key. The query might eventually discard or aggregate these rows, but they must at least be transiently generated. Most of the time joins deal with one-to-many relationships, but when you work with a many-to-many relationship between two tables, the amount of intermediate state can easily grow large. This can lead to high-memory usage in the leaf nodes of the execution engine. Note that even in cases where the memory usage is not an issue, this can cause the query to run slowly. In some cases you can control this expansion of data by adjusting the query. The Cross Join query recipe in the following section for calculating concurrency of operations is an example of how you can design the join so that the number of intermediate rows is manageable.

Regrettably, there is no simple prescription for dealing with these errors. Hopefully, we have at least given you enough information to identify the parts of the query that are causing the error and ideas for how to work around the error. Fortunately, as the execution engine evolves over time and expands its capabilities, these errors will be less common and you can forget this section!

Recipes

This section is organized as a grab bag of queries that are useful in reporting applications. We have tried to concentrate on queries that look fairly different from a similar query over data stored in a relational database. It is worth skimming this chapter to get a sense for the types of reports being addressed. That way, when you do encounter a report that seems tricky to generate using BigQuery, you will know if this section has a pertinent recipe and can return to it to look up the details.

Pivot

The operation of pivoting or transposing a table is common when shaping data for reports or visualization. In SQL the natural way to generate totals broken down by multiple dimensions is to use a grouping clause with required dimensions. This works well because it generalizes to an arbitrary number of dimensions. However, when working with two dimensions, especially when one dimension has only a handful of possible values, it is useful to have a column for each value of the dimension. For example, you might be interested in finding the longest 100 words across the plays of Shakespeare together with the counts for how often they appear in each work.

```
SELECT word, corpus, corpus_total
FROM (
  SELECT
    word,
    LENGTH(word) AS word_len,
    corpus,
    SUM(word_count) AS corpus_total
  FROM [publicdata:samples.shakespeare]
  WHERE LENGTH(word) > 10
  GROUP BY word, word_len, corpus)
ORDER BY word_len DESC
LIMIT 100
```

This query does not quite do what we set out to do because each row corresponds to a word and corpus pair. We will fix it as we pivot the data.

If you are only interested in a specific set of his works, it would be more convenient if you could have a column for the count of the word in each of the works of interest. In addition, you can then ensure that you collect 100 separate words because each row will correspond to a single word. You can achieve this by adding multiple aggregation columns with conditional expressions.

```
SELECT
  word,
  SUM(IF(corpus = 'kinglear', corpus_total, 0)) AS kinglear,
  SUM(IF(corpus = 'tempest', corpus_total, 0)) AS tempest,
  SUM(IF(corpus = 'macbeth', corpus_total, 0)) AS macbeth,
  SUM(corpus_total) AS [total]
FROM (
  SELECT
    word,
```

```
      LENGTH(word) word_len,
      corpus,
      SUM(word_count) corpus_total
    FROM [publicdata:samples.shakespeare]
    WHERE LENGTH(word) > 10
    GROUP BY word, word_len, corpus)
  GROUP BY word, word_len
  ORDER BY word_len DESC
  LIMIT 100
```

This query generates three columns for the counts of the longest words in King Lear, Tempest, and Macbeth. It also includes a total column that is the total across all the works in the table. As you might guess, most of the counts are zero because long words are unique and tend to be limited to a single corpus.

In many cases the values to pivot are not known up front. Even in this query we picked three works at random. In realistic reports there is usually a better way to select the columns. For example, we could identify the three largest works and use those in our column expressions.

```
SELECT CONCAT(
        CONCAT("SUM(IF(corpus = '", corpus),
        "', corpus_total, 0)")
FROM (
  SELECT corpus, SUM(word_count) total
  FROM [publicdata:samples.shakespeare]
  GROUP BY corpus
  ORDER BY total DESC
  LIMIT 3)
```

If the number of columns grows large, the query can be tedious to write, but usually such queries are generated programmatically. The previous query generates the individual column expressions. In practice, you might not actually want BigQuery to handle your formatting, but the query illustrates how you might feed a query result into a string-formatting library to generate the final query.

Cohort Analysis

When trying to make sense of Big Data, it is common to discuss cohorts that are basically sets of entities that have a specific property, for example:

- Users who accessed a given application on their phone
- Wikipedia contributors that edited a particular title
- Cities that have more than one ZIP code

In most cases it is not possible to determine if an entity belongs to a particular cohort by inspecting a single record. Here you investigate how to compute a condition that spans multiple rows and use it in a cohort analysis query.

TIP In this chapter we have mostly used explicit field references in GROUP BY and ORDER BY clauses. This generally makes the query a little easier to understand. The older SQL standard and many popular implementations also support using column indices in these clauses. BigQuery also supports this feature, and we have used it in the queries that appear in this recipe and also in other chapters. Often it is useful when you are experimenting with queries, and in some cases it even improves the readability of the query. However, the feature is not standardized, so if that is a concern, you may want to avoid it in your production code.

In the Wikipedia example, because each record contains a single edit, you must look at all the edits for a given contributor to determine if the contributor belongs to the cohort. You can evaluate each record to see if it establishes membership or not, but then you need to combine all the results to see if there is *at least* one record where the condition evaluates to true. The SOME and EVERY aggregate functions perform the logical aggregation required for this operation. SOME computes the disjunction of its inputs; it is true only if there is at least one input that is true. EVERY computes the conjunction of its inputs; it is false if at least one input is false.

```
SELECT bush_all, bush_some, obama_all, obama_some,
       COUNT(1) AS num, AVG(edits) AS avg_edits
FROM (
  SELECT contributor_id,
    EVERY(bush_edit) AS bush_all, SOME(bush_edit) AS bush_some,
    EVERY(obama_edit) AS obama_all, SOME(obama_edit) AS obama_some,
    COUNT(1) AS edits
  FROM (
    SELECT
      contributor_id,
      (LOWER(title) = 'george w. bush') AS bush_edit,
      (LOWER(title) = 'barrack obama') AS obama_edit
    FROM [publicdata:samples.wikipedia])
  GROUP EACH BY 1
  HAVING bush_all OR bush_some OR obama_all OR obama_some)
GROUP BY 1, 2, 3, 4
ORDER BY 1, 2, 3, 4
```

The innermost query could have been collapsed into the containing query, but it is often more readable if you have a query that solely computes the conditions on individual records, especially if a condition is used more than once in the containing query as is the case here. The GROUP EACH BY nested within a GROUP BY query is typical for cohort analysis. The EACH query is collecting and summarizing all the records for every user. It is common to need EACH because there are usually a large number of entities, so shuffling the data among nodes avoids hitting resource limits. This inner query produces one record per user with fields that describe the properties of interest. The outer query then counts the number of users falling in each cohort, where the cohort is defined by specific values for the properties computed. In our example, the properties are "user has edited *at least* one Bush page," "user has *only* edited Obama pages," and so on. This grouping does not have an EACH because the number of different cohorts tends to be small for any given query, in our example, just 5. You can accumulate multiple statistics in one pass; for example, this query computes the number of unique users in each cohort and the average number of edits per contributor in a cohort.

To illustrate more complex cohort conditions that can be implemented using the same basic strategy, imagine defining a cohort based on the relative times of the first edit.

```
SELECT
  IF(bush_some AND obama_some,
     first_bush < first_obama, NULL) AS bush_earlier,
  bush_some,
  obama_some,
  COUNT(1) AS num,
  AVG(edits) AS avg_edits
FROM (
  SELECT
    contributor_id,
    MIN(IF(bush_edit, ts, 99999999999)) AS first_bush,
    SOME(bush_edit) AS bush_some,
    MIN(IF(obama_edit, ts, 99999999999)) AS first_obama,
    SOME(obama_edit) AS obama_some,
    COUNT(1) AS edits
  FROM (
    SELECT
      contributor_id,
      timestamp AS ts,
      (LOWER(title) = 'george w. bush') AS bush_edit,
      (LOWER(title) = 'barrack obama') AS obama_edit
    FROM [publicdata:samples.wikipedia])
  WHERE bush_edit OR obama_edit
  GROUP EACH BY 1)
GROUP BY 1, 2, 3
ORDER BY 1, 2, 3
```

The main feature to observe is that you can compute cohort membership in the top-level query. In this case, you can subdivide the cohort of contributors that have edited the pages of Obama and Bush into separate cohorts depending on which page was edited earlier. You can also see that we tweaked the rows being considered for the total statistics by moving the condition from the HAVING clause to the WHERE clause, limiting the query to rows involving the pages of interest, which is a condition we can apply prior to the aggregation.

The essential piece of this technique is using a nested GROUP EACH specifying the fields that identify the entity that is being evaluated for inclusion in a cohort. After you have a handle on this bit, you can play with the row filter conditions and aggregations at different levels of the query to extract the information you need.

Parallel Lists

When you design schemas for BigQuery, it is best to organize repeated data so that fields that repeat together are collected into a RECORD type field that is repeated; this allows for simpler queries over the data. Unfortunately, there are times when you have to deal with data that is structured as independent lists where elements at equal indexes are related to each other. For example, consider this table representing mappings between numbers in different representations.

```
[
  {"name": "src_id", "type": "string"},
  {"name": "dst_id", "type": "string"},
  {"name": "src", "type": "string", "mode": "repeated"},
  {"name": "dst", "type":"string", "mode": "repeated"}
]
```

Ideally, you would have preferred a schema that paired the source and destination values into a single record.

```
[
  {"name": "src_id", "type": "string"},
  {"name": "dst_id", "type": "string"},
  {"name": "map", "type": "record", "mode": "repeated", "fields": [
    {"name": "src", "type": "string"},
    {"name": "dst", "type": "string"}
  ]}
]
```

Fortunately, if you are stuck with the former schema, you can still arrange for the pairs to be constructed on-the-fly.

You can use the POSITION function to access the index of each value, but you need to include a FLATTEN operation because the fields accessed are independently repeating.

```
SELECT src_id, dst_id, src, dst
FROM FLATTEN((
  SELECT src_id, dst_id,
         POSITION(src) AS src_index, src,
         POSITION(dst) AS dst_index, dst
  FROM [bigquery-e2e:ch10.parallel]),
  src)
WHERE src_index = dst_index
```

This works well enough, but keep in mind this is quite a bit more expensive than the simpler queries possible with the more appropriate schema. The execution engine has to generate the cross product of the elements in the list before it can filter it down to matching the entries with the matching positions. Just to demonstrate that you can actually do something useful with the result of this query, here is a version that does a little more than pulling the entries together.

```
SELECT src,
  GROUP_CONCAT(CONCAT(dst_id, CONCAT(":", dst))) AS dst_list
FROM FLATTEN((
  SELECT
    src_id, dst_id,
    POSITION(src) AS src_index, src,
    POSITION(dst) AS dst_index, dst
  FROM [bigquery-e2e:ch10.parallel]),
  src)
WHERE src_index = dst_index
  AND src_id = "decimal"
GROUP BY src
ORDER BY src
```

This approach generalizes to more than two parallel lists. Each additional repeated field requires a nested FLATTEN. You should also place the WHERE clauses, applying the position equality filter in the nested queries, rather than collecting them all at the top-level to reduce the number of intermediate rows generated by the cross product. That means one such condition following each FLATTEN invocation.

Exact Count Distinct

The COUNT(DISTINCT *field*, *N*) aggregation function is approximate and intended to be a quick way to roughly determine the cardinality of a given field. It is exact for cardinalities less than *N*, so it is tempting to simply use it with a large value of *N* to determine the exact cardinality. This is problematic because it consumes memory proportional to N causing these kinds of queries to fail. There is a straightforward way to determine the exact cardinality of a field, and it also scales to larger cardinalities. The query is slower because it involves a shuffle operation, so rather than using the approach outlined next all the time, reserve it for when you have to compute exact cardinalities for large sets.

Here is the simplest version of the query that highlights how the shuffle is used to collapse duplicate values in a given field.

```
SELECT COUNT(1) AS unique FROM (
  SELECT 1 FROM [publicdata:samples.shakespeare]
  GROUP EACH BY word)
```

The inner query buckets each input row into a group associated with a distinct word. The SELECT 1 is perhaps a little confusing. The query would remain the same if you change it to SELECT word, but you can use a constant expression here to emphasize that you do not care about the actual value of the word outside the grouping clause. COUNT(1) similarly indicates that we are interested in the number of rows rather than any particular field. This approach scales to millions of distinct values because EACH distributes the aggregation operation.

It is fairly common to want to determine distinct values broken down across one or more dimensions. Daily active users over the last seven days or distinct HTTP user agents by URL are examples of such queries. All you need to do is add an additional field to the grouping clause and thread it through to the outer query.

```
SELECT wp_namespace,
  COUNT(num) AS unique,
  SUM(num) AS total
FROM (
  SELECT wp_namespace,
    COUNT(1) AS num
  FROM [publicdata:samples.wikipedia]
  GROUP EACH BY wp_namespace, contributor_id)
GROUP BY wp_namespace
ORDER BY wp_namespace
```

In addition to cardinality, this query also records the total counts broken down by the same dimension. It is common to want both together, so it is helpful to fetch them in a single query.

One nice capability of COUNT(DISTINCT *field*) is that a single query can determine the cardinality of multiple fields. With a little cleverness you can modify your exact version to do the same.

```
SELECT wp_namespace,
  SUM(IF(field = 'ID', 1, 0)) AS unique_id,
  SUM(IF(field = 'ID', INTEGER(num), 0)) AS total_id,
  SUM(IF(field = 'IP', 1, 0)) AS unique_ip,
  SUM(IF(field = 'IP', INTEGER(num), 0)) AS total_ip,
FROM (
  SELECT wp_namespace, field, COUNT(1) AS num
  FROM (
    SELECT wp_namespace,
      'ID' AS field,
      HASH(contributor_id) AS val
    FROM [publicdata:samples.wikipedia]
    WHERE contributor_id IS NOT NULL
  ), (
    SELECT
      wp_namespace,
      'IP' AS field,
      HASH(contributor_ip) AS val
    FROM [publicdata:samples.wikipedia]
    WHERE contributor_ip IS NOT NULL)
  GROUP EACH BY wp_namespace, field, val)
GROUP BY wp_namespace
ORDER BY wp_namespace
```

This query is fairly complicated, but it has the advantage that you do not need to run and wait for a query job for each field that you need to analyze. The pivot by field type in the top-level SELECT clause is not actually required, so you could replace that with a simple aggregation by field type and simplify the query a little.

Trailing Averages

With the introduction of window functions, it is fairly easy to generate trailing (or other moving averages). The main issue to deal with is some of the restrictions around the use of window functions. To demonstrate how to construct the query, we have created a synthetic dataset (`bigquery-e2e:ch10.sessions`) corresponding to user sessions on some hypothetical service. Each record has a user ID and a start and end timestamp.

```
[
    {"name": "user_id", "type": "string"},
    {"name": "start", "type": "timestamp"},
    {"name": "end", "type": "timestamp"}
]
```

The metric we are going to smooth is the daily active users. We start with an inner query that computes the base metric and then wrap it in a query that uses window functions to fetch trailing rows. The outermost query combines the trailing values into a weighted average paying attention to missing values.

```
SELECT
  start_date,
  ((num_0 +
    IF(num_1 > -1, num_1, num_0) * 0.5 +
    IF(num_2 > -1, num_2, num_0) * 0.25) /
    1.75) AS smooth_num
FROM (
  SELECT
    start_date,
    num_0,
    LAG(num_0, 1, INTEGER(-1))
      OVER (ORDER BY start_date) AS num_1,
    LAG(num_0, 2, INTEGER(-1))
      OVER (ORDER BY start_date) AS num_2
  FROM (
    SELECT
      DATE(start) AS start_date,
      INTEGER(COUNT(1)) num_0
    FROM [bigquery-e2e:ch10.sessions]
    GROUP BY start_date))
ORDER BY start_date
```

This method is easy to follow but there is one important caveat. If there are missing days from the inner query, then the moving average will be wrong because the missing day will not be treated as zero, rather the first nonzero day before it will be used. If your data can suffer from gaps, you may want to consider forming the union of the inner query and table containing a zero entry for every day of interest to ensure there are no gaps.

Finding Concurrency

Now continue with the session dataset used in the previous recipe to illustrate an interesting way to leverage CROSS JOIN. The goal is to compute the maximum number of concurrent sessions observed for each hour of a given day, performing the calculation at minute granularity.

The basic idea is to determine all the sessions that were live during a given minute. You can do this by cross-joining each session with every minute of the day and then discarding all the minutes that do not fall within the start and end time of the minute. Then group the values by minute and count the occurrences. Finally group the minutes by hour and take the max count over all the minutes in the given hour.

```
SELECT
  INTEGER(minute / 60) AS hour,
  MAX(active) AS active
FROM (
  SELECT m.index AS minute, COUNT(s.user_id) AS active
  FROM (
    SELECT
      user_id,
      INTEGER((TIMESTAMP_TO_SEC(start) -
              TIMESTAMP_TO_SEC(TIMESTAMP('2014-01-15'))) /
              60) AS start_min,
      INTEGER((TIMESTAMP_TO_SEC(end) -
              TIMESTAMP_TO_SEC(TIMESTAMP('2014-01-15'))) /
              60) AS end_min
    FROM [bigquery-e2e:ch10.sessions]
    WHERE start > '2014-01-14 23:00:00'
      AND end < '2014-01-16 01:00:00') s
  CROSS JOIN [bigquery-e2e:ch10.minutes] m
  WHERE s.start_min <= m.index AND m.index <= s.end_min
  GROUP BY minute)
GROUP BY hour
ORDER BY hour
```

To make this work you need to load a file containing the minutes. Actually all you need is a table with a single column containing the integers [0, 24 * 60]. We have generated the table *bigquery-e2e:ch10.minutes* by simply loading a text file containing these integers. If your input is spread across tables covering different time periods, then you need to adjust the query for sessions that span the boundaries of your tables. Since this example only uses a single table, all you had to do was ensure that the inner WHERE clause selected sessions from an interval slightly larger than the day you are analyzing.

Abstracting a bit from this specific problem, there are two important points to note. Firstly, JOIN, and CROSS JOIN in particular, allow you to expand the number of input rows, effectively *multiplying* the left table with the right table. Second, although the ON clause in BigQuery joins is restricted to equality comparisons, you can always use the WHERE clause to apply more general filtering conditions to the generated rows. The only danger to avoid is both tables being large in which case the cross product is prohibitive.

Summary

This was a long chapter, heavy on examples and details, yet it covered only a small part of what can be done with BigQuery. For programmers familiar with procedural languages, SQL can initially seem awkward. However, given some time, you may find yourself warming to the notion that the language is well suited to the task of transforming structured data. The examples covered are merely a starting point for all the interesting queries you can run to extract meaningful information from your data.

One other important point is that BigQuery is constantly evolving the capabilities of its SQL implementation. Over time, various awkward restrictions have been dropped, and additional functions and language features have been added. You will find that more of your analysis can be done easily within the service.

Inevitably you will hit a problem that seems intractable in SQL. Consider reaching out to the BigQuery StackOverflow forum mentioned in the introduction or the broader SQL community for ideas on how to tackle the problem. Even if we cannot solve your challenge, we are interested to learn about the different kinds of problems people are trying to tackle. Who knows, your question may lead to the next round of new language features or functions.

Managing Data Stored in BigQuery

The previous chapters cover how BigQuery simplifies analytics over large datasets. BigQuery also has features to simplify data management and the integration of analytics into an application. This chapter covers those features and how to handle common data warehousing tasks using them.

Query Caching

As discussed in Chapter 7, "Running Queries," BigQuery has an auto-caching feature that enables it to reuse results across identical queries. This feature is convenient because it is transparent to the user but is limited to instances in which the service can guarantee that existing results from a prior query job are identical to the results that would be generated by running the query again, which we will elaborate on below. The application developer, on the other hand, knows a great deal more about the use case. So when the application can trade freshness for execution cost, it is possible to further reduce query costs by directly managing caching. With many data warehousing systems, it is necessary to utilize a separate caching framework, for example Memcached, to reduce load on the query engine or the latency of operations in a front end. With BigQuery it is usually feasible to avoid a separate caching framework for query results by leveraging the feature that query results are actually new tables that can be assigned an explicit name. Different parts of the application can interact with the same query result by accessing the appropriate named table. Next you see how this works.

Result Caching

To understand how named query results are useful, look at how to build a page in your application that renders the top 100 most active Android applications over, for example, the last 6 hours. Imagine something like a leaderboard for applications, which could perhaps serve as a navigational element leading to information about a specific application. First, you need to formulate the query that can generate the information that needs to be displayed:

```
SELECT
  running.name AppName,
  AVG(running.memory.total) MemUsage,
  COUNT(running.name) Running
FROM (TABLE_DATE_RANGE(logs.device_,
                       DATE_ADD(CURRENT_TIMESTAMP(), -1, 'DAY'),
                       CURRENT_TIMESTAMP()))
WHERE
  (TIMESTAMP_TO_SEC(CURRENT_TIMESTAMP()) -
   TIMESTAMP_TO_SEC(ts)) < 60 * 60 * 6
GROUP BY 1
ORDER BY 3 DESC
LIMIT 100;
```

This is a simple query capturing application usage over a 6-hour rolling window. Note that this query is not cacheable because of the use of CURRENT_TIMESTAMP and the continuously updated source tables. The cost of this query is going to be proportional to the number of records in the source tables, which is expected to be large. If you plan for the page displaying this table to be accessed frequently, for example, once per minute, you would need to run this query approximately 1,500 times a day.

If it is reasonable for the contents of the page to be up to 1 hour behind the current contents of the source table, fewer distinct queries need to be run. One simple way to do this is to tweak the query so that BigQuery considers it auto-cacheable. For example, you could generate a timestamp that is rounded to a 1-hour boundary and include it as a constant expression in place of CURRENT_TIMESTAMP() in the query. This works well at handling queries that generate identical results. However, this does not work if the underlying tables are changing frequently because the query needs to be rerun at least as frequently as the underlying table is changing. For a table that is continuously updated via streaming inserts, this implies that the query can never be cached.

You can structure the dashboard data generation differently to cache results in a manner tuned to the application. The general idea is to run the query from a background process that stores the results in a known location. The dashboard rendering code can then simply retrieve the results rather than actually issue the query. The details of how you trigger the periodic refresh depend on the application framework. For example, if you are using AppEngine this is easily done using the scheduled tasks feature (`https://developers.google .com/appengine/docs/python/config/cron`). Chapter 8, "Putting it Together," covers the details of setting up such background tasks. Here we focus on how to explicitly cache and read query results. Listing 11.1 contains functions to refresh the contents of a query result cache table and a function to read back the results.

Listing 11.1 Caching query results

```
def cache_query(jobs, query, cache_id):
  # Must use Jobs.insert() because Jobs.query() does not
  # support a named destination.
  resp = jobs.insert(
    projectId=auth.PROJECT_ID,
    body={
      'configuration': {
        'query': {
          'query': query,
          'destinationTable': {
            'projectId': auth.PROJECT_ID,
            'datasetId': CACHE_DATASET,
            'tableId': cache_id
          },
          'writeDisposition': 'WRITE_TRUNCATE'
        }
      }
    }).execute()
  if 'jobReference' in resp:
    job_id = resp['jobReference']['jobId']
    while not resp.get('jobComplete', False):
      resp = jobs.getQueryResults(
        projectId=auth.PROJECT_ID,
        jobId=job_id,
        # Do not need the data.
        maxResults=0).execute()
  else:
    raise SystemError('Query failed: %s' % json.dumps(resp))
  return resp
```

continues

Listing 11.1: *(continued)*

```
def read_cache(tabledata, cache_id):
  rows = []
  resp = {'pageToken': None}
  while 'pageToken' in resp:
    resp = tabledata.list(
      projectId=auth.PROJECT_ID,
      datasetId=CACHE_DATASET,
      tableId=cache_id,
      pageToken=resp['pageToken'],
      maxResults=10000).execute()
    rows.extend([[cell.get('v') for cell in row.get('f')]
                 for row in resp.get('rows', [])])
  return rows

def update_top_apps(jobs):
  return cache_query(
    jobs,
    '''
SELECT
  running.name AppName,
  AVG(running.memory.total) MemUsage,
  COUNT(running.name) Running'''
# FROM (TABLE_DATE_RANGE(logs.device_,
#                        DATE_ADD(CURRENT_TIMESTAMP(), -1, 'DAY'),
#                        CURRENT_TIMESTAMP()))
# Daily tables are protected so we substitute a sample table.
'''
FROM [bigquery-e2e:ch11.sample_device_log]'''
# Drop the where clause since the sample table is static.
# WHERE
#   (TIMESTAMP_TO_SEC(CURRENT_TIMESTAMP()) -
#    TIMESTAMP_TO_SEC(ts)) < 60 * 60 * 6
'''
GROUP BY 1
ORDER BY 3 DESC
LIMIT 100''', TOP_APPS_ID)
```

The background task would need to periodically invoke `update_top_apps(jobs)` and the dashboard page will read the cached results using `read_cache(tabledata, TOP_APPS_ID)`. Following are three points to note:

- The update is atomic.
- Results pagination will be consistent even with the background update. (See Chapter 7, "Running Queries.")
- Accessing the rows from the result table is fast and cheap (free).

The first two points deserve further explanation. In cases in which the results cannot be fetched in a single request, BigQuery guarantees consistent pagination even if the table is changing underneath the reader. This means that no additional coordination (locking, for example) is required between the background task and the dashboard handler. Also it is worth noting that the background task does not bother to wait for the completion of the job or check for success. In the rare event that there is a failure for some reason, the results will be a little staler than usual but the next scheduled invocation will fix the problem. Note that the age of the results can be determined by observing the modification time of the table. If it is appropriate, the dashboard page can either report an error or directly run the query if the results in the cache are too old.

The aim of the strategies discussed in this section is to cache the results of your queries. Often, this can be achieved by simply adjusting the query. In other cases, you need to control how frequently the query is executed. Let's go back to the question of how many times this query would need to be run. With this cron-based scheme, it would be executed roughly twice an hour or approximately 50 times a day. At the modest usage levels we assumed, that is a 30-fold reduction in query volume compared to a design that runs the query for each request. In addition, the latency of the dashboard page will also be reduced.

Intermediate Results

As you have seen, query results are tables, so they can be used as sources for further queries. This feature can be useful in a variety of application scenarios. For example, consider the problem of exploring the mobile records collected according to the hour and state in which they were collected. Potentially interesting statistics are:

- Counts by hour summed over all states
- Relative distribution by state in a particular time range
- Hourly distribution for a given state

Running any one of these queries on the base data each time a page is rendered can be expensive. Because each result would require a unique query, a simple cache would not be effective. But a single intermediate table can make all these queries have a fixed, lower cost independent of the underlying table size. You can construct this intermediate table with the following query:

```
SELECT
  DATE(l.ts) Day,
  HOUR(l.ts) Hour,
  z.state State,
  COUNT(l.ts) Num
FROM [bigquery-e2e:ch11.sample_device_log] l
INNER JOIN [bigquery-e2e:reference.zip_codes] z
  ON  z.zip=l.location.zip
GROUP BY 1, 2, 3
ORDER BY 1, 2, 3;
```

The result table is not suitable for direct rendering because it has $7 \times 24 \times 50 = 8400$ rows but is small enough that the cost of a query on the table is negligible. A further rollup query, one that performs additional aggregation, on this result table can be used to generate a summary view. Filter queries that select a subset of rows corresponding to specific states and time ranges can be used to explore details. Also note that identical queries referencing this table will benefit from the auto-caching feature because this result table is effectively frozen until the query that generated it is run again. By virtue of this feature, frequently accessed graphs will end up being cached and returning immediately. It is also worth noting that the size of this intermediate table can be scaled by 2 to 3 orders of magnitude without noticeably impacting query latency, allowing the intermediate table to hold more granular records.

In traditional databases, query results are usually ephemeral and special action has to be taken to stash them in temporary tables or external stores. BigQuery takes a different approach, making query results available for 24 hours or indefinitely if assigned a name. This section illustrated how applications can take advantage of this behavior.

Table Snapshots

BigQuery provides table management features that make it simple to handle many aspects of the data life cycle, including backups and snapshots of changing datasets to enable historical analysis. Developers should, of course, consider integrating separate backup systems when appropriate; Chapter 12, "External Data Processing," which covers exports, might be useful in that regard. This section focuses on facilities available within BigQuery.

These features are enabled by BigQuery's capability to cheaply create copies of tables. This is achieved by running a table copy job that specifies a source and destination table. This job usually completes in less than 1 minute independent of the table size. Although the job is free, it is subject to the overall job quota, and storage charges begin to accrue for both copies of the data. See the `copy_table()` function in Listing 11.2 for the details of how a copy job is configured.

Now look at a concrete archiving requirement to see how this might be utilized. In the sample application you have an AppEngine Datastore table, `devices`, in which you can record all current installations of the mobile app. In the next section, "AppEngine Datastore Integration," you learn how a snapshot of this table is made available for queries in BigQuery. Because rows in this table are continuously updated, it is useful to have access to historical versions because you can then compare how installations vary over time. The goal is to have a new snapshot of this table every day but retain some number of older versions. Listing 11.2 illustrates how you can combine the update step with copy jobs to meet this requirement.

Listing 11.2 Backups using copy

```
EXPIRATION_MS = 30 * 24 * 60 * 60 * 1000

def wait(jobs, job_ref):
  '''Helper function to block for completion.'''
  start = time.time()
  done = False
  while not done:
    time.sleep(10)
    result = jobs.get(**job_ref).execute()
    print "%s %ds" % (result['status']['state'], time.time() - start)
    done = result['status']['state'] == 'DONE'
  if 'errorResult' in result['status']:
    raise SystemError(json.dumps(
        result['status']['errorResult'], indent=2))

def copy_table(jobs, src, dst):
  '''Insert and wait for a copy job with src and dst.'''
  resp = jobs.insert(
    projectId=auth.PROJECT_ID,
    body={
      'configuration': {
        'copy': {
          'sourceTable': src,
          'destinationTable': dst,
          'writeDisposition': 'WRITE_TRUNCATE'
        }
      }
    }).execute()
  print json.dumps(resp, indent=2)
  wait(jobs, resp['jobReference'])

def make_table_ref(table_id):
  return {
    'projectId': auth.PROJECT_ID,
    'datasetId': 'ch11',
    'tableId': table_id
  }

def load_device_data(jobs, dst):
  # This method simulates loading data from datastore by
  # simply copying a sample table to a new location.
  copy_table(
    jobs,
    src=make_table_ref('devices'),
    dst=dst)

def load_and_backup(bq, date):
  # Get the latest data.
```

continues

Listing 11.2: *(continued)*

```
daily = make_table_ref('devices_' +
                       date.strftime('%Y%m%d'))
load_device_data(bq.jobs(), daily)

# Make the snapshot representing the latest.
current = daily.copy()
current['tableId'] = 'devices_current'
copy_table(bq.jobs(), daily, current)

quarters = {
  '0331': 1,
  '0630': 2,
  '0930': 3,
  '1231': 4
}
quarter = quarters.get(date.strftime('%m%d'), None)
if quarter:
  quarterly = daily.copy()
  quarterly['tableId'] = (
    'devices_%dq%d' % (date.year, quarter))
  copy_table(bq.jobs(), daily, quarterly)

# Finally set the daily version to expire.
bq.tables().patch(
  body={
    'expirationTime': long(time.time() * 1000 +
                           EXPIRATION_MS)
  },
  **daily).execute()
```

This code ends up retaining daily versions of the table for the last 30 days, by virtue of the expiration time set on the daily snapshots, and quarterly versions indefinitely. Figure 11.1 illustrates how the data is moved between the daily, current, and quarterly tables. This aligns well with classic versioning schemes that retain a larger number of recent snapshots and older snapshots at a coarser resolution. This enables analyses at higher resolution over recent time intervals and lower resolution analyses over longer intervals.

A backup strategy serves as a defense against data loss, but also as a safeguard against inadvertent data corruption due to bugs in software or operator error. Cloud storage has an excellent track record for data durability because providers have a lot of experience building redundant fault-tolerant systems. However, these measures do not help with a bug that corrupts the stored data. This is another scenario in which the table copy feature can be used effectively to prevent such corruption from occurring, especially in the management of tables that are being periodically updated by appending new data. One way to do this safely is to load the new data into a staging table. Then run a suite of verification queries against the new data. Note that the verification suite can easily be set up to combine the new and old data to simulate the table contents that appears after the update is completed, if this is required for determining validity. After the suite passes, the table copy operation can be used to append the staged data into the table that needs to be updated. The reason this works is that the copy job accepts a write disposition just like the load job, and with disposition set to append, it adds the data rather than truncating existing contents.

```
jobData = {
  'configuration': {
    'copy': {
      'sourceTable': source,
      'destinationTable': destination,
      'writeDisposition': 'WRITE_APPEND'
    }
  }
}
```

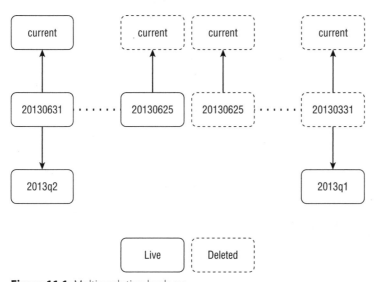

Figure 11.1: Multiresolution backups

The advantage of this scheme over simply performing a backup before modifying the table and then rolling back on corruption is that queries can continue to operate on the table, and they will never encounter corrupt data. With a rollback-based scheme, there is a window between corruption and rollback when queries will potentially be returning incorrect results.

One final scenario is covered in which table copy is useful; although it is not quite related to data backup. When a query is run without a destination table specified, the default mode, the results are stored in a service-assigned anonymous table. This anonymous table cannot be shared because it lives in a dataset that cannot have its ACL modified, and further, it is automatically garbage collected. If the results do need to be shared or saved, there is no need to rerun the query with a new destination. Instead, the anonymous table can simply be copied to the new destination, which can be shared or retained indefinitely. It is worth mentioning that this is how the BigQuery UI implements the Save as Table feature.

AppEngine Datastore Integration

Chapter 6, "Loading Data," briefly described how AppEngine Datastore backups can be imported into BigQuery to allow analytics over the contents. The mechanics from the BigQuery side were pretty much the same as loading CSV or JSON data from Google Cloud Storage. In fact, in some ways it was simpler because the table schema was not required because it is derived from the contents of the backup. However, this final step of loading a backup into BigQuery is a relatively small part of the overall Datastore-BigQuery integration. This section covers the details on the AppEngine side and covers important features and caveats in the integration. Developers who have used Datastore will find that the material is familiar, but it is still useful to see how the features of the service relate to BigQuery. If you are not familiar with Datastore, the section can serve as a quick introduction to its capabilities and help you evaluate if it could be used as a component in your analytics solution.

Briefly, Datastore is a NoSQL data storage service that is well suited to transactional workloads. It supports:

- Efficient writes, reads, and lookups of individual records
- A well-defined consistency model and transactions
- Secondary indexes
- Structured records
- A whole lot more

You can learn all about the service at `https://developers.google.com/datastore/`. The two most important characteristics with respect to BigQuery are:

- Relatively slow and expensive full scan queries
- NoSQL, records are not required to adhere to a schema.

The cost of full scan queries is what makes BigQuery integration interesting. In general, Datastore has a high cost for low selectivity queries where a large fraction of rows have to be inspected. If a primary or secondary index cannot be used to limit the amount of data that needs to be read from a large table, the query is generally prohibitively slow and expensive on Datastore. Further, the query language supported by BigQuery is much richer and permits much more complex queries than the query language supported by Datastore, which is intended mainly for record lookup operations. The second point, the NoSQL nature of Datastore, is probably the main source of complexity in the integration of the two services.

By now you have seen that schemas are strictly enforced on BigQuery tables. In Datastore terminology tables are *kinds*. A set of *entities* in Datastore have the same *kind* if certain parts of their Datastore *key* are the same. Although entities are structured, namely they have fields with values rather than being a binary or text blob, they are not required to all have a uniform structure. In fact, even entities of the same kind are not required to have the same structure. However, it is common for entities of the same kind to have a uniform structure. This is generally enforced at the application layer, and the commonly used Datastore client libraries are geared to this kind of usage. The service does not enforce this behavior, and there are examples of applications that take advantage of this flexibility. When entities of a given kind have a uniform structure, the integration with BigQuery is quite transparent, and the kind maps neatly to a BigQuery table. Now start with an example that fits this simple usage model and then explore what happens when a non-uniform structure is introduced.

To fully work through the examples in this section, you need an AppEngine project and a Google Cloud Storage project. Sample data is available so that some of the examples can be tried with just a BigQuery project.

Simple Kind

As part of the sensor application developed for this book, we stored information about the devices registered with the application to stream logs. We chose to store this data in Datastore as the `Device` kind. Each entity of this kind represented a single device registered with the service and stored information that was pretty much constant for a given device so that each log record did not have to duplicate this information. Here is the Python code used to describe the information stored in these entities:

```python
class Device(ndb.Model):
    """Registration record for a device logging to the service."""
    owner = ndb.UserProperty()
    added = ndb.DateTimeProperty(indexed=False, auto_now_add=True)
    type = ndb.StringProperty(indexed=False, choices=('phone', 'tablet'))
    make = ndb.StringProperty(indexed=False, validator=_validate_str)
    model = ndb.StringProperty(indexed=False, validator=_validate_str)
    os = ndb.StringProperty(indexed=False, choices=('android', 'ios'))
    os_version = ndb.StringProperty(indexed=False,
                                    validator=_validate_version)
    storage_gb = ndb.IntegerProperty(indexed=False)
    screen = ndb.LocalStructuredProperty(Screen)
```

```
carrier = ndb.StringProperty(indexed=False)
home_zip5 = ndb.StringProperty(indexed=False, validator=_verify_zip5)
```

This snippet is from the `models.py` file in the sample application described in Chapter 8, "Putting it Together." Even without understanding all the details of the client API, it should be apparent this is defining something very much like a schema. By default, the client API uses the name of the class as the *kind* of the records. Note that there is no explicit table creation step. A kind exists as long as one or more entities with the appropriate key exist. Here is a code snippet for creating a `Device` entity:

```
device = Device(id=base64.b64encode(os.urandom(9), '-_'))
device.owner = user
device.type = self.request.get('type')
device.make = self.request.get('make')
...
device.put()
```

The sensor application supports the creation and deletion of these device records to allow users to register and unregister their phones and tablets with the application.

When the client component of the sensor application logs a record from a device, it includes the ID stored in the registration record for the device. You can easily imagine that a lot of interesting queries would be possible if it was possible to join the log records with the device records using the ID. Fortunately, you can get this done easily if you can accept a snapshot of the data in Datastore. For the purpose of the sensor application, a daily snapshot works well, and it is quite likely that a similar approach would work for a variety of applications. So, the task at hand is to get this data from Datastore into BigQuery where you can mix it with other data to generate useful results.

Generating a Snapshot

The first step is to generate a backup or a snapshot of the entities of a given kind in Datastore. You can use the AppEngine administration console to manage the process. The list of AppEngine applications you can manage is located at https://appengine.google.com/. Selecting a project from the list takes you to the dashboard with a navigation panel on the left. To administer Datastore select the Datastore Admin link under the data section in the panel. If this is the first time you are using this feature, you will be prompted to enable the feature; accept to continue. You will see a panel, shown in Figure 11.2, listing the kinds stored in your application.

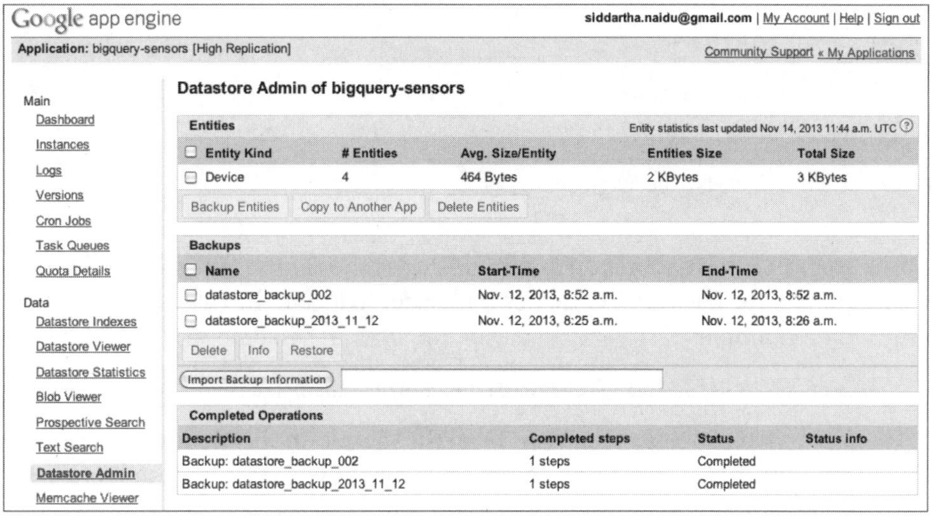

Figure 11.2: Datastore backup console

For the sample application you need to select the Device kind and click Backup Entities. For this sample you have just one kind, but AppEngine supports saving multiple kinds in a single operation. This takes you to a form where you can specify the details of the backup. The most important backup option is the destination. The entities can either be saved to Blobstore or to Google Cloud Storage. BigQuery does not support reading from AppEngine Blobstore, so you must select the Google Cloud Storage option. With the GCS option you need to specify a bucket. You are not restricted to a top-level bucket; you can specify a path within the bucket. It is helpful to specify a unique path for each backup because it makes it much simpler to locate the files when you have many backups. This is especially important when loading the backup into BigQuery because you need to pass the name of the backup file in the load job configuration. After the form is complete, click the Backup Entities button to initiate the backup. You will be taken to a page where you can monitor the underlying MapReduce job performing the snapshot. If you go back to the Datastore Admin page, you see the backup you scheduled either in pending or completed state. When a backup is complete you can select the backup and click information to see the details of the backup as shown in Figure 11.3.

Figure 11.3: Datastore backup information page

The piece of information you are interested is the *Handle,* which is effectively the location of the backup. In practice it is easier to locate the relevant files using `gsutil`, for example:

```
$ gsutil ls gs://bigquery-e2e/data/backup/datastore/001/*.backup_info
```

We have made a couple of backups from the sample application world readable so that you can try the BigQuery commands even if you do not set up your own copy of the AppEngine sample application. Running the command previously shown lists two files of the form:

```
gs://bigquery-e2e/data/backup/datastore/001/handle.Device.backup_info
gs://bigquery-e2e/data/backup/datastore/001/handle.backup_info
```

These are metadata files describing the contents of the backup. The first file stores information specific to the backup of a single kind. The second file stores information about the backup that is common across all the kinds.

With the backup completed you are now ready to load this data into BigQuery.

Loading a Backup

Chapter 6 mentioned the capability to load Datastore data in the context of explaining the `sourceFormat` option in the load job configuration. Now we are in a position to explain the full details. A BigQuery load job with the `sourceFormat` set to `DATASTORE_BACKUP` expects a single source URI, the backup metadata file for the kind that needs to be imported. Note that the metadata file for the overall backup is not relevant here. In addition you need to specify the destination table that will receive the contents of the file. You can perform the operation using the command-line client.

```
$ bq mk ch11
$ BACKUP_PATH='gs:// bigquery-e2e/data/backup/datastore/001'
$ BACKUP_HANDLE='. . .'
$ bq load --source_format=DATASTORE_BACKUP \
```

```
ch11.devices \
${BACKUP_PATH}/${BACKUP_HANDLE}.Device.backup_info
```

For the most part this looks like a regular load job, but there are a couple of caveats:

- The WRITE_APPEND write disposition is not supported.
- The schema is not specified in the job.

The write disposition restriction is primarily to avoid operator error because it is usually not sensible to load multiple copies of a Datastore backup into the same table. The second restriction is more interesting. Because Datastore is a NoSQL store, the schema for the destination table has to be derived. The backup metadata contains the full set of fields (and their types) encountered while generating the backup. BigQuery uses this data to generate a schema that can hold all the entities in the backup. Hence the user is not permitted to specify a schema in the job configuration.

Querying the Data

The first thing to try is to look at the schema of the destination table, as shown in Listing 11.3.

Listing 11.3 Schema of the table generated from a Datastore backup

```
$ bq show ch11.devices
Table 317752944021:ch11.devices

  Last modified                   Schema              Total Rows   Total>
 ----------------   ---------------------------------  ----------  ------>
  12 Nov 00:34:16   |- added: integer                     3          567
                    |- os: string
                    |- make: string
                    |- home_zip5: string
                    |- os_version: string
                    |- carrier: string
                    +- owner: record
                    |   |- email: string
                    |   |- userid: integer
                    |- model: string
                    |- type: string
                    +- screen: record
                    |   |- diagonal: float
                    |   |- res_x: integer
                    |   |- res_y: integer
                    |   +- __key__: record
                    |   |   |- namespace: string
```

continues

Listing 11.3: *(continued)*

```
|   |   |- app: string
|   |   |- path: string
|   |   |- kind: string
|   |   |- name: string
|   |   |- id: integer
|- storage_gb: integer
+- __key__: record
|   |- namespace: string
|   |- app: string
|   |- path: string
|   |- kind: string
|   |- name: string
|   |- id: integer
|- __error__: string (repeated)
|- __has_error__: boolean
```

Comparing this with the model definitions used in the AppEngine application, you can see that all the fields declared in the model are present in the schema. In addition there are a couple of special fields that are added by the import job. These fields contain additional information captured during the transformation from Datastore entities to BigQuery records.

- __has_error__: Indicates if an error occurred while transforming the row.

- __error__: A repeated field containing descriptions of the transformation errors.

- __key__: The Datastore entity key, so that you can locate the corresponding entity. Note that every nested entity includes this field, but it is usually empty because nested entities are commonly purely local to the containing entity.

The fields under __key__ correspond to the terms documented in the Datastore key reference available at https://developers.google.com/appengine/docs/python/ndb/keyclass.

It is convenient to have access to the kind, id, and name properties, but it is the path field that uniquely locates an individual entity. It is a string representation of the array returned by the Key.flat() method in the Datastore client library.

Outside of these special fields the table constructed from the snapshot behaves just like a regular BigQuery table. Here is a simple query to look at errors that occurred when the snapshot was loaded:

```
$ bq query \
    'SELECT __key__.name, __has_error__, __error__
    FROM ch11.devices'
+---------------+---------------+----------+
| __key___name | __has_error__ | __error__ |
+---------------+---------------+----------+
| H1JInRKWgXoU |          false | NULL      |
```

```
| WOBWlk3th8HW |                false | NULL       |
| cVDuditLBGN_ |                false | NULL       |
+--------------+----------------+-----------+
```

In this case there were no errors encountered when the data was loaded. The reason errors occur during transformation is that the Datastore type system and BigQuery type system differ, and this results in some values being unsupported. For example, BigQuery has a 64 K limit of the string type, but Datastore has no hard limit on the size of `TextProperty` fields, so values are truncated. An error will be added to the record to indicate that a loss-y transformation was applied to a field.

Finally take a quick look at the actual data that appears in the table:

```
$ bq query \
    'SELECT __key__.name, owner.email, make, model
    FROM ch11.devices'
+--------------+-----------------------+-------+-------+
| __key___name |       owner_email     | make  | model |
+--------------+-----------------------+-------+-------+
| H1JInRKWgXoU | bigquerye2e@gmail.com | nexus | s     |
| WOBWlk3th8HW | bigquerye2e@gmail.com | nexus | 7     |
| cVDuditLBGN_ | bigquerye2e@gmail.com | nexus | 10    |
+--------------+-----------------------+-------+-------+
```

This is not a particularly interesting query, but it gives you an idea of how you might use this data inside BigQuery. The sample application has a couple of examples that illustrate how this table can be joined with the logs to produce useful aggregations by device property.

Automation

Creating a backup through the Datastore Admin console is convenient but not at all suitable for performing regular backups. The Datastore documentation describes how to set up a periodic backup using the AppEngine cron feature. This documentation is available at https://developers.google.com/appengine/articles/scheduled_backups.

We recommend using a variation of the basic instructions. The cron job as described will end up placing all the backups under the same GCS path. This is inconvenient because it makes it somewhat harder to discover when the backup for a particular date has completed. If instead the date could be included in the GCS path, it would be simple to detect the completion of the backup. You can achieve this by installing a custom handler that is invoked by the AppEngine cron system. In the custom handler you simply invoke the backup handler but use the current date in the value passed to the `gs_bucket_name` parameter. The handler URL will look something like this (newlines and indentation have been added for legibility):

```
http://ah-builtin-python-bundle.application_id.appspot.com/
  _ah/datastore_admin/_ah/datastore_admin/backup.create?
    name=daily-date&
    kind=kind1&
    kind=kindN&
    queue=default&
    filesystem=gs&
    gs_bucket_name=bucket/path/date
```

This scheme allows you to easily detect when new data needs to be loaded into BigQuery. You schedule a separate cron that runs periodically. It looks for the presence of a load job for the current date and also the backup info file for the current date. If no job is present but the file is present, it inserts a load job passing the file it found as the source URI. A little more care has to be taken if you want to be resilient to retry-able job failures, but even that is quite straight-forward with a naming scheme for the job that includes an attempt counter. You can also use AppEngine task queues instead of a separate cron job, but the individual steps are basically the same. Refer to the sample application for the complete implementation of this periodic loading scheme.

Mixing Types

The start of this section discussed that going from NoSQL storage to a strictly typed storage introduces complications. However, in the previous example everything seems to have gone smoothly. This is because we did not actually use any of the NoSQL flexibility. Now take a look at what happens when you do exercise some of the features. When we defined the model for Device entities, we chose to use an `IntegerProperty` to represent the number of gigabytes of storage present in a device.

TRUE STORY

This example may seem a bit contrived, but one of the authors actually ran into this scenario. Developing the application in 2013, it was easy to assume that every phone model would have a couple of GB of storage. When an actual catalog of models was consulted, there were a number of models with less than 1 GB of storage released as recently as 2012.

Say you need to update your model to support fractional gigabytes. You could update your model to use a `FloatProperty` for the field instead.

```
class Device(ndb.Model):
    ...
    storage_gb = ndb.FloatProperty(indexed=False)
    ...
```

Observe that we have updated the type of the field but retained the same name. When we update the application and add a new device, everything works just fine. Datastore does not mind that we have some entities with an integer for `storage_gb` and others with a floating-point value.

If you run through the same steps of the Datastore snapshot and import the results into a new table, you end up with a schema that is different from the original table. Here is the schema of the resulting table:

```
$ bq show ch11.devices_multi_type
Table 317752944021:ch11.devices_multi_type

   Last modified              Schema              Total Rows    Total Byt>
 ----------------- ------------------------------- ------------ ---------->
  12 Nov 00:56:18   |- added: integer                 4             796
                     . . .
                    +- storage_gb: record
                    |   |- float: float
                    |   |- integer: integer
                    |   |- provided: string
                     . . .
```

The difference is that the `storage_gb` field has been promoted from a simple integer field to a record field. This is to allow the field to represent both integer values and floating-point values. For entities that have an integer value for `storage_gb`, the `integer` subfield will contain the value, the `float` subfield will be `NULL`, and `provided` will contain the value `integer`. For entities that contain a floating point value for `storage_gb`, it will be the other way around. In this fashion the strictly-typed schema represents the flexibility of the NoSQL storage model. In this case it is relatively simple to use the field in queries. Here is an example of how you could query the field:

```
$ bq query \
    'SELECT IF(storage_gb.float IS NULL,
              FLOAT(storage_gb.integer),
              storage_gb.float) storage_gb
    FROM ch11.devices_multi_type'
+------------+
| storage_gb |
+------------+
|       16.0 |
|       16.0 |
|       32.0 |
|        0.5 |
+------------+
```

This coerces the field to a simple floating-point value at query time.

Although the service can handle the representation of general NoSQL entities, you should be wary of relying on this feature. If the types of fields vary substantially across entities, you will end up with unwieldy schemas that are not convenient to work with in queries. If you are in a position to design your storage scheme, it is good to strike a balance between leveraging the flexibility of NoSQL and having uniform entities that are convenient to query.

Final Thoughts

It may be a little surprising that we have devoted so much space to Datastore in a section on managing data in BigQuery. We have devoted a fair amount of space to this topic because Datastore and BigQuery complement each other. They are good examples of platform components that can be combined so that the overall solution is more than just the sum of its parts. In fact, in this chapter we have even used GCS as a conduit between the services. Over time we expect this integration to become more seamless, but it is already possible to do a lot by putting them together.

Metatables and Table Sharding

When compared to traditional databases, there is a proliferation of tables in BigQuery. There are a few reasons for this difference:

- Every query result generates a new table.
- The unit of deletion is a table.
- Query costs are proportional to table sizes, so partitioning can help manage costs.

Tables in BigQuery feel a bit like files in a filesystem. A database with thousands of tables would be regarded with suspicion, but filesystems containing thousands of files are the norm. This section covers the features the service offers to deal with this abundance of tables. The unifying theme is that these features allow tables (in contrast to the contents of tables) to be treated a bit like data and to be included in expressions rather than just static references.

Time Travel

Tables in BigQuery are mutable, and you have seen how you can grow tables over time using jobs with the WRITE_APPEND disposition or by inserting individual records. In this chapter you have also seen how to save a snapshot of a table prior to modifying it so that you can retain a historical copy. The ability to retrieve earlier versions of data is a useful feature in any data storage system. It is quite likely that you are familiar with filesystems that allow you to access historical views of the filesystem or the ability in Google Docs to access revisions (https://support.google.com/drive/answer/190843). BigQuery supports similar access to table revisions. Almost anywhere that you can pass a table name, you can instead pass a reference to a slice (in the time dimension) of the table. This section discusses this type of metatable and how to use it to implement common data management solutions.

YOU NEED YOUR OWN COPY OF THE SAMPLE TABLE

In most cases we provide sample tables for queries in a shared dataset so that you can test queries without building your own version. In this case it is not possible because BigQuery collapses revisions older than 7 days. Instead, you have to build your own fresh copy to try the examples. It also means that you have to adjust all the time-stamps appropriately.

First create a table that is particularly amenable to time slicing. The table may seem a bit contrived, but it clearly illustrates how the slicing expressions function. Here is the recipe for building the sample table:

```
$ bq query --destination_table=ch11.time_lapse \
    'SELECT 0 index, 0 millis'
$ for i in $(seq 10); do
    echo $i
    bq query --append_table --destination_table=ch11.time_lapse \
      "SELECT ${i} index, INTEGER(NOW()/1000) millis"
    sleep 10
  done
```

Here you use a query to append a row to a fixed destination table (ch11 .time_lapse) that includes a timestamp and row index. Each query run is a job and the jobs are the *atom* of change that BigQuery tracks. You cannot reference changes smaller than that made by a single job because its effect is atomic. Here is what the table looks like after the command completes:

```
$ bq head ch11.time_lapse
+-------+---------------+
| index |     millis    |
+-------+---------------+
|     0 |             0 |
|     1 | 1395214708049 |
|     2 | 1395214719589 |
|     3 | 1395214731135 |
|     4 | 1395214742932 |
|     5 | 1395214754874 |
|     6 | 1395214766503 |
|     7 | 1395214778642 |
|     8 | 1395214790355 |
|     9 | 1395214802060 |
|    10 | 1395214814200 |
+-------+---------------+
```

The key property to keep in mind is that the `millis` field of a given record is approximately the same as (it will be a little before) the completion time of the query that added it to the table.

The syntax for referencing a time slice of a table is:

```
<table name>@[-]<start time>[-[<end time>]]
```

It will be easiest to understand the various options by trying examples of each variation. Start with the simplest variant, a reference to a table as it existed at a particular point in time:

```
$ START_TIME='1395214700000'
$ bq head ch11.time_lapse@$((${START_TIME} + 5 * 10 * 1000))
+-------+----------------+
| index |     millis     |
+-------+----------------+
|     2 | 1395214719589  |
|     4 | 1395214742932  |
|     0 |              0 |
|     1 | 1395214708049  |
|     3 | 1395214731135  |
+-------+----------------+
```

If you are wondering why the rows do not appear in order, keep in mind that BigQuery does not guarantee a stable ordering of rows in a table. Only the result of a query with an explicit ORDER BY clause has well-defined ordering.

This is the table as it existed before the fifth row was added. You can see that the value used for the timestamp is the timestamp that appears at index 5 in the full table. The timestamp is encoded as the milliseconds since the UNIX epoch (1970-01-01 00:00:00 UTC). If you pick a time that is earlier than the table creation time, you will, unsurprisingly, get a NOT_FOUND error. Instead of an absolute time, you could use a relative time by adding a leading hyphen. The value specified as the relative time is interpreted as an offset in milliseconds with respect to the current time. The absolute time is computed by subtracting the offset from the current time.

```
$ date +%s; bq head ch11.time_lapse@-850000
1395215611
+-------+----------------+
| index |     millis     |
+-------+----------------+
|     2 | 1395214719589  |
|     4 | 1395214742932  |
|     0 |              0 |
|     1 | 1395214708049  |
|     5 | 1395214754874  |
|     3 | 1395214731135  |
+-------+----------------+
```

The value 0 refers to the table's oldest available version. Table history is retained for 7 days so this version is that old unless the table was created more recently.

```
$ bq head ch11.time_lapse@0
+-------+--------+
| index | millis |
+-------+--------+
|     0 |      0 |
+-------+--------+
```

The previous examples refer to the table as it existed at a particular point in time. You can also reference the set of changes that occurred in a specific time interval. For example, to see all the rows added, you could use:

```
$ bq head ch11.time_lapse@$((${START_TIME} + 6 * 10 * 1000))-
+-------+---------------+
| index |    millis     |
+-------+---------------+
|     8 | 1395214790355 |
|     9 | 1395214802060 |
|     7 | 1395214778642 |
|    10 | 1395214814200 |
+-------+---------------+
```

The trailing hyphen indicates that the upper bound for the time interval should be the current time. Again, adding a leading hyphen causes the value to be treated as an offset with respect to the current time.

```
$ date +%s; bq head ch11.time_lapse@-850000-
1395215622
+-------+---------------+
| index |    millis     |
+-------+---------------+
|     8 | 1395214790355 |
|     9 | 1395214802060 |
|     7 | 1395214778642 |
|    10 | 1395214814200 |
+-------+---------------+
```

Finally, here is how you would reference a closed interval:

```
$ AROUND_3=$((${START_TIME} + 3 * 10 * 1000))
$ AROUND_7=$((${START_TIME} + 7 * 10 * 1000))
$ bq head ch11.time_lapse@${AROUND_3}-${AROUND_7}

+-------+---------------+
| index |    millis     |
+-------+---------------+
|     4 | 1395214742932 |
```

```
|      6 |  1395214766503 |
|      5 |  1395214754874 |
|      3 |  1395214731135 |
+-------+----------------+
```

This covers the full range of options that you can use to address a historical view of a table. Now take a look at a couple of different ways you can use these references. Here is a query that accesses only part of the table:

```
$ bq query \
    "SELECT MIN(index), MAX(index)
     FROM [ch11.time_lapse@${AROUND_3}-${AROUND_7}]"
+-----+-----+
| f0_ | f1_ |
+-----+-----+
|   3 |   6 |
+-----+-----+
```

Note that the table reference has to be quoted because it is not a valid identifier. Other than that it behaves just like a regular table. An important feature is that you are billed only for the portion of the table you scanned. You can see this using the show command:

```
$ bq show ch11.time_lapse
Table 317752944021:ch11.time_lapse
```

Last modified	Schema	Total Rows	Total Bytes	Expi>
13 Nov 14:27:04	|- index: integer	10	160	
	|- millis: integer			

```
$ bq show ch11.time_lapse@${AROUND_3}-${AROUND_7}
Table 317752944021:ch11.time_lapse@1384381608691-1384381619201
```

Last modified	Schema	Total Rows	Total Bytes	Expi>
13 Nov 14:27:04	|- index: integer	4	64	
	|- millis: integer			

The number of rows and bytes in the slice are a fraction of the rows and bytes in the full table. In addition, a dry run query on a slice can be used to probe how many bytes a query will scan. This feature is helpful for applications that need to frequently query the most recently added data to a table. They can avoid paying for the cost of scanning the full table by using a table reference that limits the query to changes that occurred in the time window of interest. The sample application uses this feature to generate graphs of recent logs.

Table Recovery

When we discussed the table copy job we described how it could be used to prevent corruption due to a bad load job. With time slices of tables, we have a tool to recover from inadvertent table corruption even if no copy was created prior to the load operation. The idea is straightforward: Copy the table, as it existed prior to the job, to a new table. Then the corrupted table can be deleted (or truncated) and replaced with the recovered table.

```
$ bq cp ch11.time_lapse@1384381614244 ch11.recovered
Table '317752944021:ch11.time_lapse@1384381614244' successfully \
copied to '317752944021:ch11.recovered'
$ bq head ch11.recovered
+-------+---------------+
| index |    millis     |
+-------+---------------+
|     5 | 1384381611449 |
|     2 | 1384381603871 |
|     4 | 1384381608691 |
|     3 | 1384381606536 |
|     1 | 1384381601244 |
+-------+---------------+
```

You can see that the recovered table is missing the last 5 rows added to the original table. We picked the timestamp of the sixth row (1384381614244), so the sixth row and all rows after it have been dropped. The main challenge with using this technique is finding the right timestamps. Unfortunately, the timestamps correspond to the completion time of the job that added the data, rather than the last modification time of the table, which can differ slightly. To remove data added by a job, you must find the job metadata or adjust the timestamp via trial and error. We will leave it as an exercise for you to figure out how to fix a table that has bad data sandwiched between good data, for example when a valid import follows a bad import.

Caveats

Tables being updated via the streaming API deserve special attention. Time slices that have no end time will include all rows that have been inserted successfully (subject to the caveats discussed in Chapter 6 with respect to streaming). Beyond that the behavior is loosely defined. Behind the scenes, rows are buffered and then inserted in batches. Each batch insertion behaves like a job, and all the rows in the batch appear atomically at a specific timestamp. The fact that a row is associated with two separate timestamps, row insert and batch insert, leads to surprising behavior when slicing these tables. However, it is reasonable to use slices to isolate recently added records, namely an interval with no end time. This will *at least* fetch all the rows added since the start time but possibly additional rows that were inserted at an earlier time.

When we introduced these time slicing references, we mentioned that they could be used in most places where a table name is expected. A notable exception is in mutation operations. For example, you cannot use a time slice as the destination for a load or query job. Deleting a time slice would be useful but is not currently permitted. It is conceivable that some of these restrictions may be lifted in the future, but for now you are restricted to using time slices as sources of data.

Selecting Tables

The list operation on the REST table resource allows clients to paginate through the list of tables in a dataset. If there are only a handful of tables in a dataset, this works great. However, finding one or a few tables in a large dataset can be cumbersome using this paginated approach. To simplify locating tables, the service provides a metatable that contains a record for each table in the dataset:

    <dataset>.__TABLES__

Listing 11.4 offers a quick tour of its features.

Listing 11.4 Using the dataset metatable

```
$ bq show ch11.__TABLES__
Table 317752944021:ch11.__TABLES__

  Last modified                     Schema                      Total Rows   Total B>
  ----------------   --------------------------------   ------------   ------->
  13 Nov 22:44:52    |- project_id: string                  4
                     |- dataset_id: string
                     |- table_id: string
                     |- creation_time: integer
                     |- last_modified_time: integer
                     |- row_count: integer
                     |- size_bytes: integer
                     |- type: integer

$ bq query \
    'SELECT table_id, MSEC_TO_TIMESTAMP(last_modified_time)
     FROM ch11.__TABLES__
     ORDER BY 2 DESC'
+--------------------+---------------------+
|      table_id      |         f0_         |
+--------------------+---------------------+
| recovered          | 2013-11-14 06:44:52 |
| time_lapse         | 2013-11-13 22:27:04 |
```

```
| devices_multi_type | 2013-11-12 08:56:18 |
| devices            | 2013-11-12 08:34:16 |
+--------------------+---------------------+
```

You can use this table to easily locate tables that meet some criteria, for example, finding all tables that begin with the prefix "logs" that have been modified in the last 4 hours.

Dynamic Table Lists

The dataset metatable can be directly queried to simplify administering tables or supporting more efficient navigation of datasets in user interfaces. However, when combined with a function that allows it to be used to construct lists of tables in the FROM clause of a query, it becomes substantially more powerful. The beginning of this chapter discussed that the BigQuery data management and query pricing models encourage partitioning tables. The ability to dynamically generate a list of tables in a query simplifies recombining the partitions when queries need to span a variable number of partitions based on the value of one or more query parameters. To explore this feature, start with setting up a couple of tables:

```
$ DAY_LIST='20131108 20131109 20131110
   20131111 20131112 20131113 20131114'
$ for day in ${DAY_LIST}; do
    for kind in a b; do
      echo $kind $day
      bq query --destination_table=ch11.${kind}_${day} \
        "SELECT \"${kind}\" kind, \"${day}\" day"
    done
  done
```

Now take a quick look at what you created:

```
$ bq query "SELECT table_id FROM ch11.__TABLES__
            WHERE REGEXP_MATCH(table_id, r'^(a|b)_')"
+------------+
| table_id   |
+------------+
| a_20131108 |
|    . . .   |
| a_20131114 |
| b_20131108 |
|    . . .   |
| b_20131114 |
+------------+
```

You can see how to use the metatable to locate the tables rather than just simply listing the dataset.

If the list of tables in a query depends on the input or needs to be resolved just before running the query, you could now achieve that by issuing two queries. First, query the dataset metatable, and then use the results of that query to construct the actual query over your tables. The script `two_phase.py` in the examples for this chapter performs this two-step query. Here is the relevant bit:

```
# Query the metatable for a list of matching tables.
resp = bq.jobs().query(
    projectId=PROJECT_ID,
    body={'query':('SELECT table_id FROM ch11.__TABLES__ '
                   'WHERE LEFT(table_id, 2) = "%s_"'
                   % (sys.argv[1]))}
).execute()
# Build the list of tables.
tables = ', '.join(['ch11.' + cell(r, 0) for r in resp['rows']])
# Run a query over the list of tables.
resp = bq.jobs().query(
    projectId=PROJECT_ID,
    body={'query':('SELECT kind, COUNT(day) FROM %s '
                   'GROUP BY 1' % tables)}
).execute()
```

We have listed this code for two reasons. First, it clarifies the semantics of the function that will be introduced below and second, it illustrates the boilerplate and extra operation you can avoid by using it. The function that simulates this table listing behavior is TABLE_QUERY, and it has the following signature:

```
(TABLE_QUERY(<dataset>,
             "<conditional expression>")
```

It should appear in the FROM clause of a query just like you would use a subselect expression. Just as with subselects it must appear in parentheses. The conditional expression can be any expression that would be legal in the WHERE clause of a query over the dataset metatable. With this function the script we wrote could be replaced with:

```
$ (INPUT="a"
   bq query "SELECT kind, count(day) [count]
             FROM (TABLE_QUERY(
               ch11, 'LEFT(table_id, 2) = \"${INPUT}_\"'))
             GROUP BY 1")
+------+-------+
| kind | count |
+------+-------+
| a    |     7 |
+------+-------+
```

The conditions in the WHERE clause of the first query in the script are passed as a string to the TABLE_QUERY function. The function effectively simulates the operations performed by the script, but more efficiently because it can all happen within the service. Keep in mind that the limit on the total number of tables referenced in a single query still applies. It is easiest to work out the conditional expression using direct queries over the dataset metatable. After you figure out the correct expression, just copy that into the final query.

NO TABLES SELECTED

Both versions, script and TABLE_QUERY, will fail if the conditions lead to no tables being selected. They will fail with the same error indicating a bad FROM clause. You should plan on handling this error if you use this function.

Date Partitioned Datasets

Because time is frequently an important dimension when data is collected, it usually has a privileged role in the organization of data. A common design is to partition data into time-based buckets. The data is then managed and queried at the granularity of these buckets. For example, you may want to delete all buckets older than some age. The default time range for queries may be the last 7 days, and being able to limit the data scanned for most queries could help reduce costs. The approach that works well in BigQuery is to put data into daily tables, so the time bucket is 1 day. To simplify this use case, BigQuery has a specialization of the TABLE_QUERY function that operates on tables that conform to the following naming scheme:

```
<table prefix>YYYYMMDD
```

The function is TABLE_DATE_RANGE and has the following signature:

```
(TABLE_DATE_RANGE(<prefix>,
                  <start timestamp>,
                  <end timestamp>)
```

Whenever a calendar date appears, you have to worry about the issue of time zones. Currently, the only time zone supported is UTC, so the feature works best if you use UTC-aligned day boundaries. Otherwise, you need to shift times into the UTC time zone.

Here is a sample query using the tables we created:

```
$ bq query "SELECT kind, MIN(day), MAX(day)
            FROM (TABLE_DATE_RANGE(ch11.a_,
```

```
                              DATE_ADD(TIMESTAMP('20131114'), -3,
                                      'DAY'),
                              CURRENT_TIMESTAMP()))
                GROUP BY 1"
    +------+----------+----------+
    | kind |    f0_   |    f1_   |
    +------+----------+----------+
    | a    | 20131111 | 20131114 |
    +------+----------+----------+
```

Notice that for start and end timestamp you can supply any expression that evaluates to a timestamp. To use date constants you can cast a string to a timestamp:

```
$ bq query "SELECT kind, MIN(day), MAX(day)
                FROM (TABLE_DATE_RANGE(ch11.b_,
                              TIMESTAMP('2013-11-09'),
                              TIMESTAMP('2013-11-11')))
                GROUP BY 1"
    +------+----------+----------+
    | kind |    f0_   |    f1_   |
    +------+----------+----------+
    | b    | 20131109 | 20131111 |
    +------+----------+----------+
```

The reason this function is particularly helpful is that it can be a chore to work out the conditions that select out an arbitrary date range. It is certainly possible to implement the same functionality using TABLE_QUERY directly, but this function makes it a lot simpler and avoids common date handling errors.

This completes the discussion of metatables in BigQuery. The reason these one-row tables (or appends to a single table) were created was to illustrate how to move the computation from operations over rows in tables to operations over the tables. All the complexity of the query was inside the FROM clause with a simple boilerplate in the other clauses. Clearly this was a bit contrived. Real-world applications have most of the logic in the clauses operating on the data in the table with a little bit of logic in the FROM clause to specify a relevant set of tables (or table slices). The sample application has examples that use this functionality, which you can explore.

Summary

This chapter covered strategies for managing data within BigQuery and across the Google Cloud Platform as it relates to data warehousing. Some of these strategies are related to schemes you can use in a traditional database or data warehouse but implement in a manner better suited to operating in the cloud and within BigQuery. The sample application combines a few of these strategies to illustrate how they fit together in a realistic application. Similarly, you can find the right combination of features to support your analytics applications.

BigQuery Applications

In This Part

External Data Processing

By this point you should be getting good at using BigQuery and have an understanding of how it works. That said, sometimes it may not be convenient to use BigQuery directly via the API, generated clients, or web UI. Other times, you need to do something with your data that isn't possible inside of BigQuery.

This chapter shows you how to handle both of these situations. In data warehousing, the process of taking data out of one storage system and adding it to another one is called ETL, for Extract Transform and Load. The first section in this chapter is about Extract: You've got your data in BigQuery and you want to take it out. The next section describes different ways to Transform your data, such as running a Hadoop MapReduce on Google Compute Engine. The Load component of ETL was covered in Chapter 6, "Loading Data."

The last portion of the chapter shows some of the alternative interfaces to BigQuery that enable you to access your data from two popular spreadsheet programs: Google Spreadsheets and Microsoft Excel. You can use Google Apps Script to run BigQuery queries, which enables you to fill your Google Spreadsheets (or even Google Forms) with BigQuery data. For those of you who prefer Microsoft Excel to Google Spreadsheets, the final portion of the chapter describes the BigQuery Excel Connector that enables you to run BigQuery queries from Microsoft Excel directly.

This chapter covers only the Google-provided interfaces. Chapter 13, "Using BigQuery from Third-Party Tools," describes some of the third-party tools that have been built taking advantage of the BigQuery API.

Getting Data Out of BigQuery

Although there are a lot of things you can do with BigQuery's SQL language, sometimes you want to take your data out of BigQuery. Maybe you have a custom prediction algorithm that you want to run over your data via Hadoop; maybe you want to feed a BigQuery table into an in-house reporting tool; or maybe you just want to make a backup of your data to store somewhere else.

You can read your data out of BigQuery in two ways: The first is to extract it; the second is to read it directly. Extract is the "E" from ETL. ("T" is transform and "L" is load.) In BigQuery, you can extract your data by running an Extract job. Reading the data directly, however, can be done using the `TableData` `.list()` operation.

Extract Jobs

Chapter 5, "Talking to the BigQuery API," gave an overview of the BigQuery Jobs interface but didn't go into detail about the various types of jobs that can be run. Extract jobs are the opposite of Load jobs. A Load job takes data from somewhere outside of BigQuery and imports it into a BigQuery table, whereas an Extract job takes a BigQuery table and exports it outside of BigQuery.

To run an Extract job, you need to fill out an extract configuration of a job object and insert the job into the BigQuery jobs collection. Here is an example that uses the raw HTTP API to extract the Shakespeare word-count reference table that you've seen in several other chapters to a Google Cloud Storage bucket as newline-delimited JSON:

```
$ PROJECT_ID=bigquery-e2e
$ BUCKET_ID=bigquery-e2e
$ BASE_URL="https://www.googleapis.com/bigquery/v2"
$ JOBS_URL="${BASE_URL}/projects/${PROJECT_ID}/jobs"
$ GCS_OBJECT="data/extract/shakespeare_$(date +'%s').json"
$ DESTINATION_PATH="gs://${BUCKET_ID}/${GCS_OBJECT}"
$ SOURCE_TABLE="{ \
      'projectId': 'publicdata', \
      'datasetId': 'samples', \
      'tableId': 'shakespeare'}"
$ JOB_CONFIG="{'extract': { 'sourceTable': ${SOURCE_TABLE}, \
   'destinationUris': ['${DESTINATION_PATH}'], \
   'destinationFormat': 'NEWLINE_DELIMITED_JSON'}}"
$ JOB="{'configuration': ${JOB_CONFIG}}"
$ curl  \
      -H "$(python auth.py)" \
      -H "Content-Type: application/json" \
      -X POST \
      --data-binary "${JOB}" \
```

```
      "${JOBS_URL}"
  {
  ...
  "configuration": {
    "extract": {
     "sourceTable": {
      "projectId": "publicdata",
      "datasetId": "samples",
      "tableId": "shakespeare"
     },
     "destinationUris": [
      "gs://bigquery-e2e/data/extract/shakespeare_1395530836.json"
     ],
     "destinationFormat": "NEWLINE_DELIMITED_JSON"
    }
   }
  }
```

Downloading Data from GCS

Once you've extracted the data from BigQuery, you might want to download it locally. You can download Google Cloud Storage (GCS) files via the `gsutil` command-line tool distributed with the Google Cloud SDK. Alternatively, you might, want to download the file programmatically. Listing 12.1 shows the Python code to download GCS files in Python.

Listing 12.1: Downloading files from Google Cloud Storage (gcs_reader.py)

```python
import os
import sys

# Imports from the Google API client:
from apiclient.errors import HttpError
from apiclient.http import MediaIoBaseDownload

# Imports from local files in this directory:
import auth

# Number of bytes to download per request.
CHUNKSIZE = 1024 * 1024

class GcsReader:
  '''Reads files from Google Cloud Storage.

  Verifies the presence of files in Google Cloud Storage. Will download
  the files as well if download_dir is not None.
```

continues

Listing 12.1: *(continued)*

```python
    '''

    def __init__(self, gcs_bucket, download_dir=None):
        self.gcs_service = auth.build_gcs_client()
        self.gcs_bucket = gcs_bucket
        self.download_dir = download_dir

    def make_uri(self, gcs_object):
        '''Turn a bucket and object into a Google Cloud Storage path.'''
        return 'gs://%s/%s' % (self.gcs_bucket, gcs_object)

    def check_gcs_file(self, gcs_object):
        '''Returns a tuple of (GCS URI, size) if the file is present.'''
        try:
            metadata = self.gcs_service.objects().get(
                bucket=self.gcs_bucket, object=gcs_object).execute()
            uri = self.make_uri(gcs_object)
            return (uri, int(metadata.get('size', 0)))
        except HttpError, err:
            # If the error is anything except a 'Not Found' print the error.
            if err.resp.status <> 404:
                print err
            return (None, None)

    def make_output_dir(self, output_file):
        '''Creates an output directory for the downloaded results.'''
        output_dir = os.path.dirname(output_file)
        if os.path.exists(output_dir) and os.path.isdir(output_dir):
            # Nothing to do.
            return
        os.makedirs(output_dir)

    def complete_download(self, media):
        while True:
            # Download the next chunk, allowing 3 retries.
            _, done = media.next_chunk(num_retries=3)
            if done: return

    def download_file(self, gcs_object):
        '''Downloads a GCS object to directory download_dir.'''
        output_file_name = os.path.join(self.download_dir, gcs_object)
        self.make_output_dir(output_file_name)
        with open(output_file_name, 'w') as out_file:
            request = self.gcs_service.objects().get_media(
                bucket=self.gcs_bucket, object=gcs_object)
            media = MediaIoBaseDownload(out_file, request,
                                        chunksize=CHUNKSIZE)

            print 'Downloading:\n%s to\n%s' % (
                self.make_uri(gcs_object), output_file_name)
```

```
        self.complete_download(media)

def read(self, gcs_object):
    '''Read the file and returns the file size or None if not found.'''
    uri, file_size = self.check_gcs_file(gcs_object)
    if uri is None:
      return None
    print '%s size: %d' % (uri, file_size)
    if self.download_dir is not None:
      self.download_file(gcs_object)
    return file_size
```

To use the GcsReader, you can write code such as the following:

```
$ python
>>> gcs_bucket='bigquery-e2e'
>>> from gcs_reader import GcsReader
>>> GcsReader(gcs_bucket=gcs_bucket,
...           download_dir='/tmp/bigquery').read('shakespeare.json')
gs://bigquery-e2e/shakespeare.json size: 13019156
Downloading:
gs://bigquery-e2e/shakespeare.json to /tmp/bigquery/shakespeare
.json
13019156
```

This will read the GCS file gs://bigquery-e2e/shakespeare.json and download it to the /tmp/bigquery directory on your local machine. The data will be downloaded in 1 MB chunks using the HTTP resumable download protocol. The details of the code aren't important, but the subsequent examples in this section use the GcsReader to download files after running BigQuery extract jobs, so understanding what it does at a high level is useful.

This example uses the same authentication code from Chapter 5, but has a couple of additional tweaks. It adds a method to the auth module to get the GCS service object, similar to the method that creates an authenticated BigQuery service object. The other change to the auth module is to add the GCS OAuth2 scope to the list of required scopes. Unfortunately, this requires you to re-authenticate. In order to prevent you from getting errors when you run these examples, the saved credential file is named differently from the one used in other chapters. If you run these examples and get a HTTP 403 error "Insufficient Permissions," try deleting the saved credentials (~/bigquery_credentials.dat) and rerunning the operation.

Running Extract Jobs

By this point, you should understand how the BigQuery Jobs API works; if not, you should read the section titled "Jobs" in Chapter 5. Since we assume you're familiar with starting jobs and waiting for them to complete, the code to do so is not shown here in the text. The job management code used in the subsequent listings is encapsulated in the `JobRunner` object defined in `job_runner.py` file. This file is included within the supplemental download material for this chapter.

Listing 12.2 runs a BigQuery Extract job via a `JobRunner` and then downloads the results using a `GcsReader`, which was defined in the previous listing.

Listing 12.2: Exporting a table via an Extract job (extract_and_read.py)

```
import json
import logging
import sys
import time

# Imports from local files in this directory:
import auth
from gcs_reader import GcsReader
from job_runner import JobRunner

def make_extract_config(source_project_id, source_dataset_id,
                        source_table_id, destination_uris):
  '''Creates a dict containing an export job configuration.'''

  source_table_ref = {
      'projectId': source_project_id,
      'datasetId': source_dataset_id,
      'tableId': source_table_id}
  extract_config = {
      'sourceTable': source_table_ref,
      'destinationFormat': 'NEWLINE_DELIMITED_JSON',
      'destinationUris': destination_uris}
  return {'extract': extract_config}

def run_extract_job(job_runner, gcs_reader, source_project_id,
    source_dataset_id, source_table_id):
  '''Runs a BigQuery extract job and reads the results.'''

  timestamp = int(time.time())
  gcs_object = 'output/%s.%s_%d.json' % (
      source_dataset_id,
      source_table_id,
      timestamp)
  destination_uri = gcs_reader.make_uri(gcs_object)
  job_config = make_extract_config(
      source_project_id,
      source_dataset_id,
      source_table_id,
      [destination_uri])
  if not job_runner.start_job(job_config):
    return

  print json.dumps(job_runner.get_job(), indent=2)

  job_runner.wait_for_complete()
  gcs_reader.read(gcs_object)
```

Because the details of running a job and downloading a file from GCS àre abstracted away from this listing, the code is short and straightforward. The method `run_extract_job` picks a GCS path name based on the timestamp and name of the table being downloaded, and then creates an Extract job to write to that GCS path. Once the job completes, the listing downloads the object using the `GcsReader`. The following snippet is an example usage of this code that exports the table `publicdata:samples.shakespeare` and downloads the results:

```
$ python
>>> project_id='bigquery-e2e'
>>> gcs_bucket='bigquery-e2e'
>>> from gcs_reader import GcsReader
>>> from job_runner import JobRunner
>>> import extract_and_read
>>> extract_and_read.run_extract_job(
...      JobRunner(project_id=project_id),
...      GcsReader(gcs_bucket=gcs_bucket,
...               download_dir='/tmp/bigquery'),
...      source_project_id='publicdata',
...      source_dataset_id='samples',
...      source_table_id='shakespeare')
{
  "status": {
    "state": "PENDING"
  },
  "kind": "bigquery#job",
  "statistics": {
    "creationTime": "1395596962435"
  },
  "jobReference": {
    "projectId": "bigquery-e2e",
    "jobId": "job_1395596963"
  },
  "etag": "\"Ny_MVtklP3Cn04wt1Sr9PinHZEI/-ytBLaKo_odhSBz-AVUT8r4aR7M\"",
  "configuration": {
    "extract": {
      "destinationUri":
        "gs://bigquery-e2e/output/samples.shakespeare_1395596964.json",
      "destinationUris": [
        "gs://bigquery-e2e/output/samples.shakespeare_1395596964.json"
      ],
      "sourceTable": {
        "projectId": "publicdata",
        "tableId": "shakespeare",
        "datasetId": "samples"
      }
    }
  },
```

```
  "id": "bigquery-e2e:job_1395596963",
  "selfLink": "https://www.googleapis.com/bigquery/v2/projects/..."
}
PENDING 1s
PENDING 7s
PENDING 12s
PENDING 17s
RUNNING 23s
RUNNING 29s
DONE 35s
JOB COMPLETED
Downloading:
gs://bigquery-e2e/output/samples.shakespeare_1395596964.json to
/tmp/bigquery/output/samples.shakespeare_1395596964.json
```

The default extract format, like the default in Load jobs, is CSV. If you have tables with nested and repeated fields, CSV won't work because you can't represent a repeated field as a comma-separated row without introducing new formatting—at which point it isn't actually CSV anymore. If you don't want to export your data as CSV, you can specify a `destinationFormat` of `NEWLINE_ DELIMITED_JSON`, which outputs each row as a JSON element, with each row separated by a newline character (\n). Table 12.1 lists all the configuration options for an Extract job.

Table 12.1: Extract Configuration Fields

FIELD	TYPE	DESCRIPTION
sourceTable.tableid	string	Table ID of the source table
sourceTable.datasetId	string	Dataset ID of the dataset containing the table to export
datasetReference.projectId	string	Project ID of the project that owns the table to be exported
destinationUris	string array	Where to write the output
destinationFormat	string	Either CSV or NEWLINE_ DELIMITED_JSON, depending on the wanted format of the output. The default is CSV.

FIELD	TYPE	DESCRIPTION
printHeader	boolean	Whether to include a header row with the names of the fields. This is only valid for destinationFormat = CSV.
fieldDelimiter	string	Single character to use to separate fields. This is only valid when destinationFormat = CSV. The default is ", ."

Most of these parameters are relatively straightforward; however, the destinationUris could benefit from a little bit of extra explanation. The destinationUris value should contain a path that the user running the job has write access to in GCS. GCS paths look like gs://bucketname/objectname. Although you can specify additional slashes in the name to make it look like a directory, there is no real directory hierarchy. A path like gs://bucket/directory/subdir/object just refers to an object named directory/subdir/object in bucket bucket. This is mentioned because you don't have to worry about creating subdirectories before exporting a table.

There are a couple of other special options that you can use when specifying a destination URI or URIs, which are described next.

Pattern Export Paths

BigQuery won't export files larger than 1 GB to a single filename. Because a single file can't be written in parallel, a large destination file is inefficient to emit. If you export large tables, you can use a pattern path, which allows as many files to be written as necessary.

You shouldn't make any assumptions about the size or number of these files, other than that they will all be smaller than 1 GB in size. Small tables will likely just be exported as a single file, and larger tables will be broken into a larger number of pieces. BigQuery often moves data around to make it easier to query, so if you export the same table more than once, it might be split a different way each time.

To create a pattern export path, specify the glob character * somewhere in your destinationUris field. Glob patterns operate like command-line glob matching (for example, foo*.txt), rather than regular expressions (where you'd specify foo.*\.txt). The glob patterns will be replaced by a shard number padded to twelve digits, which starts at 000000000000 and increments by one for each file that is written out. For instance, if you pass the filename `gs://bigquery-e2e/data/extract/zipcodes*.json`, BigQuery may write out these objects:

```
gs://bigquery-e2e/data/extract/zipcodes0000000000.json
gs://bigquery-e2e/data/extract/zipcodes0000000001.json
gs://bigquery-e2e/data/extract/zipcodes0000000002.json
```

These files generally are written out in parallel (up to a limit, of course), so using a glob pattern can drastically reduce the time it takes to export a table. It is a best practice to always use a glob when exporting, since a glob pattern allows you to export data without worrying about the size of the source table.

Partitioned Export

Nobody likes waiting around for data. Often the reason you want to export your data is because you want to use it right away somewhere else. For example, you might be running a Hadoop job over your data in Google Compute Engine, or you might be exporting analysis results into your local MySQL database. In those cases, you don't necessarily want to wait until every last byte is ready because it is probably going to take you a while to consume the data. Ideally, you'd like to start processing the data as soon as possible.

If you have a number of parallel readers (as in the Hadoop case), you can tell BigQuery to write your data out to multiple patterns immediately. When the `destinationUris` field has more than one path, the export goes into a special "partitioned" mode, where the target file sizes are smaller and the parallel writers work on separate patterns immediately. When the writer finishes, it writes a special 0-row file to signal completion.

This mode can be extremely useful when you export data to use as input to a Hadoop job. In this case, each Hadoop worker will be looking for a single pattern and will continue to poll for new data until a 0-byte object is found. GCS shows only files after they have completed.

Listing 12.3 demonstrates an example of how you would use partitioned export.

Listing 12.3: Parallel export readers (extract_and_partitioned_read.py)

```
import sys
import threading
import time

from apiclient.errors import HttpError

# Imports from local files in this directory:
from gcs_reader import GcsReader
from job_runner import JobRunner

class PartitionReader(threading.Thread):
```

```python
'''Reads output files from a partitioned BigQuery extract job.'''
def __init__(self, job_runner, gcs_reader, partition_id):
  threading.Thread.__init__(self)
  self.job_runner = job_runner
  self.partition_id = partition_id
  self.gcs_reader = gcs_reader
  self.gcs_object_glob = None

def resolve_shard_path(self, path, index):
  '''Turns a glob path and an index into the expected filename.'''
  path_fmt = path.replace('*', '%012d')
  return path_fmt % (index,)

def read_shard(self, shard):
  '''Reads the file if the file is present or returns None.'''
  resolved_object = self.resolve_shard_path(self.gcs_object_glob,
                                            shard)
  return self.gcs_reader.read(resolved_object)

def start(self, gcs_object_glob):
  ''' Starts the thread, reading a GCS object pattern.'''
  self.gcs_object_glob = gcs_object_glob;
  threading.Thread.start(self)

def wait_for_complete(self):
  ''' Waits for the thread to complete.'''
  self.join()

def run(self):
  '''Waits for files to be written and reads them when they arrive.'''

  if not self.gcs_object_glob:
    raise Exception(
        'Must set the gcs_object_glob before running thread')

  print "[%d] STARTING on %s" % (self.partition_id,
      self.gcs_reader.make_uri(self.gcs_object_glob))
  job_done = False
  shard_index = 0
  while True:
    file_size = self.read_shard(shard_index)
    if file_size is not None:
      # Found a new file, save it, and start looking for the next one.
      shard_index += 1
    elif job_done: break
    else:
      # Check whether the job is done. If the job is done, we don't
      # want to exit immediately; we want to check one more time
      # for files.
      job_done = self.job_runner.get_job_state() == 'DONE'
```

continues

Listing 12.3: *(continued)*

```
        if not job_done:
          # Didn't find a new path, and the job is still running,
          # so wait a few seconds and try again.
          time.sleep(5)
      print "[%d] DONE. Read %d files" % (self.partition_id, shard_index)


def make_extract_config(source_project_id, source_dataset_id,
                        source_table_id, destination_uris):
  '''Creates a dict containing an export job configuration.'''

  source_table_ref = {
      'projectId': source_project_id,
      'datasetId': source_dataset_id,
      'tableId': source_table_id}
  extract_config = {
      'sourceTable': source_table_ref,
      'destinationFormat': 'NEWLINE_DELIMITED_JSON',
      'destinationUris': destination_uris}
  return {'extract': extract_config}

def run_partitioned_extract_job(job_runner, gcs_readers,
    source_project_id, source_dataset_id, source_table_id):
  '''Runs a BigQuery extract job and reads the results.'''
  destination_uris = []
  gcs_objects = []
  timestamp = int(time.time())
  partition_readers = []
  for index in range(len(gcs_readers)):
    gcs_object = 'output/%s.%s_%d.%d.*.json' % (
        source_dataset_id,
        source_table_id,
        timestamp,
        index)
    gcs_objects.append(gcs_object)
    destination_uris.append(gcs_readers[index].make_uri(gcs_object))

    # Create the reader thread for this partition.
    partition_readers.append(
        PartitionReader(job_runner=job_runner,
                        gcs_reader=gcs_readers[index],
                        partition_id=index))

  job_config = make_extract_config(source_project_id, source_dataset_id,
      source_table_id, destination_uris)
  if not job_runner.start_job(job_config):
    return

  # First start all of the reader threads.
  for index in range(len(partition_readers)):
```

```
    partition_readers[index].start(gcs_objects[index])
# Wait for all of the reader threads to complete.
for index in range(len(partition_readers)):
    partition_readers[index].wait_for_complete()
```

This code has two main parts: the `PartitionReader` class that downloads files when they become available and the `run_partitioned_extract_job` method that launches the partitioned read and waits for it to complete. The `PartitionedReader` extends Python's `Thread` object and periodically polls for new files to be available. Once the BigQuery job is complete, no more new files will arrive, so it exits after reading all remaining files.

The `run_partitioned_extract_job` method starts the job, and then starts all of the `PartitionedReader` threads to read and download the files in parallel. It returns after waiting for all of those threads to complete. The following code snippet shows how to use the `run_partitioned_extract_job` to download the `publicdata:samples.shakespeare` table in three partitions:

```
$ python
>>> from extract_and_partitioned_read import run_partitioned_extract_job
>>> from job_runner import JobRunner
>>> from gcs_reader import GcsReader
>>> project_id='bigquery-e2e'
>>> gcs_bucket='bigquery-e2e'
>>> run_partitioned_extract_job(
...     JobRunner(project_id=project_id),
...     [GcsReader(gcs_bucket=gcs_bucket,
...                download_dir='/tmp/bigquery') for x in range(3)],
...     source_project_id='publicdata',
...     source_dataset_id='samples',
...     source_table_id='shakespeare')
[0] STARTING on gs://bigquery-e2e/...shakespeare_1395605954.0.*.json
[1] STARTING on gs://bigquery-e2e/...shakespeare_1395605954.1.*.json
[2] STARTING on gs://bigquery-e2e/....shakespeare_1395605954.2.*.json
Downloading:
gs://bigquery-e2e/...shakespeare_1395605954.1.000000000000.json to
/tmp/bigquery/output/samples.shakespeare_1395605954.1.000000000000.json
Downloading:
gs://bigquery-e2e/....shakespeare_1395605954.0.000000000000.json to
/tmp/bigquery/output/samples.shakespeare_1395605954.0.000000000000.json
Downloading:
gs://bigquery-e2e/...shakespeare_1395605954.2.000000000000.json to
/tmp/bigquery/output/samples.shakespeare_1395605954.2.000000000000.json
[1] DONE. Read 1 files
[2] DONE. Read 1 files
Downloading:
gs://bigquery-e2e/...shakespeare_1395605954.0.000000000001.json to
/tmp/bigquery/output/samples.shakespeare_1395605954.0.000000000001.json
[0] DONE. Read 2 files
```

TableData.list()

If you want to read data out of a table, the alternative to an Export job is to just read the data directly using the `TableData.list()` method. Chapter 5 demonstrated using `TableData.list()` to read rows of data from a table. You can also use the same method to read an entire table, one page of rows at a time.

There are drawbacks to this approach, however. `TableData.list()` has two paging modes: using the row index and using a page token. Page tokens are the easiest to use because you get back a page token after you start reading the table, which you can then use in your next request to pick up where you left off. When no page token is returned, it means you are at the end of the table. A page token also reads from a single point in time, so if the table changes while you're reading from it, you still get a stable version of the table. The problem with page tokens, however, is that they force you to read the entire table serially, that is, start at the beginning and read to the end.

The other way of reading from a table, via a row index, lets you read any rows you want, whenever you want. So if you want to skip to row 1,000,000 and read from there, you can just specify that row as the start index. This makes it easier to read a table in parallel because each parallel worker can skip to the index that they want. For instance, if you have 10,000,000 rows in the table and 10 workers, the first worker would start at row 0 and read the first 1,000,000 rows, the second worker would read rows 1,000,000 through 1,999,999, and so on. There are two problems with reading a table this way: It is trickier to keep track of which rows to read by which worker, and if the table changes while you're reading it, you're going to read inconsistent data.

Listing 12.4 shows a `TableReader` class that can be used to read an entire table using `TableData.list()`. It reads one page at a time and then calls out to a `ResultHandler` class that processes each page of results as it arrives. If you use the `FileResultHandler`, it will write the results (still in the F/V row format) to a local file. The section titled "TableData.list()" in Chapter 5 shows how to translate the F/V format to a flat JSON format.

Listing 12.4: Reading a table with TableData.list() (table_reader.py)

```
import json
import os
import sys
import threading
import time

# Imports from the Google API client:
from apiclient.errors import HttpError

# Imports from files in this directory:
```

```
import auth

READ_CHUNK_SIZE= 64 * 1024

class ResultHandler:
  '''Abstract class to handle reading TableData rows.'''

  def handle_rows(self, rows):
    '''Process one page of results.'''
    pass

class TableReader:
  '''Reads data from a BigQuery table.'''

  def __init__(self, project_id, dataset_id, table_id,
      start_index=None, read_count=None, next_page_token=None):
    self.project_id = project_id
    self.dataset_id = dataset_id
    self.bq_service = auth.build_bq_client()
    self.next_page_token = next_page_token
    self.next_index = start_index
    self.rows_left = read_count
    self.table_id = table_id

  def get_table_info(self):
    '''Returns a tuple of (modified time, row count) for the table.'''

    table = self.bq_service.tables().get(
        projectId=self.project_id,
        datasetId=self.dataset_id,
        tableId=self.table_id).execute()
    last_modified = int(table.get('lastModifiedTime', 0))
    row_count = int(table.get('numRows', 0))
    print '%s last modified at %d' % (
      table['id'], last_modified)
    return (last_modified, row_count)

  def advance(self, rows, page_token):
    '''Called after reading a page, advances current indices.'''

    done = page_token is None
    if self.rows_left is not None:
      self.rows_left -= len(rows)
      if self.rows_left < 0: print 'Error: Read too many rows!'
      if self.rows_left <= 0: done = True

    if self.next_index is not None:
      self.next_index += len(rows)
    else:
      # Only use page tokens when we're not using
      # index-based pagination.
```

continues

Listing 12.4: *(continued)*

```python
        self.next_page_token = page_token
      return done

  def get_table_id(self):
    if '@' in self.table_id and self.snapshot_time is not None:
      raise Exception("Table already has a snapshot time")
    if self.snapshot_time is None:
      return self.table_id
    else:
      return '%s@%d' % (self.table_id, self.snapshot_time)

  def make_read_message(self, row_count, max_results):
    '''Creates a status message for the current read operation.'''
    read_msg =  'Read %d rows' % (row_count,)
    if self.next_index is not None:
      read_msg = '%s at %s' % (read_msg, self.next_index)
    elif self.next_page_token is not None:
      read_msg = '%s at %s' % (read_msg, self.next_page_token)
    else:
      read_msg = '%s from start' % (read_msg,)
    if max_results <> row_count:
      read_msg = '%s [max %d]' % (read_msg, max_results)
    return read_msg

  def read_one_page(self, max_results=READ_CHUNK_SIZE):
    '''Reads one page from the table.'''

    while True:
      try:
        if self.rows_left is not None and self.rows_left < max_results:
          max_results = self.rows_left

        data = self.bq_service.tabledata().list(
            projectId=self.project_id,
            datasetId=self.dataset_id,
            tableId=self.get_table_id(),
            startIndex=self.next_index,
            pageToken=self.next_page_token,
            maxResults=max_results).execute()
        next_page_token = data.get('pageToken', None)
        rows = data.get('rows', [])
        print self.make_read_message(len(rows), max_results)
        is_done = self.advance(rows, next_page_token)
        return (is_done, rows)
      except HttpError, err:
        # If the error is a rate limit or connection error, wait and
        # try again.
        if err.resp.status in [403, 500, 503]:
          print '%s: Retryable error %s, waiting' % (
              self.thread_id, err.resp.status,)
```

```
            time.sleep(5)
        else: raise

def read(self, result_handler, snapshot_time=None):
  '''Reads an entire table until the end or we hit a row limit.'''
  # Read the current time and use that for the snapshot time.
  # This will prevent us from getting inconsistent results when the
  # underlying table is changing.
  if snapshot_time is None and not '@' in self.table_id:
    self.snapshot_time = int(time.time() * 1000)
  self.snapshot_time = snapshot_time
  while True:
    is_done, rows = self.read_one_page()
    if rows:
      result_handler.handle_rows(rows)
    if is_done:
      return


class FileResultHandler(ResultHandler):
  '''Result handler that saves rows to a file.'''

  def __init__(self, output_file_name):
    self.output_file_name = output_file_name
    print 'Writing results to %s' % (output_file_name,)

  def __enter__(self):
    self.make_output_dir()
    self.output_file =  open(self.output_file_name, 'w')
    return self

  def __exit__(self, type, value, traceback):
    if self.output_file:
      self.output_file.close()
      self.output_file = None

  def make_output_dir(self):
    '''Creates an output directory for the downloaded results.'''

    output_dir = os.path.dirname(self.output_file_name)
    if os.path.exists(output_dir) and os.path.isdir(output_dir):
      # Nothing to do.
      return
    os.makedirs(output_dir)

  def handle_rows(self, rows):
    if self.output_file is None:
      self.__enter()
```

continues

Listing 12.4: *(continued)*

```
    self.output_file.write(json.dumps(rows, indent=2))


class TableReadThread (threading.Thread):
  '''Thread that reads from a table and writes it to a file.'''
  def __init__(self, table_reader, output_file_name,
               thread_id='thread'):
    threading.Thread.__init__(self)
    self.table_reader = table_reader
    self.output_file_name = output_file_name
    self.thread_id = thread_id

  def run(self):
    print 'Reading %s' % (self.thread_id,)
    with FileResultHandler(self.output_file_name) as result_handler:
      self.table_reader.read(result_handler)
```

This listing is a little bit more detailed than it needs to be, in order to simplify subsequent listings, which show how to read in parallel threads. The `TableReader` class can do index-based or pagination token-based reading, and will add a snapshot time to the table ID so that the listing is based on a stable snapshot of the table. This listing also handles errors, which is important if you want to be able to reliably read a large number of pages from a table. Finally, there is a `TableReadThread` class that is used in Listings 12.5 and 12.6 in order to spin up a separate thread to read a table or portion of a table. The following example uses a `TableReader` to read the `publicdata:samples.shakespeare` table in a background `TableReadThread` and saves the results to file.

```
$ python
>>> from table_reader import TableReader
>>> from table_reader import TableReadThread
>>> output_file_name = '/tmp/bigquery/shakespeare'
>>> table_reader = TableReader(project_id='publicdata',
...     dataset_id='samples',
...     table_id='shakespeare')
>>> thread = TableReadThread(table_reader, output_file_name)
>>> thread.start()
Writing results to /tmp/bigquery/shakespeare
>>> thread.join()
Read 65536 rows from start
Read 65536 rows at CIDBB777777QOGQIBCAIABAQQCAAI===
Read 33584 rows at CIDBB777777QOGQIBCAIACAQQCAAI===  [max 65536]
```

Table Decorators

BigQuery provides a mechanism called table decorators that can solve many of the problems encountered when using `TableData.list()` to read a table in parallel. Decorators can be used anywhere you otherwise would read from a table: in a Query, Copy, or Extract job, or in a `TableData.list()` operation. Chapter 11, "Managing Data Stored in BigQuery," shows some examples of how table decorators can be used for data management; here you see how they're useful in reading your data out of BigQuery.

Snapshot Decorators

Table snapshot decorators were discussed in Chapter 11. They can be used anywhere a table is read (in the API, in a query, and so on) to refer to a historical snapshot of a table at a particular time. You can use a snapshot decorator by adding `@timestamp` to a table name, where `timestamp` is the number of milliseconds since the POSIX epoch (that is, January 1st, 1970 GMT). For example, `publicdata:samples.wikipedia@1386465812000` is the BigQuery public sample table as of 1:23 AM GMT on December 8, 2013. The snapshot time must be within the last 7 days (this snapshot only worked until December 15, 2013, for example), but 7 days should be plenty of time to read a table. Note that if you're reading via page tokens, no snapshot decorator is needed because the page token implicitly specifies a snapshot time.

If you're going to read a table in parallel via row indexes, and that table might be changing, you should use a snapshot decorator. This way all the reads will be based on the same version of the table. To find a starting snapshot time, first read as of the current time. The Python `time.time()` method returns the number of seconds since the POSIX epoch as a floating-point value. To get the current snapshot time, just multiply the current time by 1000 and cast to an integer, as in: `timestamp = int(1000 * time.time())`. Then, each parallel worker should use the same snapshot time so that row 1,000,000 means the same thing for all readers.

Listing 12.5 shows how to get a good snapshot time and use it in a parallel `TableData.list()` operation. The net effect of this listing is the same as in 12.3; however, in this case you read the table directly instead of extracting it first to GCS.

Listing 12.5: Reading from a table by index in parallel (tabledata_index.py)

```
import os
import sys
import time

# Imports from files in this directory:
from table_reader import TableReader
from table_reader import TableReadThread

def parallel_indexed_read(partition_count,
    project_id, dataset_id, table_id, output_dir):
  '''Divides up a table and reads the pieces in parllel by index.'''
```

continues

Listing 12.5: *(continued)*

```
table_reader = TableReader(project_id, dataset_id, table_id)
_, row_count = table_reader.get_table_info()
snapshot_time = int(time.time() * 1000)
stride = row_count / partition_count
threads = []
for index in range(partition_count):
  file_name = '%s.%d' % (os.path.join(output_dir, table_id), index)
  start_index = stride * index
  thread_reader = TableReader(
      project_id=project_id,
      dataset_id=dataset_id,
      table_id='%s@%d' % (table_id, snapshot_time),
      start_index=start_index,
      read_count=stride)
  read_thread = TableReadThread(
      thread_reader,
      file_name,
      thread_id='[%d-%d]' % (start_index, start_index + stride))
  threads.append(read_thread)
  threads[index].start()

for index in range(partition_count):
```

First, this listing reads the number of rows in the table, so it can partition the table into row ranges. Next, it iterates through the number of desired partitions (that is, the number of parallel readers you want) and assigns each one a section of the table to read by creating a TableReader that is limited to that section. It then spins up a TableReadThread to run each TableReader. Finally, it waits for all of the threads to complete. Following is an example of running the indexed table reader to read your favorite table, publicdata:samples.shakespeare in three parallel threads:

```
$ python
>>> import tabledata_index
>>> tabledata_index.parallel_indexed_read(
...     3, 'publicdata', 'samples', 'shakespeare',
...     '/tmp/bigquery')
publicdata:samples.shakespeare last modified at 1335916045099
Reading [0-54885)
Writing results to /tmp/bigquery/shakespeare.0
Reading [54885-109770)
Writing results to /tmp/bigquery/shakespeare.1
Reading [109770-164655)
Writing results to /tmp/bigquery/shakespeare.2
Read 54885 rows at 54885
Read 54885 rows at 109770
Read 54885 rows at 0
```

Time Range Decorators

Another way to split up a table is to use a time range decorator, which allows you to read only data that was added to a table during a particular time range, for example:

```
publicdata:samples.wikipedia@1386465812000-1386465899999
```

Time range decorators create a view of the table containing only the data that was added between those two timestamps. Like a snapshot decorator, the times used in time range decorators must be within the last 7 days.

How is reading only a time slice of data in a table useful when reading out a table? It is useful because you might not *have* to read out the whole table. Maybe you read the table yesterday at time T, so today you need to read only the data that was added between T and now. If you had to read out the entire table page by page it might take a long time, but the data that was added in the last 24 hours might be much more manageable.

Because you don't always know what the current time is in milliseconds since 1/1/1970, there is another mode of address available for time range decorators. Negative numbers indicate relative numbers. For example, the table `publicdata:samples.wikipedia@-7200000--3600000` would contain all the data added between 2 hours and 1 hour ago. Don't forget: You're measuring time in milliseconds, which is why you have such big numbers.

Dynamic Partition Decorators

A third table decorator type can help when you're reading from a table in parallel: a partition decorator. This decorator type lets you partition a table into as many pieces as you like by modifying the name of the table that you use. Partition decorators are specified as `<table>$<index>-of-<count>`, where `<index>` is the partition number (starting with 0) and `<count>` is the number of total partitions. If you have 3 Hadoop workers, each one could read a different partition of the table, for example:

```
publicdata:samples.wikipedia$0-of-3
publicdata:samples.wikipedia$1-of-3
publicdata:samples.wikipedia$2-of-3
```

There are a couple of caveats with partition decorators: They do not guarantee to divide up the table range in exact chunks, and if you ask for too many partitions, the last ones will be empty. That is, if you have a 10-row table and ask for two partitions, you'll likely find that the first partition has all 10 rows and there are none in the second. The partition granularity is usually approximately 32 MB of table data (although a lot of factors can influence the size), so this is most useful when you're dealing with a large table.

Of course, you still have the same issue where the different workers start reading at different times and might be operating over different data if the table is changing. To prevent this, you can use a snapshot decorator in conjunction with a partition decorator. The snapshot decorator comes first from left to right; you can think of it as "table X, snapshotted at time T, partitioned into Y pieces." The Wikipedia table above would then be:

```
publicdata:samples.wikipedia@1386465812000$0-of-3
publicdata:samples.wikipedia@1386465812000$1-of-3
publicdata:samples.wikipedia@1386465812000$2-of-3
```

Listing 12.6 is similar to Listing 12.5 except it uses a partition decorator instead of dividing up the table by rows. This method of reading the table will likely be much faster than using the range-based indexing.

Listing 12.6: Reading from a table in parallel using partition decorators (tabledata_ partition.py)

```python
import os
import sys
import threading
import time

# Imports from files in this directory:
from table_reader import TableReader
from table_reader import TableReadThread

def parallel_partitioned_read(partition_count,
    project_id, dataset_id, table_id, output_dir):

  snapshot_time = int(time.time() * 1000)
  threads = []
  for index in range(partition_count):
    file_name = '%s.%d' % (os.path.join(output_dir, table_id), index)
    suffix ='$%d-of-%d' % (index, partition_count)
    partition_table_id = '%s@%d%s' % (table_id, snapshot_time, suffix)
    thread_reader = TableReader(
        project_id=project_id,
        dataset_id=dataset_id,
        table_id=partition_table_id)
    read_thread = TableReadThread(
        thread_reader,
        file_name,
        thread_id=suffix)
    threads.append(read_thread)
    threads[index].start()

  for index in range(partition_count):
    threads[index].join()
```

EXTRACT JOBS VERSUS TABLEDATA.LIST() FOR READING DATA IN PARALLEL

Both Extract jobs and `TableData.list()` let you read data from tables in parallel. When should you use one versus the other? The answer, unsurprisingly, depends on how you want to read the data. If you want to read the table like a file—that is, read 1 k bytes at a time—you will likely want to use the output of an Extract job. Extract produces files that live in Google Cloud Storage (GCS) that you can read multiple times and in any byte range you choose. You can download the files using standard HTTP resumable download operations.

`TableData.list()`, however, lets you read a specific number of rows but doesn't give you control over bytes. To read all the data, you need to use a page token to fetch the next section of data. This means that you can't just plug it in as-is to download your tables.

There are latency trade-offs as well. Extract jobs require you to wait for the data to be produced, but when it is ready, you can download at the speed of your Internet connection. `TableData.list()`, however, lets you read data immediately, but the effective bandwidth will be lower because the data has to be transcoded into your desired format on-the-fly.

AppEngine MapReduce

There are a number of reasons you might want to extract data from BigQuery. One common case is when a certain data transformation cannot be expressed as a query within the service. For instance, it could be any combination of the following:

- Computation is not expressible in SQL.
- It is too slow or expensive when expressed as a SQL query.
- Requires specialized functions that are not supported

If you extract your data from the service, you are then free to run your computation using a framework that supports the transformation you require. The MapReduce family of data processing frameworks is especially well suited to transformations of large datasets. Hadoop is the most popular implementation of this computation model, but it is not the only one. The AppEngine platform also supports the MapReduce model of computation, which can be used to transform BigQuery tables. This section covers using this framework to augment BigQuery.

Before diving into the nuts and bolts of using AppEngine MapReduce, it is useful to have a well-defined use case in mind. Compared to running a query within BigQuery, the AppEngine framework is going to appear rather cumbersome. This is to be expected because it is a more general-purpose computing framework. However, it does warrant a motivating example that justifies the additional complexity.

In our sample application in Chapter 8, "Putting It Together", we had captured logs from the phone that included geolocation information describing the position of the phone. The logs record the latitude, longitude, and ZIP (postal) code that most closely correspond to the coordinates. ZIP codes prove handy for joining log records with other geographic information.

Joining tables based on geographic information using latitude and longitude is actually challenging in (BigQuery) SQL because a simple equality join is not feasible. Equality joins work when the exact value in one table matches the exact value in another table. If you have latitude and longitude points, you rarely will have two points in different tables that match exactly, and typically you're more interested in proximity than exact overlap.

However, if you can bucket data into sufficiently small regions, such as a ZIP code, then you can use a straightforward equality join. You can easily imagine that in the first iteration of our application we neglected to include the ZIP code in our log records; however, we are going to use this to drive our examples for this section.

Concretely, we are going to transform a BigQuery table with latitude and longitude fields into a new table that has all the original fields, plus an additional field with the ZIP code that is the best match for the record. To avoid distractions we will use a simple source table with the following schema:

```
[
  {"name": "id", "type": "string"},
  {"name": "lat", "type": "float"},
  {"name": "lng", "type": "float"}
]
```

The transformed table will have the same schema with one additional field:

```
[
  {"name": "id", "type": "string"},
  {"name": "lat", "type": "float"},
  {"name": "lng", "type": "float"},
  {"name": "zip", "type": "string"}
]
```

Now that you have a well-specified problem, you can move on to finding a solution.

Sequential Solution

The most straightforward way to solve the ZIP-code assignment problem would be to:

1. Export the data from the table to a file on GCS.

2. Download the data to a local file.

3. Run a custom program that transforms the file.

4. Load the transformed file into the new BigQuery table.

Steps 1, 2, and 4 have been covered in detail in the first section and in Chapter 6. Although step 3 is not actually specific to BigQuery, the details of how to construct the program to transform the data are going to be relevant to how to run it in the AppEngine MapReduce framework. Listing 12.7 shows how to solve the problem if you deal with data that is small enough that you can process it sequentially. This listing is a baseline that you can compare against a parallel version.

Listing 12.7: Resolving to ZIP code (add_zip.py)

```python
import json
import sys

# Imports from files in local directory:
from kdtree import KDTree

class ZipPoint(tuple):
  '''Tuple containing a lat, long, and zip code.'''
  def __new__(cls, json_dict):
    return super(ZipPoint, cls).__new__(
      cls, (json_dict['lat'], json_dict['lng']))

  def __init__(self, json_dict):
    self.zip = json_dict['zip']

with open('zip_centers.json', 'r') as f:
  ZIP_INDEX = KDTree([ZipPoint(json.loads(r)) for r in f])

def apply(input):
  val = json.loads(input)
  closest = ZIP_INDEX.query((val['lat'], val['lng']))
  if closest:
    val['zip'] = closest[0].zip
```

continues

Listing 12.7: *(continued)*

```
    yield json.dumps(val) + '\n'
  else:
    yield input

if __name__ == '__main__':
  for line in sys.stdin:
    for o in apply(line):
      print o,
```

This listing reads records from standard input, looks up the ZIP code, and writes records with the ZIP code added to the standard output. The input records must be specified as newline-delimited JSON matching your expected input schema. The output format is similar, with the addition of the ZIP code field.

On startup, the listing loads the ZIP code database into an index (a *k*-d tree, which supports efficient lookup of the nearest points to a given point; see `https://code .google.com/p/python-kdtree/`). Then it parses each input line as a JSON object, looks up the nearest ZIP code, and emits the record with the ZIP code it located added to the record. You can run the script with the following command line:

```
$ cd appengine
$ python add_zip.py ../add_zip_sample.json
$ cd ..
```

The code has been structured so that the core computation is independent of the details of input and output. This enables you to clearly see the parts that stay the same when it is converted to a MapReduce computation. You might not be familiar with the Python `__new__` operator. This is used in order to represent the `ZipPoint` class as a tuple.

Before moving on, it is important to note that the script seems simple only because most of the complexity is hidden in the *k*-d tree library it uses. This illustrates why it is sometimes necessary to perform transformations outside of BigQuery. There are inevitably specialized algorithms that will be difficult to implement within the BigQuery query language. Furthermore, it is likely that implementations exist in some suitable external framework. In these situations you need to look for the best way to make the data stored in BigQuery accessible in the appropriate framework.

STARTING WITH THE SAMPLE

There is a fair amount of setup and boilerplate code required to get an AppEngine project configured and running. First, you'll need to create an AppEngine app from `https://appengine.google.com/start/createapp`. To simplify the setup necessary to run the examples in this section, the downloads for this chapter contain a complete AppEngine project. There is a script file provided called `setup_appengine.py` that can be used to set up your local AppEngine environment and customize the required configuration files. To use, run the following command:

```
$ python setup_appengine.py ${APP_ID} ${PROJECT_ID} ${GCS_BUCKET}
```

This command will extract the `appengine_deps.zip` file into the `appen-gine` directory and generate a `controller.yaml` file with the settings needed to complete the MapReduce example in this section. More information on setting up AppEngine is provided in Chapter 8 in the section titled "Log Collection Service.

You can then start the app by simply loading those files using the `appcfg` tool from the AppEngine SDK. This operation may take several minutes.

```
$ appcfg.py update appengine/controller.yaml
08:07 AM Host: appengine.google.com
08:07 AM Application: ...; version: 1
08:07 AM
Starting update of app: ..., version: 1
08:07 AM Getting current resource limits.
08:07 AM Scanning files on local disk.
08:07 AM Cloning 4 static files.
08:07 AM Cloning 130 application files.
08:07 AM Compilation starting.
08:07 AM Compilation completed.
08:07 AM Starting deployment.
08:07 AM Checking if deployment succeeded.
08:07 AM Will check again in 1 seconds.
...
08:20 AM Will check again in 60 seconds.
08:21 AM Checking if deployment succeeded.
08:21 AM Deployment successful.
08:21 AM Checking if updated app version is serving.
08:21 AM Completed update of app: ..., version: 1
```

Basic AppEngine MapReduce

The AppEngine MapReduce framework enables you to leverage AppEngine scalability to solve your data processing challenges. The authoritative documentation for the feature is available at `https://developers.google.com/appengine/docs/python/dataprocessing/`.

We will port our simple script to AppEngine MapReduce to show how it works with simple data inputs. Rather than use local files as inputs and outputs to the script, the AppEngine version directly reads the GCS input file and writes the output straight back to GCS.

In this example, GCS is used as the cloud equivalent of a local filesystem. We are postponing BigQuery integration a little longer so that you can focus on the difference between scripts intended to be executed on a single machine and the MapReduce version that can be scaled up.

To set up your AppEngine project to run MapReduce jobs, you need to install the AppEngine MapReduce SDK. The samples for this chapter include an AppEngine project with the SDK installed. Instructions for downloading the SDK into your application directory are available at the link previously given.

In addition, you need to install the library for AppEngine/GCS integration, which is available at `https://developers.google.com/appengine/docs/python/googlecloudstorageclient/download`.

After adding this client library to your application, you need to grant permission to the AppEngine application service account. This will let it create files in your output GCS bucket. To grant access, substitute your own AppEngine ID for `APP_ID` and your own GCS bucket for `GCS_BUCKET` and issue the following commands:

```
$ APP_ID=bigquery-mr-sample
$ GCS_BUCKET=bigquery-e2e
$ gsutil acl ch \
    -u ${APP_ID}@appspot.gserviceaccount.com:W \
    gs://${GCS_BUCKET}
Updated ACL on gs://bigquery-e2e/
```

You can run a simple MapReduce with almost no additional code beyond the previous script. You just need to set some configuration parameters and save them in a file called `mapreduce.yaml` at the top level of the AppEngine project directory. Here is an example `mapreduce.yaml` file:

```
mapreduce:
- name: Add Zip Codes
  mapper:

    handler: add_zip.apply
    input_reader: mapreduce.input_readers.FileInputReader
    output_writer:
      mapreduce.output_writers._GoogleCloudStorageOutputWriter
    params_validator: validator.adjust_spec
    params:
    - name: files
      value: /gs/bigquery-e2e/chapters/12/add_zip_input.json

    - name: shards
      default: 1
    - name: format
      default: lines
    - name: output_bucket
      default: bigquery-e2e
```

This file is basically a replacement for the last part of our script that read from the standard input and wrote to the standard output in Listing 12.7. You just need to tell the MapReduce where to get the source data and where to write the results. The `input_reader` and `output_writer` fields indicate that you want to read and write data in GCS. The `params` field contains parameters that control the behavior of these modules, in this case, by specifying the input and output location as well as the degree of parallelism. Note that files in GCS are referenced using a slightly different syntax: `/gs/bucket/object` instead of the `gs://bucket/object` format used by BigQuery.

The default output bucket is set to `bigquery-e2e`. You will not have write access to this bucket, so you can either override the value to your own GCS bucket here or you can wait until you start the MapReduce and set the value in the MapReduce settings page.

If you've modified any of the files in the AppEngine app, you'll need to re-upload the most recent version. You can do this by re-running the previous `appcfg.py` command:

```
$ appcfg.py update controller.yaml
```

After you have uploaded your application with the MapReduce SDK, you can navigate to `http://<your-app>.appspot.com/mapreduce`.

You can see a console that lists MapReduce jobs that have been created, as well as a form for creating new jobs according to the templates you defined. In this case you see a single option representing your MapReduce configuration, with form fields that allow you to edit the parameters.

Unfortunately, the automatic forms support only simple string parameters, but some of the input modules expect a list or dictionary of values. To turn the form parameters into a configuration dictionary that you need to pass into the I/O modules, you can provide a Python function to do the translation. The `params_validator` setting in the configuration provides the name of a parameter transformation and validation function. It is passed a dictionary of all the values in the form as its single argument; it can modify that dictionary to turn it into a valid MapReduce configuration. If it throws an exception, the MapReduce creation simply fails. We have defined a simple version for this pair of writer and reader in `validator.py`:

```python
def adjust_spec(params):
  params['files'] = params['files'].split()
  params['output_writer'] = {
      'bucket_name': params['output_bucket'],
      'naming_format': 'test/$id-$num'}
```

Using the validator lets you configure your MapReduces using the simple configuration file and AppEngine console, rather than requiring you to write custom code to configure and launch your MapReduce jobs.

DEVELOPMENT SERVER

It is easiest to test AppEngine MapReduce code by actually uploading it and using the live version rather than testing using the development server `dev_appserver.py`. The reason for this is that `dev_appserver.py` uses a fake GCS; therefore, you would first have to create GCS files at the appropriate location before the example can work correctly. Arguably, it would be nicer if `dev_appserver.py` had the ability to use real GCS files, but at this time it does not support that option.

This is a good time to try running a MapReduce job. Simply set the `output_bucket` parameter (just the bucket name, no `gs://` or `/gs/` is necessary) to the GCS bucket that you are using for the example, and click Run. The status page will update and list your job as now running. You can click the link to the job to follow its progress. When the job finishes successfully, you can inspect its output by listing the contents of your bucket. The sample provided writes to filenames of the form `test/<job id>-<shard>`, For example:

```
$ gsutil ls gs://${GCS_BUCKET}/test/*
gs://bigquery-e2e/test/15784101297666AC77A71-0
gs://bigquery-e2e/test/15792505778554A7B9C41-0
```

This list command displays the output file generated by your job.

BigQuery Integration

Now that you have seen how to MapReduce over files that live in GCS, you can integrate with BigQuery by coordinating the MapReduce job with a pair of BigQuery export and import jobs. You need to run a BigQuery export job to materialize the contents of a table as a set of GCS files. When that job completes you can run the MapReduce job in AppEngine to produce output files in GCS. Finally, you need to run a BigQuery import job to populate a table with the contents of the output files.

All the BigQuery-related plumbing should be familiar. The first section of this chapter covered the details of extracting data from BigQuery tables, and Chapter 6 covered loading data into tables. The main challenge is to run all this in the AppEngine environment and coordinate it with a MapReduce job.

Ordinarily, you'd run into an AppEngine limitation—all requests must finish within 60 seconds. Because BigQuery Load and Extract jobs may take longer than 60 seconds, you need to implement a complex timer-and-callback mechanism that would divide up the longer-lived BigQuery jobs into smaller chunks.

However, to simplify the code, you can take advantage of AppEngine's support for long-lived instances; you just need to write a function that sequentially performs each step. Because long-lived instances are allowed to spin up background threads and have no restrictions on the time spent on an individual request, your background thread can simply poll for the completion of each step.

Configuring long-lived instances is covered in the AppEngine documentation. The `setup_appengine.py` script creates a `controller.yaml` file that defines a suitable AppEngine module. The significant portions of this file are:

```
application: bigquery-mr-sample
module: controller
version: 1
runtime: python27
api_version: 1
threadsafe: yes
instance_class: B4
basic_scaling:
  max_instances: 1

handlers:
- url: /mapreduce/pipeline/images
  static_dir: mapreduce/lib/pipeline/ui/images

- url: /mapreduce(/.*)?
  script: mapreduce.main.APP
  login: admin

- url: .*
  script: controller.app
  login: admin

libraries:
- name: webapp2
  version: latest
- name: pycrypto
  version: latest
...
```

The common bits have been elided to highlight the portions that enable implementation of the controller script, which is defined in `controller.py`. Most of the controller script defines a simple web application that allows the process to be started by an HTTP POST request and then displays the status of individual steps in the process. A single function, `run_transform`, and a couple of helper functions handle the transformation process. Listing 12.8 contains the definition of the MapReduce job.

Listing 12.8: The RunTransform task (appengine/controller.py)

```
import cgi
import time
import threading
```

continues

Listing 12.8: *(continued)*

```python
import json

from google.appengine.api import users
from google.appengine.ext.webapp.util import login_required
from google.appengine.api import memcache
from google.appengine.api import app_identity
from google.appengine.api import background_thread
import webapp2
import httplib2
from oauth2client.appengine import AppAssertionCredentials
from apiclient.discovery import build
from mapreduce.mapper_pipeline import MapperPipeline
from job_runner import JobRunner
from config import PROJECT_ID
from config import GCS_BUCKET

credentials = AppAssertionCredentials(
  scope='https://www.googleapis.com/auth/bigquery')
bigquery = build('bigquery', 'v2',
                 http=credentials.authorize(httplib2.Http(memcache)))

g_state_lock = threading.RLock()
ZERO_STATE = {
  'status': 'IDLE',
  'extract_job_id': '',
  'extract_result': '',
  'load_job_id': '',
  'load_result': '',
  'mapper_link': '',
  'error': 'None',
  'refresh': '',
  }
g_state = ZERO_STATE.copy()

def pre(s):
  '''Helper function to format JSON for display.'''
  return '<pre>' + cgi.escape(str(s)) + '</pre>'

def run_bigquery_job(job_id_prefix, job_type, config):
  '''Run a bigquery job and update pipeline status.'''
  global g_state
  runner = JobRunner(PROJECT_ID,
                     job_id_prefix + '_' + job_type,
                     client=bigquery)
  runner.start_job({job_type: config})
  with g_state_lock:
    g_state[job_type + '_job_id'] = runner.job_id
  job_state = 'STARTED'
  while job_state != 'DONE':
    time.sleep(5)
    result = runner.get_job()
```

```
      job_state = result['status']['state']
      with g_state_lock:
        g_state[job_type + '_result'] = pre(json.dumps(result, indent=2))

    if 'errorResult' in result['status']:
      raise RuntimeError(json.dumps(result['status']['errorResult'],
                         indent=2))

def wait_for_pipeline(pipeline_id):
  '''Wait for a MapReduce pipeline to complete.'''
  mapreduce_id = None
  while True:
    time.sleep(5)
    pipeline = MapperPipeline.from_id(pipeline_id)
    if not mapreduce_id and pipeline.outputs.job_id.filled:
      mapreduce_id = pipeline.outputs.job_id.value
      with g_state_lock:
        g_state['mapper_link'] = (
          '<a href="/mapreduce/detail?mapreduce_id=%s">%s</a>' % (
            mapreduce_id, mapreduce_id))
    if pipeline.has_finalized:
      break
  if pipeline.outputs.result_status.value != 'success':
    raise RuntimeError('Mapper job failed, see status link.')

def table_reference(table_id):
  '''Helper to construct a table reference.'''
  return {
    'projectId': PROJECT_ID,
    'datasetId': 'ch12',
    'tableId': table_id,
    }

OUTPUT_SCHEMA = {
  'fields': [
    {'name':'id', 'type':'STRING'},
    {'name':'lat', 'type':'FLOAT'},
    {'name':'lng', 'type':'FLOAT'},
    {'name':'zip', 'type':'STRING'},
    ]
  }

def run_transform():
  JOB_ID_PREFIX = 'ch12_%d' % int(time.time())
  TMP_PATH = 'tmp/mapreduce/%s' % JOB_ID_PREFIX

  # Extract from BigQuery to GCS.
  run_bigquery_job(JOB_ID_PREFIX, 'extract', {
      'sourceTable': table_reference('add_zip_input'),
      'destinationUri': 'gs://%s/%s/input-*' % (GCS_BUCKET, TMP_PATH),
      'destinationFormat': 'NEWLINE_DELIMITED_JSON',
      })
```

continues

Listing 12.8: *(continued)*

```
  # Run the mapper job to annotate the records.
  mapper = MapperPipeline(
    'Add Zip',
    'add_zip.apply',
    'mapreduce.input_readers.FileInputReader',
    'mapreduce.output_writers._GoogleCloudStorageOutputWriter',
    params={
      'files': ['/gs/%s/%s/input-*' % (GCS_BUCKET, TMP_PATH)],
      'format': 'lines',
      'output_writer': {
        'bucket_name': GCS_BUCKET,
        'naming_format': TMP_PATH + '/output-$num',
        }
      })
  mapper.start()
  wait_for_pipeline(mapper.pipeline_id)

  # Load from GCS into BigQuery.
  run_bigquery_job(JOB_ID_PREFIX, 'load', {
      'destinationTable': table_reference('add_zip_output'),
      'sourceUris': ['gs://%s/%s/output-*' % (GCS_BUCKET, TMP_PATH)],
      'sourceFormat': 'NEWLINE_DELIMITED_JSON',
      'schema': OUTPUT_SCHEMA,
      'writeDisposition': 'WRITE_TRUNCATE',
      })

def run_attempt():
  global g_state
  try:
    with g_state_lock:
      if g_state['status'] == 'RUNNING':
        return
      g_state = ZERO_STATE.copy()
      g_state['status'] = 'RUNNING'
    run_transform()
  except Exception, err:
    with g_state_lock:
      g_state['error'] = pre(err)
  finally:
    with g_state_lock:
      g_state['status'] = 'IDLE'

class MainHandler(webapp2.RequestHandler):
  @login_required
  def get(self):
    current = ZERO_STATE.copy()
    with g_state_lock:
      current.update(g_state)
      if current['status'] == 'RUNNING':
        current['refresh'] = '<meta http-equiv="refresh" content="6"/>'
    self.response.write(_PAGE % current)
```

```
  def post(self):
    if not users.is_current_user_admin():
      self.abort(401, 'Must be an admin to start a mapreduce.')
    background_thread.start_new_background_thread(run_attempt, [])
    self.redirect(self.request.route.build(self.request, [], {}))
app = webapp2.WSGIApplication([
    webapp2.Route(r'/', handler=MainHandler, name='main'),
], debug=True)
```

Before you can run this code, you'll need to load the zip codes source file into BigQuery. You can do this with the following commands:

```
$ bq mk ch12
$ bq load --source_format=NEWLINE_DELIMITED_JSON \
    ch12.add_zip_input add_zip_sample.json \
    "id:string,lat:float,lng:float"
```

The `MainHandler` class that responds to requests to the `/mapreduce` URL simply spins up a background thread when it receives a POST request, which is triggered when you hit the Run button. The background thread runs a BigQuery job to extract the table to Google Cloud Storage and then runs an AppEngine mapper pipeline to add the zip code and save the output back in Google Cloud Storage. Finally, the background thread runs a Load job to import the data back into BigQuery.

There is a lot of boilerplate code that handles AppEngine MapReduce state management. We have included a function that waits for MapReduce pipeline completion so that it is clear how to poll for its status. The definition of the MapReduce pipeline, the middle operation, in code closely mirrors the configuration in the `controller.yaml` file previously discussed. We specify the outputs of the earlier step as the inputs to the next step to chain them together.

In this case, a simple sequential pipeline approach works well and makes it easy to see what is happening. If the individual steps have more complex dependencies or could run in parallel, then you could use the AppEngine pipeline framework to orchestrate the steps. More information on the pipeline framework is available at: `https://code.google.com/p/appengine-pipeline/`.

In addition, we have not covered cleaning up the files generated on GCS. One option is to add code to the function to perform the deletion explicitly. Alternatively, you can use automatic life-cycle management available in GCS to clean up the files after some duration. Documentation for this feature is available at `https://developers.google.com/storage/docs/lifecycle`.

PROGRAMMING LANGUAGE NOTE

AppEngine is a general-purpose computing environment. In our examples we have used Python, but all these features are also available in the AppEngine Java SDK, so you could use Java if it is more convenient for your application. Translating the Python APIs to Java is mostly straightforward. You should consult the AppEngine documentation for more information about the differences between the Java and Python APIs.

The AppEngine SDK contains other reader and writer modules that let you specify Datastore or Cloud SQL as MapReduce sources or destinations. Using these, you can modify the sample presented in this chapter to move data between BigQuery and AppEngine. This approach is more flexible than the Datastore backup import method presented in Chapter 11 because it allows you to transform the data before insertion into BigQuery. This can be useful when your Datastore entities have a complicated or nonuniform structure.

In addition, AppEngine also supports transferring data in the reverse direction, from BigQuery to Datastore. This can be useful to mirror data in both locations. If your application requires efficient individual object lookups, Datastore is a perfect solution; if you also require more complex analytics, having the same data also in BigQuery allows fast queries over the entire dataset. Be aware, however, that you will incur the costs of Datastore writes when performing this operation.

The AppEngine MapReduce SDK does not contain direct BigQuery input readers and writers as of the time of publication. It is quite likely, however, that they will become available in future releases. When they do the process will become even simpler—instead of supplying BigQuery job configurations in code, you will be able to specify them in the config file, like the GCS example.

Using BigQuery with Hadoop

Hadoop is more or less synonymous with Big Data. It started out as a clone of Google MapReduce and Google File System (GFS) but has since developed into a robust ecosystem for storing and processing large amounts of data. A number of tools have been built on top of Hadoop to make it easier to use; a number of companies have been formed to help customers use Hadoop, and a lot of work has gone into improving its performance.

Several BigQuery customers have migrated from Hadoop to BigQuery to perform faster, interactive queries over their data. They still, often, have a significant amount of "business logic" in their Hadoop pipelines, transforming the raw data, anonymizing it, cleaning it, and so on. For these customers, BigQuery doesn't replace Hadoop; it complements it.

You can, of course, run your Hadoop cluster anywhere: on premise, on Amazon Elastic Computer Cloud (EC2), and so on. But given that you are MapReducing over data that will either come from or go to BigQuery, it will usually be more efficient to perform the computation near where the data is stored to minimize having to copy it across the Internet (which can be expensive in terms of both time and money). For that reason, we discuss running your Hadoop cluster on Google Compute Engine.

Hadoop on Google Compute Engine (GCE)

You don't need any additional support to run Hadoop on Google Compute Engine; the GCE API is quite robust and it isn't hard to write a script to manage a cluster to run your Hadoop jobs. There are even third-party companies, such as Qubole, that have built products out of Hadoop cluster management. Hadoop is a key part of Cloud Computing, and the performance of Hadoop on GCE is a key differentiator for Google's Cloud. To make it easier to run Hadoop on GCE, Google has released special cluster-management tools and data connectors to talk to Google data sources and sinks.

These Hadoop-on-GCE tools are relatively new at the time of publication—so far, they are merely a set of scripts that can create and manage a Hadoop cluster for you. They also include connectors to allow you to access data in AppEngine Datastore, Google Cloud Storage, and BigQuery. Because at the time of this writing these tools have not yet been released to the public, we don't provide a walkthrough of how to use them, other than to mention that they will be available, and if you are a Hadoop user, options exist for running Hadoop over BigQuery data. For more information, see `https://developers.google.com/hadoop/bigquery-connector`

Querying BigQuery from a Spreadsheet

Spreadsheets allow you to generate charts and visualizations of your data, and enable advanced data manipulation features like pivot tables. However, spreadsheets aren't designed for Big Data—they tend to not scale well and become difficult to manage when they get too large. That said, the world seems to run on spreadsheets, and many data analysts want to use a spreadsheet to access their large datasets. To squeeze the large data sets into a small spreadsheet, the usual mechanism is to run a query over the raw data to pre-aggregate it into something more easily manipulated in a spreadsheet.

BigQuery provides two different mechanisms for running queries on spreadsheets, depending on what software you use. If you use Google Spreadsheets, you can use the Apps Script language to script your access to BigQuery. If you use Microsoft Excel, you can use the BigQuery Excel Connector to run your queries. The former is a richer interface that gives you a lot of control over how you run your queries. The latter is a simpler mechanism but, due to the limitations of sending HTTP requests in Excel, lacks some of the bells and whistles of the Apps Script version.

BigQuery Queries in Google Spreadsheets (Apps Script)

Apps Script is a programming language based on JavaScript that allows you to extend Google Apps to talk to outside services. You can make HTTP requests, perform a mail merge, and run queries on BigQuery. You can add buttons and menu items, and generally customize Google's apps to do things that you wish they could do but don't already.

The main use case for the BigQuery integration in Apps Script is to run queries in Google Spreadsheets. However, you also could use them to run an import job periodically from Google Cloud Storage. On the BigQuery team, we use Apps Script to automate a number of query tasks. For example, when we get a customer who reports a problem in a certain job ID, to find information about the job, we need to also have the project ID. We can use Apps Script to make a BigQuery query into our metadata table to match the job ID with the project. This is a relatively simple operation, but it saves a lot of typing.

BIGQUERY INTEGRATION IN APPS SCRIPT IS EXPERIMENTAL

Here's a caveat: The BigQuery Apps Script integration (like the Apps Script integration with several other Google APIs) is still marked experimental. This means that things can change without much notice. In the past year this has happened only once, but it can be frustrating when a script that worked yesterday stops working today.

Both the BigQuery and the Apps Script teams work hard to prevent breaking changes, and the rate of change will likely go down over time. The good part is that many things will likely get better. For example, a lot of steps are needed to start using BigQuery in an Apps Script; this will almost certainly get easier over time.

Enabling Apps Script in Google Drive

The first step toward running Apps Script is turning it on in Google Drive. This can be done from `https://drive.google.com` by clicking the big, red CREATE button and then selecting Connect More Apps, as shown in Figure 12.1. A window displays enabling you to select which apps you want to connect to Drive. The Google Apps Script option will likely be displayed on the first page of apps, but if it is not, you can search for it in the top-right corner of the dialog box. Select Google Apps Script, and click the green button to connect your account.

You may be asked to authorize Google Apps Script. In the process of getting BigQuery enabled, you may see the authorization page again; if so, you should click allow each time. The authorization that you'll be prompted for doesn't do anything particularly scary; it just allows Google Apps Script to access your data in BigQuery. This makes sense because if you want to run a BigQuery query in your spreadsheet, that spreadsheet needs to see your BigQuery data.

Creating an Apps Script in Your Spreadsheet

The hard part is over, right? Unfortunately, there are 37(-ish) other steps needed to start using BigQuery in your Google Spreadsheet. Fortunately, none of the steps are difficult.

Although you can create a standalone Apps Script directly from Google Drive, these scripts cannot be used from within a spreadsheet. It is an easy mistake to start out with a standalone script and then try to connect it to your spreadsheet; however, as we found out the hard way, this doesn't work.

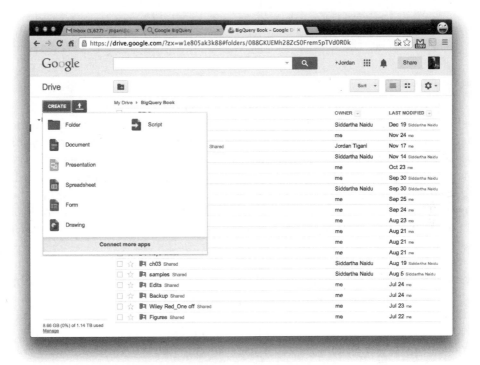

Figure 12.1: Enabling Apps Script in Google Drive

To create a Spreadsheet script, you should first open Google Spreadsheets; then select Script Editor from the tools menu. This creates a new script that can access your spreadsheet. You get a pop-up asking you what kind of script to create. Just select Blank Project. You might want to try running something on your script to verify that it works. Try entering this in your script:

```
function onOpen() {
  var ss = SpreadsheetApp.getActiveSpreadsheet();
  var menuEntries = [];
  menuEntries.push({name: "Set project", functionName: "setProject"});
  ss.addMenu("BigQuery", menuEntries);
 }

function setProject() {
  var sheet = SpreadsheetApp.getActiveSheet();
  var cell = sheet.getActiveCell();
```

```
  var value = cell.getValue();
  if (value) {
    projectId = String(value);
    UserProperties.setProperty('PROJECT_ID', projectId);
    Logger.log('Project id set to %s', projectId);
  } else {
    Logger.log('Project id not set');
  }
}
```

This installs a BigQuery menu when you open your spreadsheet and adds a Set Project menu item. Save the script, go back to the spreadsheet, and reload the page in your browser. You should now see a BigQuery menu item. Enter your project ID in a cell. With it selected, run the Set Project item from the BigQuery menu. This saves your project ID as a per-user property. This project ID will be used when talking to BigQuery, so you don't have to indicate it every time you want to run a query or hard-code it in the script. After you set your project ID, you can delete it from the spreadsheet—it has been saved and you won't need to use it again.

Switch back to your script so that you can enable BigQuery and start to write some interesting code. One pointer for checking out what you've run in Apps Script: If you go to the View menu and select Execution Transcript, you can see the output from the last operation that you ran. In this case, it shows the output from when you set your project ID from the BigQuery menu. This transcript can be helpful when debugging because it can tell you what was executed and show you line numbers of any problems you encounter.

Enabling BigQuery in Your Apps Script

You're almost there. You just need to turn on BigQuery...how hard can that be? From your script, go to the Resources menu and select Advanced Google Services. A dialog box displays showing a number of Google APIs, their version numbers, and an on-off toggle for each one. Look for the entry for BigQuery API. Make sure the version says v2, and turn on the toggle to enable BigQuery access. Figure 12.2 shows BigQuery enabled.

Don't close the dialog box yet—there may be one more step. Hopefully, by the time you read this, the extra step will be unnecessary. If at the bottom of the dialog box it says, "These services must be enabled in the Google Developers Console," you need to click through, and once again switch a toggle to turn on BigQuery. This page looks like the project setup page when you signed up for BigQuery and turned on billing. You do *not* have to sign up for billing here, and although this *does* create a project, this project is not used in a meaningful way when you access BigQuery. This project does not show up in your projects list. After enabling BigQuery from the list, you can safely forget that this project even exists.

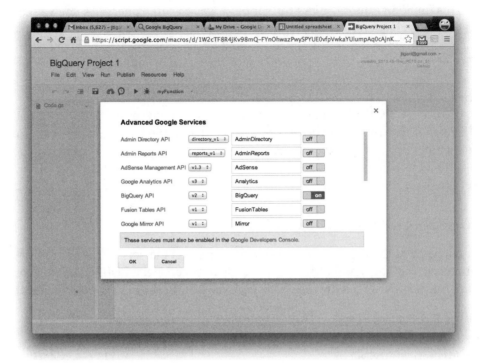

Figure 12.2: Enabling BigQuery in Apps Script

Now you can close the various dialog boxes and browser tabs that have popped up, and BigQuery access should be ready to go.

Running a BigQuery Query in Apps Script

Before returning to the spreadsheet, just write a simple function that runs a query and logs the result. This way you can verify that things are configured correctly and BigQuery works. Try entering the following function (substituting your own project ID) and pressing Save:

```
function simpleQuery() {
  var projectId = 'bigquery-e2e'; // YOUR PROJECT HERE.
  var sql = 'SELECT corpus, COUNT(*) as cnt '
      + 'FROM [publicdata:samples.shakespeare] '
      + 'GROUP BY corpus';
  Logger.log('%s: Running query: "%s"', projectId, sql);
  var resource = {
    'query': sql
  };
  var queryResults = BigQuery.Jobs.query(resource, projectId);
  Logger.log('Got query results:\n%s', queryResults);
}
```

This function is more or less the simplest way to run a query. As you've seen in previous chapters, it is far from complete; it doesn't handle queries that take longer to run than the default timeout, and it fetches only the first page of results. The advantage, however, is it lets you know whether you have BigQuery working. Select `simpleQuery` from the Select Function drop-down menu, and then click the Play button. This runs the query and writes the results to the logger.

If you open the log (under the View menu), you should see both the query and the results. If there was an error, you can see that in the log or in the execution transcript (also on the View menu). If you need more debugging support, if you use the bug icon instead of the play icon, you can step through the script and set breakpoints, and so on.

Writing Query Results to a Spreadsheet

You now have all the pieces you need to write a script that lets you send arbitrary queries to BigQuery and write the results to a spreadsheet. Listing 12.9 lets you run queries and writes the results to a Query Results sheet in the spreadsheet.

Listing 12.9: Running a query and writing the results to a spreadsheet (query.gs)

```
/**
 * BigQuery query script.
 * This script installs a 'BigQuery' menu in your spreadsheet that
 * allow you to run queries.
 *
 * To use, first enter your project ID in a
 * cell of your choosing, then with that cell selected, select the
 * 'Set project' item from the BigQuery menu. This will save your
 * project ID as a user property so you won't need to set it again.
 * You can delete the cell where you had entered the project ID.
 * To run a query, write a query in any cell or range of cells.
 * Select those cells, and then pick 'Run Query' from the BigQuery
 * menu. This will run the query you've selected and add the outputs
 * to a new sheet called 'Query Results'. If this sheet already
 * existed, it will be cleared and rewritten (so don't put stuff you
 * want to keep in the results sheet). Note that Google Spreadsheets
 * has a limit of about 400,000 cells, so if you have large query
 * results, you might find yourself hitting this limit pretty quickly.
 */

// Name of the sheet that will contain the query results. This page
// will be cleared every time the query is run.
var QUERY_RESULTS_SHEET = 'Query Results'
// Name of the user property where we save the project ID.
var PROJECT_ID_PROPERTY = 'PROJECT_ID'
// Number of results to return from BigQuery per page.
```

```
var MAX_RESULTS_PER_PAGE = 1000

/** Installs a BigQuery menu to allow you to run queries. */
function onOpen() {
  var ss = SpreadsheetApp.getActiveSpreadsheet();

  var menuEntries = [];
  // Create a menu link to the 'runQuery' function. To run a query,
  // select the cells that contain your query and then select 'Run
  // a query  from the BigQuery menu.
  menuEntries.push({name: "Run a query", functionName: "runQuery"});

  // Before you can run a query, you need to set a project ID to use
  // with the query. You can do this by selecting a cell that has the
  // project ID to use, then picking the the 'Set project" menu item
  // from the BigQuery menu. Note that after you set the project ID,
  // you can delete that cell... the project ID is remembered as part
  // of the user properties for the script.
  menuEntries.push({name: "Set project", functionName: "setProject"});
  ss.addMenu("BigQuery", menuEntries);
}

/**
 * Sets the project ID to use for BigQuery queries. User
 * should select a cell containing the desired project ID
 * and then call the setProject menu item.
 */
function setProject() {
  var sheet = SpreadsheetApp.getActiveSheet();
  var cell = sheet.getActiveCell();
  var value = cell.getValue();
  if (value) {
    projectId = String(value);
    UserProperties.setProperty(PROJECT_ID_PROPERTY, projectId);
    Logger.log('Project ID set to %s', projectId);
  } else {
    Logger.log('Project ID not set');
  }
}

/**
 * Gets the project ID property.
 */
function getProjectId() {
  var projectId = UserProperties.getProperty(PROJECT_ID_PROPERTY);
  if (!projectId) {
    throw new Error("Property PROJECT_ID is not registered");
  }
  return projectId;
```

continues

Listing 12.9: *(continued)*

```javascript
}

/**
 * Reads the query from the active selection in the current
 * spreadsheet. To read from more than one cell, just select the range
 * of cells you want.
 */
function readQuery() {
  var sheet = SpreadsheetApp.getActiveSheet();
  var range = sheet.getActiveRange();
  var values = range.getValues();
  query = values.join(' ');
  return query;
}

/**
 * Given a sheet to write to, the start row and a 2D array of
 * values, writes those values to the sheet.
 */
function writeChunk(sheet, startIndex, data) {
  var nRows = data.length;
  if (nRows == 0) {
    // Nothing to do.
    Logger.log('No results to write');
    return;
  }
  var nCols = data[0].length;
  sheet.getRange(startIndex, 1, nRows, nCols).setValues(data);
  Logger.log('Wrote %s rows to: %s', nRows, sheet.getName());
}

/**
 * Translates the .f and .v format of the query results into
 * a 2D array of values.
 */
function extractRows(rows) {
  // Append the results.
  var data = new Array(rows.length);
  for (var i = 0; i < rows.length; i++) {
    var cols = rows[i].f;
    data[i] = new Array(cols.length);
    for (var j = 0; j < cols.length; j++) {
      data[i][j] = cols[j].v;
    }
  }
  return data;
}

/**
 * Sets up a sheet with a given name which will contain our
 * query results. If the sheet already exists, it will be cleared.
```

```
  * If it doesn't exist, we'll create a new one.
  */
function setUpResultSheet(sheetName) {
  var spreadsheet = SpreadsheetApp.getActive();
  var sheet = spreadsheet.getSheetByName(sheetName);

  if (spreadsheet.getActiveSheet().getName() == sheetName) {
    // Don't run a query from the queryResults sheet -- this will
    // erase your query!
    throw new Error("Cannot write query results to active sheet");
  }

  if (sheet) {
    sheet.clear();
  } else {
    sheet = spreadsheet.insertSheet(sheetName);
  }
  return sheet;
}

/**
 * Gets a function that can be used to write out chunks of
 * data as they're being returned from BigQuery.
 */
function getChunkWriter(sheetName) {
  return function(rowIndex, rows) {
    var sheet;
    if (rowIndex == 1) {
      // If we're starting from the beginning, we need to set up
      // the result  sheet.
      sheet = setUpResultSheet(sheetName);
    } else {
      // The sheet should already exist and be ready for us to write.
      sheet = SpreadsheetApp.getActive().getSheetByName(sheetName);
    }
    writeChunk(sheet, rowIndex, rows);
    return rowIndex + rows.length;
  }
}

/**
 * Pulls the field names out of query results. Retrurns them
 * as a 2D array with 1 row, so they can be written via the
 * same mechanism we use to write rows of data.
 */
function extractHeaders(fields) {
  return [fields.map(function(field) {return field.name;})];
}

/**
 * Runs a given SQL query and writes the results to the chunkWriter
```

continues

Listing 12.9: *(continued)*

```
 * one page at a time. This is preferable to returning results, since
 * the query results may be large.
 */
function runSqlQuery(projectId, sql, chunkWriter) {
  Logger.log('%s: Running query: %s', projectId, sql);
  var resource = {
    'query': sql,
    'maxResults': MAX_RESULTS_PER_PAGE
  };
  var queryResults = BigQuery.Jobs.query(resource, projectId);

  var jobId = queryResults.jobReference.jobId;

  // The job might not actually be done; wait until it is marked
  // complete. For simple queries, it will have completed within the
  // default timeout, but for more complex queries (JOIN, etc), you
  // might find the query takes a long time.
  var sleepTimeMs = 500;
  while (!queryResults.jobComplete) {
    Utilities.sleep(sleepTimeMs);
    sleepTimeMs *= 2;
    queryResults = BigQuery.Jobs.getQueryResults(projectId, jobId);
  }

  // Write the field names as the first row.
  chunkWriter(1, extractHeaders(queryResults.schema.fields));
  // Now we've got the first page, write that out to the spreadsheet.
  nextIndex = chunkWriter(2, extractRows(queryResults.rows));

  // But wait, there's more!
  while (queryResults.pageToken) {
    queryResults = BigQuery.Jobs.getQueryResults(projectId, jobId, {
      'pageToken': queryResults.pageToken,
      'maxResults': MAX_RESULTS_PER_PAGE
    });

    nextIndex = chunkWriter(nextIndex, extractRows(queryResults.rows));
  }
}


/**
 * Runs a query from the currently selected cells and write the results
 * to a sheet called 'Query Results' in the current spreadsheet.
 */
function runQuery() {
  var chunkWriter = getChunkWriter(QUERY_RESULTS_SHEET);
  runSqlQuery(getProjectId(), readQuery(), chunkWriter);
}
```

Everything in this code listing should be familiar: The polling loop that waits for a job to complete is similar to the Python listing in Chapter 7, "Running Queries." Writing the results to the spreadsheet uses the same objects that you saw earlier when setting the project ID property.

Running this script is easy (especially when compared to the setup steps). First, write the query you intend to run in any range of cells. With those cells selected, execute Run Query from the BigQuery menu. (If this menu item isn't there, you might need to reload the page because it updates only when you open the spreadsheet.) The script then runs your query, downloads the results one page at a time, and writes the results to a Query Results sheet. If the destination sheet didn't exist, it will be created; otherwise that sheet will be reset.

This example grazed only the surface of the kinds of things that you can do in Apps Script, but hopefully it whet your appetite. For those of you who don't have the luxury of using Google Spreadsheets, the next section describes using BigQuery from Excel.

BigQuery Queries in Microsoft Excel

It is surprising (or perhaps terrifying) to realize how much of the world runs on Excel spreadsheets. During the financial crisis in 2008, there were stories about traders who managed multibillion dollar trading strategies from a single Excel spreadsheet with no backup. A coding error in an Excel spreadsheet created by an economist led to numerous national governments choosing policies that may have been economically unsound. Excel is an extremely powerful tool for making sense of your data, if you use it wisely.

Excel has built-in support for connecting to outside data sources. It can connect to databases via ODBC, import files from a myriad of other sources, and run queries on the web. The BigQuery team built a custom AppEngine app that exposes the BigQuery query API in a manner that can integrate with Excel without requiring custom macros or client-installed software. This section walks you through setting up access and querying your BigQuery data from an Excel spreadsheet. Although some of the steps or menu items involved may be different between Mac and Windows versions, or on different versions of Excel, the BigQuery Excel Connector should work with any version of Excel since Office 97.

BigQuery Excel Connector App

The first step in using BigQuery from Excel is visiting the BigQuery Excel Connector page at `https://bigquery-connector.appspot.com/`. This page should have all the instructions necessary for integration; although, some of the details can be tricky if you're unfamiliar with setting up external queries in

Excel. The first bit talks about a key, which you won't have yet, so don't worry about it for now.

Click the link that says, "Click here to download the IQY file," and save the resulting file to your local disk. The next section describes what this file is and how to use it, but for now, just remember where you saved it.

Next, you need to create an authorization key. Because Microsoft Excel doesn't support OAuth2 (which hadn't been invented yet when Excel Web Queries were created), you need to use a separate authorization mechanism. The connector app can generate a secret key that you can use to authenticate as you. You can revoke it at any time, and it is valid for an interval of your choice up to 30 days.

Scroll to the bottom of the page, pick a key lifetime, and click the Create Key button. This reloads the page, and at the top you see your new key. You can retrieve the key again by coming back to the connector page. You need to cut and paste it into a prompt in Excel.

The Web Query (.iqy) File

In the last section, you should have downloaded a file called `connector.iqy`. This file is just a simple text file that describes how Excel should make requests to the BigQuery connector. Now take a look at the contents:

```
WEB
1
https://bigquery-connector.appspot.com/data
q=["Query", "Enter a query:"]&
p=["Project","Enter a project ID:"]&
k=["Key", "Enter your Connector Key:"]
```

The first two lines, WEB and 1, are required by the .IQY specification (more information about that at `http://support.microsoft.com/kb/157482`). The third line is the address to send the queries to. In this case, it is the address of the BigQuery connector query endpoint. The last line (broken up into three lines to avoid line-wrapping issues) describes the HTTP POST request to make.

There are three parameters that need to be sent to the connector as part of the request. If you've been using BigQuery for a while, you probably can guess what they are:

1. The query that you want to send, for example, SELECT 17

2. The project that will be billed for the queries you run, for example, bigquery-e2e

3. An authorization key. This is the part that we glossed over on the original BigQuery Connector landing page.

There is some extra formatting in the .IQY file that tells Excel to prompt for the data. If you prefer, you could just hard-code your choices in the .IQY file. If you manage Excel installations in an enterprise setting, for example, you might want to just set the project ID to your company's project to save individual users this step. Alternatively, you might want to hard-code the authorization key so that users don't have to do key management. For ordinary operation, however, you shouldn't need to modify the .IQY file.

Excel Web Query

Now that you've done the external setup, open Microsoft Excel. These instructions are based on Microsoft Excel for Mac 2011, but any version since Excel 97 should work on either Windows or Mac. That said, the menu options change on virtually every version, so if your UI doesn't match the screen shots, you might have to do a little more digging to figure out how to complete the setup.

From the Data menu, select the Get External Data submenu and the Run Saved Query menu item, as shown in Figure 12.3. This brings up a file open dialog box that prompts you to find the .IQY file you downloaded from the BigQuery Connector app. To see this file listed, you may have to change the Enable selector from Text Files to Query Files. Select your connector.iqy file and click the Get Data button.

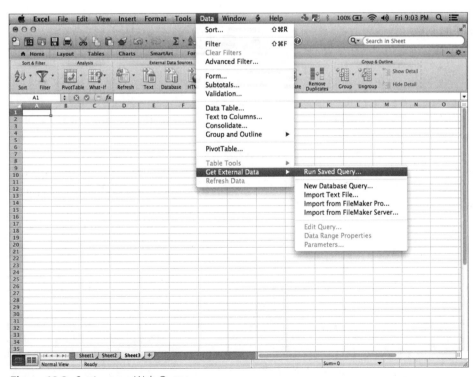

Figure 12.3: Setting up a Web Query

After you select the .IQY file, you'll be given a series of prompts to configure the query. The first prompt is the location of the output data, which is a cell or range of cells that will get the query results after the query is run. This is the one choice that you cannot change later, so pick a good spot that you'll remember. The remaining prompts come directly from the .IQY file (Query, Project, and Key). The query can either be a static query, like SELECT 17, or you can give a cell or range of cells where the query text will be drawn from. You'll usually want to give a cell or range of cells, unless you know that you'll want to run only the same query.

If your query is longer than 256 characters, you need to split it across multiple cells. This is a limitation of Excel Web Queries and can be a little bit frustrating when you run into it accidentally. We recommend specifying a reasonably large range of cells when you set up the Web Query so that you can write queries that are as long as you like. This limitation isn't all bad; it can make your queries more readable by forcing them to be split up across multiple lines.

The next prompt is for project ID, which should be the project that will be billed for your queries. (You must, of course, be a member of the project team to run queries in that project.) You should probably select the "Use this value/ reference for future refreshes" box because it is unlikely that your project ID will change.

Finally, you need your authorization key. This key can be cut-and-pasted from the key you generated when you selected the Generate key. You should also probably select the box to remember your key so that you don't have to juggle the key every time you open the document.

After completing the three prompts, you should be ready to start querying. Just enter the query in the query source range you specified, and the results should pop up within a few seconds. Depending on the version of Excel you use, you may have some additional options, like having the query results auto-refresh when the query changes or having the query run periodically. You can also specify a cell to hold the project ID and key so that you can enter them in the spreadsheet instead of via the dialog boxes. Figure 12.4 shows a query along with the results.

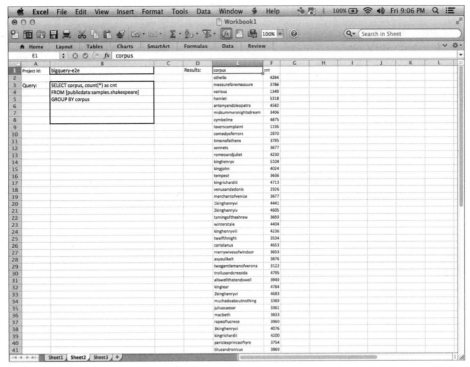

Figure 12.4: Excel Web Query and results

Summary

Sometimes you may want to use tools that operate over your raw BigQuery data or otherwise use BigQuery through other mechanisms than the BigQuery Web UI or HTTP API. This chapter showed ways to access your data when you're not using BigQuery directly. You saw how to export your data from BigQuery via export jobs and via direct download.

You saw how to access your data in parallel because when you deal with Big Data, you're going to want to take advantage of scale-out parallel architectures. MapReduce is the most common parallel architecture, and you saw how to use AppEngine's MapReduce to transform data in parallel. Google Compute Engine's Hadoop integration was introduced, which you can also use to perform MapReduces over your BigQuery tables.

Finally, you saw how to run BigQuery queries from two different spreadsheet programs: Google Spreadsheets and Microsoft Excel. The spreadsheet integration can be a good launching point for incorporation of BigQuery data into your own Business Intelligence applications.

The next chapter introduces some third-party tools that have been built on top of BigQuery that enable you to visualize your data and extend the scope of BigQuery access and usefulness.

Using BigQuery from Third-Party Tools

BigQuery was designed to be a platform for Big Data analytics that you could layer other tools on top of, rather than an all-in-one Big Data solution. A number of third parties have built tools on top of BigQuery to extend its capabilities. Some of these tools enable you to make BigQuery work just like your on-premise relational database, visualize your data in the cloud, or access your data from scientific applications. This chapter walks you through several of these types of tools; the goal is to show a little bit of what they can do and how they integrate with BigQuery.

There are three parts to this chapter:

- **BigQuery adapters:** If you currently use ODBC or JDBC to connect to your database, you can use BigQuery without writing any code just by using the Simba ODBC driver. This section also discusses client-side encryption.

- **Scientific data processing:** R is the de facto standard for scientific data analysis. See how to use the `bigrquery` R package to connect to BigQuery from R. Also see BigQuery in the Python Data Analysis Library (aka pandas).

- **Data visualization:** See how to visualize your BigQuery data using two popular commercial applications: Tableau and BIME.

These are only a representative sampling of the third-party tools that integrate with BigQuery. Google keeps track of a number of them at `https://developers`

`.google.com/bigquery/third-party-tools`. There is also a handy BigQuery sub-reddit (`http://reddit.com/r/bigquery`) that is a more crowd-sourced collection of applications of BigQuery. Before starting on a new project, it might be helpful to check these locations to see if someone has already done a lot of the hard work for you!

BigQuery Adapters

There are two ways to try to incorporate BigQuery into your production processes: You can either adapt your code to talk to BigQuery or you can adapt BigQuery to talk to your code. If the latter route sounds silly, it needn't be; some third-party tools adapt BigQuery to make it look like a standard relational database.

For instance, if your code uses "standard" Open Database Connectivity (ODBC) connections, you can use a freely available ODBC driver to start performing BigQuery queries without having to change your code. The Simba ODBC driver translates Standard SQL into BigQuery SQL and allows BigQuery to be used virtually anywhere an ODBC-compatible database can be used. Alternately, if you use Java to talk to your database, you can use the StarSchema Java Database Connectivity (JDBC) connector to allow you to talk directly to BigQuery. Both of these mechanisms have limitations, however, which are discussed later in this section.

There is another type of connector discussed in this section: the Encrypted BigQuery (`ebq`) connector, which adapts BigQuery to look like BigQuery, but with a twist: It encrypts all the data locally so that the server never sees the unencrypted data. The `ebq` connector performs a number of mathematical tricks to allow you to access your data normally and do most of the same types of queries you do on your unencrypted data.

Simba ODBC Connector

ODBC is one of the oldest ways to talk to a database; it is a well-understood standard that is used by a wide range of software and has connectors for a wide range of databases. Simba is a Canadian company that specializes in writing ODBC drivers. It has been around for almost as long as ODBC has and has built ODBC drivers for virtually anything that you can think of—from SAP to MongoDB to Hive. One of its most recent ODBC drivers provides access to BigQuery.

The Simba driver has two modes of operation. The first, native mode, allows you to run queries directly in BigQuery SQL. That is, you write the same queries that you'd write if you were using the BigQuery web UI, and the Simba driver passes them to BigQuery. The other, translated mode, translates standard SQL queries into BigQuery SQL. So if you already have code that writes SQL queries, you can switch to BigQuery just by switching ODBC drivers.

Depending on your use case, you may decide to use one native or direct mode. The advantage of the direct mode is that you always know what BigQuery is going to execute, and you can run the exact same queries by hand in the BigQuery web UI. Translated mode, however, will let you swap out BigQuery as your query back end without making any changes to your queries.

Unlike JDBC, ODBC drivers are platform-dependent. That means that an ODBC driver that works on Windows won't work on a Mac or Linux machine. The Simba driver currently comes in two flavors: Windows and Linux. However, as of this writing, only the Windows version is available for free. This platform dependence is something to consider when choosing the connector.

One additional note in favor of the Simba driver, however is that Simba is *the* expert in ODBC, and its driver is fully fledged and full-featured. Simba charges for many of its drivers, and because of this, it has a higher standard of documentation and support. Now, let's move on before starting a war between the forces of open and closed source.

Like the SQL standard, ODBC is a wide standard that includes a lot of pieces. Simba has implemented most of these pieces except Data Definition Language (DDL). Because BigQuery doesn't support CREATE TABLE or ALTER TABLE commands, the Simba ODBC driver doesn't handle them either, even in translated mode. If your analysis setup requires creating temporary tables or changing schemas, you might need to write code that specifically handles these cases by making direct BigQuery calls (such as the Tables.insert() or Tables.update() REST calls described in Chapter 4, "Understanding the BigQuery Object Model").

The Simba driver also has limited support for prepared statements and parameter substitution. BigQuery does not support prepared statements, and although translated mode could emulate them, this support isn't currently available in the driver.

Installing and Configuring

If you go to the Simba website, it wants to charge you to download the BigQuery ODBC driver. However, the Windows versions of the driver are available on the BigQuery third-party tools page at https://developers.google.com/bigquery/third-party-tools. If you need the Linux version, want tech support, or merely want to get updates, you can get those from Simba at http://www.simba.com/connectors/google-bigquery-odbc. The remainder of these setup instructions assume you use Windows 7, although the steps won't be much different whether you run Windows XP or Windows 8.

To install the Simba driver and create a DSN, you can do the following:

1. Download the Simba BigQuery ODBC driver that matches your operating system and hardware (the 64- or 32-bit versions as necessary) and run the installer. This registers the BigQuery ODBC connector with the operating system. (Note it also requires administrator privileges on your machine.)

2. After the driver is installed, you need to create a Data Source Name (DSN), an antique Windows term for a connection to a database. To create your DSN to connect to BigQuery, open the Control Panel, select the Administrative Tools (see Figure 13.1) and open the Data Sources (ODBC) applet. You might have to change your Control Panel view to large or small icons to see Administrative Tools.

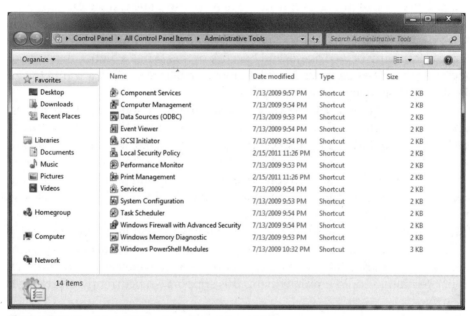

Figure 13.1: The Administrative Tools Control Panel folder

3. After you open the Data Sources Control Panel applet, click Add in the User DSN tab. This creates the connection for just a single user; alternatively you could use a System DSN if you want to create the connection for all users of the machine. The Add button brings up a dialog box asking you to select the DSN type. Choose Simba BigQuery ODBC driver from the list, and it displays the BigQuery-specific settings dialog box.

4. Create a name for the DSN (**bigquery1**, for example). This is the name that you will use later when you use the DSN to connect to BigQuery.

5. The DSN encapsulates authorization for BigQuery, so to set it up, you'll need to tell BigQuery who you are and perform the OAuth2 sign-in process. Click the Sign in button, and it pops up a web browser. Google requires that OAuth2 be done in a web browser, which can make this type of login flow a bit awkward. The rationale is that this prevents you from having to type your password into anything that isn't a web browser; presumably you already trust your web browser with your password. The good part is that you have to do it only once, when you set up the DSN.

6. You'll be prompted to log in (if you're not already logged in) and asked whether you want to allow access to your BigQuery data. After you accept, you'll be given a code that you need to cut and paste into the Confirmation Code box in the Connection dialog box. When you paste in the confirmation code, it automatically fills in the refresh token. After authentication, your Connector Setup dialog box should look something like Figure 13.2.

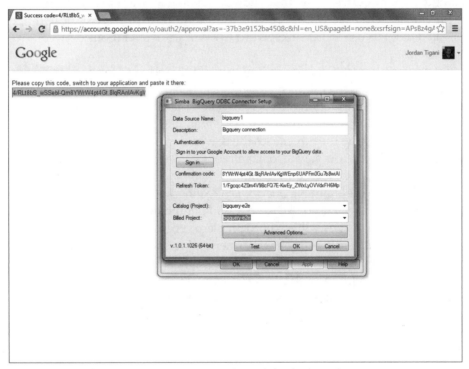

Figure 13.2: Simba BigQuery ODBC Connector Setup dialog box

7. The last step in setting up your BigQuery connection is selecting a project. The Catalog project will be the project that datasets and tables will be

drawn from; you'll have an opportunity to select the actual datasets and tables later, but they all must come from this project. By default, all queries you perform will be billed to this same project. If, however, you want to read from a different project than you want charged for the queries, you can set the Billed Project to something different. These settings can also be overridden later, so you shouldn't worry too much about what you set them to here.

8. Press Test to verify that the connection is working. It will pop up a dialog box that lists the datasets in the catalog project—if this succeeds it means that it could connect to BigQuery and authorize successfully. Press OK to dismiss, and it takes you back to the Connector Setup dialog box.

As previously mentioned the Simba driver transparently rewrites standard SQL into BigQuery SQL. Often, this is exactly what you want; you may have a tool that generates standard SQL, and you want to use BigQuery without changing your queries. Sometimes, however, you may want to express a query in BigQuery SQL exactly. Maybe you want to take advantage of nested and repeated data, or use the EACH keyword to allow JOIN operations between two large tables.

If you want to write queries in BigQuery SQL and not Standard SQL, you can tell the Simba driver to pass through the SQL statements exactly and not perform any transformations. To do this, click the Advanced Options button, which hides an important check box: Use Native Queries, which defaults to unchecked. Checking the box causes the driver to pass through queries exactly as they are written. You may also have the option of overriding these options when you create an ODBC connection.

In ODBC terms, the Simba BigQuery ODBC connector maps a project to an ODBC catalog; this means you need to choose ahead of time which project you will use. For most practical purposes this is not a problem because most people use a single project in their queries. When you write queries, you should use the dataset name and table name only; the project name will be implicit. For example, the query you might run in the BigQuery web UI SELECT COUNT(*) FROM [publicdata:samples .shakespeare] would look like SELECT COUNT(*) FROM samples.shakespeare when using the ODBC driver; the publicdata project ID must be specified in the connection settings.

ODBC Queries from the .NET Framework

ODBC is a platform-dependent mechanism; if you use ODBC to talk to your data source, you're probably using Windows. The most common programming environment on Windows is the Common Language Runtime (CLR), which allows you to program in a number of different languages using identical APIs.

The flagship programming language under the CLR is C#. Because we expect that C# will be the most relevant language for users of the Simba BigQuery ODBC driver, we've provided C# sample code to talk to BigQuery via ODBC in Listing 13.1.

Listing 13.1: Simple ODBC query application (C#) (bigquery_odbc.cs)

```csharp
using System;
using System.Collections.Generic;
using System.Data;
using System.Data.Odbc;
using System.Linq;
using System.Text;
using System.Threading.Tasks;

namespace BigQueryE2E
{
  /**
   * Helper class to build an ODBC Connection to connect to a Simba
   * BigQuery ODBC Driver.
   */
  class ConnectionBuilder {
    public String Dsn;
    public String Catalog;
    public String ExecCatalog;
    public bool UseNativeQuery;

    public OdbcConnection Build() {
      if (Catalog == null || Dsn == null) {
        throw new ArgumentException(
            "Missing required Connection setting");
      }

      StringBuilder connectionString = new StringBuilder();
      connectionString.AppendFormat("DSN={0}; Catalog={1};",
          Dsn, Catalog);
      if (ExecCatalog != null) {
        connectionString.AppendFormat("ExecCatalog={0};",
            ExecCatalog);
      }
      if (UseNativeQuery) {
        connectionString.Append("UseNativeQuery=1");
      }

      OdbcConnection conn = new OdbcConnection();
      conn.ConnectionString = connectionString.ToString();
      return conn;
    }
```

continues

Listing 13.1: *(continued)*

```
  }

/**
 * Simple console program that runs a query against BigQuery,
 * prints the results, and waits for a user to hit any key
 * before exiting.
 */
class Program {
  private static String Query =
      "SELECT corpus, SUM(word_count) " +
      "FROM samples.shakespeare " +
      "GROUP BY corpus";

  private static void PrintResults(OdbcDataReader reader) {
    for (int ii = 0; ii < reader.FieldCount; ii += 1) {
      System.Console.Write("{0}{1}",
          reader.GetName(ii),
          ii + 1 < reader.FieldCount ? "\t" : "\n");
    }
    while (reader.Read()) {
      for (int ii = 0; ii < reader.FieldCount; ii += 1) {
        System.Console.Write("{0}{1}",
            reader.GetValue(ii),
            ii + 1 < reader.FieldCount ? "\t" : "\n");
      }
    }
  }

  static void Main(string[] args) {
    ConnectionBuilder builder = new ConnectionBuilder();
    // Set this to the name of the ODBC dns you created:
    builder.Dsn = "bigquery1";
    // This is the default project that will be used to resolve tables
    // in the job:
    builder.Catalog = "publicdata";
    // Set this to your own project ID so that Jobs are run under
    // this project:
    builder.ExecCatalog = "bigquery-e2e";

    string state = "creating connection";
    try {
      state = "opening connection";
      using (OdbcConnection connection = builder.Build()) {
        connection.Open();
        state = "creating command";
        using (OdbcCommand command = connection.CreateCommand()) {
          command.CommandText = Query;
          state = "running query";
          using (OdbcDataReader reader = command.ExecuteReader()) {
            PrintResults(reader);
          }
        }
```

```
      }
    } catch (Exception ex) {
      System.Console.WriteLine("Error {0}: {1}", state, ex);
    }
    // Wait until the "any key" is pressed.
    System.Console.ReadKey();
  }
 }
}
```

Most of the sample code is boilerplate that you would use to talk to any data source using ODBC. The BigQuery-specific parts are actually involved only in creating the connection; because of this, we've separated out the ConnectionBuilder into its own class that lets you easily create an ODBC connection to talk to your BigQuery data.

To use the ConnectionBuilder, you need to specify the DSN name; this is the name of the connection you created in the ODBC setup steps. We created the DSN as bigquery1, so we set that as the DSN name. You also need to specify a catalog, which is the project from which to read the tables. The code talks about catalogs, which are ODBC terms, but for BigQuery connections catalogs are synonymous with projects. If you are going to be reading data from the same project that you want to bill queries to, this is all the information that you need. However, if you want to bill a different project, you can set the billing project independently. The final option, which we don't specify in the following code snippet because we don't use it, is to turn on Native mode, which can cause the ODBC driver to pass your queries directly through to BigQuery without modification.

Here is the code that creates a connection to the DSN bigquery1 using the project publicdata and bills queries to the bigquery-e2e project:

```
ConnectionBuilder builder = new ConnectionBuilder();
builder.Dsn = "bigquery1";
builder.Catalog = "publicdata";
builder.ExecCatalog = "bigquery-e2e";
OdbcConnection connection = builder.Build();
```

The ConnectionBuilder takes this information and turns it into the ODBC connection string DSN=bigquery1; Catalog=publicdata; ExecCatalog=bigquery-e2e. When you run this code, you should fill in your own project ID as the builder.Catalog.

There are a couple of limitations to the ODBC driver. Some ODBC features, like prepared statements and parameter substitution, may not work; you should test them to try them out before relying on them in your code. In addition, by default, when you build a C# program, it is targeted as "anycpu," which means that it can run on either 32-bit or 64-bit platforms. However, the Simba ODBC driver that you install will be tied to a particular processor type. When you build your program, you need to make sure to specify a processor target that matches the processor type of your Simba driver. If the processor type is set to the wrong processor target, you'll get an error that it doesn't match the ODBC driver.

How to Find Out More

To find out more about the Simba ODBC driver, the page at `http://www.simba` `.com/connectors/google-bigquery-odbc` has installation instructions and documentation on what, exactly, is supported. The Quick Start guide shows how the ODBC driver can be used to connect Microsoft Excel to your BigQuery tables. Chapter 12, "External Data Processing," shows how to connect to Excel via the BigQuery Excel Connector. The Simba ODBC driver provides another option.

You should note that the default way to connect to an ODBC source in Excel is to download the entire table; this may not be what you want if you have large tables. As a workaround, you can create a small table with the query results you want to use in Excel. Alternatively, you can use the Microsoft Queries tool provided with Office to create the query that will be used.

The previous example for connecting to the ODBC driver relies on Microsoft's .NET runtime and is written in C#. If you're not a fan of C# but still want to use the ODBC driver, you can try pyodbc, which lets you make ODBC connections from Python. Pyodbc seems to be robust and well supported. It is available at `https://code.google.com/p/pyodbc/`.

JDBC Connection Options

If you write code in Java, the most obvious database connection type to use is JDBC, not ODBC. JDBC performs most of the same types of tasks as ODBC but in a platform-independent way. You shouldn't have to worry about whether you're going to be running on Windows or Linux, let alone whether your processor type is 32 bit versus 64 bit. Unfortunately, although there are a couple of JDBC driver options, they all have limitations.

The most straightforward way to use JDBC with BigQuery is to use the Simba ODBC driver and use the ODBC to JDBC bridge that is built into Java, via the `sun.jdbc.odbc.JdbcOdbcDriver` class. However, according to Oracle's official documentation at `http://docs.oracle.com/javase/7/docs/technotes/` `guides/jdbc/bridge.html`, this class is being deprecated in Java 8. So if you use this class to connect to your ODBC connections, you may have a difficult time upgrading to a newer Java runtime.

There is a native JDBC driver that can connect to BigQuery, developed by StarSchema and released as open source at `https://code.google.com/p/` `starschema-bigquery-jdbc/`. Although this JDBC driver does work, it is not under active development and using it may not be as simple as plugging it into your current system like other JDBC drivers. The good news is that because it is open source, if you need to tweak it, you should be able to update it yourself.

Client-Side Encryption with Encrypted BigQuery

Many potential BigQuery customers aren't comfortable storing their production data in a public cloud. As the value exposed by "the cloud" increases, more people are getting over their hesitations. That said, as a rule of thumb, if you absolutely depend on keeping something secret, you must encrypt it yourself before using any cloud product, and you should decrypt it only in your client. The problem is that in order to run interesting queries, the query engine needs to see unencrypted data. For example, under ordinary circumstances, you can't compute the sum of an encrypted field or order by an encrypted value.

As a side note, if you want to protect your data from a government, your best bet is to store the data in a computer that you never turn on and have sealed in a lead box. If government X wants your data, it will get it. We don't want to get involved in speculation about Google's relationship with any government, other than to say that it is the opinion of the authors that your data is going to be safest from spying, government or otherwise, in Google's cloud.

Encrypted BigQuery (`ebq`) is a tool that enables you to encrypt your data client side and then upload it to BigQuery. The unencrypted source data never gets sent over the network; the encryption key is never sent over the network either. As such, there is no way that anyone at Google can decrypt your data. This means you need to be careful with your key because if you lose it, you'll lose access to your data irrevocably.

You might notice that `ebq` commands look a lot like commands in the `bq` command-line client; this is because Encrypted BigQuery is an open source fork of `bq` that adds in client-side encryption functionality. Although researchers at Google wrote Encrypted BigQuery, it uses only publicly documented interfaces. If you'd like to implement your own client-side encryption, or expand upon what is done in `ebq`, it is relatively easy to do so. You can check out the code or the official documentation at the project website here: `https://code.google.com/p/encrypted-bigquery-client/`.

Installing and Configuring

If you have Python setuptools installed, installing Encrypted BigQuery is as simple as running the command:

```
$ easy_install encrypted_bigquery
```

Of course, nothing is ever that easy. If you're on a Mac, you might need to prefix the command with `sudo`. You might also need to install XCode, which is available from the Mac App Store. If you can't or don't want to use `easy_install`, you can do a manual installation by following the steps at `https://pypi.python.org/pypi/encrypted_bigquery/1.0`.

After you install Encrypted BigQuery, you can run the `ebq` command:

```
$ ebq --helpshort
Python script for interacting with BigQuery using encrypted data.
USAGE: ebq [--global_flags] <command> [--command_flags] [args]

Global flags:

/usr/local/bin/ebq:
  --master_key_filename: The path of the file containing the master key
    to use in encrypting to use in encrypting table data.

Run 'ebq help' to see the list of available commands.
Run 'ebq help <command>' to get help for <command>.
```

Using Encrypted BigQuery

To start, get some data that you want to encrypt. For our examples, we export the public Shakespeare table and re-import it with encryption. Note that you have to download the data locally—the encryption must happen on the client side, so you can't encrypt a file that is already stored in Google Cloud Storage.

```
$ GCS_BUKET=biquery-e2e
$ bq extract --destination_format=NEWLINE_DELIMITED_JSON \
    publicdata:samples.shakespeare \
    gs://${GCS_BUCKET}/shakespeare.json
Waiting on bqjob_ ... (26s) Current status: DONE
$ gsutil cp gs://${GCS_BUCKET}/shakespeare.json .
```

Now look up the schema of the table and save it in a file named `table.txt`.

```
$ bq --format=prettyjson show \
    publicdata:samples.shakespeare > table.txt
$ cat table.txt
...
  "schema": {
    "fields": [
      {
        "name": "word",
        "type": "STRING"
      },
      {
        "name": "word_count",
        "type": "INTEGER"
      },
      {
        "name": "corpus",
        "type": "STRING"
      },
      {
        "name": "corpus_date",
```

```
        "type": "INTEGER"
      }
    ]
  },
...
```

To create an encrypted version, run an `ebq` load job with some special schema options. Edit `table.txt` so that it just has the schema fields, and for each column, indicates what type of encryption you want to do. Save the resulting file as `encrypted_schema.txt` (this file is also distributed with the downloads for this chapter, which can save you some typing.).

```
$ cat encrypted_schema.txt
  [
    {
      "name": "word",
      "type": "STRING",
      "encrypt": "probabilistic"
    },
    {
      "name": "word_count",
      "type": "integer",
      "encrypt": "homomorphic"
    },
    {
      "name": "corpus",
      "type": "STRING",
      "encrypt": "pseudonym"
    },
    {
      "name": "corpus_date",
      "type": "integer",
      "encrypt": "none"
    }
  ]
```

You may notice a new entry in each field: `encrypt`. This tells `ebq` how to encrypt that field of the schema. The following section on encryption modes describes the meaning of these values. First, however, create a dataset that will hold your encrypted tables. The command line is the same as the normal `bq` usage:

```
$ ebq mk ch13
```

To encrypt and load the data, you can use the following command:

```
$ ebq --master_key_filename=ebq.key load \
    --source_format=NEWLINE_DELIMITED_JSON \
    ch13.enc_shakes shakespeare.json encrypted_schema.txt
```

You must specify a master key file via the *master_key_filename* flag; this is the encryption key that will be used. If the encryption key doesn't already exist, a new key file will be created. Otherwise, loading the encrypted table looks just like a standard `bq load` command line. The encryption process can be slow; you should allow plenty of time for the data to be encrypted and the encrypted load operation to run. Because a special type of encryption is being used, it is much slower than you might expect. The Shakespeare table, which is not a large table, may take an hour or so to complete encryption.

After the data has loaded, you can get information about the encrypted table via `ebq show` (which is similar to the `bq show` command):

```
$ ebq --master_key_filename=ebq.key show ch13.enc_shakes
Table bigquery-e2e:ch13.enc_shakes

    Last modified                    Schema                    Total Rows
 ------------------  ----------------------------------------  ------------
   07 Feb 19:45:16    |- word: ciphertext (required)             164656
                      |- word_count: ciphertext (required)
                      |- corpus: ciphertext (required)
                      |- corpus_date: integer (required)
```

If you try to read the data outside of `ebq`, it will look like garbage. The column names get rewritten to contain the encryption type. For example `corpus` becomes `p698000442118338_PSEUDONYM_corpus`. The values themselves get rewritten as Base-64 encoded binary values; `hamlet` in pseudonym encryption becomes something like: `ztYxwmeiiZB/yDPC4W8u6g==` (depending, of course, on the encryption key). Figure 13.3 shows what the `enc_shakes` table looks like in the BigQuery web UI.

Encryption Modes

The encryption modes used in this example are pseudonym, homomorphic, and probabilistic. These don't tell `ebq` which encryption algorithm to use—it always uses standard AES. Instead of describing which encryption algorithm to use, the encryption modes describe desired properties of the encrypted data. The available encryption types are:

- `none`: Not actually encrypted. Use this value for fields you don't care if an attacker sees, or numeric fields that aren't meaningful on their own.

- `pseudonym`: This is the simplest encryption mode that always encrypts the same data the same way, given a particular key. This allows you to check whether two values are equal, lets you JOIN on encrypted values, and lets you GROUP BY the encrypted values. The downside is that this type of field can be vulnerable to attackers who can use correlation attacks or known-frequency attacks to find out the plaintext. Once they have decrypted the value once, they know everywhere it appears.

- `probabalistic`: Encrypts the same text differently every time. This makes it harder for known-plaintext and correlation attacks to operate.

- `homomorphic`: Encrypts numeric fields with special mathematical properties that allow mathematical operations (specifically, sums) to be performed on the encrypted data that yield an encrypted result.

- `searchwords`: Encrypts data such that you can find a particular word within a longer string. Note that each individual word will be encrypted the same way each time, so this can allow known plaintext attacks or linguistic frequency attacks. The advantage of this type of encryption is that it lets you find records that have a particular word embedded in a longer string without the query engine seeing anything except encrypted data.

- `probabilistic_searchwords`: Combines probabilistic encryption with `searchwords` encryption. Encrypts each separate word with probabilistic encryption, so it will be different each time. This allows you to pull out individual words and compare them.

Figure 13.3: Encrypted BigQuery table as seen in the BigQuery web UI

Attacks Against Encrypted Data

We've mentioned a lot of attacks against the encryption; what do these actually mean? An active attacker can glean information about encrypted data without being able to break the encryption directly. For example, say that an attacker has access to an encrypted table and wants to know the words that are used in *Macbeth*. The attacker knows that there are six Shakespeare plays where the name of the play is also a character, one of which is *Macbeth*. He could use this information to find the rows in the table where the corpus field equals the word field. He might also know that of the six plays where the name of the play is also a character, only two were written in the same year: *Macbeth* and *Othello*. So with this information he could narrow the field down to only two plays by finding out which plays had an encrypted year that matched another one. He can further narrow this down to one with the knowledge that *Macbeth* is shorter than *Othello*, so it should have fewer words.

Without decrypting the data, the attacker can now find the exact rows that represent *Macbeth*. Of course, he can't decrypt the words, so you're safe, right? Not quite; say he knows the words in *Othello*. He can also tell which encrypted words are in *Othello* because it is the other one from the same year. He can then find out which words in *Macbeth* are also in *Othello*.

As you can see, by cleverly using outside knowledge and some of the plaintext values, an attacker can start to pick apart your encryption. Encrypted BigQuery has a clever way around this: *probabilistic encryption*. This means that the same data may be encrypted in different ways. The value Macbeth might be encrypted one way in one row and another way in the next row. This would thwart the attacker because he wouldn't be able to perform correlations.

The `"encrypt": "probabilistic"` entry in the encrypted Shakespeare schema instructs ebq to encrypt the field a different way each time it is seen. The downside of probabilistic encryption is that it makes the field a bit harder to use; you can decrypt it only when you select it; you can't do a GROUP BY or an EQUALS check on the field.

However, the corpus field uses *pseudonym encryption*, which encrypts the same value the same way every time. Pseudonym encryption is useful for filtering or grouping by values. For example, you can GROUP BY and even ORDER BY the corpus field because it uses pseudonym encryption.

```
$ ebq --master_key_filename=ebq.key query "
    SELECT corpus, COUNT(word_count)
    FROM ch13.enc_shakes
    GROUP BY corpus"
```

However, if you group by the word field, you'll get an error because you can't group by something that uses probabilistic encryption, since it is encrypted differently every time.

```
$ ebq --master_key_filename=ebq.key query "
    SELECT word, COUNT(word_count)
```

```
    FROM ch13.enc_shakes
    GROUP BY word"
Error in query string: Cannot GROUP BY probabilistic encryption.
```

Another interesting encryption mode is homomorphic, which can be used only for numeric fields (integers and floats). This tells Encrypted BigQuery to encrypt the fields in a way that you can still do math on them. One downside of encrypting numbers normally is that they no longer act like numbers. That is, the query engine doesn't know how to sum them, for example, unless you decrypt them first. Fear not, homomorphic encryption to the rescue! Although describing the math behind *homomorphic encryption* is beyond the scope of this book, we can say that it is a special encryption form that allows you to add two encrypted values to get their encrypted sum without ever decrypting the data.

There is a special SQL function that the BigQuery query engine implements to allow the addition of encrypted values—PAILLIER_SUM(). Encrypted BigQuery turns your SUM() aggregations over encrypted fields into PAILLIER_SUM(). You can use PAILLIER_SUM on your own to perform homomorphic encryption; you don't need to rely on ebq to do it for you. The following query sums the homomorphically-encrypted field word_count and filters by the pseudonym-encrypted field corpus.

```
$ ebq --master_key_filename=ebq.key query "
    SELECT sum(word_count)
    FROM ch13.enc_shakes
    WHERE corpus = 'hamlet'"
Waiting on bqjob_... (1s) Current status: DONE
+-----------------+
| SUM(word_count) |
+-----------------+
|         32446.0 |
+-----------------+
```

You can see that this is the same value we'd get from computing the sum on the unencrypted table:

```
$ bq query "
    SELECT SUM(word_count)
    FROM publicdata:samples.shakespeare
    WHERE corpus = 'hamlet'"
Waiting on bqjob_... (0s) Current status: DONE
+-------+
|  f0_  |
+-------+
| 32446 |
+-------+
```

For more information on `ebq` and available encryption modes, check out the Encrypted BigQuery docs available from `https://pypi.python.org/pypi/encrypted_bigquery`.

Scientific Data Processing Tools in BigQuery

Sometimes, pure SQL isn't enough for your data analysis needs. Maybe you'd like to train a machine learning model on your data or apply advanced statistical functions to squeeze meaning from your tables. A number of scientific and mathematical processing tools are available to perform these types of analyses.

This section shows how to use BigQuery with two popular free scientific processing applications: R and Pandas. R is a popular programming language and runtime environment for statistical data processing. Pandas, while it is somewhat less ubiquitous than R, has the advantage that it enables you to work directly in Python. If you're already using Python, pandas can be easier to integrate with your existing tools and libraries. Both R and pandas have good support for BigQuery. R can interact with BigQuery via an extension package written by a researcher from Rice University. Pandas, on the other hand, has direct BigQuery support available in the library.

If you use a different tool that doesn't have direct support for BigQuery, it is likely you can connect to BigQuery via ODBC, which makes BigQuery look like any other relational database. The "BigQuery Connectors" section earlier in this chapter has more information to help out in these cases.

BigQuery from R

R is an open-source statistical analysis tool/programming environment that lets you perform powerful analyses without writing a lot of code. The core language has a convenient syntax for manipulating structured data; there is a relatively simple notation that enables you to perform operations over vectors and matrices. R also has a data frame data type that acts like a table for many purposes but can also include additional metadata.

R is a dynamically typed language, which allows various operations to "do the right thing" when they get different types of data as input. If you sum a vector, you'll get a number, but if you sum a table, you'll get a vector of sums of the columns. Conversely, the lack of strong typing can also make it much harder to figure out when something goes wrong. We won't say anything else negative about dynamic typing here for fear of igniting a war between the static and dynamic typing proponents.

One limitation of R, however, is that it requires all the data it operates on to reside in memory. If you want to analyze a billion-row dataset, it is unlikely that you'll have enough memory to handle it. This limitation is important when working with BigQuery; you probably wouldn't want to download an entire BigQuery table at once, and if you could, it likely wouldn't fit in memory.

The real power of R is in the extension packages; there are hundreds of curated open-source extensions that can do sophisticated analyses that range from unsupervised clustering to Bayesian prediction. You can browse the available extension packages and read the documentation at `http://cran.us.r-project.org/web/packages/available_packages_by_name.html`. Many of these extensions are optimized C or Fortran code, which can run orders of magnitude faster than programs written in R. To download and install, `visit http://www.r-project .org` and select the download for your operating system.

Bigrquery Extension

The bigrquery extension enables you to interact with your BigQuery tables from R. Because, in general, your BigQuery tables will be larger than you'll want to manipulate directly in R, bigrquery enables you to run BigQuery queries and download the results as an R data frame. These data frames preserve information about the original table and allow you to manipulate, plot, or further analyze the local copy of the data. They do, however, eagerly download all of the data, which can be slow. A future enhancement to bigrquery may allow you to access data lazily, so you can leave as much of the data as possible in the cloud and download it only when you need it.

Installing Bigrquery

Bigrquery is a standard R extension that lives in CRAN—the central R extension repository. Like any CRAN package, you can install it directly from the R command line by running:

```
> install.packages("bigrquery", dependencies=TRUE)
```

Adding the `dependencies=TRUE` argument should ensure that the transitive dependencies are installed as well. The Rook package is also needed to perform authentication; the rjson package is needed to parse JSON responses coming from BigQuery. These commands will get you the latest bigrquery version from CRAN. To install the latest version released by the tool author, you can install it using `devtools`:

```
> install.packages("devtools", dependencies=TRUE)
> devtools::install_github("assertthat")
> devtools::install_github("bigrquery")
```

After bigrquery is installed, you will need to perform authentication. Authentication is triggered the first time you try to run a query; in this case, just run a dummy query to force authentication to occur.

```
> library(bigrquery)
> billing_project <- "bigquery-e2e"
> query_exec("publicdata", "samples", "SELECT 17",
             billing=billing_project)
starting httpd help server ... done
Waiting for authentication in browser...
```

This pops up a browser window that prompts you to log in (if you're not already logged in) and asks you if you want to allow access to your BigQuery Data. Press Allow. Then it displays a page that says Authentication Complete - You Can Now Close This Page and Return to R. When you return to the R window, you should see:

```
starting httpd help server ... done
Waiting for authentication in browser...
Authentication complete.

  f0_
1  17
```

If you see the result 17, it means that bigrquery is working correctly.

Running Your First BigQuery Query from R

Now that you have bigrquery installed and can authenticate with BigQuery, try running a simple query:

```
> query <- "SELECT corpus, max(corpus_date) as date, count(*) as c
  FROM [publicdata:samples.shakespeare]
  GROUP BY corpus ORDER BY date asc"
> results <- query_exec("publicdata", "samples",
                        query, billing=billing_project)
```

The publicdata and samples arguments to the query_exec function may be surprising. The first two positional arguments are the default project and data-set for tables referenced in a query. As of the current version of bigrquery, you need to specify these even if you use fully qualified table names (for example, publicdata:samples.shakespeare) in the query. The advantage of specifying the defaults is that it makes your queries simpler because you can specify only the table name, not the project or dataset. To specify which project gets billed for the query, you should use the billing argument. The authenticated user must be a member of the project team to run queries, so you can't run queries as publicdata. If you don't pass the billed project, BigQuery attributes the query to the project ID passed as the first positional argument.

After the query completes, the entire results will be downloaded into an R data frame. For queries returning large results, this can take a lot of time and space. Even though this query only returns 42 rows and 3 columns, it is still a good idea to use `head()` rather than `print()` to display the results. If there are more than a few dozen results, it won't be particularly useful to list them all to the screen, so `head()` will just show the first few rows.

```
> dim(results)
[1] 42   3
> head(results)
          corpus date    c
1        various    0 1349
2        sonnets    0 3677
3    1kinghenryvi 1590 4441
4    3kinghenryvi 1590 4076
5    2kinghenryvi 1590 4683
6 kingrichardiii 1592 4713
```

R Example: Predicting Shakespeare

Now that you've seen how to use bigrquery to run BigQuery queries in R, let's try a more interesting example: See if we can predict, based on the words in a Shakespeare play, whether the play is a comedy, a history, or a tragedy. This type of classification is an example of something that is easy to do in R but cannot be done directly from SQL.

We use a naïve Bayesian classifier to classify the plays. Although this might sound, well, naïve, this is a powerful prediction mechanism. For example, naïve Bayes is the basis for most spam filters. If you think about it, predicting whether a play is a comedy, history, or tragedy from word usage is similar to predicting whether an e-mail is spam. Perhaps in the 17th century, people worried about "unsolicited histories" that they'd have to sit through when what they actually wanted was a light comedy. In that case, our classifier would have been able to tell them whether they should stay home instead.

To start, first find a filtered list of all the words used in Shakespeare plays. Exclude the words used in every play because they don't provide any predictive power. Exclude, also, the words that are used only in a single play because they could lead to overfitting the data. Here's the query that gets all the words in Shakespeare that show up in more than 1 and fewer than 35 plays:

```
SELECT word, word_count, corpus
FROM [publicdata:samples.shakespeare]
WHERE word IN (
  SELECT word
  FROM (
```

```
        SELECT word, COUNT(*) as corpus_count
        FROM [publicdata:samples.shakespeare]
        GROUP BY word
        HAVING corpus_count > 1 and corpus_count < 36
    ))
```

This can serve as the core of your query. There is a technique in Information Retrieval called TF-IDF, which means that you compute the term frequency (TF) and multiply by the inverse document frequency (IDF). In other words, for each word in the corpus, you divide the number of times that word occurs by the number of total words in the document. This mechanism lets you compare relative frequencies for documents that are different sizes. You can apply TF-IDF to your Shakespeare results by dividing each word count by the number of words in the corresponding play:

```
$ QUERY="
SELECT s1.word AS word,
    10000 * s1.word_count/s2.total_words AS tfidf,
    s1.corpus as corpus
FROM (
SELECT word, word_count, corpus
FROM [publicdata:samples.shakespeare]
WHERE word IN (
  SELECT word
  FROM (
    SELECT word, COUNT(*) AS corpus_count
    FROM [publicdata:samples.shakespeare]
    GROUP BY word
    HAVING corpus_count > 1 AND corpus_count < 36
))) s1
JOIN (
  SELECT corpus, SUM(word_count) AS total_words
  FROM [publicdata:samples.shakespeare]
  GROUP BY corpus
  ) s2
ON s1.corpus = s2.corpus"
```

You could do the rest of the work in R, but there are still a lot of results here to import directly (more than 100,000). So you can perform one more step in BigQuery—pivot in the corpus so that you have one row per word and one column for each play; the values will be the computed TF-IDF for the word/play combination. Now save the query results as the table ch13.shakespeare_tfidf to make it easier to refer to in the future. You can do this with the following command:

```
$ bq query --destination_table=ch13.shakespeare_tfidf "${QUERY}"
```

The final query to perform the pivot is a bit verbose because you need to list each play you're interested in as the column name. Note that you're going to ignore anything that isn't a comedy, history, or tragedy (the sonnets and the poem "Venus and Adonis," for example). Here is the full query to compute the pivoted TF-IDF values:

```
> query <- "
SELECT word,
SUM(IF (corpus == '1kinghenryiv', tfidf, 0)) AS onekinghenryiv,
SUM(IF (corpus == '1kinghenryvi', tfidf, 0)) AS onekinghenryvi,
SUM(IF (corpus == '2kinghenryiv', tfidf, 0)) AS twokinghenryiv,
SUM(IF (corpus == '2kinghenryvi', tfidf, 0)) AS twokinghenryvi,
SUM(IF (corpus == '3kinghenryvi', tfidf, 0)) AS threekinghenryvi,
SUM(IF (corpus == 'allswellthatendswell', tfidf, 0))
    AS allswellthatendswell,
SUM(IF (corpus == 'antonyandcleopatra', tfidf, 0))
    AS antonyandcleopatra,
SUM(IF (corpus == 'asyoulikeit', tfidf, 0)) AS asyoulikeit,
SUM(IF (corpus == 'comedyoferrors', tfidf, 0)) AS comedyoferrors,
SUM(IF (corpus == 'coriolanus', tfidf, 0)) AS coriolanus,
SUM(IF (corpus == 'cymbeline', tfidf, 0)) AS cymbeline,
SUM(IF (corpus == 'hamlet', tfidf, 0)) AS hamlet,
SUM(IF (corpus == 'juliuscaesar', tfidf, 0)) AS juliuscaesar,
SUM(IF (corpus == 'kinghenryv', tfidf, 0)) AS kinghenryv,
SUM(IF (corpus == 'kinghenryviii', tfidf, 0)) AS kinghenryviii,
SUM(IF (corpus == 'kingjohn', tfidf, 0)) AS kingjohn,
SUM(IF (corpus == 'kinglear', tfidf, 0)) AS kinglear,
SUM(IF (corpus == 'kingrichardii', tfidf, 0)) AS kingrichardii,
SUM(IF (corpus == 'kingrichardiii', tfidf, 0)) AS kingrichardiii,
SUM(IF (corpus == 'loverscomplaint', tfidf, 0)) AS loverscomplaint,
SUM(IF (corpus == 'loveslabourslost', tfidf, 0)) AS loveslabourslost,
SUM(IF (corpus == 'macbeth', tfidf, 0)) AS macbeth,
SUM(IF (corpus == 'measureformeasure', tfidf, 0))
    AS measureformeasure,
SUM(IF (corpus == 'merchantofvenice', tfidf, 0)) AS merchantofvenice,
SUM(IF (corpus == 'merrywivesofwindsor', tfidf, 0))
    AS merrywivesofwindsor,
SUM(IF (corpus == 'midsummersnightsdream', tfidf, 0))
    AS midsummersnightsdream,
SUM(IF (corpus == 'muchadoaboutnothing', tfidf, 0))
    AS muchadoaboutnothing,
SUM(IF (corpus == 'othello', tfidf, 0)) AS othello,
SUM(IF (corpus == 'periclesprinceoftyre', tfidf, 0))
    AS periclesprinceoftyre,
SUM(IF (corpus == 'romeoandjuliet', tfidf, 0)) AS romeoandjuliet,
SUM(IF (corpus == 'tamingoftheshrew', tfidf, 0)) AS tamingoftheshrew,
SUM(IF (corpus == 'tempest', tfidf, 0)) AS tempest,
SUM(IF (corpus == 'timonofathens', tfidf, 0)) AS timonofathens,
SUM(IF (corpus == 'titusandronicus', tfidf, 0)) AS titusandronicus,
SUM(IF (corpus == 'troilusandcressida', tfidf, 0))
    AS troilusandcressida,
```

```
SUM(IF (corpus == 'twelfthnight', tfidf, 0)) AS twelfthnight,
SUM(IF (corpus == 'twogentlemenofverona', tfidf, 0))
    AS twogentlemenofverona,
SUM(IF (corpus == 'winterstale', tfidf, 0)) AS winterstale,
FROM [ch13.shakespeare_tfidf]
GROUP BY word"
```

You can set this as the query in R and fetch the results:

```
> results <- query_exec("bigquery-e2e", "ch13", query,
                        billing=billing_project,
                        max_pages=Inf)
3.6 megabytes processed
Retrieving data: 28.7s
> summary(results)
     word            onekinghenryiv      onekinghenryvi      twokinghenryiv
 Length:16281    Min.   :  0.0000    Min.   :  0.000    Min.   :  0.0000
 Class :character 1st Qu.:  0.0000    1st Qu.:  0.000    1st Qu.:  0.0000
 Mode  :character Median :  0.0000    Median :  0.000    Median :  0.0000
                  Mean   :  0.7842    Mean   :  0.738    Mean   :  0.8419
                  3rd Qu.:  0.0000    3rd Qu.:  0.000    3rd Qu.:  0.0000
                  Max.   :631.0000    Max.   :435.000    Max.   :614.0000
...
```

This command creates a data frame with more than 16,000 rows, one row for each word that is used in more than one play but not all of them. The first column is the word; the subsequent columns are the TF-IDF values of the word in each of the plays. You can drop the first column at this point because you won't need to know which word it is to perform the prediction. However, you can store the word as the name of the row in the data frame in case you need it again.

```
> rownames(results) <- results$word
> results$word <- NULL
```

Next, you need to know whether a particular play is a comedy, a history, or a tragedy. You can look this information up from the list at http://www .opensourceshakespeare.org/views/plays/plays.php and compute a lookup table by hand:

```
> categories_str = "
corpus, type
onekinghenryiv, history
onekinghenryvi, history
twokinghenryiv, history
twokinghenryvi, history
threekinghenryvi, history
allswellthatendswell, comedy
antonyandcleopatra, tragedy
asyoulikeit, comedy
comedyoferrors, comedy
```

```
    coriolanus, tragedy
    cymbeline, tragedy
    hamlet, tragedy
    juliuscaesar, tragedy
    kinghenryv, history
    kinghenryviii, history
    kingjohn, history
    kinglear, history
    kingrichardii, history
    kingrichardiii, history
    loverscomplaint, comedy
    loveslabourslost, comedy
    macbeth, tragedy
    measureformeasure, comedy
    merchantofvenice, comedy
    merrywivesofwindsor, comedy
    midsummersnightsdream, comedy
    muchadoaboutnothing, comedy
    othello, tragedy
    periclesprinceoftyre, history
    romeoandjuliet, tragedy
    tamingoftheshrew, comedy
    tempest, comedy
    timonofathens, tragedy
    titusandronicus, tragedy
    troilusandcressida, tragedy
    twelfthnight, comedy
    twogentlemenofverona, comedy
    winterstale, comedy"
> categories = read.csv(text=categories_str)
> summary(categories)
                        corpus            type
 allswellthatendswell: 1    comedy :15
 antonyandcleopatra  : 1    history:12
 asyoulikeit         : 1    tragedy:11
 comedyoferrors      : 1
 coriolanus          : 1
 cymbeline           : 1
 (Other)             :32
```

Now do the same thing with the play names in the categories table that you did in the results table—you can use the play name as the row name and drop the first row:

```
> rownames(categories) <- categories$corpus
> categories$corpus <- NULL
> summary(categories)
```

Now, you have all the data you need to run the naïve Bayesian classifier. There are a couple of different implementations of the naïve Bayes in R; the example uses the one from the e1071 package. You need to make sure it is installed first before you can use it:

```
> install.packages("e1071")
. . .
> library(e1071)
```

You can train your naïve Bayes classifier by giving it a table of plays with their TF-IDF values and the actual values we're looking for (that is, whether the play is a comedy, history, or tragedy). Note that you need to transpose the results because the `naiveBayes` function expects that each row will be a different sample, with the columns being the features, whereas your results table has the columns as samples (that is, plays) and the rows as features (that is, TF-IDF values for a particular word). In R, you can transpose with the `t()` function:

```
> classifier <- naiveBayes(t(results), categories[,1])
```

Finally, with the classifier trained, you can predict whether a play is a comedy, history, or tragedy with the `predict()` method:

```
> predictions <- predict(classifier, t(results))
> predictions
 [1] history history history history history comedy  tragedy comedy
 [9] comedy  tragedy tragedy tragedy tragedy history history history
[17] history history history comedy  comedy  tragedy comedy  comedy
[25] comedy  comedy  comedy  tragedy history tragedy comedy  comedy
[33] tragedy tragedy tragedy comedy  comedy  comedy
```

To test the validity of your predictions, you can check against the actual values:

```
> table(predictions, categories[,1], dnn=list('predicted','actual'))
           actual
predicted   comedy  history  tragedy
   comedy      15        0        0
   history       0       12        0
   tragedy       0        0       11
```

We can see here that the classifier predicted correctly for all Shakespeare plays you gave it. You might notice that we're cheating here a little bit—we're predicting over the same data that was used for training. In practice, you'd want to keep a holdout set from the training data or perform cross-validation, but that is beyond the scope of this example.

Finding Out More Information

CRAN is generally the first place you should look to find out more about anything in R. The bigrquery package on CRAN at `http://cran.us.r-project .org/web/packages/bigrquery/index.html` has documentation of the available commands and how to use them. This will likely be more up to date than this book, so be sure to check it out.

The version of bigrquery on CRAN may not be the most recent, however. Bigrquery is currently under active development; the Open Source project for bigrquery is on github at `https://github.com/hadley/bigrquery`. If you'd like to read the source code to see how bigrquery works (or even submit a patch to add new functionality), you can check out the github bigrquery project. There is nothing mysterious or magical; the most interesting parts may be the OAuth2 authentication and the job management code. This code is all open source, licensed as GPL v3, so you can copy it and make changes and extensions to it as you want.

Hadley Wickham, the creator of the bigrquery package, also has a more ambitious project called dplyr that can use BigQuery (among other back ends). Dplyr simplifies applying operations to local or remote tabular data. If you're interested in using BigQuery on R, you might also be interested in checking it out—it is available on CRAN at `http://cran.us.r-project.org/web/packages/dplyr/index.html`.

Python Pandas and BigQuery

One of the downsides of R is that it is poorly integrated with things outside of scientific and statistical analysis. If you want to perform unsupervised clustering, it is great, but if you want to integrate it with other code you have written, it can be more difficult. R has fantastic library support for scientific applications but lacks an ecosystem that can let you do things like request and parse data from a website as easily as in other languages. Although R is a Turing-complete programming language, nobody writes much code in R unless they have to, so it remains a niche language.

Scientific Programming in Python

Python is used in a wide range of general-purpose programming environments. It lacks, however, the kind of scientific and mathematical functions that you get with R. Because Python is general purpose and a hugely popular language, people have started to make up the gap between Python and R by adding a number of libraries, most of which are implemented in C++ or Fortran for performance reasons. Here is a list of the primary Python mathematical and scientific libraries:

- **NumPy:** Fast matrix manipulation and linear algebra
- **SciPy:** More scientific computing goodies
- **SymPy:** Symbolic math library
- **Pandas:** Data analysis library

These libraries provide a lot of mathematical and scientific functions in Python and make up some of the gap between Python and R (or even commercial scientific computing environments such as Matlab or Mathematica). These don't, however, provide the syntactic sugar that makes R so easy to work with. Although writing Python code may be easier than writing C++, the Python command shell is not as nice for scientific workloads as the R shell. But Python has a library for that, too; iPython provides a convenient notebook interface that enables you to save and annotate your environment, much like the R shell.

But what if you want some functionality that is only available in R, or functionality that you're used to in R and for which you don't want to learn a new method? For these cases in which you really want to use something in R, there is the RPy library, which enables you to call out to R functions from within your Python code. RPy can turn pandas data frame into an R data frame automatically. You can also use RPy to plot your graphs via R's nice plotting functions, or you can use the matplotlib library to plot graphs directly from Python.

Pandas BigQuery Module

The Python data analytics library, pandas, has an experimental module called `pandas.io.gbq` that enables you to query your BigQuery tables and turn the results into pandas data frames. This library is functionally similar to the bigrquery package in R. Most BigQuery operations other than queries need to be done outside of the Python environment, however, although there is limited support for creating a BigQuery table from a Python data frame.

Installing Pandas and Related Dependencies

The installation method to use for installing pandas can depend highly on your operating system and version. Python has a number of package managers, from pip to setuptools to MacPorts to Anaconda, any of which can be used to install pandas. On Mac OS X, running `easy_install pandas` may be sufficient. However, if you want to use SciPy (which is used in the examples in this section), you might need to download and install additional components, such as XCode and even Fortran libraries.

Anaconda is a prepackaged suite of Python scientific computing and data analysis tools. This may be the easiest option, since it provides everything you need, from pandas to iPython to SciPy and NumPy. Even if you already have some of the components, Anaconda can be easier than trying to manage all the configuration bits and pieces that you'd otherwise need. One downside of Anaconda is that it is a separate installation; this means that you need to install the Google Cloud SDK inside of an Anaconda terminal window to get it to integrate correctly. (This last point may be addressed by the time you read this, however.)

Running Your First BigQuery Query with Pandas

The `pandas.io.gbq` module performs authorization in a different way from most other tools; it decides to let somebody else take care of the problem. The `gbq` module reuses the authorization information saved by the `bq` command-line tool. It also reuses the default project ID set by `bq`, so you don't have to pass a project ID with all your requests. If you have not installed `bq` or have not authorized your Google account using it, you should follow the instructions in Chapter 3, "Getting Started with BigQuery."

Assuming you have authenticated with `bq` or the Google Cloud SDK, it is easy to run a query in pandas:

```
$ python
>>> from pandas.io import gbq
>>> data_frame = gbq.read_gbq(
   'SELECT COUNT(*) FROM [publicdata:samples.shakespeare]')
Waiting on bqjob_r2f6dcee956cff5bd_0000014460593881_1 ... (0s)
Current status: DONE
>>> print "%s" % (data_frame,)
     f0_
0  164656

[1 rows x 1 columns]
```

If the `gbq.read_gbq()` command works without returning an error, then you're all set to begin using BigQuery from pandas.

Pandas Example: Clustering Shakespeare

In the R example, we tried to classify Shakespeare texts into genres; whether they are tragedies, histories, or comedies. To do so, we needed to know the genre in advance for some of the plays in order to train our machine learning model. Wouldn't it be nice if we didn't have to know any genres in advance, but we'd still be able to classify the plays? We could divide up the plays into the "natural" buckets and go back and see if those buckets have any real-world meaning. That is, instead of providing classifications at the beginning, we can provide them after we've already sorted the plays into buckets. Of course, the buckets may not correspond to genre, but they might also show some hidden similarity between the plays, or align themselves in other ways, like early or late plays or even plays that were written by Shakespeare's evil twin brother.

This type of analysis is called unsupervised learning, and there are a lot of different algorithms you can use to approach the problem. One of the standard algorithms is called *k-means clustering*, which groups unlabeled data into a fixed (k) number of clusters. K-means clustering is provided in the `scipy.clustering.vq` package.

We'll use a k of 2, which means we're going to be dividing up the plays into two different buckets. We don't have a lot of data (there are only 38 plays that we know about), so dividing up the plays into a lot of clusters may not be particularly instructive. After clustering, we'll see if this binary division makes any intuitive sense.

The Python file `clustering_shakespeare.py` has the entire script for computing the clusters, but we will walk you through the individual pieces. Start with the import statements:

```
>>> from numpy import array
>>> from numpy import asarray
>>> from pandas import DataFrame
>>> from pandas.io import gbq
>>> from scipy.cluster.vq import vq, kmeans, whiten
```

Note that you need numpy, pandas, and scipy to be installed. If they're not, or they have problems, you'll see errors either here or when you try to use them. A bit of forewarning—if you don't have everything installed correctly, the errors can be a bit cryptic because the thing that fails to load often isn't the thing that is missing. If module A imports module B, you might see module A fail to load, but module B might be the missing one, and you may not get an error message telling you why.

Next, after you verify that you have all the libraries that you need, run a BigQuery query to get the data you need:

```
>>> query = """
    SELECT word,
      SUM(if (corpus == '1kinghenryiv', tfidf, 0)) as onekinghenryiv,
...
      SUM(if (corpus == 'winterstale', tfidf, 0)) as winterstale,
    FROM [ch13.shakespeare_tfidf]
    GROUP BY word
    """
>>> data_frame = gbq.read_gbq(query)
```

This is the same query from the Predicting Shakespeare example in the section on R; it relies on the same intermediate table, `ch13.shakespeare_tfidf`, which contains relative frequencies for all the words in all Shakespeare's plays. You can run the query using the pandas `gbq.read_gbq()` method and save the result in a data frame. A pandas data frame is similar to an R data frame; it is a bit like a matrix but can have additional metadata, such as column and row names.

The first column of the data frame is `word`; this contains nearly every word that is used somewhere in Shakespeare. The subsequent columns are the normalized frequencies of the corresponding word's usage in each of Shakespeare's plays. The column names (other than `word`) are the names of the plays. You don't actually use the word in the clustering step; the learning process doesn't know anything about words; it just cares about the relative frequencies that make up the feature matrix. Because you don't need the actual words, you can drop the `word` column from the data frame.

```
>>> del data_frame['word']
```

To run k-means clustering, you need to turn the data frame into an array where each row is a vector describing the sample. That is, you want each play to represent one row, while the word frequencies are columns. To coerce the data into this format, you can create a numpy array containing the transposed results:

```
>>> features = asarray(data_frame.T)
```

After you create the features matrix, pass it to the clustering function:

```
>>> codes, _ = kmeans(features, 2)
```

K is set to 2, which means you're just trying to find two clusters. Another way of looking at it is that you're creating a hyperplane dividing the Shakespeare word frequency matrix into two parts, where the hyperplane is defined as all the points that are equidistant from the two cluster centroids. If that sounds confusing, don't worry; it was just an excuse to get to write the word "hyperplane."

The first result from the `kmeans()` function is the "code book"; this is a k by N matrix (where k is the number of clusters and N is the number of samples) that defines the centroids of the clusters. In this case, the code book contains two columns, one for each cluster. The rows contain the expected frequency of each word in the play for the corresponding cluster.

After you find the two clusters, sort the Shakespeare plays into which cluster they are closest to. You can use the `vq()` (short for "vector quantization") method for this.

```
>>> assignments, _ = vq(features, codes)
>>> results = {
      'play' : array(data_frame.columns.values),
      'cluster' : assignments}
```

The assignments will be an array of cluster indexes indicating which cluster each sample was closest to. That is, there will be a value of 0 or 1 for each Shakespeare play that says whether that play was in the first or second cluster.

A DataFrame is pandas' version of R's data frame that represents a matrix of values with some additional metadata. You can match the cluster with the play name with a little bit of DataFrame magic; combine the column names from the result of the BigQuery query (which are the play names) with the cluster assignments and then sort by the cluster. The sort operation enables you to see all the plays that showed up in the same cluster, which can give you a good picture of which plays were assigned to which cluster.

```
>>> result_frame = DataFrame.from_dict(results).sort(['cluster',
                                                       'play'])
```

The assignment matrix is reproduced here:

	cluster	play
5	0	allswellthatendswell
6	0	antonyandcleopatra
7	0	asyoulikeit
8	0	comedyoferrors
9	0	coriolanus
10	0	cymbeline
11	0	hamlet
12	0	juliuscaesar
19	0	loverscomplaint
20	0	loveslabourslost
21	0	macbeth
22	0	measureformeasure
23	0	merchantofvenice
24	0	merrywivesofwindsor
25	0	midsummersnightsdream
26	0	muchadoaboutnothing
27	0	othello
28	0	periclesprinceoftyre
29	0	romeoandjuliet
30	0	tamingoftheshrew
31	0	tempest
32	0	timonofathens
33	0	titusandronicus
34	0	troilusandcressida
35	0	twelfthnight
36	0	twogentlemenofverona
37	0	winterstale
13	1	kinghenryv
14	1	kinghenryviii
15	1	kingjohn
16	1	kinglear
17	1	kingrichardii
18	1	kingrichardiii
0	1	onekinghenryiv
1	1	onekinghenryvi
4	1	threekinghenryvi
2	1	twokinghenryiv
3	1	twokinghenryvi

[38 rows x 2 columns]

This is a cool result—given no information other than relative word frequencies of various plays, the clustering algorithm has divided up Shakespeare's output into two buckets—one that contains all the histories, and one that contains all of the other plays. This was done without saying which plays are histories or even what history means.

Visualizing Data in BigQuery

One of the problems with Big Data is that it becomes difficult to build an intuition about your data. If you have a thousand rows in a table, you can scan it, see whether one column is always numeric, or whether there are `null`s, and if there are, figure out what the `null`s represent. When you have a million rows, however, it is harder to get a feel for the data—you're not likely to want to read through all the data.

Data visualization tools can help you make sense of your data; good ones make it easy to "see" various aspects of data, interactively. If you want to plot one column by another, it is usually quite trivial, or if you want to get statistics about unique values, the tool usually computes them for you. Most data visualization tools work great on your million row table; however, if you have a billion rows, they may start to take minutes to compute simple values, or hours to produce a graph.

There are a number of data visualization tools that combine with BigQuery to get the performance you'd expect from a small dataset on your Big Data tables of virtually any size. This section introduces two of them that take two different approaches to data visualization: Tableau and Bime.

Visualizing Your BigQuery Data with Tableau

Tableau has quickly become the gold standard for data visualization; it makes it easy to get a feel for your data in a way that is difficult when you're just writing queries. You can drag and drop fields to plot one against another, apply aggregations, and so on. It has a lot of automatic intelligence built in so that it can pick the best type of graph for your data.

Tableau's main visualization product, Tableau Desktop, is a thick client. This means that a lot of the visualization work is being done on your machine, rather than in the cloud. At a time when everything seems to be moving to the cloud, this feels like a bit of a throwback. However, there are good reasons to do work on the client: It enables you to build much snappier visualizations because you don't have to wait until some remote server decides to process your request.

There is a downside to performing the work on the client—it usually means that you need the data to exist on the client as well. For big datasets, requiring client-side data can mean spending a lot of time reading your data (especially if that data is stored in the cloud).

When interacting with BigQuery (and other Big Data sources), however, Tableau takes a hybrid approach: It issues BigQuery queries to perform aggregations and then downloads the results of those queries locally. This means that only the query results need to be transferred to the client, and it doesn't need to rerun the BigQuery queries unless the aggregations change. In this model, many data manipulations can be done with only local data.

There are a couple of potential "gotchas" when using BigQuery with Tableau. The first is that you don't have much control over the SQL that is generated. Tableau currently uses the Simba BigQuery ODBC driver to issue standard ODBC requests (as Standard SQL). This doesn't allow usage of specialized BigQuery SQL syntax, such as using the EACH keyword to group by a field that has a lot of distinct values. Tableau treats BigQuery like a standard data source, so it doesn't have many specializations that would make BigQuery perform better.

It is possible that by the time you read this, Tableau will have released a custom connector that can more effectively handle BigQuery data sources. Tableau has specialized data connectors for other data sources (for Apache Hive, for example). A specialized connector would mean that you wouldn't need the Simba ODBC driver; you could run in environments in which the ODBC driver isn't available (such as on a Mac).

Tableau has a free 14-day trial that you can use to try out the BigQuery integration. To sign up, just navigate to http://www.tableausoftware.com/ in your web browser and click the Free Trial button. Select the Tableau Desktop option and follow instructions from there to download and install the software.

WARNING: VISUALIZATION TOOLS CAN RUN A LOT OF QUERIES

In Tableau, when you drag and drop a field to indicate you want it to represent the rows of your chart, or change the aggregation from SUM() to COUNT(), it issues a query. If you tweak the parameters a lot, it can cause you to run a lot of queries. If you run a lot of queries over a large table, it is going to get expensive.

Other Visualization tools such as BIME, have the same issue. They trade off ease of use for understanding exactly which queries are going to be executed and when. Visualization tools frequently issue queries to get statistics about certain columns, or in response to interactions you make in the UI.

The automatic caching that BigQuery does can help out here—if a query has already been issued within the last 24 hours, the cached results will be retuned rather than running a separate query. That said, if you have billions of rows in your table, you should know that every time you tweak something it might cost you money.

Connecting Tableau to Your BigQuery Tables

Tableau has built-in support for BigQuery; to connect to a BigQuery table, follow these steps:

1. Open Tableau to a blank workspace; then click Connect to Data. This opens a menu that lists the different types of data sources Tableau can communicate with.

2. Under the On a Server menu, select Google BigQuery. This pops up a browser window that prompts you to log in to your Google account.

3. Log in to your Google account, and accept the OAuth2 prompt asking you whether you want to allow Tableau Desktop to have access to your BigQuery data. After you accept, your OAuth2 refresh token will be cached, and you won't have to log in again unless you reinstall or revoke the token. Tableau does not ever see your login credentials. Figure 13.4 shows the prompt to allow Tableau access to your data and shows the Connect to Data" dialog box in the background.

Figure 13.4: Granting Tableau access to your BigQuery data

4. After granting authorization, you'll be prompted for which table you'd like to use. For this example, use the public Shakespeare table. Select `publicdata` from the Project menu and `samples` as the dataset. You can select Projects and Datasets from a list, but you need to type the table name in manually. Type **shakespeare** for the table name and press OK. It automatically creates a connector name to use for the table based on the information you entered. Figure 13.5 shows the populated connection dialog box.

Figure 13.5: Tableau BigQuery Connection dialog box

5. After creating the connection, you see another prompt asking how you want to connect to BigQuery. You should select the Connect live and check the Always Do this For BigQuery box. This tells Tableau to leave as much of the data as possible on the BigQuery servers. You almost certainly want this option when dealing with large tables because the other alternative is to download all your data locally.

Creating a Visualization

At this point you should connect to your BigQuery tables in Tableau—so how do you make pretty graphs and visualizations? Although a lesson on how to use Tableau is beyond the scope of this book, it is intuitive to use. We will walk you through producing a simple visualization that shows how easy it can be to create graphs that extract meaning from your data.

Tableau is a drag-and-drop environment; if you don't like using the mouse, you might just have to put away your mouse-o-phobia for a little bit if you want to create fantastic pictures. In order to graph anything, you need at least two fields; the graph lets you see how the first field varies in relation to the second one. This is true for almost any kind of graph: A bar graph plots a name against a height, and a line graph plots an ordered series against another value. Even a pie chart needs at least two variables: the names of the pie slices and their sizes.

You're actually not limited to plotting two variables in Tableau; you can use color, size, or even tooltip text as other dimensions. And you're not limited to pie, line, or bar graphs either; if you have geographic data, you can easily plot the data on a map in dozens of different ways. You're also not limited to values that are actually present in raw form in your data. Tableau can perform a number of different types of aggregations: SUM(), COUNT(), and so on and can apply them automatically to make the graph make more sense. Probably the best way to figure out what is available is just to play with it for a while and see what you come up with.

As a demonstration, however, we can create a bar chart of the word count of each Shakespeare corpus in the Shakespeare dataset. The fields from the table are divided up into dimensions and measures; the dimensions are the text fields and the measures are the numeric fields. Tableau automatically categorizes fields into dimensions and measures based on statistics about the fields such as number of unique values and whether they are numeric types. For the Shakespeare table, the dimensions are `corpus` and `word`; the measures are `corpus_date` and `word_count`. There are a couple of other special dimensions and measures, such as Measure names, Number of Records, and Measure Values, which aren't in the actual dataset but can be computed on-the-fly. You can drag the measures and dimensions between the boxes to create visualizations.

Did Shakespeare Get Lazy as He Got Older?

As a way of demonstrating the use of Tableau on BigQuery data, let's see if we can figure out whether Shakespeare got wordier as his career progressed, or whether he got lazy and started wrapping up his plays as soon as possible. You could, of course, do this with a query; but because the results are multidimensional (play versus word count versus date), it can be tricky to grok the patterns from a table of results by itself. You can get this information in a single numerical result using a correlation query:

```
SELECT CORR(count, date)
FROM (
  SELECT SUM(word_count) AS count, MIN(corpus_date) AS date
  FROM publicdata:samples.shakespeare
  GROUP BY corpus)
```

This returns 0.41—a high positive correlation. Sounds like maybe Shakespeare stopped listening to his editor telling him to "wrap it up" after he got a little bit of fame. Not quite, however. If you look at the extreme values of the data, there are two corpora with a `corpus_date` of 0: sonnets and various. Because they were written over a period of time, there is no one date that makes the most sense; whoever created the dataset has the date set to 0. The collected sonnets are shorter than any play, and the various other writings are only one-fifth as long as the shortest play. These two values are going to completely skew the correlation calculation; if you remove them by adding the filter WHERE corpus_date > 0, you see that the actual correlation coefficient is actually negative, although quite small: −0.21.

This mistake highlights why data visualization is so powerful; if you rely on the raw numbers without looking closely at them, you run the risk of making mistakes if you have outliers or data you don't expect. Data visualization, in general, makes these types of issues much more obvious. To see this, walk through how you could visualize this relationship in Tableau.

To start out, drag the corpus measure to the Columns box. This indicates that you want to plot something against the Shakespeare corpus name (for example, *Hamlet* or *Merchant of Venice*). To generate a nice bar chart, all you need to do is drag word_count from the Measures pane to the Rows box. It automatically selects SUM as the aggregation and plots the corpus name as the bar label versus the total word count of the play. From this, it is easy to see that *Hamlet* and *Richard III* have a lot of words, whereas *The Comedy of Errors* is significantly shorter (which may be, in fact, how you like your Shakespeare). This graph displayed in Figure 13.6 is the equivalent of running the query:

```
SELECT corpus, SUM(word_count)
FROM [publicdata:samples.shakespeare]
GROUP BY corpus
```

If you'd rather see the number of distinct words, you can right-click the SUM(word_count) icon and change the aggregation to CNT(word_count) via the Measure submenu. Remember that each row in the underlying table has a single word and the number of times it appears in a particular corpus. The sum is the total number of words in the corpus; the count is the number of *different* words.

Now add another dimension to the table (or actually, another measure). Drag the corpus_date measure to the Color box in the Marks window. This tells Tableau to let the color of the bar be proportional to the value of that measure. A darker bar will correspond to a later date, a lighter one will correspond to an earlier one. Because corpus_date doesn't vary independently for a particular corpus (for example, all records for *Hamlet* will have the same corpus date—the date that Hamlet was published), the aggregation you choose here isn't important—we'll suggest AVG(corpus_date), but you could just as easily use MIN or MAX because all the values for a single corpus will be identical.

The date dimension, however, is going to be skewed by the corpora that you saw earlier that don't have publication dates: various and sonnets don't have a single date, so they're recorded as 0. You can see this immediately because it skews the coloring so that you can't see the difference in gradations between the other plays. To fix the skew, you can change the scaling. Right-click AVG(corpus_date), choose Edit Colors, then click Advanced. In the Advanced menu, you can set a custom range; set it to start at 1590 and end at 1620, which is the range of Shakespeare's writing career. After you make this adjustment, you should see lighter bars for the earlier plays, such as *King Henry VI*, and darker ones for the later ones, such as *The Tempest*. Figure 13.6 shows this graph; see if you can tell whether Shakespeare got longer-winded as he got older.

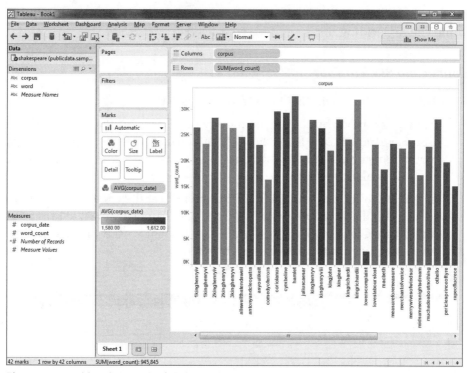

Figure 13.6: Tableau bar graph of Shakespeare corpus versus word count

Visualizing Your BigQuery Data with BIME

Do you find it a little bit odd that to visualize your data in the cloud, you have to install software on a Windows desktop machine to access your data? After all, your data lives in the cloud, so why can't you access it via the cloud?

For the cloud-o-philes, BIME Analytics offers a robust cloud-based data visualization option that works from any flash-enabled web browser. This enables you to analyze your data that lives in the cloud while keeping it in the cloud. BIME can connect to dozens of different types of data sources, including BigQuery, and visualize them live. It also offers an option to pull your data out of whatever datastore it is currently in and store it in a BigQuery dataset. It provides a variety of extract, transform, and load (ETL) options to help finesse your data into a format that makes it easy to query. We won't go into the ETL option further, but using BIME to automatically import your data into BigQuery can be a great way to save you the overhead of managing it yourself.

BIME may be cloud-based, but it is not free. You should consult the pricing page at `http://www.bimeanalytics.com/pricing.html` to determine whether it is within your budget. BigQuery is only available in the Big Data pricing tier, which might seem cheap if you're running a large enterprise, but it might seem expensive if you just have a couple of tables you'd like to turn into pretty graphs. Like Tableau, BIME has a free trial that you can use to try it out while you're deciding if it is right for your needs.

Connecting BIME to Your BigQuery Tables

In order to use BIME with BigQuery, follow these steps:

1. Sign up for BIME by clicking on the Try BIME Free button at `http://www.bimeanalytics.com/index.html`. After you complete the signup process, you will receive a custom URL that you can use to connect to the service. For our trial, it was `http://bqtrial.bimeapp.com`.

2. Navigate to the custom BIME URL and click on the Create Connection, which should be visible on the landing page. After clicking it, it brings up the Create Connection dialog box. Figure 13.7 shows the various options, with BigQuery in the bottom-left corner.

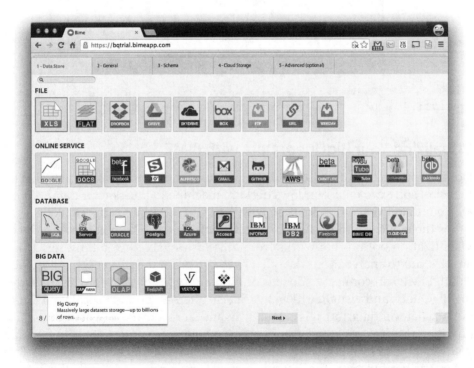

Figure 13.7: BIME create connection dialog box

3. Select BigQuery and then press Next. You'll be prompted to name the connection; call it **Shakespeare** because you want to connect to the public `shakespeare` table.

4. Click the Connect with Google button. This brings up a web page with the standard Google OAuth2 prompt. It asks you to log in to your Google account (if you're not already logged in), and then whether you want to allow BIME to view and manage your data in BigQuery. After you approve the access, you have to cut and paste a verification code that BIME then uses to access your BigQuery tables in the future.

5. Next, click the … next to the Table prompt. This brings up the BigQuery Explorer dialog box, as shown in Figure 13.8, where you can select the project, dataset, and table that you'd like to connect to. For this example, select `publicdata`, `samples`, and then `shakespeare`. Press Select, and it takes you back to the General tab with the table name filled out.

Figure 13.8: BIME BigQuery Table Explorer dialog box

6. Click on Next one more time, and BIME will pull down the schema of the table and present you with a dialog box that lets you select columns. If you want all your columns to be available in your visualizations, you can just ignore this dialog box and press Next again.

7. The Cloud Storage tab is where you can tell BIME where you want to store your data if you want to store it elsewhere. If you have Oracle data, for

example, that you want to visualize by storing it in the cloud in BigQuery, you can select Google BigQuery, and BIME can take care of ingesting all your Oracle data into BigQuery. Because the Shakespeare table is already in BigQuery, you can just select None and press Save. Because this was the last required tab, it then takes you to the Analysis screen, where you can create your visualizations.

Creating a Visualization

To compare BIME to Tableau, we will create the same bar graph that you did in the Tableau section. You should note that like Tableau, BIME often runs queries as a result of small changes you make in the UI; these queries can add up in cost, especially if you're visualizing large tables. To create the Shakespeare corpus length graph:

1. Select the Shakespeare connection that you just created, because you want to analyze the Shakespeare table and click Load. This brings up the analysis pane, which looks a lot like a Tableau workspace.

2. Drag the corpus entry from the Axis of Analysis menu to the Columns bar, which means you're going to be visualizing on a per-corpus basis. Then drag the word_count measure to the Measures bar. (Note there are two places labeled Measures; you want the one on the right that doesn't already have word_count listed.) This will bring up a table showing word counts per corpus.

3. To create a bar chart with this information, click Grid to open up the visualization menu and then Column to create a columnar bar chart. Now you should see each corpus listed along the bottom row with the word count as the height of the column.

4. Since our desired visualization uses color to indicate the date the play was written, drag corpus_date to the Color tab. You should then see red and green bars.

5. The default aggregation that is used is SUM(), but for corpus_date, this doesn't make sense; adding multiple dates together doesn't mean anything. Moreover, the SUM() aggregation doesn't make sense here because the corpus_date entries matching a particular corpus all have the same value. MIN() is a better choice, although MAX() or AVG() would also produce the same visualization. Select the drop-down menu in the Color tab and pick MIN() from the available options.

6. Remember from the Tableau example that two of the corpora have a date of 0, which skews the coloring. On the right side, under Measures, there are sliders that let you select the range to use. Pick something like 1500 as the minimum, which should give enough dynamic range so that you

can see the difference between the various plays. Figure 13.9 shows the final visualization, which shows the variation between the corpus date and corpus length of Shakespeare's oeuvre.

Figure 13.9: Shakespeare corpus versus word count in BIME

Other Data Visualization Options

There are a lot of ways you can visualize your BigQuery data; you have just seen two commercial solutions. If you're cost-sensitive, or just want to make a quick graph or two, Tableau and BIME might not be the most cost-effective option. (Although both do have free trials to let you decide if they're right for you.) There is an up-to-date list of popular third-party visualization tools at `https://developers.google.com/bigquery/third-party-tools`, which includes both Tableau and BIME but also other options such as Metric Insights and QlikView.

If you don't want to spend money on your visualizations, you can also build nice graphs via your favorite spreadsheet software. Microsoft Excel has advanced charting features, and we've shown two different ways to use it with BigQuery (via the BigQuery Excel Connector, described in Chapter 12, or via the ODBC driver, described earlier in this chapter). Google Docs' graphing capabilities are more limited, but it has the advantage of being free, and it works from any web browser.

You can also build any visualization you want by writing a little bit of custom code; this may sound like a lot of work but is simpler than it sounds. In addition, writing your own graphing code lets you customize your graphs to show exactly what you want to show, not what some tool decides to show you. Chapter 8, "Putting It Together," provided sample code to build dashboards for a data collection app, using Google's charting API, Gviz (`https://developers.google.com/chart/interactive/docs/reference`) for bar graphs and dygraphs (`http://dygraphs.com/`) for time series graphs.

If neither of those is powerful enough for you, d3 (`http://d3js.org/`) is a general-purpose, open source JavaScript library for turning data into HTML DOM elements. It can build some impressive graphs and animations, and there are a number of extensions available for building different types of charts. That said, it is also more involved and can be a lot of work to set up even fairly simple graphs.

Summary

This chapter walked you through a number of third-party tools built on top of BigQuery. Some of these tools, such as Tableau and BIME, enable you to visualize your data; others, such as the Simba BigQuery ODBC driver, enable you to integrate BigQuery into your existing software with little or no changes necessary. The section on Encrypted BigQuery showed how you can encrypt your data client side, such that Google's servers never see the unencrypted data.

In addition, this chapter described two different mechanisms for scientific computing using BigQuery: bigrquery, which lets you run BigQuery queries from R, and Python pandas, which lets you do the same from Python's scientific computing environment. Both of these systems are open source, so if you want to see how they work or reuse any of the components, you can do so fairly easily.

Along the way, you graphed the relationship between the lengths of Shakespeare's plays and when he wrote them, built a machine-learning model to classify Shakespeare plays by genre, and clustered those plays into histories and other plays.

Finally, you saw only a sampling of the currently available third-party tools for BigQuery; the SAS connector, visualization options such as QlikView, and ETL tools such as Informatica and Pervasive were not mentioned. It is likely that by the time you read this chapter, still more options will be available. To see more up-to-date sampling of available third-party tools, check out the list at `https://developers.google.com/bigquery/third-party-tools`.

Querying Google Data Sources

For users of certain Google services, BigQuery enables more direct access to their data contained in the service. The current set of services supporting BigQuery enhanced access includes:

- Google Analytics
- AdSense
- Google Cloud Storage (GCS)

These services, as part of their core functionality, have dashboards that enable you to access summarized views of your data with varying degrees of customization available in their interfaces. What is generally true is that a fair amount of aggregation is applied to the underlying data in your account before it is rendered. These views are designed to cover the common use cases. However, if you have more advanced analysis requirements, especially if you need to combine the data in the service with external data sources, you end up wanting direct access to the data. These services support using BigQuery to give access to the un-aggregated data. Note that this has the advantage that you do not have to download the data to perform useful analysis. For heavy users of these services, this is quite important because the volume of data collected by these services can be substantial, and simply downloading and storing the full data can be challenging, to say nothing of analyzing it efficiently. Of course, you can still use BigQuery to export or download your data if required.

Unfortunately, the access method is not at all uniform across these services, so each of the services just listed is covered in a separate section. BigQuery-based access is considered an advanced feature of these services, so we assume that you are already familiar with the basic functionality of the service. The focus is on enabling access and the details of how the data appears in BigQuery as it relates to formulating queries.

Google Analytics

Google Analytics (`http://www.google.com/analytics`) is one of the leading web traffic analysis services. It enables you to monitor and analyze the behavior of your users across your web properties and mobile applications. The service records *hits*, a page view, or any other developer-defined action from individual users and organizes them into *visits*, where a visit roughly corresponds to a session of activity. Developers can instrument the logging to include a variety of custom dimensions or values that are saved as part of the hit or visit. The service front end allows you to view this data in a variety of reports and dashboards that support a substantial amount of customization. Direct access to individual hits organized into visits is available via BigQuery, but it requires that you have a *Premium account*. A Premium account requires a USD 150,000 annual contract, so the target audience is high-traffic sites that are generating a substantial amount of data. Hopefully, in the future this feature will be available to additional account types.

Setting Up BigQuery Access

When Google Analytics is integrated with BigQuery, it pushes a copy of your daily traffic data into BigQuery every day. When this data is in BigQuery, you can manage it independently of your Google Analytics account. For example, you can control the ACL and lifetime or make additional copies as you see fit. To start you need to contact your Premium support manager `https://support.google.com/analytics/answer/3437618`) and give him two bits of information:

- BigQuery project ID that should receive your data
- Google Analytics view ID

Your Google Analytics account can handle multiple properties and each property can have more than one view. A view is a subset of the data (defined by custom filters) collected for a single property. By default, every property has a single view that contains all the data for the property. Currently Google Analytics supports only exporting a single view per property to BigQuery, so most likely you want to have this unfiltered view pushed into BigQuery because then you can run queries over all the data for your property. When you submit this request, you will be instructed to modify the ACL of your project so that Google Analytics can write data to your project. Specifically, you will be asked to add edit permissions on the project for the account:

```
analytics-processing-dev@system.gserviceaccount.com
```

After you have done this, support updates your account configuration so that a nightly job pushes your data into the project. A dataset will be created with a name equal to the view ID you specified in the request, and within that dataset a daily table will be created some time after the end of the day. The tables have the following naming pattern:

```
ga_sessions_YYYYMMDD
```

Table Schema

Fortunately, you can experiment with this feature without going through all this setup or even signing up for a Premium account. The Google Analytics team provides a sample dataset that you can use to understand the nature of the data generated. You can add this data to your view in the BigQuery UI by adding the project `google.com:analytics-bigquery` using the project menu (the drop-down next to the project name, Switch to Project ⇨ Display Project). Alternately, you can navigate to the BigQuery UI link `https://bigquery.cloud` `.google.com/project/google.com:analytics-bigquery`.

After you add the project, the sample dataset (LondonCycleHelmet) appears in the navigation panel. It contains two tables:

- `ga_sessions_20130910`
- `refunds_201309`

For now you can ignore the second table. The first table is the sample table that contains data that corresponds to what Google Analytics collects when users interact with a web property. Selecting the table displays a complicated schema that has a large number of fields, as shown in Figure 14.1.

Figure 14.1: Google Analytics sample data

This schema is a great example of leveraging BigQuery's capability to represent nested and repeated structures in a record. To help understand the schema, it is useful to look at a stripped down version that highlights the most important properties and nested structures. We have used italics to indicate fields that are records containing nested fields and boldface to indicate fields that are repeated. Note that we have fields that are bold and italic to indicate that they are repeated records, and we have repeated fields that appear within a repeated field.

- visitorId
- date
- *totals*
- *trafficSource*
- *device*
- ***customDimensions***
- ***hits***
  - time
  - referrer
  - *page*
  - *transaction*
  - ***customVariables***
  - ***customDimensions***
  - ***customMetrics***

This structure may appear rather complex, especially when compared to schemas in relational databases. However, it is quite natural considering the data collected. As we discussed, Google Analytics organizes user actions (hits) on your web property into sessions (visits). Each record in this table corresponds to a single visit, and the visit contains the corresponding list of hits. Each visit has a field describing data that is common across all the hits in the visit, for example, the device used to access your property. Each hit subrecord contains data specific to the hit, for example, the page that was accessed.

As we mentioned earlier, the data collected can also be customized. Google Analytics allows you to instrument your application and add data to each record; these are recorded in the repeated `custom[Variables/Dimensions/Metrics]` fields. Dimensions that are common across hits appear at the top level, and hit-specific custom properties appear within each hit record.

The `totals` field that appears at the top level is actually a summary of the hits collection. In principle it is possible to compute the information present in the totals from the collection of hits, but it is convenient to have these visit metrics precomputed.

Querying the Tables

Now that you have a basic feel for the shape of the data, try a simple query. In the queries that follow, the table name has been abbreviated to meet formatting requirements, but the queries in the supporting material for this chapter use the fully qualified name.

```
SELECT
  device.browser,
  SUM(totals.bounces)/SUM(totals.visits) bounce_rate
FROM [LondonCycleHelmet.ga_sessions_20130910]
GROUP BY 1
```

This is a simple query that generates the *bounce rate* broken down by browser. This query is quite uninteresting because you could easily access the same data along with a nice chart with the Google Analytics web interface. It is worth verifying that the results you get from a simple query match what you see in the web interface. This can help verify that the correct data is being transferred to your dataset. But, you are actually interested in the new analysis that becomes feasible after you can access the raw hit data. Here is a query that leverages the structure of the data and BigQuery's more advanced query features to compute a more interesting result.

```
SELECT
  yellow,
  orange,
```

```
  SUM(TotalTime)/SUM(Visits) avg_time
FROM (
  SELECT
    MAX(IF(hits.page.pagePath CONTAINS 'yellow', 1, 0))
      WITHIN RECORD yellow,
    MAX(IF(hits.page.pagePath CONTAINS 'orange', 1, 0))
      WITHIN RECORD orange,
    totals.timeOnSite TotalTime,
    1 AS Visits
  FROM [LondonCycleHelmet.ga_sessions_20130910])
GROUP BY 1, 2
```

The "Repeated Fields" section in Chapter 10, "Advanced Queries," introduced the scoped aggregation feature that allows you to control aggregation operations. The feature is used here to compute new derived properties for visits:

- orange indicates whether a user visited a web page with "orange" in the path.
- yellow indicates whether a user visited a web page with "yellow" in the path.

You can then use these derived properties as dimensions and compute the average time spent per visit broken down by these dimensions.

After you understand the schema of the records, you can work with the data in these tables just like any other table in BigQuery. As mentioned earlier, one of the most useful features of having your Google Analytics data accessible in BigQuery is that you can join it with other data you have uploaded. The sample dataset contains a refunds table with a TransactionId field that can be joined against the hits.transaction.transactionId field in the traffic data table. For completeness here is a query that performs a join to compute the average refund broken down by traffic source. All the techniques used in the query should be familiar from Chapter 10. Note the use of FLATTEN to allow joining with a repeated field.

```
SELECT
  traffic_data.source,
  SUM(refunds.RefundAmount)/COUNT(traffic_data.tid) refund
FROM FLATTEN(
  (SELECT
    trafficSource.source source,
    hits.transaction.transactionId tid
  FROM
    [LondonCycleHelmet.ga_sessions_20130910]
  ), tid) traffic_data
INNER JOIN
  [LondonCycleHelmet.refunds_201309] refunds
  ON traffic_data.tid=refunds.TransactionId
GROUP BY 1
```

The discussion of querying this data wraps up with a recipe for dealing with custom dimensions, metrics, and variables. These dynamic properties can be a bit awkward to work with because they do not fit comfortably in a query language intended to work with explicitly specified fields. You can use the WITHIN operator to *pivot* these fields in an inner query so that the outer query can treat your custom property as a regular field. Here is a sample query:

```
SELECT * FROM (
  SELECT
    visitId, hits.hitNumber,
    MAX(IF(hits.customDimensions.index = 1,
          hits.customDimensions.value, NULL))
      WITHIN hits.customDimensions Item,
    MAX(IF(hits.customDimensions.index = 3,
          hits.customDimensions.value, NULL))
      WITHIN hits.customDimensions Level
  FROM [LondonCycleHelmet.ga_sessions_20130910])
LIMIT 100
```

In the example, the outer query was a trivial limit query. A realistic query would use the generated Item and Level fields to do something useful.

Beyond querying, you can also export these tables to GCS if you want to access the data as JSON. Because the tables have a nested schema you cannot directly export them as CSV. However, you could run a query and export the resulting table as CSV. You also need to manage the lifetime of these tables because they count toward your storage usage in BigQuery.

Google AdSense

Google AdSense is a publisher product that allows content owners to use advertisements from Google's inventory, collected from its network of advertisers, to generate revenue from their sites. The Google AdSense interface allows publishers to monitor the performance of ads on their sites and discover the ad units that work well with their sites. For large publishers it is more useful to have programmatic access to this data and AdSense provides an API to access this data and now also provides access to this data through BigQuery. The data accessible through either method does not provide details of individual impressions or clicks. Instead it provides daily rollups along important dimensions (ad unit, domain, channel, and others). The amount of data can still be substantial because a large site might display thousands of distinct ads each day, so it is still important to filter and aggregate the data, which is simple in BigQuery.

The data is made available differently from Google Analytics. All users access the same dataset:

```
google.com:adsense-reports:Reports
```

Once again you can display this dataset in the BigQuery UI by navigating to the dataset URL `https://bigquery.cloud.google.com/project/google .com:adsense-reports`.

This dataset is readable by any BigQuery user, but the contents of the table depend on the user querying the table. The data made available corresponds to the AdSense accounts that you are authorized to access. This has the advantage that there is no special required setup; if you have access to BigQuery, you have access to your AdSense data in BigQuery. However, it has the disadvantage that it is not actually possible to share queries because different users see different data, and you do not have any control over the lifetime of the data. The result of a query over these tables is a regular (either anonymous or named) BigQuery table, which you can preserve indefinitely and share independently of the source data.

Table Structure

The AdSense dataset contains five different tables, as shown in Figure 14.2, which represent the same ad serving data aggregated by different dimensions.

- `DailyDomainReport`
- `DailyReport`
- `DailyAdUnitReport`
- `DailyUrlChannelReport`
- `DailyCustomChannelReport`

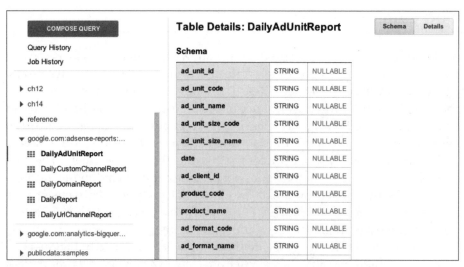

Figure 14.2: AdSense dataset in BigQuery

Each of these tables has a date field so that you can access daily records. They have a common set of metric fields that measure the performance of ads:

- ad_requests
- matched_ad_requests
- individual_ad_impressions
- clicks
- earnings
- page_views (only present in DailyReport and DailyDomainReport)

In addition, there are a few dimension fields present in all the tables:

- ad_client_id
- product_code
- product_name

The remaining dimension fields vary across the five tables and are described next in the description of each table. The fields in these tables should be familiar to users who have managed AdSense accounts. For a full explanation of individual fields, refer to the AdSense API documentation (https://developers. google.com/adsense/management/).

DailyDomainReport

The domain-level report is the least granular, broken down only by the domain of the web page hosting the ads. It has a single dimension in addition to the common dimensions.

- domain_name

Here is a query that extracts page views for all days since January 1, 2014, for a single domain:

```
SELECT date, page_views
FROM [google.com:adsense-reports:Reports.DailyDomainReport]
WHERE domain_name = 'www.asciiflow.com'
  AND date >= '2014-01-01'
ORDER BY 1
```

Note that the date field in these tables is a string field formatted as YYYY-MM-DD.

DailyReport

Here are the dimensions available in the `DailyReport` table:

- `ad_format_[code, name]`
- `bid_type_[code, name]`
- `targeting_type_[code, name]`
- `platform_type_[code, name]`
- `country_[code, name]`

You can see that each dimension comes in code and name variants. The name is a human-friendly representation of the code. It is often nicer to work with codes because they are more strictly specified. For example, the `country_code` field follows the ISO 3166-1 alpha-2 standard for specifying countries. You can easily generate a table containing the mapping from code to human-readable representation.

```
SELECT ad_format_code, ad_format_name
FROM [google.com:adsense-reports:Reports.DailyReport]
GROUP BY 1, 2
```

The results of this query are shown in Table 14.1.

Table 14.1: Ad Format Code to Name Mapping

AD_FORMAT_CODE	AD_FORMAT_NAME
dynamic_image	Animated image
Flash	Flash
Html	Image
text	Text

You can save the resulting table permanently for use in joins to map from codes to readable values. If you do this, you would want to periodically regenerate the map because it can grow over time depending on the ads served on your site.

DailyAdUnitReport

This table contains metrics for each of the ad units that you have defined across the sites in your account. Because you control the definition of ad units, the amount of data in this table depends on how many separate ad units you define. The following dimensions are available in the table:

- All the dimensions available in the `DailyReport` table
- `ad_unit_id`

- ad_unit_[*code*, *name*]

- ad_unit_size_[*code*, *name*]

Three separate fields, the id, code, and name, identify an ad_unit. AdSense assigns the id and code, and the account manager chooses the name for the unit. Because you can control the name, it is the simplest field to use for joining against other data you might have describing the ad unit. Here is a query that shows the sizes of ad units served on a given day:

```
SELECT ad_unit_name, ad_unit_size_code
FROM [google.com:adsense-reports:Reports.DailyAdUnitReport]
WHERE date = '2014-01-04'
GROUP BY 1, 2
```

Because this table has all the dimensions present in the DailyReport table, it may seem like it makes that table redundant. However, note that the page view metric is only available in the DailyReport table. Because a single page view can contain multiple ad units, it is not possible to associate a page view with rows in the ad unit table, which is why the metric does not appear in this table. To use page views (generally to normalize totals by the number of page views) you must work with the DailyReport table.

DailyUrlChannelReport

Just as the DailyAdUnit table is a breakdown of daily totals by ad units, the DailyUrlChannelReport table contains the metrics broken down by the URLs on which the ad unit was served. However, you must explicitly create URL channels to track the URLs you are interested in before data will be collected for a channel. The AdSense documentation describes how to set up a URL channel. The dimensions in this table are:

- All the dimensions available in the DailyReport table

- url_channel_id

- url_channel_name

Like with the ad unit name, you control the channel name when you configure it. Here is a sample query over this table that computes click-through rates by URL channel:

```
SELECT
  url_channel_name,
  SUM(clicks)/SUM(individual_ad_impressions) ctr
FROM [google.com:adsense-reports:Reports.DailyUrlChannelReport]
WHERE date >= '2014-01-01'
GROUP BY 1
```

DailyCustomChannelReport

You can configure custom channels in your accounts much like you can define URL channels. However, with custom channels you control the channel an ad unit is assigned to rather than have it be fixed by the URL path. Again, this table is a breakdown of the `DailyReport` table with fields added to identify the custom channel.

- All the dimensions available in the `DailyReport` table
- `custom_channel_id`
- `custom_channel_[code, name]`

The coverage of the individual tables concludes with a final example computing the revenue rate broken down by custom channels.

```
SELECT
  custom_channel_name,
  SUM(earnings)/SUM(ad_requests) revenue_rate
FROM [google.com:adsense-reports:Reports.DailyCustomChannelReport]
WHERE date >= '2014-01-01'
GROUP BY 1
```

Leveraging BigQuery

As you have seen, all these tables have simple flat schemas, so constructing queries is straightforward. These kinds of results are accessible in the AdSense UI, but the advantage of using BigQuery is that you can use your own reporting and dashboard framework rather than relying on the AdSense user interface. For example, you could use a tool like Tableau or the BigQuery Excel Connector to analyze your data. You could also join the data in these tables with other data you have, but keep in mind that you do not have much control over the values of the fields, so it may be necessary to transform your data to have field values suitable for joining against these tables.

You may also want to save a full copy of your data to your own tables. The advantage of doing this is that you can manage the lifetime of the data and share it with other users without granting them access to your AdSense account. A "SELECT *" query with the `allowLargeResults` flag set and a destination table specified will do the trick. The only downside is that you will have to pay for storage and queries (currently, queries over AdSense data are free) over your copy of the data. However, given the volume of data this should not be significant.

Google Cloud Storage

Throughout this book we have used GCS as a way to move data in and out of the Google Cloud. The most common use case for GCS is to host static content in web applications and for sharing large binary files. In these scenarios it is useful to inspect GCS access logs to understand how the content is used. GCS supports configuring buckets so that operations on objects in the bucket are eventually exported to a different logging bucket. These files can be imported into BigQuery, so you can analyze GCS logs without having to download and process the files. This section discusses how to set up and manage this process.

The process for setting up logging in GCS requires choosing a bucket that will be used to store your logs and then using the `gsutil` tool to update the bucket you need to track with configuration indicating that access and usage logs should be written to the logging bucket. The full details are available at:

```
https://developers.google.com/storage/docs/accesslogs
```

Here are the `gsutil` commands you need to start collecting logs:

```
$ LOG_BUCKET="bigquery-e2e"
$ gsutil mb gs://${LOG_BUCKET}
$ gsutil acl ch -g cloud-storage-analytics@google.com:W \
    gs://${LOG_BUCKET}
$ LOG_PREFIX="chapters/14/log"
$ SERVING_BUCKET="my-serving-bucket"
$ gsutil logging set on \
    -b gs://${LOG_BUCKET} \
    -o ${LOG_PREFIX} \
    gs://${SERVING_BUCKET}
```

The first command is required only if the bucket does not exist. The second command grants access to a service group that will be writing the logs, and the final command actually enables logging for the bucket. Note that these commands will work only if you update the variables in the snippet to reference GCS buckets that you administer.

When logging is enabled, two types of files, usage and storage, will periodically be added to the bucket you specified. The usage files contain the operations performed on the bucket and the storage files contain the byte-hours of storage consumed over a 24-hour period. Both of these files contain CSV formatted data. The storage files are not particularly interesting because they are trivial and contain only a single record. The rest of this section focuses on the usage files that have a lot more information.

The usage file contains a number of fields that provide a detailed description of every operation performed on the bucket. Table 14-2 lists the fields available.

Table 14-2: Fields in the GCS Usage Records

FIELD	DESCRIPTION	TYPE
time_micros	Time (microseconds since the Unix epoch) the request was completed	Integer
c_ip	IP address of client	String
c_ip_type	IP address type: 1=IPV4, 2=IPV6	String
c_ip_region	Currently not supplied	String
cs_method	HTTP request method	String
cs_uri	Request path (does not include the host)	String
sc_status	HTTP status code returned to client	Integer
cs_bytes	Request bytes	Integer
sc_bytes	Response bytes	Integer
time_taken_micros	Time (microseconds) taken to process the request	Integer
cs_host	HTTP request host	String
cs_referer	HTTP referrer header value, if present	String
cs_user_agent	HTTP user agent header value, if present	String
s_request_id	Server assigned request ID	String
cs_operation	GCS operation performed	String
cs_bucket	Target bucket	String
cs_object	Target object	String

Because the usage log is CSV formatted, it is immediately compatible with BigQuery, so you can load the data into a BigQuery table with a suitable schema. GCS provides a reference schema that you can download.

```
gsutil cp gs://pub/cloud_storage_usage_schema_v0.json /tmp/
```

If you prefer to use different names for the fields, you can modify the field names in the downloaded schema; the command to load the data will still work.

For the command to load the data into BigQuery, you need to specify the list of files. The log files generated conform to a naming scheme:

```
gs://<log bucket>/<log prefix>_usage_YYYY_MM_DD_hh_mm_ss_<id>_v0
```

The ID following the timestamp on the file is a system-generated string to avoid name collisions. For example, you might be saving the serving logs of 2 different buckets to the same log bucket and prefix. In the event that log files are generated in the same second, the ID ensures that one of them does not clobber the other.

A reasonable scheme is to load all the logs for a day after the last log for the day has been generated. Because logs are generated hourly, you could set up a cronjob that executes a couple of hours after midnight UTC to load the previous day's logs. Assuming you have a suitable dataset created in BigQuery, the command would look something like this:

```
$ LOG_DATASET='ch14'
$ bq mk ${LOG_DATASET}
$ bq load \
    --skip_leading_rows=1 \
    --schema=/tmp/cloud_storage_usage_schema_v0.json \
    ${LOG_DATASET}.gcs_usage \
    "gs://${LOG_BUCKET}/${LOG_PREFIX}_usage_2014_02_*"
```

You could keep the table more up to date by loading files through the day as they appear, but this requires additional bookkeeping to track which files have been loaded. One strategy is to use load job IDs that contain the suffix of the name of the file that is being loaded. Then you could have a periodic job that checks to see which files have been scheduled by enumerating jobs and scheduling jobs for files that have no corresponding job ID.

After the data is loaded into BigQuery, you can run all sorts of interesting queries on your usage data. Here is one to get you started:

```
SELECT
  HOUR(time) traffic_hour
  SUM(get_bucket) bucket_gets,
  SUM(put_bucket) bucket_puts,
  SUM(head_object) object_heads,
  SUM(get_object) object_gets
FROM (
  SELECT
    USEC_TO_TIMESTAMP(time_micros) time,
    IF(cs_operation = 'GET_Bucket', 1, 0) get_bucket,
    IF(cs_operation = 'PUT_Bucket', 1, 0) put_bucket,
    IF(cs_operation = 'HEAD_Object', 1, 0) head_object,
    IF(cs_operation = 'GET_Object', 1, 0) get_object
  FROM [bigquery-e2e:ch14.gcs_usage])
WHERE
```

```
    time >= '2014-02-19 00:00:00' AND
    time <  '2014-02-20 00:00:00'
GROUP BY 1
ORDER BY 1
```

This query computes counts of different types of GCS operations broken down by the hour for a single day. The USEC_TO_TIMESTAMP conversion is required because we used the reference schema that defines time_micros as an integer field.

Keep in mind that your data has been copied into BigQuery, so you have two copies of your logs. Depending on how you intend to use this data, you may want to retain only a single copy. Because your GCS logs are regular files in GCS, you are charged for the storage they consume.

Summary

This chapter presented a handful of Google products that make large volumes of data more useful to their customers by exposing it through BigQuery. BigQuery is useful in this context because it provides a way for customers to operate on their data rather than simply expose it as bytes they must download and process before extracting value from it. Although the current list of products enabling this access is a small fraction of Google services' universe, over time more products will follow suit. Hopefully, the manner in which the data is exposed will also become more uniform across Google products. For now, if you are a user of one of these products, you can use the recipes described in this chapter to get more mileage from them.

Index

SYMBOLS

`**` (asterisk/double), Python, 198

`()` (parentheses)
  nested fields, 120
  parenthesis matching, query editor, 54

`%` (percent symbol), modulo operator, 321

`|` (pipe symbol), Tab-Separate-Values, 176

`"` (quote character)
  bulk loads, 177
  table names, 224

`[]` (square brackets), JSON, 179

A

AaaS. *See* Analytics as a Service

`ABS()`, 321

abstractions, 69–70

`Access`, 127

access, `Datasets()`, 129

access control list (ACL)
  anonymous tables, 209, 357
  datasets, 77–78, 87, 126
  `Datasets()`, 130
  `Datasets.insert()`, 127
  `Datasets.list()`, 129
  `Datasets.patch()`, 131
  GCS, 165
  Google Analytics, 480

jobs, 85
mobile client, 259
permissions, 73
Project resource, 123
`Tables.list()`, 136

access tokens
  API client library, 103
  OAuth, 101–102, 259–260
  server-side validation, 260

`accessDenied`, HTTP errors, 156

`access.domain`, 127

`access.role`, 127

`access.specialGroup`, 127

`access.userByEmail`, 127

ACID. *See* Atomic, Consistent, Isolated, Durable

ACL. *See* access control list

adapters, third-party tools, 436–452

ad-hoc queries
  relational database, 298
  Sensor, 42–43

Advanced Options, 56

advanced queries, 305–348
  advanced SQL, 306–318
  query errors, 334–338
  recipes, 338–348
  SQL extensions, 318–334

advanced SQL, 306–318
  analytic function, 315–318
  subqueries, 307–309
  tables, 310–315
  window functions, 315–318

aggregation
  `WITHIN`, 327–328
  cohort analysis, 343
  Google Analytics, 483
  query language, 225–227
  window functions, 317

aliases, 326

`allowJaggedRows`, 178

`allowLargeResults`, 205, 213, 221
  materialize queries, 295
  query errors, 336

`allUsers`, 150

`ALTER TABLE`, 22, 437

Amazon EC2, 35, 418

Amazon Redshift, 8, 25

analytic function, advanced SQL, 315–318

Analytics as a Service (AaaS), 26–29
  asynchronous job execution, 28–29
  global data namespace, 26–27

Android app, 67
  AppEngine, 248
  mobile client, 242–252
  Sensor, 40–41

Android Development Kit, 242

anonymous tables, 209–210
  ACL, 357
  garbage collection, 357–358

anti-`JOIN`, 314–315